WAR IS BEAUTIFUL

Also by James Neugass

Rain of Ashes

Also by Peter N. Carroll

The Odyssey of the Abraham Lincoln Brigade:
Americans in the Spanish Civil War

The Good Fight Continues: World War II Letters
from the Abraham Lincoln Brigade (*with Michael Nash and Melvin Small*)

Facing Fascism: New York and the Spanish Civil War
(*with James D. Fernandez*)

They Still Draw Pictures: Children's Art in Wartime
from the Spanish Civil War to Kosovo (*with Anthony L. Geist*)

Also by Peter Glazer

Radical Nostalgia: Spanish Civil War Commemoration in America

WAR IS BEAUTIFUL

AN AMERICAN AMBULANCE DRIVER
IN THE SPANISH CIVIL WAR

JAMES NEUGASS

EDITED AND WITH AN INTRODUCTION BY
PETER N. CARROLL AND PETER GLAZER

THE NEW PRESS

NEW YORK
LONDON

This book was funded in part by a grant from the Program for Cultural Cooperation between Spain's Ministry of Culture and United States Universities.

© 2008 by Abraham Lincoln Brigade Archives, Inc.
All rights reserved.
No part of this book may be reproduced, in any form, without written permission from the publisher.

Requests for permission to reproduce selections from this book should be mailed to: Permissions Department, The New Press, 38 Greene Street, New York, NY 10013.

Published in the United States by The New Press, New York, 2008
Distributed by W. W. Norton & Company, Inc., New York

Library of Congress Cataloging-in-Publication Data

Neugass, James, 1905–1949.
War is beautiful: an American ambulance driver in the Spanish Civil War / James Neugass ; edited with an introduction by Peter N. Carroll and Peter Glazer.
    p.   cm.
Includes bibliographical references.
ISBN 978-1-59558-427-4 (hc.)
1. Spain—History—Civil War, 1936–1939—Personal narratives, American.
2. Spain—History—Civil War, 1936–1939—Participation, American.
3. Spain—History—Civil War, 1936–1939—Medical care.   I. Carroll, Peter N.
II. Glazer, Peter.   III. Title.
DP269.9.N48 2008
973.8'67—dc22   2008023065

The New Press was established in 1990 as a not-for-profit alternative to the large, commercial publishing houses currently dominating the book publishing industry. The New Press operates in the public interest rather than for private gain, and is committed to publishing, in innovative ways, works of educational, cultural, and community value that are often deemed insufficiently profitable.

www.thenewpress.com

Book design by Cinqué Hicks
Composition by The INFLUX House
This book was set in Bodoni and Hoefler Text

Printed in the United States of America

2   4   6   8   10   9   7   5   3   1

To Dr. Edward K. Barsky
and the men and women of the
American Medical Bureau
to Save Spanish Democracy

Abraham Lincoln Brigade Archives, Tamiment Library, New York University.

Figure 1: Dr. Edward K. Barsky, as head of the Joint Anti-Fascist Refugee Committee, speaking on behalf of Spanish exiles in the 1940s.

CONTENTS

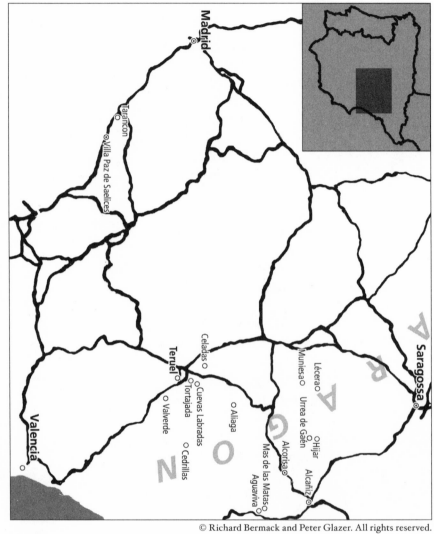

Figure 2: A map of the cities important to James Neugass during his time in Spain, and major roads.

© Richard Bermack and Peter Glazer. All rights reserved.

ILLUSTRATIONS

INTRODUCTION

The outbreak of the Spanish Civil War struck with stark immediacy on July 18, 1936. From the earliest moment, there was fighting in the streets of otherwise functioning cities; blood pooled on sidewalks, bodies were left to broil in the sun. Spain would continue to bleed for another thirty-two months and then some, in the war's cruel aftermath. But the war was not just about Spain. As the English writer George Orwell (himself a volunteer soldier) later wrote, "The outcome of the Spanish war was settled in London, Paris, Rome, Berlin—at any rate, not in Spain."

Five years earlier, King Alfonso XIII had abandoned the throne, allowing Spain's Parliament to create an elected republic. The new regime introduced changes—gave women the right to public education, permitted secular marriages and divorce—and promised land reforms to aid the rural poor, while cutting the size of the army. Such programs antagonized various entrenched groups, especially the Catholic clergy (which lost control of schools and family life), landed and industrial elites (who resisted agricultural and labor reforms), and military leaders (who faced a loss of authority and jobs).

Meanwhile, the Republic faced serious economic crises associated with the worldwide Depression as well as intense divisions among competing political parties. Often the constitutional government found itself caught between hostile groups, for instance, when labor unions resorted to violence or landowners used their own police to prevent land reform. Right-wing groups denounced the Republic for failing to control social change and lawlessness. In turn, anarchist groups, especially powerful in the province of Catalonia, demanded extensive social reforms.

In February 1936, a coalition of left-wing groups known as the Popular Front (which included liberal Republicans, Socialists, and a small Communist party, but not the Anarchists, who formally rejected cooperation) won the closely contested parliamentary elections. The military, led by General Francisco Franco and supported by anti-Republican leaders and the Falange (a Spanish version of fascism), began conspiring for armed insurrection. During the spring, street fighting between right-wing and leftist factions erupted spontaneously; public violence took various forms, including political assassinations and church burnings by anarchist groups.

After months of disorder and tension, uprisings led by top army officers commenced among military units stationed in Spain's colonies in Morocco, North Africa, and the Canary Islands, catching the Madrid government by surprise. As the rebellion spread to army bases in Spain, loyal Spaniards spontaneously organized civilian resistance, particularly in cities with strong labor unions and civil militia. Indeed, in Madrid, Valencia, and Barcelona, the Loyalists effectively stopped the insurrection. In other cities, the rebels succeeded in seizing power. Nonetheless, Republican leaders remained confident that the uprising would soon collapse.

What enabled the rebellion to continue and ultimately to succeed in wresting power from the elected government was the intercession of other European military powers. By 1936, Italy's Benito Mussolini and Germany's Adolf Hitler made no secret of their intentions for global conquest. Both had violated agreements with the League of Nations and built their armies. When Franco and the rebels appealed to the Fascist dictators for military support, those leaders seized the opportunity to test their military prowess and destabilize Europe. Thanks to Italian and German aviation and naval support, Franco managed to convey his Army of Africa, including Moorish mercenaries, onto the Spanish mainland. Fighting brutally, making no distinctions between Loyalist soldiers and civilians, the rebel army began marching toward Madrid.

The elected Republic appealed to the democratic countries for assistance. But Britain, under the Conservative leadership of Prime Minister Neville Chamberlain and still stung by the enormous casualties of the First World War, wanted to avoid conflict with Italy and Germany. France, under the Socialist Leon Blum, indicated some interest in allowing materiel to reach Spain, but dared not oppose Britain and risk being left alone to face Mussolini and Hitler. In the end, the western "Allies" adopted a policy known as "Non-Intervention," prohibiting the sale of arms to either side of the conflict and setting up an international committee to monitor compliance. Italy and Germany happily became parties to non-intervention and, as happily, ignored its terms. Britain and France feared to upset the diplomatic balance any further.

Republican Spain eventually persuaded Soviet Russia to provide arms and munitions in exchange for a treasury of gold. But transporting weaponry was complicated, and eventually the flow from Russia dried to a trickle. Mexico also sold the Loyalists some limited arms. The United States, still a relatively minor power and locked into a policy of isolationism, followed the British, blocking arms sales under various Neutrality Acts of the 1930s. By early 1937, the State Department stamped all U.S. passports "Not Valid for Travel in Spain."

The Soviet Union also lent another kind of assistance to the Spanish Republic. Aware of the crucial role of German arms for Franco and of Hitler's vow to expand German power into the Ukraine, Soviet leader Josef Stalin encouraged the world Communist movement to provide voluntary aid to Spain. By the autumn of 1936, Communist parties around the world were organizing both humanitarian aid and volunteer soldiers to support the Republican cause. In the end, some 35,000 men and women from over fifty countries made their way to Spain: German anti-Fascists formed the Thaelmann Battalion, Poles the Dabrowski, and Italians named themselves the Garibaldis. In addition, nearly 3,000 volunteers came from the United States. Those who left before the United States initiated passport restrictions were able to travel directly to Spain, but even those eventual restrictions didn't stop the flow of U.S. volunteers, many of whom shipped off to France instead. With the assistance of French officials and civilians sympathetic to the Republican cause, they made their way through France to the Spanish border and walked across the Pyrenees to join the struggle.

The first U.S. volunteers to fight for the Spanish Republic left New York City the day after Christmas, 1936. Naming themselves the Abraham Lincoln Battalion (part of the 15th International Brigade), they saw action at Jarama in February 1937 and stayed in the front lines continuously until June. By then, additional volunteers had created a new George Washington battalion. Both American groups fought at Brunete in July 1937, sustaining so many casualties that the units were merged as the Lincoln-Washington Battalion. By the late summer, North Americans formed yet another battalion, named MacKenzie-Papineau after two Canadian patriots. Other U.S. volunteers were attached to transportation groups (Regiment de Tren), the John Brown artillery battery, or the Transmissions (communications) units. Collectively, the American volunteers were known after the war as the "Abraham Lincoln Brigade." Nearly 800 U.S. men were killed in Spain.

While Americans from almost every state joined the fight, a second stream of volunteers offered their services to the American Medical Bureau

to Save Spanish Democracy. Part of a nationwide effort to provide humanitarian and medical aid to Spain, the organization's recruitment of doctors,
nurses, laboratory technicians, and ambulance drivers drew wide support
from people of all political persuasions. Most donated small sums to pay for
ambulances, medicine, or condensed milk for Spanish children. Others offered their professional services. None was more influential in this campaign
than Dr. Edward K. Barsky, who organized the first American hospital unit,
which sailed to Spain in January 1937. Within a month, they established a
fully functional surgical hospital near the front lines to treat casualties from
Jarama. Barsky returned to the United States in the summer of 1937 to raise
additional funds for medical aid. Returning to Spain a few months later, he
met the thirty-two-year-old writer who would become his personal driver,
James Neugass.

Isidore James Newman Neugass was born in New Orleans, January 29, 1905.
He came from a well-to-do Jewish family. His maternal grandfather, Isidore
Neumond, changed his name to Newman when he emigrated from Germany
in 1853, and, though he arrived in steerage, went on to become one of New
Orleans's leading industrialists and philanthropists—a founder of the local
stock exchange and of the Isidore Newman School, which remains one of
the foremost private day schools in New Orleans. Newman's grandson James
Neugass began writing as a teenager. "I have been writing poetry since I was
seventeen," he stated in 1933, "lots of it and nothing but it." At that time,
editor Edward J. Fitzgerald of the *American Poetry Journal* called his talent
"forceful, dramatic, and modern." By the time Neugass left for Spain, his
work had appeared in the *Atlantic*, the *Dial*, the *Nation*, and other publications. His education included time at Exeter, Yale, Harvard (Mayan archeology), the University of Michigan (mining engineering), and Oxford (history),
although it's unclear whether he received any degrees.

At the age of twenty, Neugass was working for a newspaper in Paris. A
passport issued by the American consulate in Nice in 1929 indicates three
years of travel to countries including Germany, Italy, Switzerland, Spain, Algeria, and Yugoslavia. He returned to the United States late in 1932 and sold
shoes, wrote book reviews, taught fencing, and worked as a cook, a social
worker, and a janitor. During this period, he also helped organize a department store workers union. And he continued to write and publish poetry,
short stories, and book reviews.

In October 1937, in preparation for his journey to Spain, Neugass applied
for a new passport. U.S. law still permitted humanitarian and medical work

ers to enter Spain, so unlike the soldiers in the Lincoln Brigade, Neugass did not have to lie about his intended destination. He arrived in that war-torn country in mid-November and served with the American Medical Bureau until the following April. During this five-month period, as Neugass's journal reveals, the war's course changed dramatically. Assigned to the American hospital at Villa Paz, Neugass immediately realized that the Loyalist armies were preparing for a bold initiative to block recent Fascist advances on the Aragon front. He was restless for the chance to see action, and before long, his ambition would be fulfilled. In December of 1937, the Republican armies launched a surprise attack to seize the strategically positioned city of Teruel. Neugass's medical unit was relocated near the front and found themselves in the thick of battle.

Neugass was soon driving his ambulance through the perilous combat zone, assisting the medical teams in setting up hospital units, dodging Fascist bombers and fighter planes, and ferrying the wounded and the dead. Along with the military units, he experienced the terror of war, witnessed the suffering of civilians, and felt the extreme emotional highs and lows of victory and defeat. Always, he knew the omnipresence of hunger and exhaustion.

The initial Loyalist triumph at Teruel brought powerful counter-attacks and terrible fighting. As Neugass's ambulance carried casualties to the hospitals, he saw the tide of war shifting. Neugass himself received several shrapnel wounds, but nothing stung him as much as the sheer superiority of Franco's military technology, which was the result of Nazi and Fascist support. Meanwhile the so-called democracies were allowing the Republic to starve, literally. In the end, through extraordinary personal courage and luck, Neugass survived the calamitous actions that became known as the Great Retreats, in which the Loyalist armies were ripped to shreds and forced to flee across the Ebro River to Republican-held territory. James Neugass, the ambulance driver, had to engage in hand-to-hand combat to save his life. But after driving himself, Dr. Barsky, and other medical personnel to safety, he was utterly exhausted. Barsky saw his condition and advised Neugass to go home.

Back in the United States, he continued to write. In 1939, he married Myra Shavell, a child of Russian immigrant parents. A son, Paul, was born in 1943, and James followed in 1948. During this period, Neugass supported the family as a cabinetmaker and as foreman of a machine shop, but he devoted substantial intellectual energy to a long, florid novel, titled *Rain of Ashes*, which was based on his family in New Orleans and the move to New York in his youth. The manuscript was accepted for publication by Harper & Brothers in 1949. In a brief biographical statement Neugass wrote for the publisher, he made no mention of his service in the Spanish Civil War—an omission that was not surprising, given the political climate of the times. By then, the United States was enmeshed in a domestic cold war against communism, and the American veterans of the Spanish Civil War were now viewed—and often treated—as political subversives.

Neugass did not personally experience the predations of anti-communism. He died suddenly of a heart attack in the Sheridan Square subway station in Greenwich Village on September 17, 1949. His neighbors took up a collection to assist the family, and six months later, Myra and her two children moved to southern California, where she had relatives. *Rain of Ashes*, Neugass's only novel, was published posthumously.

War Is Beautiful: An American Ambulance Driver in the Spanish Civil War (originally subtitled *Journal of an American Ambulance Driver in Spain, 1937–1938*) was handwritten during Neugass's time in Spain. The text must have been typed soon after his return, probably by Myra, and was sent to at least one publisher. It was rumored that some years after he died, Neugass's papers were destroyed in a flooded cellar. Fortunately, he had sent his typescript to someone for review, and, by luck, it survived.

The version published here has been trimmed from the original by approximately 10 percent to eliminate repetition and remove material extraneous to the story or of limited historical value. In the text that remains, we made only occasional revisions. Handwritten edits appeared throughout the typescript, invariably improvements, and we took them as the author's preference.

Neugass encountered scores of people in Spain who appear in this memoir. Some are mentioned once or twice, some are present throughout. Many are alluded to by only their first names, others by an alias or an abbreviation. One of our earliest editorial decisions was to research these names, and if we could, provide brief biographical profiles as footnotes. Neugass brings his own perspective to the daily lives of American volunteers and others in the International Brigade, and we felt it important to help the reader know who these people were.

Paul Neugass, James Neugass's older son, remembers a scene from his childhood. "When I was three or four he and I were relaxing," Paul recounts. "I was rubbing his large forehead, his eyes were closed—he'd told me I took his headaches away. I again saw the large thick scar that covered the top of his thigh and gently touched it; bumpy and smooth, I had memorized the look and feel of it and asked if it still hurt. He told me that it was from a downhill skiing accident when he chose to hit a tree instead of a child. Somehow I instinctively knew this was not the truth. I knew it did not come from sport. I knew he was protecting me from a terrible memory of a war." When James Neugass died in 1949, Paul was six and his brother Jim was eighteen months old. It wasn't until Neugass's journal of his five months in Spain came to light more than sixty years after it was written that his sons, Paul and Jim, learned the real story behind that scar, and discovered, in his memoir, a father they barely knew.

"The need for sleep has dulled the edge of my memory," James Neugass wrote in his journal on January 6, 1938. "I know: I ought to be able to recall what I have seen and done. Phrases smooth as oil should roll off the end of my pencil. Something big and something terribly human. Pity and terror, mercy and pain, all between drawn lips." This is but one of many passages that suggest, beyond much doubt, that this manuscript was written in the moment, day by day, battle by battle. "The *Asaltos* ask me what I'm writing," he notes a week later, feeling a certain embarrassment about revealing his journal. "'A letter to my *novia* [girlfriend],' I answer. They approve, and admire my leather covered, zipper-bound notebook." He carried this notebook back to the United States when he returned from Spain in April. That very same year, brief excerpts of his saga were published in *Salud!*, a pamphlet of writings on Spain. "The sketches by Neugass are samples from a new 100,000-word manuscript," *Salud!* editor Alan Calmer stated.

What happened to this manuscript? We know it was never published. We know that in the year 2000, a 500-page typescript by Neugass was found by bookseller Burton Weiss in a Vermont bookshop, likely among the papers of Max Eastman, radical critic, poet, and editor of the *Masses*. Accompanying the typescript were handwritten queries ("The main question to decide is: Is this a book that will help the fight, and the building up of the people's movement against fascism?") and ideologically inflected and detailed editorial comments, perhaps by Eastman ("The title, 'War Is Beautiful,' is a Fascist slogan. If this is naïve and misdirected irony, it is very dangerous . . . "). The typescript was clearly the 100,000-word document Calmer referred to in 1938; it contains the passages reprinted in *Salud!*

Through Weiss, the work made its way to the Rare Book and Manuscript Library at the University of Illinois Urbana-Champaign. When co-editor Peter Glazer was seeking permission to reprint a poem by Neugass, he spoke with Neugass's son Paul, who mentioned the typescript and asked if Glazer would like to read it. He did, and shared it with co-editor Peter N. Carroll. They immediately recognized it as a lost gem and worked with the Neugass family to secure the rights on behalf of the Abraham Lincoln Brigade Archives; now, thanks to The New Press, it is available to the general public. "This is the most important thing that has ever happened in my life," Jim Neugass said after reading his father's book for the first time. "This man was a ghost to me." The book reveals a great deal about its author, and about being on the ground in the middle of one of the most complex, tragic, and significant military conflicts of the twentieth century. Jim Neugass knew as little of his father as most people know about the war in which he participated.

It's rare to encounter a book such as this. We've been fortunate to spend time in its company.

Peter N. Carroll and Peter Glazer
Belmont and Berkeley, California
May 2008

WAR IS BEAUTIFUL

Rich in bankruptcy, to the world
I leave my heart, to the Republic my gun
To men's slow eyes my unvanishing footsteps.

James Neugass

AFTERWARDS

It is possible to walk down New York streets without being shot at, to work without listening for sirens, to sleep in a bed and to take many showerbaths. There is much food to be bought and the water is good to drink. All over New England are weekend lakes each with its sunlight, birches and pines, canoes, laughter and sunsets. Along the seacoast it is possible to lie in the sand and later, when the light begins to fail, to look out over the ocean towards Spain until vision melts into darkness and night blinds the eyes.

Four shellshocked infantrymen stood solemnly at the side of the road, powerless as mileposts, to dig for their comrades who had just been buried by a shell. Captain R. lost his hand-knotted winter socks when the laundress blew up in her home with her father, mother and two small brothers. We took the blood out of four asphyxiated cavalrymen before they were cold and ran it into the arms of wounded. We did not talk of women, we did not dream of women, and there were no dirty jokes. Acorns, olives pulled off the trees by moonlight and wild onions taste good. No surgeon has amputated a hand so neatly as a bomb sheared the suede gloved wrist of a nurse. Lieutenant E. had his teeth fixed in Barcelona for ten packages of Lucky Strikes.

Was it really true that the English anti-tank company had cut a week's firewood with explosive shells when there were no axes? How is it possible for a driver to keep on the road for sixty hours and why is it possible to sleep at the wheel without crashing? How had the Companies of Steel in the early days stopped tanks, planes and cavalry with their big hearts and bare hands? Why did the wounded lie so still and so seldom cry out? Why did the sight of an old woman at midnight far from any town hobbling her way towards the Rear affect us more than rows of dead?

How could so little hatred have been possible? Quietly the newspapers in the cities talked of "the Invaders" or, more simply, of "Them." No one read

or spoke of "the enemy" or of "the fascists." Since hatred was the daily business of life, since They always performed exactly as we knew They would,
there was little anger no fists brandished at the sky no loud-mouthed radio
denunciations no cursing in the streets or up at the lines unless a very close
friend got what all of us, sooner or later, knew he would get.

If there were bands I did not hear them. Medals, reviews, gold braid and
dappled neurotic martial horses had always been missing and were not re-
gretted. There was little saluting in the cities and less at the front. We had
the best semi-professional army ever to be wholly recruited, trained and sea-
soned, against the wish and with the opposition of most of the War Nations,
during wartime in Europe. Hungry for Their infantry, our steel jaws could
snap only at the air. Our ravenous squinting eyes so seldom sighted down the
barrels of our rifles anything that was human.

We always had the feeling of having our hands held behind our backs.
The Republic was flogged like a horse tied up short at the head by enemies
it could not reach.

We killed naturally and with constant gnawing desire to kill more and
more, but we hated death and war and we could never manage to think of
ourselves precisely as soldiers.[1, 2]

---

1. Captain R. is Norman Rintz (1906–86), a graduate of Jeffries Medical College in Philadelphia and a volunteer physician with the American Medical Bureau to Save Spanish
   Democracy (AMB).
2. Lieutenant E., Dr. Abraham Ettleson, a graduate of the University of Illinois College
   of Medicine, was a brain surgeon from Chicago. His wife Dora also served with the
   AMB as a nurse.

PART ONE
Base Hospital

Fredericka Martin Photographs Collection (image #1:1:17), Abraham Lincoln Brigade Archives, Tamiment Library, New York University.

Figure 3: James Neugass and members of the American Medical Bureau. Left to right, back row: Edward K. Barsky, Katherine Purviance, Edwin S. Weisfield, James Neugass; front row: Carlton C. Purviance, Avemaria Bruzzichesi, Leo Eloesser.

By the time James Neugass arrived in Spain in November of 1937 as an ambulance driver for the American Medical Bureau, an estimated 600 Americans had been killed and 1,300 wounded. Neugass was stationed seventy miles southeast of Madrid, outside the town of Saelices at Villa Paz, an abandoned royal estate taken over by the American Medical Bureau to establish their third field hospital. At that time, the 15th International Brigade, in its ongoing efforts to defend Madrid, was preparing to attack Rebel forces on the Aragon front.

ᥱᶾ

Dec. 5, 1937. Villa Paz de Saelices. Near Madrid

At two o'clock in the afternoon, Santiago, the fifteen-year-old boy who crossed Rebel lines down on the Cordoba front to enlist in the Loyalist army, set a turkey feather in his khaki worsted cap and climbed on top of the largest ambulance drawn up in the base hospital courtyard. Photographs were taken of the seven chófers, the five surgeons, the eight nurses, the field kitchen staffs and of the entire group.[1]

The Commissario, the former dental mechanic from Brooklyn, ran out of the administrative offices with two cartons of American cigarettes, a box of chocolate bars and a spare sweater.[2] The cook contributed a paper bag of onions. Patients waved their crutches in the air as the kitchen *chicas* led off in the singing of their favorite song, "The Four Generals," and the four cars which were leaving for the Front passed through the archway and moved down the hill.[3] Papadapoulos, the Greek sentry whose stomach had been ruined by poisoned water at Brunete, fired a one-cartridge salute.[4]

We were glad to leave Villa Paz not only because we were going to see action but because we had been under stand-by orders for four days. In each of the four chófers' pockets were sealed orders containing *salvo conductos* for themselves and *vales* for gasoline, but none of us knew where we were going or

---

1. "Chófer," a term commonly used among the volunteers, is Spanish for *driver*. Neugass served as a chófer in Spain.
2. Joseph Highkin (1888–1971) served as political commissar at Villa Paz and returned to the United States from Spain in 1938.
3. This song (in Spanish, "Los Cuatros Generales") was also known in English as "The Four Insurgent Generals" (Franco, Mola, Sanjurjo, Queipo de Llano). This was perhaps one of the most famous songs to come out of the war. Based on a Spanish folk melody, it was recorded by Ernst Busch, Paul Robeson, and Pete Seeger, among others.
4. "Papadopoulos" is probably Louis Priovolos, a Greek American guard at Villa Paz.

how long we would be on the road or whether the Brigade was going to attack
or to be attacked. The Major sitting beside me told a nurse who had asked
him if we were headed for Huesca, with his usual misplaced sense of humor,
that we were going to Madrid to take in a few movies and night clubs.[5]

In a convoy, the slowest cars travel first, so that none of them can get
lost. Marty, in the autochir, had orders to turn off towards Valencia at the
Madrid turnpike and thenceforth not to stop until he was told.[6] The autochir
is a green and gray camouflaged truck the size of a moving van. Made and
equipped in Switzerland, it contains about fifteen thousand dollars' worth
of surgical instruments, x-ray equipment, linens, autoclaves, drugs and catgut and rubber gloves, a gasoline-powered electricity generator and a heavy
demountable operating table. Marty and Bernie are each trained mechanics,
truckdrivers and sterilizers.[7] Marty is a twenty-seven-year-old ex-salesman
of anti-freeze mixture from Philadelphia and Bernie, twenty-two, was a
printer's apprentice back in New York. Both of them came to Spain through
the international underground railway which sends *voluntarios* to fight in the
International Brigades, and both had been transferred from the infantry into
our front-line surgical unit because of their special technical skill. When you
ask them how they got into Spain, they say they came to Europe to study
marine engineering and one day, when they were studying the docks of Mar-
seilles, they decided to take a swim, got lost and wound up at Barcelona.
Marty is famous for the amount of time he spends looking for something to
eat and for his soft ways with the girls. Bernie is known for his love of argu-
ing and his curiously worried optimism. I do not believe either one of them
has in his lifetime heard a more lethal noise than the backfiring of a car, but
neither have I. The distant explosions we heard a few days ago from the Villa

5. "The Major," Dr. Edward K. Barsky, a legendary New York surgeon, organized and
served as Chief of the American Medical Bureau. During the Spanish Civil War, he directed the frontline hospitals, performed innumerable life-saving surgeries, developed
innovations in military medicine, and acted as Chief of Republican Spain's hospitals
until Barcelona fell to Franco in 1939. He later headed the Joint Anti-Fascist Refugee
Committee in the United States, organized to aid tens of thousands of Spaniards dis-
placed during the war. His political activities against Franco's Spain antagonized the
House Committee on Un-American Activities, which held him in contempt, resulting
in a six-month jail sentence and loss of his medical license in New York during the anti-
Communist attacks of the 1950s. Ernest Hemingway called him "a saint."
6. Martin Grumet, real age twenty-three, was born in Pittsburgh. "Autochir" was a term
coined during World War I for a mobile surgical hospital, from the French, *Ambulance
Chirurgicale Automobile*.
7. Bernard Gerber, real age twenty-five, was born in Brooklyn in 1911.

Paz hilltop may have been the bombing of Tarancon, but, after all, we really were not under fire ourselves. Naturally we are all anxious to be able to write home that someone has taken a shot at us.

We have all come to Spain with the notion of having done something big, and the sublime emotions which ran through us like organ-music as we watched the powerful hips of Miss Liberty merge with New York's comic-strip skyline cannot be allowed to simmer out in an endless base-hospital houseparty.

Marty and Bernie carry two of the nurses on a wide seat of their cab, for company and to relieve the congestion in the light-wounded compartment of the big evacuation ambulance "Donated by the Students and Faculty of Harvard University" in which some fifteen of the kitchen staff, ward nurses and instrument girls travel, driven by Smitty the shrimp, of Chicago, whose head hardly rises above the steering wheel.[8] Smitty has been evacuating wounded to the warm climate of Murcia for convalescence. Since the South is a five-hundred-kilometer run and Smitty has been making the round trip without sleep three and four times a week, his physique will be able to endure the hardship of the Front, about which we have heard so much and fear so little. After all, we are a hospital and there is something sacred about our errand. We may lose a little sleep and miss a few meals—and we will soon heroically be able to write home that we are lousy—but we cannot quite be considered the enemies of our enemies.

"Bring your warmest clothing," the Major told us this morning. "Take all you have that's warm." Sounds like Catalonia. But the Aragon is a quiet front. Perhaps we are going to attack. I wish I knew more about war and about medicine. All I know is to drive, to take care of my car and to speak Spanish and to take orders. I am the Major's personal driver and secretary, or adjutant. My car is a long low limousine with the lines and glass windows of a hearse and the rear doors of a delivery wagon. I am told that it can be used for a truck or to carry two heavy wounded after the removal of the two rear seats or to carry nine light wounded or nine of the staff. It does not seem to me that I am going to be very useful. I can always get into the infantry if I become too angry, I suppose. I can drill and shoot, although I do not yet know if I will be able to keep my head. Maybe I will stay up at the Front just long enough to learn how to imitate the sounds of different kinds of guns going off and shells flying through the air to impress girls at studio parties back in the States, and then desert. Perhaps I will pick myself a soft job driving for a

---

8. John Smith (real name) was an ambulance driver from Chicago.

base hospital. I'm not sure. I don't know. I'm certain that I don't like Franco and that I like democracy but I have seen nothing of fascism so far and much too much democracy. In my three weeks in Spain I believe I've learned that military strictness is necessary for the successful conduct of any war, that elections during wartime seem a little absurd and that the degree of discipline necessary to win the war counterfeits what many people might think was fascism. We don't have enough strictness. Few of us can bring ourselves to salute the Major or call him anything but "Doc."

Since my car is the fastest and the most maneuverable, I bring up the rear. Ahead of me roll the dental autochir and the supply truck. The dentist, Handsome Jack, can play Bach fugues on his mandolin and the far more complicated revolutionary songs which the Andalucians have transformed from their *flamencos*, and which the *chicas* sing all day long.[9] His chófer, George, a mechanic from Harlem, seems to know only one Spanish word, *matrimonio*, which he repeats to all the *guapas* he meets.[10] From his easy-going ways, you would never think that George knows how to take apart a carburetor with a hairpin and his fingernails.

Ahead of George is the supply truck piled high with mattresses, beds, sheets, plaster of Paris, airplane splints, gauze, adhesive and all the drugs and supplies necessary to set up a reception room, which we call a *"triaje,"* and a twenty-patient ward. Ben, a St. Louis aviator, came to Spain to enter the Air Force shortly after foreigners had ceased being accepted.[11] He brought with him a full length horsehide coat lined with sheep-skin and electric filaments. He swears that he could plug himself into his plane's ignition and that this coat of his was worth two hundred and fifty dollars. Four days after Ben got to Spain, he met a motorcycle driver who was blue with cold. The *"enlace,"* as dispatch runners together with their machines are called, wore a light horsehide coat. Ben was sorry for the *enlace* and swapped coats with him. Two days later the runner deserted to the fascists, coat and all. "I don't care about being cold," Ben says, "and besides, my horsehide was really too long to wear inside a car, but what I don't like is having to ride all around Spain in a ———ing lousy fascist coat. And when will I be able to get a new one? Maybe

---

9. Jack Klein, a New York dentist, served with the AMB for eighteen months.

10. George Walter Waters, originally from San Francisco, was only eighteen when he went to Spain and served in the transportation group, known as the Regiment de Tren.

11. Ben Levine, aka Ben Lane, studied at the University of Southern California before going to Spain, where he served with various medical groups.

after we get to the front, if somebody is my size . . . ." He looks at Marty, who wears a good U.S.A. lumberjack. . . . "No you won't," Marty says, "I'll live longer than three of you."

Artie the Finn, who drives the small front-line ambulance, wears a bottle-green windbreaker faded to almond-white across the shoulders. I do not know much about Finn, except that he talks very little, that he says "cluts" for "clutch," that he talks about the parts of his car as if they were portions of his body—i.e., "my radiator, my crankcase," etc.—that he once drove a soda-water delivery truck in Winnipeg and that he does not like Franco. "Look at that shon of a bits!" he said the other morning when we saw what we thought was a fascist plane. Artie's tow hair stands up stiff as bleached straw and the grin which is almost always on his face cracks it in half like a Halloween pumpkin. He has small piglike green eyes and no eyebrows.[12]

Late in the afternoon, Ben began to have trouble with his carburetor. The whole convoy finally drew up on top of a desert-red treeless plain. We had been eating up forty-five miles of the Castilian plain, bare but for isolated dwarf oaks and mirages of wheatfields and vineyards, ever since lunch-time. I was glad for the rest because I had come out of two days of dirt fever only that morning. Dirt fever is our name for the variety of grippe which cuts so deeply into the ranks of our effectives. Hacking night-coughs, jaundice, sores, itches, diarrhea and constipation are the occupational diseases of war in Spain. Constipation is the least serious of them, since it is often cured by the sight and sound of planes of which we have seen little thus far. All scratches and cuts seem to infect. I have been wearing adhesive on a pin-scratch in my thumb for the past two weeks, and it keeps getting worse.

Ben's carburetor trouble turned out to be water. If Finn had not been able to fix it, not only would we have had to leave the supply truck behind us, but the Major would have had to tell Ben where he was going. Since the movements of the Medical Corps of which we are a part predict and reflect the movement of troops, our whole plan of campaign might have been given away. I do not think the Major is psychotic about spies. Five months ago the American hospital at Romeral was bombed, and at night. A wide circle of burning coals had been placed in the field outside the main building as a target for

---

12. Matti August Mattson, born in Fitchburg, Massachusetts, in 1916, was the only Finnish American frontline ambulance driver in the 15th Brigade. He was responsible for the small frontline ambulance. "I wore my hair very short," he wrote in 2008. "I certainly do not fit the comical character portrayed in the few words that you read to me—being instead a taciturn and too serious a person for that to be true."

the aviators. A few weeks later we noticed that Rudolf, the sprightly efficient young German who had supposedly escaped from a concentration camp and had come to Spain with the best credentials, had too much money and was far too well dressed. Rudolf was the only officer who had an orderly and who was in favor of an officer's mess. Up to that time, and ever since, the officers had and have always eaten with the men. Everyone began to complain that the time for Rudolf's arrest was overripe. Individual threats were made, and still he was not locked up. Rumors began to spread that Rudolf had protection among the higher-ups and that the whole Loyalist General Staff must be infested with spies, fascists and Trotskyists. At length Rudolf was arrested. With him went a whole ring of spies to the amount of fifteen or twenty. The secret police had known about the Gestapo chief ever since the bombing. If he had been taken at that time, he would have been arrested alone. As it was, the police waited until Rudolf had given away his whole circle. I never heard what became of these gentlemen. Perhaps they are still in jail.

While Ben's car was being repaired, we had dinner: a slice of bread and half of a tin of bully-beef per *soldado*. When we were ready to move on, night had fallen, after a swift and spectacular sunset. The six chófers drove for many hours through mountains, down ravines and across unlit towns dead as darkness towards Valencia.

Never once during the long afternoon had I seen a cannon, a man in uniform, a field which looked fertile, a habitable house or a village which was anything but utterly wretched. Once as we stopped for gas, a little girl ran up to my car and asked for a newspaper. I had none. Then she asked for "anything printed." I finally found a torn three-weeks' old part of a Madrid paper. The little girl was quite contented. I am told that books, newspapers, magazines or printed matter has for so long been so rare in the average Spanish village that even very old newspapers are valuable.

Near midnight the convoy coiled through the dark wide empty streets of Valencia under faint blue street lamps and past the sudden bells of shadowy unlit streetcars. The *Delegación*—or barracks—of the International Brigade post welcomed us with coffee, bread and salami which was not more that one-third corn-meal. Officers and drivers signed the multiple war-time form-blanks of the Hotel Ingles and walked up marble stairs to the spacious bath-rooms, warm water and soft beds of the best hotel in Valencia. The women stayed at the *Delegación*. In what other war have girls slept unmolested in army barracks?

I slept without dreaming. I seem to have left the nightmares which drove me to Spain buried in the suburban New York garden among the roots of the irises and flowering bushes which were the best that the salary of a minor Civil Service employee could buy. Such of my plants which can take care of themselves will sprout next spring, manured by the burned out ashes of conscience-nightmares.

"When we attack," said the Major not many weeks ago in the saloon of the ocean liner which was bringing us from the old American world to the new Spanish world, "we handle many wounded. When we are attacked and retreat, well, ——."

Dec. 6. Again in Villa Paz

"Turn the cars around," said the Major after a breakfast of *café con leche*, of solid tasteless and ageless bread wet by jam of unfixable flavor and consistency. "Turn the cars around. Back to Villa Paz. We're not going to the Front. We never were going to the Front and we never will. No, there's nothing the matter, nothing went wrong. And there isn't time for shopping or sight-seeing. What do you think war is, a picnic? Don't let it get you, don't let Spain get you. Come on now, back into your cars and don't stop off to pick flowers. Somebody'll be picking flowers for you soon enough."

Flowers? I have seen no blossoms or buds but the suspicious purplish swellings in the clump of asphodel which grow near the hospital dump.

I had wanted to take another bath, to order high boots and a uniform and to buy oranges, mandarines, hazelnuts, candy and any other food I could find. Pepita had wanted to visit her cousins. Our two Leica-maniacs had thought they would be able to have films printed. Marty had believed he could have located the *chica* he had left behind on his last trip to town, and Lieutenant R. had thought he would have been able to pick up the socks he had arranged to have knitted for him. All of us were disappointed that no one would shoot at us for quite some time now.

We should have been able to cover the three hundred kilometers back to Villa Paz in seven hours, but Ben again had trouble with his carburetor. Eventually we left him on the road with our best set of end-wrenches. The convoy broke up and each carload of heavy hearts wound home under the leaden winter skies. At ten o'clock in the evening I trudged into the stable-dormitory to find my bed taken. All of the other beds in this vast dim windowless chamber of coughs and snores and slumbering monologuists were full, so I had to put up in the convalescent ward. I have not yet got used to sleeping in hospitals, although the other chófers seem to think that a ward-bed is the best place to sleep this side of the lower floors of the Hotel Florida, in Madrid.

The drifting moist haze which ebbed about the hospital set on a hilltop like a mushroom at the point of a volcano was no less dank than the globules of liquid fever that ran down the walls of the stable dormitory all day and night, no less gray than the morale of the men and women who wandered about the courtyard. Coffee is the bugle by which we get up. If anyone wants to sleep right through coffee, he may. I believe that this is wrong. Rare as copper is in this country, there should be a morning bugle or a siren or some sort of whistle.

Since my car had travelled some hundreds of miles without being looked after, I spread an oilcloth over the wet cobbles under her and went to work. The Major has violent and ununderstandable opinions about the care of our transport. He believes that ambulance drivers should sleep on the stretchers in their ambulances—Finn has not spent a night away from his Tampa sweetheart for months—that they should wander never more than a hundred feet away from their steering wheels during daytime, that a taillight is an offense, we should use lock-tops for our gas tanks, all doors should be locked at all times and that self-starters should never be used, and that drivers should always refuse to loan each other tools, tires or inner tubes.

I was very short of tools and went to the electrician's shop. Luna, the Filipino second electrician, refused to let me have the wrench I needed. Swede, the chief, was more liberal. The two of them have charge of the generators which not only pump water from the irrigation ditch at the bottom of the hill but furnish us with all our light.

During the later part of the morning, I built a wood tool-chest. Eufemio the head carpenter gave me all the tools and screws and help I needed. The shed in which he constructs coffins of packing-case wood from the States, at the rate of three or four a week, is one of the most cheerful spots I have found in the entire Villa Paz establishment because of the fire of chips which is never allowed to die.

El Generál, who keeps the fire going, is either shellshocked or a lunatic. He appears to be at least fifty years old, although I am told that he isn't over thirty-five. His skinny legs double so completely under him as he squats looking into the flames that the grin which never seems to come out of the silver stubble of a beard on his nutcracker face seems to hang between his legs. The carpenters, like most Spaniards—and most Internationals—talk little, especially when they work. I wish I could understand the constant stream of chatter which bubbles out of the General's thin lips. The carpenters seldom speak to him or answer his questions. Months ago he turned up at the hospital and asked for bread. We gave him a loaf, and he never left us. Meticulously dressed in the baggy khaki ski pants—"*pantalónes*"—which are or should be the lower part of an infantry uniform—and khaki windbreaker, he wanders about the grounds looking for some way to pay for his keep. We let him chop wood or dig or carry off litter, but he soon grows tired of each task and goes to another. Once I saw him speaking savagely to three of the big blue and white magpie-looking birds. Once the General disappeared. After a few days he returned, bearing three large loaves of stale bread, which we were forced to accept. Today the weather is so bad that he stays by the fire, telling us how the battle of the Arganda Bridge should have been fought, and strumming *flamencos* on his stick as he sings.

The weather cleared off a little during the afternoon and we heard the sound of an engine in the sky. There is talk of digging a trench.

The drivers, used in times of inactivity as labor gangs, went out to mend the road at the bottom of the hill. We gathered the stone which lies far more thickly on the plains of Castile than in New England highlands and raised the level of the ruts above the mud which filled them. Shovels are almost more an emblem of war than bayonets, and more frequently used. "What's won with the rifle is held by the spade," say the Spanish.

Menu at Villa Paz

Breakfast 1. Coffee, tasting of chicory and parched wheat, sweetened by condensed milk.
2. Army bread in measured amounts. The oval flat loaves lack the taste of flour or yeast and shortening. Tasteless even when fresh, I wonder how it could grow stale.
3. Watery acid-tasting orange-peel jam.

Lunch 1. Bread
2. Soup, flavored by potatoes and tomato.
3. Garbanzos. These are dried chick-peas, mostly imported from Mexico. They are the size and shape of chicken's brains. When boiled they develop a thick velvety skin. Salt and pepper, small amounts of onion and of tomato paste heighten their nutty flavor.
4. Coffee

Dinner 1. Bread
2. Garbanzos thinned out into soup.
3. Boiled mule-ribs flavored by potatoes.
4. Vino. Good rich Spanish red wine, slightly cut

Menu for the Patients

The same as above, with the addition of condensed milk
and small amounts of eggs, breakfast cereals, vegetable
essences imported from the States and oranges.

Some of us remember that there was cheese for breakfast and eggs for the
staff. I believe that during the early days someone ate ham. If there was
ever butter, it has been forgotten.

There is no officer's mess. Our officials eat with us. Dishes, cups and uten-
sils are of tin.

There are no table cloths or napkins.

Second servings are not given.

After dinner much of the hospital staff drifted into the hall near the offices. The generators had again failed. By candle-light, chófers and officers
cleaned their pistols. The victrola was played, and a couple listlessly danced
in the half dark, between tables and chairs. Some of the sparse talk was of
the Cordoba expedition. We had sent a surgical team to that front. They had
seen little action.

At eight-thirty the lights again turned on, and it was possible to carry
through the trials of two patients, for drunkenness.[13]

Ambulatory patients and staff members to the number of some eighty assembled in the dining hall. The Commissario, about whose duties I must
soon write many pages, presided. One of the criminals was a young Frenchman. His arm was held at the height of his neck by a special sort of wire
splint. Thick black hair, burning blue eyes, thin white face with cheek bones
made more prominent by vivid color, and wavy, untilted mouth gave him an
almost girl-like look. The other criminal was a tough-looking Belgian whose
neck was in a plaster cast.

Patients who had been in action with the two wounded Internationals testified. The records were good. Both the Frenchman and the Belgian had vol-
unteered in the terrible early days of the defense of Madrid. Kleber trained
them with three shots at a target, strapped cartridge belts over their civilian

---

13. Such tribunals, usually run by the political commissars who were attached to every
branch of the military, reinforced the idea of a "people's army" that operated by prin-
ciples of self-discipline among the rank and file.

jackets and took them out to San Martin de la Vega and to Casa del Campo, where the Brigades held their ground against artillery, tanks and planes.[14]

Both men had decent political and trade-union histories in the countries from which they had come.

The French youth spoke. He said that his arm did not pain him, that he was tired of waiting for it to get well, that he was fed up with listening to Toulouse over the radio. The Belgian seemed apt to defend drinking as a natural part of every man's life. He denied that he had been drunk. Man after man from the Belgian's ward then testified that their comrade's ravings had kept them awake many a night.

The Commissario called the keeper of the *cantina* to the stand. Ramon, the Cuban-American who dispenses the weak muscatel wine and the bitter vermouth which are the sole stock of the *cantina*, but for meager supplies of shoelaces, wallets, belts, razor-blades and soap, stated that he never served one man more than three drinks. Patients were able to get drunk only if their friends bought them additional drinks. How was he able to watch?

Speaker after speaker, each infected by the other's oratory, took the floor. Each address began with statements of devotion to the Spanish Republic, to democracy, to the People's Army and to the world-wide working class movements. The interpreter who had conscientiously rendered every word spoken into Spanish and English began to be disregarded. The Belgian, still insisting that he never had been drunk since he had come to Spain, broke out into throbbing mixture of German, French and Dutch which someone told me was Walloonish.

For the second time that evening the Commissario spoke, in Brooklyn English. He asked the patient who had admitted his guilt to sentence himself. The Frenchman rose, and in the dead silence which had come over us swore that he would never get drunk again. To show that he meant this, he asked that his next ten days' pay be turned over to the Spanish Red Cross. The Belgian then had this chance. "But I wasn't drunk," he insisted. "And now I'm going to show you that I'm as faithful a proletarian as any man or woman in this room. I sentence myself to the loss of twenty days' pay, all to be turned over to the Socorro Rojo."[15]

While the dining hall still rocked with applause, the Commissario took the vote. Not quite unanimously, the self-sentences were accepted. After the

14. Emil Kleber, a Hungarian Jew, trained as a military leader in the Soviet Union and led the defense of Madrid by the first International volunteers in November 1936.

15. Socorro Rojo Internationale (SRI) was a Communist-organized aid organization.

local secretary had made an appeal for funds to buy an electric light generator which would not break down and after the liberal collection had been
taken, the meeting ended.

That night the French youth again got drunk. He had too many friends,
too much pain and too light a head.

I walked through the dark wards to my bed. My way led through the tor-
ture chamber in which patients lay "in traction" each inside what looked like
a loom hung with complicated systems of weights and pulleys, each with a
knitting needle through an arm or a leg. There is no other way to lengthen
a shortened limb. I imagine that much of our valued morphine goes to the
traction-ward.

Few of our patients cry out.

Dec. 7. Still in Villa Paz

For forty-eight hours the six cars of the convoy which was turned back to
Valencia have stood motionless in the second courtyard; gas-tanks full,
needle-valve and timing systems adjusted to a millimeter, springs, generators
and water-pumps brimming with oil. What went wrong? Did something go
wrong? To what end did we burn up five or six hundred liters of the Ministry
of War's hard-gotten gasoline? The general feeling is that either Major B. or
the staff of the 15th Brigade blundered. Faced with a loss of prestige, the Major says nothing. I would appreciate lectures on military-medical strategy.

"There will be some days," someone told me, back in New York, "when
there is nothing to do. These times are the hardest to endure."

This is the fifth consecutive day we have been under stand-by orders. The
Major refuses to allow anything but personal baggage to be unloaded. "Take
it easy," Finn tells me. "Sleep. Pretty soon we go to Front and then you will
be sorry." But how many hours a day can a man sleep? How many times have
I climbed to the top of the rocky knoll which lies back of the hospital and
searched the horizon and the sky? Far away camions rush loads of wheat,
rice and frozen Argentine beef to Madrid. Otherwise nothing moves but the
wind, and there are no other sounds but the luscious baritone gurgling of
magpies.

Al R., a lieutenant machine-gunned at Brunete, thinks that the guns on
the Jarama Front can be heard when the wind is right.[16] He braces himself on
one crutch and points with the other at the positions on the hills across the

---

16. Albert Robbins, aka Isidore Cohen, was a student at City College New York before
    going to Spain.

valley at which he would set up the Maxims if we were attacking Villa Paz. The giant mongrel St. Bernard [that] the Infanta Christina Paz left behind in her flight stands behind us, sniffing into the damp winter wind. I cannot understand why this dog is petted so much and fed so well. Some of us call him *"perro,"* which is Spanish for "dog." Others seem to know that his name is "Rex." Unreasonably, I hate the beast. "You're only a dog," I think. "Yours is not the responsibility. Fascists can be dogs but dogs cannot be fascists. The Infanta could not have fed you as well as we do. You are the stomach and the eyes she left behind her. Whenever I look at you I think of her."

Why do I hate the Infanta? All that I know of her, thus far, is that she and her sister and their ancestors owned all the land within sight of their twin hilltop manors, and that Christina was so fond of music that she had not missed the Mozart and Wagner festivals in Munich for years. But yesterday the rock with which we mended the road was taken from a wrecked building which had been, I was told, the Infanta's private jail, in which she had the right to lock up those of her peasants she judged had offended herself or society. During the very first days of the outbreak, the peasants had dynamited the roof off of the Princess' jail. Why should they have done this? The jail was a trim little white-walled house in a grove of poplars next to the brook which fills the irrigation ditches unimproved since the days of the Moors. It would have been useful. After a few more days of road-mending, nothing will remain of the former jail but a rubble-festered scar on the lean earth.

The dynamiting of the Villa Paz jail had been the only act of violence, the only instance of the use of explosives in this part of Cuenca province. This one explosion was the high noon cannon which had ended the past and announced the birthday of the future.

Two hundred men and women are lodged in the two-storey double quadrangle which had formerly been the Infanta's manor and country home; seventy-five staff members and a hundred and twenty-five patients. We have a capacity of two hundred beds. The hospital is as quiet as the Front. Since our capture of Belchite and Their conquest of the North, there has been little surgery and less machine-gun fire. The war-news in the Madrid and Valencia newspapers (each political party has its own system of daily newspapers) with which the hospital is so plentifully supplied tells us that "today on the Huesca front there was an artillery duel. Our guns succeeded in localizing the enemy. Light machine-gun fire in the Penarroya sector. In Guadarrama a bombing party, sent out at sunset, not only destroyed the machine-gun nest which was its objective, but returned with four prisoners. At Teruel, nothing new. Three Italian planes coming from the direction of Palma de Mallorca or from Sardinia attempted to bomb Barcelona but were driven off by our patrols. One of them was observed to have fallen in the sea, but the remains have not yet been recovered."

We wonder why there is so little action. Will the attack come at Guadalajara or from the Aragon? Will Franco continue his tactics of concentrating all his best material and troops at the single point he wants most, or will the attack come like a tidal wave all up and down every front? Where has he sent the tanks, batteries and planes he used in taking Vizcaya and Asturias? Certainly not back to Berlin and Rome.

There is almost one staff member for every patient, not because we are overstaffed, but because of the policy of giving easy work to the light wounded. The eight members of the guard who man the sentry-box at the archway are all unfit for service at the front. Cockney John Milly, the sergeant of the Guard, is a t. b. suspect.[17] Bregman, a radio mechanic from Pittsburgh, "folded up after driving a truck too long."[18] Steve Tandrik, Jugoslav *responsable* of transport, who books, loads, inspects and dispatches all cars, has insomnia.[19] "I haven't slept for four years," he explains. "I sit in bed and think all night and when I collapse I sleep a little but my eyes stay open." Steve has a nervous stomach. Joe Young, West Coast seaman and storekeeper, got a lung-wound out of Brunete.[20] Night after night, arguments about the Brunete campaign of last August surge up and down the wards.

"The war only lasted five minutes for me," says Moe Fishman, a frail twenty-year-old Brooklyn boy with the look of a rabbinical student.[21] "Marty (this was Captain Martin Hourihan, of New Orleans and the United States Army) orders us up Mosquito Hill.[22] I got up to the top and pulled

---

17. John Millie was an English guard assigned to the Villa Paz hospital suspected of having tuberculosis.

18. "Bregman" is probably Maurice Freeman, one of the guards at Villa Paz who described himself as a "radio technician."

19. Steve Tandaric, aka Emil Tandarich, a Croatian-born steelworker from Hammond, Indiana, used his brother's passport to travel to Spain and to return to the United States. His later claim to be a U.S. citizen, however, resulted in his deportation to Yugoslavia in 1959.

20. Joe Young, born in Bellefonte, Pennsylvania, became a seaman on the Pacific coast after the war. During the Great Retreats, he was captured by the enemy and held at San Pedro prison and exchanged after Franco's victory.

21. Moe Fishman was a New York volunteer. He later served as National Secretary of the Veterans of the Abraham Lincoln Brigade (VALB) for many years, until his death in 2007.

22. Martin Hourihan, a battalion and regimental commander, was seriously wounded at

back my breech-bolt. I picked out a big greasy Moor for myself but before I
had the chance to fire, they drilled me." Moe is all plaster of paris from the
waist down.

"We never should have been ordered to take that hill," somebody else says,
from his bed. "They had hills that looked right down on us and enfiladed
every position we had. Whoever gave that order bollixed the works." "Listen
to him rave!" comes a voice from under a sheet, "his temperature is up again.
We had to take Mosquito Hill. It wasn't anything to us but a pain in the ass,
but They could have commanded the whole valley from the hilltop." "Yeah,"
says the first man, "but we didn't hold, did we?" "All of you *soldados* don't
know dash-all. Sure we couldn't hold Mosquito Hill. Nobody ever thought
we could. We were a line of resistance, that's what we were. The Republic
had to push some meat out there in front, and we were elected. That's what
you call war. You fellows forget that we are shock troops and shock troops
are to metal what a sponge is to water. We're high-grade sponges, that's what
we are, nothing but the best. The human body is eighty-four cents' worth of
fertilizer"—"eighty-nine cents' worth, you mean"—"do you comrades think
you're going to live forever? The only kind of immortality your transcenden-
tal souls will have. . . . "

"Ow!" says another bed, "listen to the big greasy six-bit words! That intellectual hurts me more than my busted neck."

At the pronouncing of the battle-cry word "intellectual," the entire ward
begins to howl. Nurses trot down the aisles without being able to stop the
racket. "They thought the seamen were going to be so good. Robbie made a
whole company out of nothing but stokers and deck hands, and everybody
says, 'watch the seamen. They know how to scrap.'[23] But what happens at
Brunete?" "Yeah, what happens," says a sailor, "what happens. We took Brunete, didn't we?"

"Sure we did. But after Brunete, they broke up the Robbie's company and
put some good intellectuals and white collars into it, didn't they?"

More howling breaks out at the sound of the one unstomachable fighting
word, "intellectual." The Commissar enters the ward.

"Now," he asks, "will all you military experts answer a question? What is
the chief advantage Franco has over us? Anybody who gives the right answer
will be made a Colonel as soon as he can stand without crutches. Or if he

---

Brunete in July 1937.

23. John Quigley Robinson, "Little Robbie," an Irish American seaman, served as a company commissar in Spain.

doesn't want a Colonel's stripes, we'll issue him a whole package of Lucky Strikes."

Silence. Then, "I'll take the cigarettes."

"Well," says the Commissario, "the advantage Franco has over us is that he has no intellectuals on his side."

Mosquito Hill got its name not because it was a breeding ground for Jersey tigers but because machine-gun bullets under certain conditions are said to sound exactly like giant mosquitos.

I am slowly developing a sense of inferiority because I have not been under fire. Yet none of the men seems to nourish the slightest rancor for me.

I ask someone about my position:

"Listen," he says, "you're new, aren't you?"

"How did you know I was new?" I answer.

"Well, you haven't got that 'gone' look on your face. Don't worry, you get it soon enough. We're all here doing our jobs and if we do them, our fares to Spain weren't wasted."

I notice that the worst fire-eaters and the wearers of the heaviest side-arms are men who have never been at the Front.

"Mosquito Hill" will never be written on the memorial banners of the 15th Brigade of the International Battalions. If that position had not been held while we were bringing up our artillery and tanks, Franco could have been able to wipe out all of the gains made during the twenty-one days of agonizing fighting in the worst heat of the summer. In the face of Franco's most fully developed mechanical attack, and under the motors of his heaviest planes, we took the hilltop and lost it seven times in twelve hours. The story is told that Colonel Lister, watching the men go up open slopes, was told that "these troops are Communists." "You didn't need to tell me that," the Colonel answered, "I knew they were Communists when I saw them go up the hill."[24]

It's a good story, except that the Fifteenth is not made of Communists. Their political faiths range from the child-like humanitarianism of Doukhobor colonists from Canada to the adventurism of Wobblies from the West Coast, solid Non-Partisan League Minnesota farmboys and romantic pacifists from Park Avenue.[25] I know one infantryman who says he came to Spain

---

24. Enrique Lister was a Communist general of the 5th Regiment.
25. The Doukhobors were a Christian pacifist group. Wobblies were members of the militant Industrial Workers of the World (IWW). The Non-Partisan League was a midwestern Socialist political organization.

because he was bored by playing bridge for a living and because the hunting was better than in the Adirondacks. Stuart will have to confine himself to solitaire, when and if he gets back to the States, because he has lost his left hand.[26]

Half our patients are Americans. There are a good many French, quite some Belgians and Germans, Scotchmen, and a sprinkling of Dutch, Poles, Spanish, Scandinavians, Irish—but to complete the list I would have to mention every country in Europe and many in Asia. I haven't yet heard of the Zulu or an Esquimaux, or a Russian, although there are several American Indians among us and the son of an Abyssian dedjasmatch who came to Spain, non-politically, for the open season on Italians.

The staff members are at least half Spanish. For each of our American Registered Nurses, two Spanish *chicas* are in training. Before the outbreak there was not one single trained nurse in Spain. The sick were cared for by nuns who had no formal instruction. I understand that most of these nuns are still at their duties. One of them, who now dresses as a woman and has let her hair grow into a handsome mannish bob, has in a very few months learned almost everything she could be taught at an American nursing school. Romance? Plenty, but all of the traditional war-time broken-hearted variety. Elsa, the five-foot, hundred and fifty-pound American pharmacist and laboratory technician, is said to lose twenty pounds every time she falls in love, and to gain an exactly similar amount whenever the object of her affection gets well and leaves for the Front. One of the nurses is passionately devoted to the Captain whose leg and waist are in plaster. The colored nurse from Ohio is the widow of the negro machine-gun company commander who fell in the street-fighting at Belchite.[27] All of the other nurses have strings of admirers, and many of the men are put to sleep at night by a sedative dreaminess of unrequited love, thus saving us much luminal. Few couples are able to manage the simultaneous vacation which glows with Elinor Glynnish promise of three days of fool's paradise under the palms of Murcia.

It would be difficult to understand how it is possible that each girl's scores of followers do not turn her head if it were not true that quite a few of the plainer girls have developed a queenly and exclusive manner. As for myself, I haven't yet seen anything on this hilltop that would have pleased me back

26. Yale Stuart, aka Skolnik, lost his left arm in the Ebro offensive of 1938.
27. Salaria Kea, born in Georgia and raised in Akron, Ohio, was the only African American woman to serve with the AMB. She also served in the U.S. Army Nursing Corps in World War II.

home, and after three weeks in Spain I'm still particular. One of the girls has nice big brown eyes. I danced with her the other evening, my enormous waterproof boots scraping on the rough cement floor to the sound of a rhumba hashed out of a senescent victrola with a needle rustier than the teeth of a worn-out pitchfork. Ski-pants, sweater and all, she's not such a bad little business—but I'd better keep clear of the autogenerative scandal and intrigue and gossip which breeds out the walls and flooring of any institution in which a number of people must by force of circumstance stay together and depend exclusively on each other's society. If I could locate something big, something of the genuine Tristan and Isolde, Sheean and Prohme, Liebestraum, hands-across-the-table, five-dollar-an-ounce Paris perfume magnitude, I should really have something to write about.[28] Out of devotion to his political convictions, from a mountain-top he covers the retreat of an entire Army Corps, she feeds the belt into his maxim, the sun starts to go down, they kiss, then the Moors take care of both of them, and like the Babes in the Woods, planes cover their interlocked bodies with shrapnel, but not until he has time to write it all down.

Unfortunately no small voice calls out my name from an American crib; and my mother so fervently believes that I am doing "administrative work" so far out of rifle-range that she wanted to make sure that I brought my tailcoat and white tie with me. It is true that I carry four snapshots of a very beautiful girl in my hat-band, and a perfumed letter in the pocket of my shirt, between my passport and a spare pair of glasses. I am extremely nearsighted. If it were not for my eyes, I might be in the infantry. I'm still ashamed of driving an ambulance. I don't like the literary, intellectual, here-to-be-revolted-by-the-horror-of-war, later-to-write-a-book, Allan Seager mock heroism tradition that lies behind my job.[29] First comes Jurgen, in the sophomore year at some hated Eastern college, then an ambition to write, then an apartment in the Village, then a number of book-reviews and equally unfortunate copulatory romances, then a war and then the ambulance, and ever afterwards, a Harris tweed jacket, a collection of James Joyce firsts, a wife with dough and a house on the dunes of Cape Cod. But all of those fellows were non-political. Art kept them pure and art embalms them.

---

28. Sheean and Prohme are journalists and friends Vincent Sheean and Rayne Prohme. Prohme reported on the Chinese Revolution; Sheean was thought to be in love with her and dedicated his book *Personal History* in her name.

29. Probably a reference to the poet Alan Seeger (1888–1916), well known for "I Have a Rendezvous with Death."

I am here in Spain, I imagine, because history forever breeds men in the example of Spartacus who have either to give action to words or else become neurotic with self-mortification. Give me an army of introspectives, any day. We can take it. From time to time I expect to write how well I am taking it, and why I have come to Spain. To a certain extent, going to war is like visiting the Pyramids: everyone knows all about them, but once you've been to Egypt, then you can tell people that you have seen the pyramids.

Night fell and we were still under stand-by orders. I grew tired of reading newspapers by candlelight—the generators broke down again—of listening to discussions of the price of shoes in Madrid and Valencia, of talk about who has the best pistol and how much he paid for it, had the anarchist extremists ever really lifted our cigarettes from us as they came through Barcelona, who was wounded and when and where and had he died, and what would you eat first when you got to Paris—ham and eggs or a steak or a gallon of ice-cream. The ham and the eggs generally had it. The discussion ended after Mike ("I-know-your-type") Hill, the Cordoba veteran who writes the weekly English broadcast for EAR in Madrid, said that he would like to drowse in a luke-warm bath while listening to Respighi's "Fountains of Rome" eating marzi-pan and looking through a book of photographers' nudes, with Great [sic] Garbo waiting for him in the next room between peach-colored silk sheets.[30] The Spanish do not pretend to be so sensuous: each man thinks being able to plow his piece of land without having to keep one eye on the sky, and of his right to his job and his share of the natural wealth of Spain, of which there seems to be so little. If there is wealth in this country I have not seen it, but in the landscapes and the really extraordinary sunsets.

Since I soon grew tired of talking about what I would eat when the war was over, I went upstairs to the ward in which I have secured a bed, always with the understanding that I may have to vacate it if there should be a sudden attack up at Madrid and a sudden rush of wounded to Villa Paz.

I pulled my duffle bag out from under my bed and again went over its contents trying to cut down my outfit.

I wear a pair of dark brown corduroy trousers made into a rather good imitation of the standard baggy ski-pants by means of cords passed through the cuffs. My shoes are waterproof but very loose and impossible to shine. I wear two pairs of woolen socks. A suit of moderately soft long underwear

---

30. Mike Hill, aka Aaron Aronberg, whose real name was Myron Ehrenberg, a writer
    from Boston, served as political commissar at Villa Paz and handled publicity for the
    AMB aimed at U.S. radio audiences. EAR was a Madrid radio station.

serves as a foundation for the heavy khaki flannel jacket which is the only
military part of my costume, and for a heavy blue crewneck sweater, a sleeve-
less sheepskin vest and a heavy hiplength horsehide coat lined with wool.
The secret of avoiding dirt fever is to put on your coat whenever you come
indoors.

I cannot very well leave behind the heavy rubber poncho which may be
used either for a raincoat or a ground sheet. Neither can a spare set of long
underwear, an extra shirt and a pair of socks be left behind. Two extra pairs
of glasses, my voluminous notebook, a valuable flashlight which generates
its own current, a box of matches and a candle, three secret packages of
American cigarettes, razor, comb, toothpaste, a bar of French soap and my
very valuable passport complete my present outfit. I cannot very well cut
it down.

I have decided never to sleep without a spare pair of glasses and my passport in the breast-pocket of my shirt. Against my own best advice and that
of my comrades I have decided that the passport may someday save my life.
My captors would see that I am an American citizen born in New Orleans,
and this would of course save me from being shot. I have heard no report or
rumor which should justify this hope. Quite a few Internationals have been
captured. Those of us who are taken disappear. Yet I have a childish kind of
faith in my passport. The Germans and Italians among us carry pistols to in-
sure their not being sent back to their native lands by Franco. The other day
I read the speech of Jesus Hernandez, the Republican minister of Education,
to the Italian prisoners we had captured at Brijuete:

"You thought that we hated you, that we were going to kill you," he said,
"but we do not hate the people of Italy. You are not our foe. Reluctant but
helpless, you were deceived into embarking for Abyssinia. When the ships
that should have taken you to Africa steamed into Spanish harbors, your re-
luctance turned to disgust. Overwhelmed by the eyes of your officer's pistols,
no protest was possible. In battle at Guadalajara, you were surprised that you
faced long-lost Italian brothers. Defeated by superior tactics and the heavy
artillery of our morale, you surrendered not in shame but with honor.

"In a few hours, Italian comrades, a train will take you to Franco. From
there you will return to your fatherland. We wish you to tell the men and
women what kind of treatment you had from us. Some day we will come
to Italy to help you liberate the Italian people from fascism and from him
who calls himself your leader, just as the comrades of the Garibaldi Brigade
helped in our struggle of liberation from Hitler, Mussolini and their Spanish
puppet generals. . . . "

What became of the trainload of Italian soldiers? Did they reach Italy, and if they did, what happened to them once they were "home"? Perhaps only tombstone cutters can tell.

I forgot: Tarancon, eighteen miles away on the road to Madrid, with its two large American hospitals and its American garage, was bombed today, but not seriously. Our patrols arrived in time to make the four or five Italian Fiat biplanes waste almost all of their cargo on the open fields. Late in the afternoon, when the news reached us, earth began to fly from the trench we are digging just below the lip of the hill.

Al, the wounded Lieutenant, gave me my first lesson in the art of trench-making. "Always mark the earth before you begin to dig. Trenches on a ridge should never show against the skyline. None of them should be straight, not even a communication trench. Zigzags, themselves irregular, ought to be six to eight feet long and no longer. A light bomb or a hand grenade or a trench-mortar shell bursting in a straight trench will hit everyone within a hundred feet, but could not kill more than five in a scientifically built ditch. The earth ought always be thrown towards the enemy and never away from him. All rocks must be removed from the parapet. A bullet which strikes earth is only one bullet; one which hits rock becomes many. Trench parapets should be camouflaged with bushes or tree limbs because of the planes. In no case must we dig deeper than three or four feet, even in the most solid earth, without the use of timbers."

Is the attack coming this way?

Dec. 8. The Seventh Consecutive Day of Stand-by Orders

The rumor which ran through the wards and the dining room that orders had come led me to load my duffle bag. I went to the kitchen to get water for my radiator. Cabbage, the first fresh vegetable which I have seen since I came to Spain, was being prepared by *chicas* and *guapas* in neat white aprons. Between breakfast and dinner, a musician seated in the kitchen concert hall might make a fairly complete study of what the invasion has done to Spanish music, which was and is mostly vocal. The *flamencos* of Andalucia, consisting mostly of wordless chorus, lend themselves easily to new sentiments, but they are entirely too gay for the vengeance and boastfulness which identify war music from all other kinds of songs but football anthems. The ludicrous flabby anti-climaxes of the For-God, For-Country and For-Yale spirit is entirely absent.

"If Queipo comes here"—then about two minutes of arabesque arpeggios—"We're going to kill him and all of his men"—then three more minutes of arabesques. The name of this song is "*Golondrero*." Does this mean "Sparrowcatcher"? Another song, called "The Four Generals," runs "The Moors wish to pass"—trill trill trill, in the Madrileño style—"but, dear mother, nobody will pass" and then some more trilling. The effect is gay rather than Wagnerian. Even the national anthem, "Hymno de Riego," is so light-footed that the words which the Brigade has made up to it, beginning with "Oh Barnum and Bailey are coming to town, Barnum and Bailey are coming to town" do not seem sacrilegious. Another favorite concerns Lina Odena, "fresh as the rose," who tragically drove a truckload of munitions into the Moors. The most somber song is a romance, with the chorus, "how beautiful she was," sung over and over again. In all of this music occur the breaks and sudden speeding up of time which are only found, as far as I know, in the Hungarian Chardas and the Jugoslav kolo. Slowly the bicycle of the tempo pedals up a hill: then the summit is reached; the riders balance for a perilous second, and race off wildly down the descending slope; pulling up short at the bottom of the next hill. Western music seems barren of this device; but judging by the frequency with which Liszt rhapsodies are played to raise the curtains of midwestern movie-houses, the Moors or Slavs who many years ago invented this device found a kind of adrenalin with which to speed up the beating of the human heart.

Still killing time, I help with the woodchopping. The boss of the woodshed is one of the Infanta Paz' original retainers.[31] He was a carriage driver.

Since anyone could remember, the Paz family had been grandees and had kept in their stomach the large gulp of Castilian soil some king or other, certainly nicknamed "The Liberator," had brought to them on a golden platter. Within the memory of at least eighteen generations, the Paz family had done nothing for their land but to build the castle whose ruins give the name of Castilejo, contracted from Castel Viego, to the convalescent home of the Infanta's sister which lies across the valley. It was the Moors who had dug the excellent system of canals. For six centuries, families of land-diggers—I avoid the use of the word "serf" for the benefit of those possible future readers who may have tender political stomachs—families of plowmen had been born and had died in the rabbit-hutch waterless, stoveless one-fireplace apartments that ring the broad second courtyard of the Infanta's birthright. Six hundred years of progress, science and civilization had wormed their way into Villa Paz to produce Donna Christina's bathroom, her heating plant,

---

31. Many of Spain's landed aristocrats abandoned their estates for safety behind Franco's lines.

the nineteenth century Turkish imitations of petit-point tapestry, her flimsy French copies of Spanish antique furniture and a large portrait of herself. Perhaps there had been heirlooms, long ago sold to pay the debts of a nephew who played the ponies at long-champs[32] or the tables at Cannes or the girls of Madrid too hard.

Madame Paz had lived little in her home. Because the climate of Castile is fit in winter only for those who cannot move away, she liked to pass this time of year in Munich, studying the flute and spending long mornings of adoration in the sunlit Gothic rooms of the Alte Pinacothek, dreaming among the crushed-jewel colors of Madonnas, triptichs and tortured Saints. In the spring of each year, the Princess returned to Castile for an interview with the local *cacique* who did her financial and human bookkeeping while she was away. There probably was not a malign sinew or neurone in the old lady's body.

It happened that she was in residence in the early summer of 1936, arranging for the reception of the Madrid priests who spent their summers each year in the breezes of her hilltop.

The Infanta's peasants blew the roof off of the jail in which they had been for centuries punished at the discretion of the Paz family on the advice of the *cacique*.

"We are very sorry for what has happened." Perhaps this was the first time that these men had stood in the Princess' personal part of the manor. "We hope that your headache is better. Of course, Donna Christina, things won't change. You'll stay here with us and we will give you many shares of what we produce. No one but the *cacique* must go."

He had already gone.

The Infanta was satisfied, but not satisfied. Her peasants had taken down the fence which separated her lands from the fields of the neighboring village of Saelices. Plows were already driving past the ancient boundaries in longer furrows than this part of Cuenca province had ever seen. The plowmen said that this way horses became less tired in turning and that much time was saved. Somebody talked of socialization, someone else of collectives, and many others of scientific agriculture. When Eufemio, Donna Christina's devoted carpenter (who now is our coffin-maker), was elected head of the Saelices de Tarancon Collective, she left for Madrid. With much difficulty and at some expense, her peasants sent her cartloads of food and as much money as they could spare. One day the cart returned from Madrid with the news

---

32. The French horse-racing track Longchamps.

that the mistress of Villa Paz had gone to Munich for the Mozart festival. The peasants were relieved. By this time many of them had said novenas for brothers, sons and nephews who had died in the defense of Madrid. Rumors had reached them that aeroplanes were dropping bombs on the working-class neighborhoods of many Spanish cities. The Infanta had gradually come to be identified by her people with the Generals, Senoritos, Curas, Tercios, Italianos and Moros in whose path blood was everywhere flowing fuller than the Manzanares River in winter.

Assassinated by History, Frau Christian Paz now lives in concert halls and the Gothic splendour of one of Europe's finest museums.

Why did I come to Spain?

In six months American money, American technical skill, American hands and sweat have helped the Spanish establish and organize what must be a fair imitation of a first-class American hospital in the Infanta's former home. We lack flowers and much else. The board floors on the second floor have been covered with tiles bought after the entire staff had donated ten days' pay. So now we will have a dependable lighting system. The old days, when operations were finished with flashlights or candles, when eggs were boiled in wine and hot water bottles filled with soup because there was suddenly no water, are finished. We ask for little more than cases. The unnatural truce-like calm which now exists must come to a violent end before long. Meanwhile, peasants come to us from all Cuenca province with the ills which have afflicted them for centuries, expecting miracles. The Saelices doctor, one of the few medical men of this region who did not skip to the fascists, complains that we are taking away his trade. He is so unfamiliar with modern medicine that it would be unwise for us to take him in with us or to set him up in a village clinic. Should we take fees from his former patients? A new world is not born without agony.

Why did I come to Spain?

Not, certainly, to go to dances; but last night I went to the festival the English Hospital had prepared for the staff of Villa Paz.

Either because the Major must have received definite orders that the expedition to the Front had been called off or because he had noticed that the morale of his group needed bracing, he ordered Smitty to unpack the big Harvard bus and take us to the party in it.

After jolting over back roads for an hour and a half, we pulled up in front of Huete Base Hospital. Formerly a combined prison and convent, the long dank half-lit corridors, tremendous walls and massive cut stone archways made me think of Piranesi, Bel Geddes and Victor Hugo. Eventually we reached an outdoor stone stair which descended to a rectory. The orchestra consisted of guitar, violin, cello and accordion. The last two instruments were played by a doctor and a nurse who were unmistakably English. The girl had the cool green pre-Raphaelite eyes, the page-boy blonde hair and the clear transparent skin of the type of young lady I had always wished to take walking under Addison's oaks in the deer park of Morton College in Oxford in spring, but had never met. Standing outside the shuffling throng of villagers, patients and nurses, I waited my chance; but soon learned that the lady with the accordion was the wife of the blond-bearded English doctor who played *jotas* so conscientiously on his cello. Perhaps my only romance in Spain will be with a shell from a 75.

I was unable to enjoy the dancing although, out of a sense of political duty, I danced with Pepita, the ugliest and most carefully gotten-up of the Villa Paz *chicas*. The raciness, jazz-madness and glamour of wartime Paris cabarets was not present. Ragged uniforms ornamented only by side-arms, collarless shirts, arms held high in wire splints, black cotton dresses; nothing but the white aprons and the eyes of some of the girls were restful. Imperialist conflicts have a tone which social wars lack.

Later in the evening, the English girls gave a private party for the Villa Paz Internationals in the club-room they had arranged in their quarters; low whitewashed walls, soft chairs, indirect lighting and a deep-toned radio; and vermouth tasting of quina. After three drinks and a dance to a rhumba broadcast from a London night club, my spirits began to soar above the undersea level in which I have been brooding ever since the Major gave the order to turn back from Valencia.

"Do you know what," I said to the girl of the accordion, "I wish I were in a night club back home full of sloe gin fizzes listening to jazz bluer than Valencia street lights."

"You do-oo-ooo," she answered, surprised, and for the first time really looking at me. "Well, what I wish was that the war were over. I wish this killing would stop."

I had said the wrong thing. The romance was over.

I was even more sorry when the entertainment began and my lady sang, tone-perfect without accompaniment, an aria from Purcell and then one of Haydn's, her eyes fastened inside the melody or perhaps Spain's future.

Dec. 9. Still in V. P., Waiting, Waiting
Stupidly, the day was made of trench-digging and more digging, road-mending and tire-pumping. I have been put in charge of the trench. Again

we saw a plane, again of undetermined politics. The Infanta's dog, Rex, has become much interested in the trench. Is he spying for Franco? It was all I could do to keep from heaving earth at him. Jowl-eyed and wet-mouthed, he looks and waits and waits and looks. He seems to want us to know that he will be here when all of us have gone.

Waiting, waiting. I wish I had a pistol. I don't know why, but I wish I did.

Dec. 11. Villa Paz

I skipped a day's writing, for a very good reason.

Yesterday before lunch the man ahead of me in the trench lifted his head and stood still, sniffing into the wind like a bird-dog.

"Jesus Christ," he said.

As I leaned on my shovel I heard something like the noise of half a dozen distant motorcycles.

Finn came down the hill. Behind him were at least fifteen men with shovels.

"What's up?" I asked Finn.

"Nossing, Dzim, we shovel fast, yes?"

For the first time since we had begun to dig, earth and rocks flew with the silence that meant business. Again and again I had dreamed of motors in the sky, white aprons running down the hill, stretcher-bearers emptying out the wards.

At lunch time there was much talk of planes.

"I saw them. There were five."

"No, three. Red wing-tips. Ours."

"I saw six. If they were ours, why in hell did they dive on that pine grove the other side of Castilejo, emptying their machine-guns."

"They didn't."

"They did."

After lunch the Commissario made the speech we had been expecting.

"Because of the planes we saw this morning," he said, "all cars will immediately be taken out of the hospital courtyards and parked in separate places at least two to three hundred yards away from the building and the same distance away from each other. Each car should be camouflaged by blankets—no, we haven't any to spare—by bushes and branches. Swede will have a siren installed on the roof before nightfall. The laundresses should lay nothing white outside the hospital to dry. After dark, there must be no lights whatsoever in the courtyards, and all windows must be shut and the cracks stuffed with rags.

"One thing more. After lunch, line up for cigarettes in front of my office."

"Joe thinks we're afraid," someone whispered to me, "That's why the cigarettes."

"What are you, nuts?" was answered. "Today is cigarette day. What do you take, chocolate or smokes?"

Once a week we are given our choice of a bar of chocolate and a package of American cigarettes. Two bars of chocolate have a value, in trade, of twenty tailor-mades.

After lunch I went down the hill to cut a good big dwarf oak for camouflage. Several of the branches were long and straight enough to be used as supports for the oak-leaf bower I would build for my car. The heavy wax-grained trunk, ideal for knees and frames in small sailing vessels, could be used for firewood. Two more years of war and no tree will stand between here and Madrid.

The ax was dull. Unused to this type of heavy labor I soon grew tired.

Then the blade, at the back of a stroke, stayed as still as a bird held motionless for an instant by the wind.

Dull sounds, not altogether unlike the blows of an ax far heavier than mine, distinctly reached me from over Castilejo hill and the two American hospitals in Tarancon.

"This is it," I thought. "Now I hear it for the first time. This is it. What do I do? What do I think?"

I peeled off my horsehide, spit on my hands, and putting all the keenness of my eyes and the weight of my shoulders behind each slow swing, goose-flesh from calves to back, went after my enemy as if this were not a tree I was cutting down, but fascism itself.

Marty came running down the hill.

"Get into your car and tear like hell for Tarancon. Report to Captain Jungerman."

"Marty, did you hear those sounds?"

The chófer sucked on the twig he chews when he has no tobacco.

"Yes I did. Sometimes you can hear the heavy stuff at Jarama."

"Sometimes."

"Well, what are you standing there for?"

Fifteen kilometers down the road I saw a tall, voluminous curtain of black smoke mixed with steam unfolding and coiling with the horrible deliberate grace of an octopus's arms. Several ambulances, proceeding at what I estimated was belly-case speed, had passed me. Outside Tarancon itself carts piled high with mattresses and pots appeared, men straining at the bits of the mules that pulled them, old women and children trotting at the rear. A fifteen-foot gash in the rocky earth beside the road cheered me. Not every bomb had reached its mark.

I entered the town. Steering between bomb-holes as deep as four feet, I passed a dead mule, blood streaming down the gutter from between his teeth. A voice called out at me from beside the belled-out sheet metal door of the hospital garage. "Say, wait a minute. Stay right where you are."

I got out of my car and was pacing off the length of the stream of blood that flowed from the dead mule's mouth when I saw Captain J.[33]

"What in the hell do you think you're doing," he said pleasantly.

"Some day I'll have to write about this—four, five, six paces; that's about eighteen feet. Well, Doc, what are my orders? Do I get a load?"

"Bloodthirsty, aren't you. No, you don't get a load. Sixty ambulances have pulled out of here already."

"*Sixty?*" Sixty loads meant at least a hundred and eighty heavy wounded and two hundred light. The dead, of course, stay with us. Tarancon was such an innocent objectiveless little burg; two hospitals, two garages and a gas-pump.

I reported to Hospital Number One, and stood on the curb catching the mattresses, light wood beds and dusty bloodstained sheets and pillows thrown from the ruined wards overhead. A man and a woman, their faces smeared with a black rouge of powder, red swollen lips and tongue clubbed into shapelessness by concussion, lay on stretchers. Both civilians, these were the first dead I had seen since, many years ago, I had looked at my father's painted face framed by the silver and plush of the window in his coffin. I had always been afraid of the moment when I should see my first war-dead. "How dirty they look," I thought, knowing that no one would wash their faces and hands or dress them in clean clothes. There was so little time. By nightfall, both hospitals and our garage must be moved to the new site which has already been chosen.

At my feet lay a four-inch shell-head and the neat suede-gloved hand of Ysabel, one of our nurses. A surgeon would have been proud of the precision with which the amputation had been made.

I kicked at the little mongrel cur which sniffed the hand.

Before the sun went down, wards, kitchen, laboratory, dining hall and

---

33. Captain Tales Wolf Jungerman-Jungery was a Polish doctor who studied medicine in Yugoslavia.

garage were clean. Four ambulances and two staff cars had been caught in the garage. We towed their wreckage out of town. Nobody knew when the planes are coming back to put the last finishing touches on the job so well executed in the morning.

I drove back to Villa Paz whose *triaje*, hallway office and even stairs were crowded with civilians of both sexes, of all ages, to pick up the night Guard from Tarancon.

All of the stars, which hang as low as the lights of a distant hilltop city in these Southern latitudes, were out. We cursed the moon. I was to stand six hours of duty in front of No. One, then sleep, and drive the Guard back to Villa Paz in the morning. The town was entirely dark but for the few candles by which demented men still dug for their relatives. Have not seen a lantern thus far in Spain. Kerosene has always been too expensive.

Guards stalked and leaned in every shadow. It must be remembered that the vote in 1936 was very close. Plenty of Those whose planes visited us this afternoon are in every hamlet and city of Republican Spain. Looting is almost uglier than assassination and sniping. Although I had no gun but my flashlight, I felt no fear. I don't know why. Often, at night alone in the woods of Maine, I had felt afraid. I hope that I will soon be able to get hold of a pistol. I do not like the atmosphere of these bombed, disorganized towns at night. "Pistols are more useful in the Rear than at the Front," the Major tells me. "Every chófer should carry a pistol." I don't fully understand what this means.

Guard duty at night is a lonely, monotonous, depressing thing. All of the world is black and soundless. Robbed of their power of observation which might make the time grow faster your eyes stare aimlessly at black, gray and blue shapes and shadows. All sounds but the infrequent tramping of feet are indeterminable.

I was relieved at 2 A.M. and found the fire which had been lit, among hundreds of labelless tin cans and mounds of potatoes, in the one unwrecked room of the *Intendencia*.

The mickies we made of the undersized potatoes of Castile were the best thing I had tasted since I came to Spain. We ate marmalade by the can, cold cooked tomatoes and two tins of sardines. It is never difficult to assemble a Guard for a wrecked *Intendencia*.

"I wonder," said Arlington George Watt Bassett (real name), "fphwat the payperrs'll have to sye aboot this in Scutland."[34]

---

34. Arlington George Watt Bassett was, in fact, a Scottish volunteer.

"This ought to make page one all over the world."

"Did anyone see Matthews of the Times?"[35]

"No."

"Then this is how it will run, at the bottom of a page sixteen interview with Franco stating that no one feels the tragedy of civil war more than he, and that the object of his uprising which came just in time to forestall a bolshevik holocaust . . . "

"Fphwat the hell is a holo . . . ?"

"Never mind. 'Loyalist sources aver that the Tarancon, a town of some four thousand inhabitants on the lifeline'—'how newspaper men love that word 'lifeline'—'to Valencia, purportedly of no military importance, was bombed by several planes which they indicate were of Central European manufacture. . . . '"

"Are Messerschmidts made in Tahiti?"

"Shut up. ' . . . with the loss of lives and some damage to property. It could not be determined if the two American-staffed hospitals which are said to be located in Tarancon were hit.' Finis."

"They weren't Messerschmidts. They were Junkers. Three of them came over low enough at eleven this morning—hey, you, go out and get some more wood for the fire. That's one thing I like about these bombed towns. Plenty of firewood."

"Not three Junkers. Four, and they were Caproni's."

"Listen, fellows," I said. "I wasn't here this morning and I like to get the story straight. Bregman, you're not tongue-tied like Jock. . . . "

"I came down from V. P. early this morning to let Doc Jungerman bang my stomach. He thinks he knows what's wrong with it. So do I. Swallowing too much of you guys' hot air."

"At eleven, three planes came over. . . . "

"So low that you could see the markings. Red wing-tips. 'Ours,' everybody yells, 'Neustras. Neustras Gloriosas.' Now I've been at the Front down in Cordoba, and as soon as I heard that 'Neustras' yell go up, I vaulted over a fence and landed in a nice deep ditch only half full of garbage, and watched the women and the kids run out into the streets to say hello to our Glorious Airfleet. The three biplanes leveled off and slowly floated by. When they were just about over the main square, wads of leaflets drifted out of the cockpits

---

35. Herbert Matthews, reporter on the Republican side for the *New York Times*. His memoir, *Two Wars and More to Follow* (1939), includes journalistic reportage on the U.S. volunteers in Spain.

which all the kids ran to get. I don't know why they have to keep so many of the children here in a town so near the Front."

"Is seventy miles near?"

"By air it is. So: before the dummy leaflets hit the ground—I got one later and it was just a blank sheet of paper—the three Gloriosos, only they weren't ours, let go hand-grenades and double-caliber machine-guns out of the floor of their fuselages, climbed and showed the black fascist emblems on their lousy wing-tops. Meanwhile, nine big bastards which had been hiding up high in the clouds dive on us and drop one bomb apiece. The kids got plenty, but the hospitals weren't hit. While we carried the patients down into the trench . . . "

"So you didn't stay in your ditch. . . . "

"Well, you know how you feel when—Jungerman, Doc Rintz, Sonia, Dorothy the technician and some of the others helped in the *triaje*, into which the civilians had begun to pour; and when I say 'pour' that's just what I mean.[36] We plugged holes and sprayed antiseptic and snipped off legs and feet and hands and arms. We ran out of tourniquets and I had to use my belt but the guy died anyway and now I've got it back. Each time the planes came over—they gave it to us five times in two hours—we flopped in the corners of the room. If there had been a time fuse on the one that got the roof of the ward right over our heads, I wouldn't be worrying about repatriation right now."

"You should of seen Les," another guard said. Leslie is a mechanic.[37] "He finds himself a ditch, takes down his pants just to make sure, and jumps. He always takes down his pants. That's how we know when the planes are coming over. His stomach is that way. The other morning I was out walking with him in the country, thinking we could run across a farmhouse and trade a bar or two of soap for some eggs, and he starts fingering that belt of his. Before it occurred to me that Les could have been feeling Nature without no planes being over, I run two or three hundred yards and nearly bust my leg. But Les is a good guy."

"Sure, Les is a good guy. After the first time they came over, we went back to the garage to tow the cars out. He was right there with us. Before we get

<hr>

36. Sonia Merims, head nurse at Tarazona, received head injuries in a bombing and had to be evacuated to Paris. Her husband left the United States aboard a ship to join her, but died of a heart attack en route. After returning home, she gave an ambulance in his memory. Dorothy Fontaine, Massachusetts-born and a graduate of Boston College, served as a laboratory technician with the AMB.

37. Leslie Hutchins went to Spain with the first AMB unit. He was the brother of celebrated driver Evelyn Hutchins.

the last car out, the roof come in on us. The rest of the raid I was in a big bomb hole outside the town. Now don't let anybody tell you that they never fall on the same spot twice, because right after I changed for another hole which looked more friendly to me, an egg landed right where I had been."

"Where I was, a big piece landed on my hip, not hard, but hard enough. 'Get out of here,' she says. The biggest piece I saw since I came out here. Most of it is nice and small."

"Too small to hurt, hey?"

"They don't make shrapnel too small to hurt if it comes fast enough. Speed is what counts."

"When your number comes up, it comes up. That's all. All of us are behind the eight-ball. Shock troops. Don't forget we're shock troops, and sooner or later. . . . "

"I'll take mine later. Before I die I want another piece of hump."

"You mean you feel as if you could handle another piece of hump. On this diet . . . "

"It's not the diet, it's the strain."

We talked about narrow escapes and the way we wished we could want a girl and the way we really wanted a good meal until a dispatch rider came and told me that a truck had broken down halfway to V. P. and that I was ordered to tow it.

It was early morning when I got home. The hall had partially been cleared of stretchers. The figures that lay on those that remained might have been dead, for all that they moved or moaned.

When I saw the Major stretched out in a chair, bloodstains on his trousers, I thought that he was asleep.

"Did you get the pigs?" he asked me with a start.

"Well . . . but I got about two dozen rabbits."

"I ordered you to find those pigs."

"The others brought three of them in."

"Well, why didn't you say so. I don't give a —— who brings them in. What we wanted were the pigs. Why can't you talk straight?" I was glad for the abuse. The Major still must have been operating all night.

"How do you feel?" he asked me.

"I feel fine."

"Well, help with the stretchers, then."

Because of my height, I am useful carrying the back end of a stretcher up the stairs.

Long after sunrise, Major B. was still in the hall, sprawled in a chair.

"Why don't you get some sleep, Doc?"

Expressionless as ever, he stared at me.

"How do you feel?" he again asked.

"I feel fine."

"Get yourself a few hours of sleep. In your car all the beds are full. Don't forget we're still under stand-by orders."

"Listen, Doc."

"Yeah?"

"What was that column of smoke I saw? It wasn't in the town."

"A powder magazine. They got it."

"And afterwards, just for the fun of it, they came back to finish off the hospitals and Tarancon. How many casualties were there, Doc?"

"Forty-eight dead and twenty wounded."

"But sixty ambulances loaded out of that town."

"I said forty-eight dead and twenty wounded, Jim."

"But —— ."

"But nothing. Your job is to keep your car running and your eyes on the road. You don't have to think anything or know anything. Just keep your car in good shape, stay near it, and don't run off the road. Did you fix that loose stud on the door-frame?"

"Well —— ."

"Either it's fixed the next time I ride in that car or there'll be an order out for your arrest . . . and by the way," he added as I turned to go, "sometimes, Jimmy"—he knew I hated to be called Jimmy—"there are things that everybody can't know. It wouldn't be good for the morale of this neighborhood to know how many casualties there really were in Tarancon this afternoon. But don't let it get to you. Now where are you going to sleep? Not that I care, but I may need the car."

"I'll sleep in it."

Hoar-frost lay on the cobblestones on the courtyard. Good. Perhaps the weather was going to be bad.

My car was bundled high with sleeping figures that looked like corpses. I recognized a few of our stretcher-bearers. All bodies which do not move have begun to look like corpses.

I crawled into the cab of the still loaded supply truck and fell asleep.

Where had our planes been? Do we have planes?

December 15. No Chance to Write for Four Days
Chronological account follows:

Dec. 11. V. P.

<u>Night.</u> Late in the afternoon, word spread that the Major and I were going to Madrid. I gathered that he was tired of stand-by orders, that he wished to order a pair of highboots, an overcoat and a uniform, and to inspect the International Brigade rest home in the Capital. Nurses and chófers crowded around my car. I was asked to buy sweaters, stockings, oranges, cakes; to call for photographs and to buy films. I knew that the little time I would get for shopping should be used to dig myself up a pair of pants and some high boots, but meticulously wrote each commission in my notebook. We have much money. There is little to buy.

The road, endlessly arching over bare infertile hill-like plains, was empty of all but food trucks. Towards sunfall, we reached the outskirts of the city. With my ears peeled for the sound of gunfire, I passed beautifully built trenches and barbed wire of fourth, fifth and sixth reserve positions, *chevaux-de-frise* lying ready to be strung across the road. Gas stations were underground and well outside of the towns. I saw an immense dummy pump painted bright red. The nearer we got to the Front, the more apparent were the evidences of organization.

By the time we had reached the gates of Madrid, it was quite dark. The road had filled with gasoline tankers, gigantic diesels, trolley cars and all kinds of Army trucks. As far as I have been able to observe, there are about fifty trucks and two motorcycles on the road for every passenger car, and all of the latter belong to staff officers or civil officials. There are no private cars in Spain. Last to be confiscated, the taxicabs of Barcelona were militarized by the Ministry of War last September.

A few street lights were single electric bulbs painted blue, under opaque shades. The dim headlights of the trucks were blue, and those of the unlit trolleys were the same shade. Here and there a slit of light appeared in the shuttered windows. Not a tail-light was to be seen. The sidewalks were as full of people as the streets were with cars, trucks and carts. I had to drive very carefully. The trucks could often be seen coming; people, not until the last few feet.

We put up in one of the expensive lower rooms of the Hotel Florida. The upper rooms are cheaper because they are more in the line of the shells which come from Mount Garabitas.

The clerk in the dark lounge told us that the hot water would go on at nine that night. I hadn't bathed since that memorable afternoon in the marble tub of the public bathhouse in Barcelona, three weeks ago, except for inefficient efforts with a basin and a sponge, at V. P.

"How's tricks, comrade?" I asked the desk clerk.

"Quiet," he said. "Two hundred shells today."

"What's a busy day?"

"Five hundred shells is *regular*. It begins to be interesting at a thousand shells."

"Where do they land?"

"Oh, it changes. Everywhere. When They miss the *Teléfonos*, across the street from us, They hit our upper stories. Will you two comrades have dinner in the hotel tonight?"

The Major answered that we would not, much to my relief.

We ate in the dining hall of Casa Lukacs, named after a General who did not die in bed. Lukacs, the Hungarian commander of the Internationals, absorbed a shell on the Huesca front last autumn.[38] The enlarged black-bordered photograph which hung over the gilded marble Louis Something-or-other fireplace told me nothing about what sort of man he could have been. Contours and features were those we pass hundreds of times a day on the streets of any city in any country. The expression in the narrowed eyes was one of amusement, cynicism, confidence. I should like to think that these were Comrade Lukacs' feelings when he heard death whistling at him from over the desert Aragon hills.

A wild-looking Irish boy came into La Dame aux Camelias' sitting room, which lacked nothing but a polar bear's skin for the fireplace. Barefoot, shoes in hand, he jabbered a mixture of Gaelic and Brigadese Spanish as his khaki pantaloons dropped into a raspberry colored overstuffed satin chair.

"Shellshocked and drunk. A bad combination," someone whispered to me. "The only case of it I've seen among us."

"Why doesn't he put on his shoes instead of carrying them?"

"He thinks that no Irishman dies in his shoes. He's sure he's going to be killed any minute."

"What's to be done, move him out of Madrid where he won't hear the sound of a gun going off?"

"Then he'd never get well. The doctors think that here, in town, he'll hear so much that he'll get used to it."

---

38. "General Lukacz" was the nom de guerre of Hungarian writer Mata Zalka, aka "Kémeny," killed in action in 1937.

"But what's to be done about the way he drinks?"

What's to be done about the holes in the telephone building and the torn power lines of Tarancon? What's to be done about the big rheumatic eyes of the kids? What's to be done about the surface of the Madrid–Valencia highway? Where are our planes and our anti-aircraft?

The genuine lard in the two cakes I had after my evening beans and the real crystal sugar grains on top of them so warmed my stomach and bones and brain that I could already feel the warm water of the tub in the Hotel Florida on my sleeping skin, and the fragrant sheets wrapped around my neck.

I stepped out of the gravel paths of the garden. By the light of the stars I was glad to see that the plants and flowerbeds had not been neglected.

A door opened and slammed. Someone came running out of Casa Lukacs towards me.

"Are you Major B.'s chófer?"

"Yes. What's up?"

"He wants you to fill up with gas and pull around to the front of the house."

"What's doing?"

"Oh, I don't know. He was called to the telephone a few minutes ago. Sounded as if you're going to the Front. Wish I were going with you."

When I had buried my face in the cold leaves and flowers of the first sweet-olive tree I had seen since I left my home in New Orleans, many years ago, and, memory-drunk, was breathing privet-like wet boxtree oleander scent, a cannon boomed from faraway Garabitas. The sound was like that of a great tree falling in a forest on a quiet night, or like the shutting of a distant door.

No bath, no bridal bed, no uniform, no high boots, no sight-seeing and question-asking in Madrid. No beautiful Madrid *guapa* to fall in love with after dances and drinks in a night-club.

We were soon on the road. "*Ambiete*," ordered the Major. I immediately remembered the location of this town. For weeks I have been using my spare time to study my road-maps. Ambiete, one of the small towns in which the 15th Brigade was billeted, was halfway between Madrid and Tarancon.

Because road-guards were few and signposts indistinct, for the first time I had something of the sensation of being lost near the Front. There was really no danger, but not knowing exactly where you were was a little disquieting.

My fuse blew out. I had no spare. Car-parts and accessories are extremely rare and valuable. We fixed the fuse with a piece of tinfoil from a cigarette wrapper.

Cigarette Ethics and Mores

Not since a truck-load of Canary tobacco was captured on the Cordoba front, not since entire cases of Italian Macedonias were taken during the rout of the Fascist Expeditionary Force at Guadalajara has anyone in Spain smoked anything but vile, strong, dry Hebra, but occasional French cigarettes and Russian ones.

When food is insubstantial, tobacco becomes very important. Barcelona stank of the eucalyptus-smelling weed, chief among the products of the flourishing wartime industry of tobacco-substitute manufacturing.

Because of our friends at home, the International Brigades have more and better tobacco than any other part of the population or of the People's Army, with the exception of the Tank Corps, the Aviation and possibly the anti-aircraft. We are issued one package of American cigarettes and are allowed to buy one package of Hebra picaduro a week. Occasionally pillowslips of loose-rolled cabbage turn up, and anti-tanks. The latter are small tight pills of the proportions of anti-tank guns. These continually go out. Cigarettes enclosed in letters from the States reach us in a mashed-up condition, missing what the censors unofficially tax us, but can easily be re-rolled.

An intricate system of loans of tobacco exists among us. We are all hopelessly in debt to each other. It is not dishonest to deny the possession of anything that can be smoked, although extremely bad form to smoke among the tobacco-less. If you receive a whole carton from home, the moral thing to do is to distribute half and hoard the rest.

Matches are also rare. Most of us carry tinder lighter—*mecheros*—which constantly run out of almost unobtainable *mecha* and flint. Gasoline lighters are hard to get.

If a man has a cigarette but nothing with which to light it, and gets a light from someone who has fire but no smokes, he is levied a cigarette. The sensible thing to do, under such conditions, is to wait until you see someone smoking, and then ask for a light. If the smoker, however, stands in the company of two or three weed-hungry men, these have the right to ask tobacco of you. The possession of tobacco and a lack of paper run you into similar difficulties.

If you have an entire package in your pocket, it is insane to show it. Instead, you secretly slide a hand into your pocket and fish out a single pill.

After morning coffee, the smokeless have the right to ask for "first drags," "second drags," and "butts."

Since the Internationals, and particularly the Americans, possess sources of tobacco which Spaniards lack, the rationing of cigarettes is a delicate
political matter. A certain proportion of all we get from the States is issued
to the Spanish brigades nearest to us.

"Nobody but the Americans have cigarettes," said a Spanish militiaman
to me, bitterly, after I had told him that what I was smoking was a *huerfano
de guerra* or war orphan.

"Well, it's true that we have more than the others. . . . But I want to ask
you a question. When you enlisted and left for your training camp, what
did your mother give you, a rabbit or a chicken?"

"Two chickens."

" . . . and your family doesn't live far away?"

"A hundred kilometers, at present."

"They send you things to eat?"

"Yes."

"Well, our families live many thousands of miles away. We can't get
things from them easily. Do you understand?"

"Yes, I understand," the militia kid answered. "Have you a cigarette?"

When you have a cigarette, by far the best idea is to go out under a tree
to smoke it.

We pulled through a jam of trucks and trotting dark figures into the courtyard of a large chalet-style water-mill. Here in the darkness I had my first
sight of the Fifteenth. The faces and voices were those of college boys following the home ball team to an out-of-town game; but the bats they passed
into the open trucks were Lewis guns and the caps were of steel. It was hard
to think that these were political troops.

Convoys of twenty and thirty camions lay all about the neighborhood taking on water, air, gas, oil, guns and men.

When we got back to the highway, it was four o'clock in the morning.

"Tired?" the Major asked me. He had noticed that I was uppercutting my
chin with the palm of my right hand. "Want me to take the wheel?"

"No, I'm not tired." Driving with dims on a road like this was not restful,
but I knew that the Major needed repose. The mind that soon should be responsible for the correct maneuvering and the safety of so many of us should
not be loaded with the task of keeping a car on the road in the early hours of
the morning.

By the time we reached V. P., I had seen my second consecutive sunrise. I have decided that the only real hardship in Spain is being under fire and that I am going to disregard all other trials.

For a time I helped with the repacking of the supply truck. Word came to us that Hawk and his sweetheart were stuck in the mud at the bottom of the hill.[39] It was mid-morning before we got her out. She was a nice big English Bedford, captured by the Fifteenth last September in Belchite. Her wiring is a tangled mass of rotting insulation, her radiator needs filling every half hour and one of her lamps is out, but she can hold the road at sixty miles an hour and that is what matters most. "If it works," says Bernie, the second driver of the autochir, about cars, "that's the main thing."

I went to the bedside of my only friend from the States, to say farewell.

"Some people have all the luck," said Lieutenant Al R. "Two days of action, and I've been in bed four months."

"Al, I saw the infantry last night. I wish I were going with them."

"You'll change your mind." I wondered what he meant.

"Well . . . so long."

"Don't forget that we're shock troops. Keep your head down. If you get home and I don't, you know who to see and what to tell them."

"Or vice versa," I answered. "So long, Al."

For the second time in a week the convoy filed through the hospital gate and we left for the Front. There was less gayety and more tension than there had been seven long days ago. We had had first-hand contact with our enemies, although we had not seen them.

I had no notion of where I was going or of how long it would take me to get there, but I was very, very glad to be leaving Villa Paz.

---

39. Al Hawk, aka Hawke, real name Albin Hauke, was a volunteer from Milwaukee.

PART TWO
In Reserve

Courtesy of Jim Neugass. Used by permission.

Figure 4: James Neugass in Spain.

*The Lincolns were on the move, as was Neugass. He began to drive Dr.
Edward K. Barsky (aka the Major), as well as other doctors, wounded soldiers, and supplies to and from a number of cities and towns in the Aragon
region: industrial Valencia on the Mediterranean coast, Alcañiz, Hijar,
and Alcorisa, where the 15th Brigade eventually set up its base. The Lincolns were twelve miles away at Aquaviva and the British and Canadians
in nearby Mas de las Matas. Three days before Christmas, during one of
the coldest Spanish winters in decades, they all celebrated the capture of the
strategically significant city of Teruel, a provincial capital, by the Spanish
Republican Army. Since the International Brigades played a minor role
at Teruel, many believed this victory proved the strength of Republican
forces and foreshadowed the end of the military rebellion. By the end of
1937, however, Franco's counteroffensive to retake Teruel loomed.*

Dec. 12. Afternoon. Far from Villa Paz

Left V. P. at 2 P.M. We had no more than reached the Valencia turnpike when
we heard planes. Ours or Theirs? Headed for the Hospital? There will be no
way of knowing.

General feeling exists among the front-line group, especially those who
were not part of the Cordoba expedition, that the Major has blundered. No
one relishes the night-long run which is expected. "He always sets out so
late," said one of the less politically developed nurses, "and then we have to
drive all night. Why didn't he wait until tomorrow morning?" "—so you could
buy a pair of silk teddies in Valencia?" Jack the staff photographer answers,
with a snarl.[1]

Surtidors de Guerra or Ministry of Defense gas-pumps are about forty to
eighty kilometers apart. We stop at each and every one. Tanks must be kept
full, and spare tanks full. "Suppose a pump blew up," says the Major. "Suppose . . . " and then he lapses back into his habitual gruesome melancholia.
The pump attendants are women and kids of fifteen or sixteen. Theoreti-
cally, only enough gas should be given to carry us to the next station. All
drivers carry *hojas de ruta* stating each car's mission and route. The amounts
of oil and fuel we take on is registered, together with Army license-plates, so

---

1. Jack is probably Gabriel Jack Quiñones from the Bronx, New York, who listed his profession as photographer. He drove trucks and ambulances in Spain until wounded in a
   bombing attack of a frontline surgical tent.

that the Ministry may check up on how its valuable gasoline is being used. This system also prevents joy rides.

Sole factory visible from roadside larger than shed-size between V. P. and Valencia is the enormous cement-mill at Utiel. Every time I see a smoke-stack, a high tension power line pylon or the infrequent and small power-houses, I wonder why it has not been bombed.

Tell-tale driblets of plaster and rubble leak from the doorsills in these villages, remote as they are from the battle-zones.

Half an hour of hairpin turns lead down a cliff to the stone bridge across the Guadalquivir River. Another half hour of cliff-hung roads leads up the other side of the broad ravine. A single direct hit on the bridge or a stick of dynamite under it would tie up all Valencia–Madrid traffic for days. Glad to see that the guards at both approaches of the bridge were not merely *etapas*, or ordinary road-and-bridge guards, but blue-uniformed *Asaltos*. These were the "assault guards" belatedly recruited by the Republic as a counterforce to the notoriously disloyal patent-leather hatted Civil Guards. Politically chosen, they remained loyal almost to the last man.

Shrouded in benevolent mist and rain, we stopped late at night for dinner in Utiel. From the general *Intendencia* we obtained a ration of good thick-crusted white bread, four big cans of Russian beef. The mistress of a *parador*, or inn, warmed the meat free of charge for us and added several onions. Meanwhile Lieutenant Oscar, the man-who-knows-how-to-find-food, was able to locate and buy pickled tomatoes.[2]

Night. Five hours of sleep in a bathless hotel. Slept in the same bed with Lieutenant D., our negro oral surgeon and Commissar.[3] This was the first time I had shared a room, much less a bed, with a negro. My grandfather had been a slaveholder. Two ancestors had fought with the Confederates. The eyes of three generations of New Orleans private bankers and their women were on me as I stood in the room with D. He sensed this but made no comment. Both of us knew that I had an opportunity of permanently putting to sleep a hundred years of prejudice. This I did. For a century my family has had its laundry done by negroes, and its cooking. Negro women have taken care of the men's overflow sexual desires and the children they had with their wives.

---

2. Oscar Israel Weissman, MD, a graduate of the Long Island College of Medicine, practiced in New York before going to Spain.

3. Dr. Arnold Donowa, a dental surgeon originally from Trinidad, earned his DDS from Howard Unversity.

Dec. 13. Morning

After breakfast the Major allowed us half an hour for shopping.

We took the Barcelona seacoast highway. It took us an hour to emerge from the miserable industrial suburbs of Valencia; then miles of geranium and rambler-rose edged highway. We stopped in one of the endless orange groves to make a minor repair and began to pick oranges. A peasant came along. Flushed with ill conscience, we stood waiting under the trees, pockets and hands flaming with guilt. Pleasantly, the farmer asked us why we had stopped here, when there was an orchard not only of much riper oranges a few hundred meters up the road, but some magnificent tangerines.

From what I have seen of the Spanish thus far their nature is quiet, full of the will to please, and perhaps far too gay. Have not yet heard one of them, but for our cook, raise his voice.

Drove fast through Sagunto. This is the best-bombed town on the whole Mediterranean seaboard. Some day the Spanish language will contain a simile for speed which will run "fast as you drive through Sagunto."

Road full of troops in camions, mostly unarmed. Rifles and automatic arms of all but shock troops are evidently left in the lines when battalions go on leave or on rest or reserve. Have not seen troops on foot, nor have I seen the tanks, armored cars and cannons whose beauty we wait.

Nervously, took on gas and oil from camouflaged *surtidor* in Castellon, another well-bombed city. How this country holds together . . . in another few years anti-aircraft will be as much a part of the roofs with which man covers himself and his wealth as eaves and gutter-pipes and lightning rods. We have much to learn from the ant.

Afternoon. Mountains, mountains, mountains, one range of them after another. For what it will grow the countryside is in good condition.

Lunch: Half a tin of Russian beef and a slice of bread.

We had taken the sky-route to Alcañiz, two hundred and fifty kilometers to the northeast. General direction of the Saragossa front; and I had decided, with all of the acute military shrewdness of an ambulance driver who has never been to the Front, that the Fifteenth had been called out to stop a fascist drive southwards from the Teruel salient!

The mountains kept getting higher, colder and more barren. At their eventual summit was Morella, white-walled as Mykonos in the Dodecanese, spire-pinnacled as Mont St. Michel, precipitous as St. Flour. Roman aqueducts fed water into the treeless crag village. I wondered why they had not been bombed.

"I heard of a man who once ate an omelet and a salad in Morella," said Oscar significantly at the Major; but we drove on.

Dinner: Half a tin of Russian beef and a slice of gasoline-smelling bread, in the dark outskirts of Alcañiz. Since leaving Castellon that morning, we had seen not a battalion, not a gun, and no fortifications but for a single string of machine-gun nests under a ridge. Well, perhaps fortifications are not dug to be visible from the roads.

If we were going to attack, shouldn't we have passed troops?

We had left the mountains behind us and were now pulling north across the plains of Aragon. At eleven o'clock the Commissar issued a cigarette and a penny tablet of chocolate to each of the nine of the staff who rode in my car. Hardly any of us had spoken more than a sentence during the long day.

At length we reached Hijar, the town for which the Major had been looking. We found the Commandancia. I got out of the car with instructions to ask

1) Had the 15th Brigade arrived?
2) If it were not in this town, where was it?
3) Would it be possible for us to find quarters for the night here, in case the Fifteenth had not turned up?

I speak better Spanish than the Major.

The corporal who was the highest-ranking soldier awake in this dark unlit town had never heard of the 15th Brigade. When I asked him for billets for thirty men and women, he said that he would wake the *Presidente*, but that he doubted anyone's being able to convince the lousy fascist population of Hijar to put us up for the night.

"So this is a fascist town? In Republican territory?"

The *cabo* laughed. How long had I been in Spain? A month? He had thought so. It would be well to remember that Hijar was not the only town in Loyalist territory to have voted heavily for the Right during the 1936 elections.

"Well, turn the dirty sons of bitches out of their beds and let them sleep in the streets." My tiredness had suddenly taken the form of temper.

"They are workers" . . . why don't these Spanish ever raise their voices . . . "*son obreros*" said the *cabo* in a patient, stolid tone, "and here in Catalonia there is a law against turning people out of their homes by force."

Catalonia had much to learn, I thought. I had wanted to tell the corporal that there was no law which takes people away from good Civil Service jobs in the United States and turns them loose on the lunar mountains of Spain, but I did not speak. My first attempt at World War language and tactics had gone wrong.

The convoy moved on to the next town. Here the Major found what he was looking for—three low wood barracks on the top of a hill.

All of the other drivers went to sleep on the stretchers in their cars. Mine, rigged for carrying staff, has none. By the time that I had gone from car to car, only to find every stretcher taken, there was a single empty bed under the three naked electric light bulbs of the damp cold ward.

"You sleep here," said the Major to me, pointing at the bed.

"You take the bed, Doc, and I'll sleep in the car."

"You're much taller than me. You take the bed."

"The hell I will, Doc."

"The hell you won't. That's orders."

I took off my shoes and crawled under the first blanket, horsehide coat and all, but did not easily fall to sleep.

War is not so bad, after all. There are hardships but not much more anguish than the discomforts of a long canoe trip in Maine. The World War had certainly not been like this. Where are the swagger sticks of blasphemous aristocratic officers, the savage melancholia of the men, the incessant court-martials and the military elegance?

I went to sleep with the unpleasant feeling that if we were not so familiar with our commanders, if we were not so free to come and go, if there were more orders and bugles, at least one guardhouse and one Military Policeman, we would stand a better chance of giving to Franco what he must eventually get. Will steadfast devotion to an idea be the equivalent of that brutal blind discipline whose symbol is the officer's pistol? There certainly has never been such an army as this, not since the days of the Crusades.

December 14 and 15. Pueblo de Hijar. 36 Miles from the Inactive Saragossa Front

Two days of rain, sun, wind and more rain, spent on a desolate hilltop set with a railroad station, a large hospital and an impressive-looking beet-sugar factory. My sore throat has come back, with just enough fever to give me day nightmares. Have not yet discovered a fire or a place, indoors or out, that is warm. No sign of the brigade. We do not know why we are here, how long we will stay, or what is going on.

Captain Smyka's scouts turned up in their truck twelve hours after we had arrived.[4] The Captain is a tall young semi-walrus-mustached Czech civil engineer. Five months ago he was in this same hospital with twelve machine-gun bullet holes in his left leg, left side, shoulder and arm. That was the fourth time he had been wounded since he came to Spain. Good taste and freedom to dress as he wishes have made "Smickie," as his men call him, the best dressed officer in the Fifteenth. Blanket-coat with black hood and black trimming, a black-piped khaki overseas cap over the fine-grained chocolate corduroy uniform which fits what the nurses call his Greek figure like wall-paper.

Half of the Captain's men are American. Chief among them is a negro from Indiana who is said to be responsible for much of the creation of the brigade's Spanish-American swearwords. The others are of assorted nationalities, including a group of four Finnish seamen. The business of the scouts is to go ahead of the brigade, when new lines have just been established, to contact the enemy.

Dec. 16

After I had cleaned my air-filter and carburetor, oiled grease-cups and springs and for the tenth time tightened the many bolts which the roads had shaken loose, word came that the four brigades of the Fifteenth were rolling through the Pueblo de Hijar railroad station, after three days in box-cars from Albacete.

Immediately we knew that we should be moving. Now that we are within fifty miles of the front, we travel only at night.

Late in the afternoon I found a stove. One of the wounded who sat about it had deserted from the Rebels. He told us of life in Franco's army.

"There is plenty of food and good uniforms," he said, "but the Spanish recruits don't get them. All that is for the officers. Here I am paid eight pesetas a day at the Rear, and twelve a day at the Front. With the *fasciosas* I got thirty-five centimos at the Rear and fifty at the Front. Discipline is . . . well, worse than the World War. A man was once beaten in front of the whole company because he thought saluting the commander with the clenched fist was a joke.

"Sure, there are lots who would like to come over. Plenty of olive oil is poured into the engines of the trucks at night. Too many machine-gun locks

---

4. Captain Smyka is probably the Czech captain Radumir Smercka, who served as chief of information in the 15th Brigade.

are jammed. Few officers dare to lead their men while we are attacking. They sit on hills and watch us, with drawn pistols. One of our chófers ran his car into a ditch one night on a road which was easy for you . . . I mean, us"—all of us laughed—"to see. It was at night and we were moving up a regiment, in trucks.

"He suddenly turned his headlights on half a kilometer of road choked with parked and loaded camions. Your anti-tanks . . . I mean our anti-tank . . . guns immediately opened up. Two or three hundred men were killed and at least twenty trucks blown to hell. The driver did not escape. Of course he was shot. But there are many of us over there. . . . "

Dec. 19? Alcorisa. Aragon

Estimates of the distance the Front lies straight down the road from us vary from twenty-five to thirty-five miles. After all, we were not more than twice that far from the lines at Villa Paz. We don't exactly know where the fighting is in this neighborhood because there has been so little of it. I gather that mountains lie between us and the invaders, and that trench warfare is unknown in this area.

Some said that Alcorisa means "Good Water" in Arabic. Not only are there wells and springs, but the canal system which has been built about the Guadalope River makes this pocket in the red rock hills an oasis of terraced truck gardens, olive groves and vineyards. If you stop and listen, in almost any part of the town, you can hear all kinds of subterranean and outdoor gurgling.

Alcorisa is therefore the richest place I have yet seen in Spain; excepting the plains of orange and almond, cherry, lemon and tangerine orchards that circle Valencia.

I had always imagined, together with the rest of the world, that Spain was a fabulous place of rich, sun-drenched soil, more castled than a five-dollar Christmas edition of Grimm's fairy tales. From what I have seen of this endlessly pillaged country, palaces are as fictitious as the nobility of its grandees. Not that hulks of masonry do not deform the skyline of the pinnacles about which many of the towns are huddled, spires which may serve future generations as anti-aircraft posts, more than they served the people of the past.

The poverty of the land is reflected by the miserable construction of the villages. I have not yet seen a single gabled roof in Alcorisa. Wood is rare, money scarce, and ridge-poles much too expensive. The average house is built of sun-baked strawed mud or a weakly mortared rubble, with no cement or stucco exterior. There are no arches because there is no cut stone. The roofs are of cane wattles covered by the inevitable pinkish buff tiles.

The church is strong and beautiful. Its tower is a masterpiece of rococo brickwork. Nowhere else in Alcorisa has expensive brick been used. The village convent is an immense, solidly-built structure, not too large for the hospital which now houses, instead of the soft prayers of nuns, the cries of dead and dying. The river-bottom land, best in Alcorisa, also belonged to the church. Off on the hill, in a clump of soaring blue-black cedars, is the former sanctuary which the former bishop used as a summer home. The attitude of the Spanish towards their only church is not to be compared with that of Americans towards the Catholic Church of our country. If and when the American Catholic Church assumes the monopoly on property and wealth which was the possession of its Spanish brother organization, it will be easier for us to understand what happened in Spain. Starve a dog for five hundred years, for a thousand years, and expect him not to eat meat and not to bite the first person within reach of his teeth, once the chain breaks!

Alcorisa, garden spot of the Aragonese desert, is far richer than the villages of Castile. Few of its inhabitants live in cliff dwellings. Some of these primitive houses, of which most villages possess a few—and Tarancon, an entire subterranean community—are neat enough, with whitewashed stone chimneys and doorways. Each dark, well-swept room, smelling of resonant thorn-bush firewood, is a natural bomb-proof shelter. "And the roof does not leak," I can imagine the theorists of the Right saying. Neither do elegant roofs of the villas in Barcelona's Sarria neighborhood leak.

A writer who may still be a friend of mine wrote a book called *Virgin Spain* which, ten years or so ago, was accepted as the most up-to-date interpretation of the Spanish soul, whatever that is.[5] I never read the book, but I imagine that it proves that the Spirit of Hispania is a virgin.

"Virgin?" Hell, the emaciated lady is the most raped, undernourished, rachitic and tubercular woman in Europe, with the possible exception of some of the Balkan ladies. The Conqueror Kings and the Sailor Princes exported her blood to Central and South America, in exchange for yellow metal. The grandees cut down the forest, let silt form in the excellent canals dug by the Moors and forbade all irrigation which could not directly produce cash. For centuries the drugged spirit of "virgin" Spain has been chained to the straw bed on which she has been methodically violated by the economically un-

5. Waldo Frank, a novelist, literary critic, and social historian published *Virgin Spain: Scenes from the Spiritual Drama of a Great People* in 1926.

celibate Church hierarchy; by *señoritos* who let the nails of their little fingers grow as the living proof that they did not work, by four thousand Army officers and eight hundred Generals; and the rapists had neither the energy nor the industry to pimp for their captive.

Those are the lines of the struggle being fought here. Let theoreticians and sophists talk about "a religious" war and "a bolshevist plot," and "law, order and the renovation of Spain." This war is the international struggle of the poor peasant, the small and liberal business men, the poor priests, the unemployed, and the industrial workers against the international epaulets, mitres and gold fountain pens who lament with such demonstrations of quiet patience about the blood necessary to be spilled for the "renovating" of Spain against the lawful and orderly poverty of its "golden" age. The "Have-nots" will not be denied. The "Haves" of the world seldom understand that History must move only forward.

Why did I come here? Not so much out of love as from disgust, I suppose.

Military Angle. Technically, this neighborhood would be called "an Area of Assembly." We are equidistant from the Saragossa, the Montalbán and the Teruel Fronts, all of which are at this moment quiet. If a nasty job should turn up at either of these points, we could be on the scene with our necks out within eight hours. Franco knows this as well as we do. There is no purpose to simple surprise in this war; nothing but sudden fulminant raging surprise is useful.

Although our front-line surgical group is attached to the 15th Brigade and we must always be ready to handle its casualties as soon as the wounded can be gotten to us, it is possible that we might deliberately be sent to a spot at which no action was expected, with the sole purpose of deceiving the invaders as to our actual plans. The Staff can feint with the jaw with its Medical Corps, feint for the eyes with a Tank Company, then suddenly strike for the kidneys with all the weight of the infantry. Since this maneuvering costs much gasoline, the comparative lightness of our surgical group makes us ideal for decoy. This chess-playing depends on the efficiency of Franco's spy system. The enemy's Information services are evidently as dependable as our own.

When do we move, and where, and when?

Politics. The apartment in which we are billeted reeks with the nickel-plate gimcrack false marble taste of the engineer who lived in it until he "disappeared."

After the departure of the fascist and his family, their home became the office of the Olive Oil Collective of Alcorisa which operated during the early days of the war. Unused form blanks of many kinds, printed by the Alcañiz Typographical Collective, choke the desk of this organization's former secretary. The former Butcher's Collective is now the Army commissary storehouses, and the Wine Collective has turned over its offices to the Transport Corps. Large but faded red and black signs of other experiments peel and bake over many other doorways, tombstones to the untaught experimentation of early anarchist theoreticians who did not understand that paradise is impossible during wartime and that land cannot be socialized without the tractors. Only once have I seen a Russian tractor in the fields. The others are at the Front, pulling cannon and tanks, instead of the plow for which they are intended and may some day serve.

The political character of these interior Aragon towns had been anarchist, at the start of the war. At some other time, when I have spoken to more of the Spanish, I will try to say what Spanish anarchy has been and now is. In some of the villages all money was thrown away. Not only does the village of Alcorisa issue its own money but its tradesmen are allowed the same privilege. One day I bought a handkerchief. The price was one peseta. I had nothing smaller than a five-peseta note. The storekeeper gave me, as change, four slips of stamped white paper marked in ink, "good for four pesetas' worth of drygoods." Later I bought a bottle of vermouth in a bar but was unable to pay for it with my drygoods money. After a few days my pockets were stuffed with a worn mass of Bar-money, Drygoods Money, Bakeshop Money. Nor does the evil end at that point. Alcorisa money is not good in Alcañiz; Mas de las Matas money is not good in Alcorisa; Caspe money and Lerida and Barbastro money are not good in Mas de las Matas.

A law has lately been passed in Barcelona commanding all of this currency to be withdrawn by the first of the year. Notes in small denomination will on that date be issued to be good in any part of the country. This is an example of the kind of centralization which all over the world infantile left extremists call "betraying the revolution." Individuality cannot be cultivated by means such as allowing the individual to coin his own money.

The war has taught not only anarchists but all political parties in Spain many lessons. In general, the Spanish have learned that not even a rich nation can eat well and fight a war at the same time and the best means of organizing the mechanism behind their army is centralization under the Ministry of Defense.

Because the anarchists of Catalonia falsely believed that the International Brigades were Communist troops, because fascist provocateurs and Trotskyists and Poumists had capped this misinformation with the statement that the I. B.'s were "Stalin's policemen," we had a good deal of trouble with them when the Brigades first went into action in Aragon last summer.

A battalion would be billeted in a town which had never been bombed. Immediately there were raids. We would set up a hospital in an untouched village, and more bombs would fall. The peasants were inclined to blame their misfortunes on us. The International troops should have been using all possible time for maneuvers, for rifle and grenade practice. After entire days and weeks had been lost in picking olives, harvesting wheat, *refugio*-building and reconstruction of the destroyed houses, prestige grew. Finally, after we had played a large part in the capture of Quinto, Pina and Belchite even the wildest anarchist was able to understand, with the rest of the democratic world, why we had come to Spain.

There are three cafés in Alcorisa, each in the headquarters of a political party. The F. A. I., or café of the Anarchist Federation of Iberia, serves bitter coffee with milk and sugar. The Communist café sells coffee with sugar but no milk, rum, muscatel, vermouth and brandy. The Left Republican Party has coffee with sugar and that alone. The latter resort is patronized mainly by the village elders and tradesmen. The older industrial workers and many of the transport drivers and mechanics go to the F. A. I. At the Communist café are soldiers, peasants and the young men of the town.

The I. B.'s are impartial: Left Republican coffee without milk in the morning, Anarchist coffee with milk in the afternoon and Communist brandy at night.

Army organization. Not only because neither one of the four villages in this neighborhood is large enough to house the whole brigade, because troops are a burden upon townspeople, but because four villages are a bigger target than one, the Fifteenth and its various services are spread out over this entire area. The English Battalion and the Canadians of the Mackenzie-Papineau Battalion are billeted in Mas de las Matas; the Lincoln-Washingtons in Aguaviva. In each town are the battalion kitchens and *Intendencias*, cantines, armories and small infirmaries. Here in Alcorisa is the brigade headquarters (or Estado Major) and its Special Machine Gun company, the brigade Infirmary, Garage (or Auto-Parque), the Transmissions men, surgical unit and Central *Intenden-*

cia, and Classifications Post Staff. The Divisional Medical Corps (*Sanidad Militar Divisionario*) is eight miles away at Andorra, with its Ambulance Park and Medical General Staff. The Farmacy and the Scouts are quartered in a large farmhouse out in the country; God knows where the brigade ammunition dump is located. Field telephones have been strung between all towns and headquarters.

The sinews and synapses of our system of organization have been arranged to give us the power of putting the entire strength of the four thousand men of the 15th Brigade and all our equipment on the road within two to four hours; to rush over mountains and plains at a distant objective with the concentration and speed of a single shell; to strike hard, then spread out. Extreme mobility and swift unconcentration give a guerrilla-like character to modern warfare. I doubt that guns heavier than 155's or tanks weighing more than nine tons will be useful in the coming World War except on very flat or on quiet fronts, unless gasoline or diesel trucks can be built capable of speeding tremendous burdens at the rate of at least fifty miles an hour. Caterpillar traction is impractical, not so much because vehicles equipped with it cannot proceed fast enough, but because even the heaviest of steel treads wear out so much more quickly than rubber tires and are so much harder to replace and repair.

Handicapped as we are by the comparatively loose—but ever tightening—organization of our Army, we are spared the burden of maintaining a military police apparatus. I have yet to see the armband and the club of an M.P. anywhere in Spain. The single information officer attached to the brigade staff is able to handle the entire question of irregularities of loyalty and conduct. Turn a thousand hungry, thirsty, restless, ill-equipped and sex-deprived men who have been taught to think with guns, bayonets and bombs loose on the streets of a village and you would think there would be incidents; but not on this side of the trenches in our war. The six militia youths, two of them armed with bird-guns, who man the control posts at the approaches of the town are our only semblance of military police.

Naturally there is a whorehouse; three girls, a radio, a few bottles of muscatel. I went there the other night. We listened to a Seville broadcast (we are not forbidden to tune in on fascist stations), drank an occasional *copita* and kidded with the girls. The Spanish whorehouse, in the lack of amusements and clubs, has always been a good deal like a social club. I do not maintain that the men of the People's Army are puritanical or that they left their manhood at home with their civilian clothing: but the strain of modern warfare seems to suspend the sexual desires of the troops almost as much as their political understanding of the terms of the struggle. Perhaps this is not the whole answer for the curious lack of dirty jokes, the absence of smut sessions and camp followers and, in general, the absence of sex-strain among the troops with whom I have mixed. Probably the conduct of the A. E. F. in France and of expeditionary forces in past wars has given rise to a very broadspread misunderstanding of soldiers. But there is no getting away from the political character of this struggle. The ideas for which we fight are our military police. No general would measure the fighting power of his men by their love for whores and brandy, not even Blackjack Pershing. Give the men something to fight for and they will fight. Atrocity postcards and posters are not enough.

The Commander. "At ease!" ordered the sergeant as the Colonel and his translator entered the garage. A hundred International chófers and mechanics lit cigarettes.

"I'm very glad," said Colonel Copic, the Jugoslav ex-opera baritone and Siberian guerrilla-leader, in English, "for the opportunity of talking to you, comrades. Our transport is in a catastrophic state."[6]

The translator put the Colonel's words in Spanish and French.

"The deplorable condition of our trucks and staff cars is partially to be blamed on the Americans. The capitalist mentality of that rich country does not regard an automobile as something to be treasured. The manufacturers have impressed on American purchasers that if a car is injured, or if it goes little by little to pieces, through neglect, another car can easily be purchased.

"Our transport does not come to us in Spain easily. Each of the brigade trucks is bought with the sweat of the workers of the Republic. The dirt on the surface of our cars is reflected only by the evil condition of their engines.

"A chófer is sent to Madrid or Valencia. Right away he goes into a restaurant for a meal and leaves his car on the curb. When he has finished his meal, the chófer finds the camion gone. So what does he do? Thinking to atone to the Brigade for his carelessness and egoism, he goes out on the street and organizes another truck for us. And what is worse, look at the car he steals! An old piece of junk! . . . "

The Era of Organizing, when equipment flitted all up and down Spain from brigade to brigade, is drawing to a close. A chófer who lately lifted the

---

6. Vladimir Copic was the Yugoslavian-born commander of the 15th Brigade.

spark plugs of an armored car was rebuked and the plugs ordered returned. In the days when there was no centralized command, when Spain was being defended with rapiers taken from museums, and irregular automatic weapons bought from the military pawnshops of Brussels, organizing was a necessity. Eggs, however, bully beef, condensed milk and tire pumps are still considered fair game, provided that the victims are other soldiers and not civilians.

After Copic's speech an American chófer who had just inherited seventy-five thousand dollars took us to the Communist Party café for burned rum with sugar. This is an Aragonese specialty. We asked the heir if he were going home to collect his inheritance.

"Hell no," he said, "what do you think I came out here for?"

We were very sorry for him. None of us was sure that we would prefer war to money. The heir has promised to give a big party when and if he and some of his friends return to the States.

Another attraction of the C. P. café is the singer of *canto Aragonese* who hangs out there. This type of singing is something like the *flamenco*. It is more cheerful. At times the singer shuts his eyes, puts back his head and holds a single luscious note, like a canary warbling into the sun.

The drivers and mechanics of the front-line auto-parque have a hard life. Rushed off their feet at all hours of the day by work of unvarying urgency, the garage crew, black as chimney sweeps, eat, work and sleep in grease, darkness, silence and the fumes of gasoline. The head of the auto-parque is an American who will be replaced as soon as a Spaniard can be trained. Copic explains that we came here not only to fight for democracy, but to give our skill to our Spanish brothers.

Main Street. The holiday atmosphere of the main square is perpetual. The Divisional sound-truck, in the earlier days used for throwing propaganda into enemy trenches, gives frequent concerts at the crossroads. Toscanini and Stokowski recordings of Bach alternate with rhumbas, congas, *flamenco*, swing music, choral singing of revolutionary songs of all political parties and the world's most light-hearted national anthem, the "Hymno de Riego." Bulgarian, Catalan, English and Aragonese voices mix in the singing of the "Internationale."

All day long the old men who alone wear the Aragon costume—black silk Martinique-style bandana, open knee-breeches, white stockings and blue socks—stand in front of the wall newspaper at the doorway of the C. P. headquarters amazed by the pictures of themselves taken by the brigade photographers, by war bulletins, short articles and simple poems. Flaming and fresh posters pasted on the walls by the Brigade cultural delegate form a kind of permanent art exhibition. The crowd parts to make way for camions, each flying the flag of the political party favored by the infantrymen they carry to the front. Infrequent armored cars and artillery rouse the loudest cheers, and the travelling library, the greatest amazement.

Weather. Orders have been given for every radiator to be drained no later than ten o'clock each evening. We have neither anti-freeze mixture nor winter oil and cannot risk frozen cooling systems and cracked blocks. I open my valves, run my engine until dashboard thermometer shows 200, and shut off engine. In this way, the last drop of water is pumped out of the cylinder casings. In the morning, icicles have to be chipped off the butterfly nuts before valves can be closed.

We break the ice in the river before we can brush our teeth. The drivers of the brigade water-camions must clear the ice from the surface of Alcorisa's magnificent drinking-water trough before they can load.

The hands of the girls and women who wash laundry, pots and pans and wood furniture in the river are blue as turkey feet and almost as hard and gnarled. It is difficult to understand how the cotton-dressed, slipper-shod population endures the winter cold. Heavy rough wool mufflers drawn over the mouth take the place of overcoats.

All day long companies of white cavalry clouds charge from pinnacle to pinnacle. Sudden mists blow down into the town. There have been gusts of snow and hail but no rain.

Little charcoal remains for the braziers which for centuries have been the town's sources of heat, between the lighting of meal-time fires. If the ashes are too frequently knocked off the coals, carbon monoxide fills the room; if the coals are left too long unstirred, heat dwindles to such a minimum that not even our shoe-tips are warmed. Because of the dampness of the rooms, more clothing must be worn indoors than out.

Stowaway. Since the equipment of the American hospitals in Spain is far more plentiful than that of the British, the English at Huete were called on to contribute a total of only two ambulances and two drivers. The actual name of the driver of the converted Rolls, contributed by an English Lord, is "Percy."

When the second of the two English ambulances was unloaded, a young lady dressed in a good horsehide windbreaker, beret, breeches and high boots stepped out in front of the infirmary and asked, "I say, is this the Front?"

"Sure," she was answered. "Look out, here comes a big one . . . duck!"

Packed between mattresses and cases of serums and sterile water ampoules, Dorothy had lived for three days on bread and vermouth until she reached the spot which she believed to be her proper place in Spain.[7]

The court-martial, Major B. presiding, took place in the ward. The jury was of drivers, nurses and *soldados* with grippe, foot-troubles, and the three men wounded by the accidental explosion of a rifle-grenade.

"I'm a registered nurse and a trained operating-room assistant," said Dorothy. "I can do *triaje* work and first aid."

"Go on," said the Major.

"I can . . . well, I'm a Communist Party member . . . and . . . "

"We're not interested in your politics," said the Major, who was. "Go on, tell us why you came here."

"Well, British soldiers will be going into action, and there should be British nurses. . . . "

"You're a member of the Communist Party. Does that outfit believe in discipline?"

"Yes . . . but. . . . "

"But nothing. Ten days in the guardhouse, then back to Huete."

Since none of us had heard of a guardhouse between here and Valencia, we unanimously endorsed the Major's recommendation. He wrote out a *salvo conducto* to Huete and gave it to the stowaway.

"Go to the cookshed and get yourself something to eat. Then sleep downstairs. There are some mattresses in the supply room. In the morning take the line of evacuation back to Huete. You'll probably get there in a week or ten days."

"But Major, British soldiers will be wounded. . . . "

"Listen, Florence, if there is trouble, we'll lock you up in the dental autochir."

All through the court-martial I have been assaying Dorothy's voice and her white freckled stub-nosed face for signs of wildness, morbidity, neuroticism, egocentricity, passion and sentimentality. Everything about her was quiet; hands and mouth, eyes, manner and voice. Either it was impossible to get past the triple-ply shell of reserve and self-effacement with which a correct middle-class upbringing had coated heart and throat, or else she must have the calm, stable and determined character of the ideal revolutionary. Dorothy was not a fanatic or a martyr.

---

7. Dorothy Rutter was a British nurse.

In the morning she was gone. By nightfall our Nightingale had turned up in the battalion infirmary of the English, twelve kilometers across the mountains in Mas de las Matas. Before we had caught up with her, she had appeared in the Divisional ambulance park at Andorra. Since the Chief Medical Officer did not wish to set up a guardhouse especially for Dorothy, and since we had all grown fond of her, she was again sentenced to go back to Heute. I believe that a base-hospital assignment is sufficient punishment for all crimes up to but not including sabotage.

The drivers, from whom all rumors flow, say that Dorothy is very much in love with Bob Black, chófer of the ambulance in which she had stowed away. Even Communist Party members are human.

My third imaginary romance is therefore over. I had imagined a walk up to the Moorish ruins on the hill, three days' simultaneous leave under the palms and on the beaches of Denia, profound confessions and pledges while the sun set over the blood-dark sea. . . . and now there'll have to be someone else to bring flowers to my grave.

Fifth Column. I have been carrying as many as three loads of officers, supplies and sick volunteers a day to and from Mas de las Matas and Aguaviva. The narrow road climbs a hairpin staircase over a small but steep range of mountains. Fog, especially at night, settles in the top of the pass. Because of the number and the sharpness of the turns, more than a hundred meters of the road is seldom visible, day or night.

For a day or two I had been cursing the stones, some of them as large as watermelons, I would suddenly see on the road. I reasoned, in an idle sort of way, that they must have fallen from the carts in which material was being brought down into the towns for the reinforcement of *refugios*. The road is so narrow that you have the choice of hitting one of these blocks with your tires or of swerving off the road over the cliff on one side of the wall or the other, or of cracking the bottom of your crankcase. I grew tired of stopping my car, getting out and heaving rocks into the valley. As often as I would clear the road, it would fill up. The other drivers noticed the same thing.

One night a small boulder pitched on to the road ahead of me.

Landslide?

I picked up a grenade that night before I came back over the mountains. Not that a pistol would do much good at night, even if I had one. The next accidental landslide that falls on me is going to get blown back where it came from.

I reported the incident to Commissar Dave Doran.[8] He decided that, out of consideration for the local morale, no one but the *Presidente* can be told. We cannot put guards on every road in Spain.

"Fifth Column" is the name given to the civilians of Bilbao who shot up the streets of the Basque capital while Franco was converging on it with four other columns. He boasts that he has Fifth Columns in every other city in Spain.[9] No doubt he has. The 1936 elections were very close. We have a few fifth columns of our own, on the other side of the trenches. This is a peculiar war. I know that well, war is war and hell is hell, but when men stand on top of mountains and roll boulders at ambulances, I begin to understand what Goebbels meant when he said that international diplomacy is made with the sword and only with the sword. By "totalitarian war" Mussolini means exactly that. There seems to be nothing sacred about ambulances, after all. I've been an instinctive pacifist and a hater of flags and uniforms and, above all, martial music all my life; but I feel that if I catch the man who rolls rocks onto the Mas de las Matas road, I'd like to open him up little by little with my jackknife until I see if I can tell a fascist heart from a democratic heart. It's the actions you kill, not the man. Murder! Think of it.

Recruits. Blue with cold, three companies of eighteen- and nineteen-year-old village boys drill each morning on the river bank. In the afternoon they march out into the country. At night there are lectures and lessons in reading and writing. They are much better dressed than the International Volunteers, in Russian khaki woolen wind-breakers, pea-jackets and pantaloons, but nowhere is there a rifle, helmet, bayonet, knapsack or canteen. All arms must still be kept at the Front.

As I watched the slightly bewildered faces and listened to the singing and

---

8. Formerly part of the Young Communist League leadership in the United States, David Doran was Commissar of the 15th Brigade and one of the highest-ranking Americans in Spain. He was killed during the Retreats in March 1938.

9. As Franco's armies marched toward Madrid with four columns during the summer of 1936, the Rebels predicted that they would receive assistance from a "fifth column" of sympathizers within the city. Obviously, the war's political lines could not mirror the military situation, as dissidents on both sides found themselves in "occupied" territory. The result produced opportunities for subversion and a continuing search for spies. Everyone's loyalty was suspect, and rumors abounded, as the author's journal repeatedly indicates.

the jokes, I could not help feeling sorry for these boys. Songs cannot take the place of target practice.

Shoes. My motor-oil-greased apple-toed bennies are holding out so far all but the soles. I heard that the village shoemaker could sew high tops to them. By the time that I had reached him, he had run out of leather. Much of my spare time is spent trying to get a good pair of shoes. I go to the *Intendencia*, interview the Commissar, beg at the commissary of the other Brigades and offer large sums to the officers. In Alcañiz the other morning, I saw two recruits carrying new high boots down the hill. They were glad enough to lead me to the *Intendencia* from which they had just got them, but to no use.

After standing in line for an hour, I was able to buy a paper cornucopia of hot cakes made with genuine grease and flour and sugar. In Alcañiz I also bought a sackful of mandarins, most of them for the nurse who will eat nothing but fresh fruit, bread and onions. I was also successful in buying a yard of striped cotton, for handkerchiefs. No cigarette lighters were to be had.

Pay. Every ten days I receive a hundred and fifty pesetas. This is front-line pay. Rear pay is a hundred pesetas. The Major gets four hundred odd pesetas.

We have plenty of money but little to buy. Most of the village stores have closed down. Cheap wallets, writing paper, towels used also as mufflers, bachelor buttons, fountain pens and sometimes handkerchiefs continually run out of stock, and there is nothing else.[10]

We're getting so hungry and so tired of meat-flavored beans that there is talk of sending a truck out into the country with thousands of pesetas to buy any kind of beast or vegetable. The official sentiment is against this venture, because individual buying from the peasants encourages speculation. Are there such things as ham and cheese and butter and eggs and milk and real bread in the world? The other day a cartload of oranges drew into the courtyard of the *posada* or post-inn. Within an hour it was sold out. We can't give all of our money to the Red Aide, and not all of us can play poker. I am going to save mine for a pistol, whatever it costs.

Wall mottoes and slogans. Long live the Popular Front! All Aide to Madrid! To Resist is to Conquer! Long Live the Tribus of Aragon! (The Tribus were the troops of the three Aragon provinces.) The people of Democratic Spain

---

10. Bachelor buttons are attached to clothing by a clasp and so require no sewing.

Salute the International Brigades! Juan loves Manola. Hernan thinks he's a wise guy. Felipe stinks. To Dig Refugios is to Fortify the Family! Martyred Asturias still lives! Death to War! Homage to the Soviet Union! Long Live the Republic!

High up on the hill on the side of a detached farm-shed I read, "Free the anti-fascist prisoners in Barcelona—P. O. U. M." This referred to the prisoners taken by the Negrin government after the collapse of the May 3 Barcelona left-extremist putsch.

All over town, indoors and out, on fences and bridges and scratched in the smoky walls of fireplaces like talismans are the initials of the three anarchist and syndicalist organizations: C. N. T. (National Federation of Workers), F. A. I. (Federation of Iberian Anarchists), A. I. T. (International Association of Workers), and sometimes F. I. J. L. (Iberian Federation of Anarchist Youth).

Most of these monograms seem from their age to have been written before the invasion. There is no overestimating the swing away from anarchism and syndicalism towards the Popular Front, and the changes which have taken place inside the anarchist parties and trade unions since the beginning of the war.

The poster I like best shows five swords, each held by powerful wrists, and each lettered with the initials of a political party, pointed upwards towards the pledge alone by which we may win:

"First Win the War!"

December 21. Alcorisa. Under Stand-by Orders

... and we had just gotten used to waiting! All patience is at an end. Something must be going on. Saragossa? Teruel? Heusca? No refugees have marched into the town, so we must have advanced. Or is an attack being prepared? I don't think so. There are not enough Internationals in Spain now (15,000 to 18,000, my estimate, although at least twice that number have died here) to conduct an attack. Therefore I think that we will be used as reserves.

Did a little investigating the other morning at Aguaviva. I had asked a peasant if troops had ever been quartered in this town before us. "Of course," he said, "the Listers were with us"—proudly—"they pulled out just before you came." Where had Lister gone? "I don't know," answered the peasant, turning his eyes on the snowfields that rose to the south of us. South means Teruel. The Listers are among the best troops in Spain.

Went on car-guard duty last night. As usual, drew the 10 P.M. to 2 A.M.

shift. Cold and lonely as hell. Even the lights in the cookshed are out and the door locked, damn. You listen to the town clock, ration off a cigarette at the rate of four puffs every quarter hour, then count to the steps of your feet on the frozen road. I stood guard duty but I didn't have a gun; nothing but my patent generator flashlight which is not working so well these days, and that bomb I keep in my car.

By about 11 P.M. I hadn't heard a voice or an engine. I was out of cigarettes. Somebody said that there was a show on over at the Convent. I saw the last act. Vaudeville turns, juggler, acrobats, somehow politicalized. At the end a traveling "cultural" team from Madrid—obvious intellectuals trained more in defining the social duty of the artist than in public appearance—put on highly stylized political skits. There was a very serious reading of poetry by Lorca, the poet executed by Franco in Granada at the start of the war.[11] The Vaudeville actors had it all over the cultural boys. True social art lies some-where between the two groups.

Before the show was over ill conscience drove me back to my post.

My car was gone.

I woke up Jack, my best friend among the drivers.

"Hell," he said, "Captain S. got the keys from the Major.[12] He had to take his girl friend back to Andorra. Don't worry."

"But I drained my engine."

"If that dumb son of a bitch didn't have the sense to fill it. . . . "

"The bearings will burn out. . . . Well, I suppose it's the Infantry for me. . . . "

At about one o'clock I heard the sound of an engine. It sounded like mine. Captain S. jumped out, swearing.

"Look at me," he said.

In the dim starlight I saw that he was wet and muddy almost up to the waist.

"Why did you drain your radiator?"

"Orders."

"Lucky I looked at the dial before she burned up." S. was not permitting his anger to get the best of him. If he tried to make a stink, it would come out that he had used an ambulance for amatory purposes. "I found a ditch. There wasn't anything in the car for carrying water. I used my rubbers. . . . "

---

11. Federico Garcia Lorca was executed by Fascists in Granada in 1936.

12. Dr. Mark Straus, head of the 15th Brigade Sanitary Service, was responsible for all hospital arrangements and the various doctors.

S. appeared to be wavering between duty and discretion. I had better keep my mouth shut. Perhaps he had sneaked up to my car with his girl, pulled out fast, and didn't even know that I had left my post. " . . . but I slipped on the ice up to my waist in the ditch. . . . "

"Say, Doc, I hope that you got la——," I said as S. stalked off.

"You hope I got what?"

"Let it go."

I cannot understand why S. had to use my car. The stretchers in the small front-line ambulances are much more comfortable.

December 22. Alcorisa. Stand-by Orders; But Now We Know

Sit in my car with notebook on wheel. Much of my writing will be done here from now on. I am going to be busy. Driving Captain S. (grudge gone, happy as a lark, whistles to himself and smiles from time to time) on tour of small towns in which battalions are quartered. Are the men digging and using la-trines? Do they wait for the water trucks or drink from the ditches and the well? Is the delousing camion (called "bug-hatcher") being sufficiently used? Are the battalion infirmaries operating smoothly, with enough supplies? Has anyone broken his glasses? Should the dental autochir be sent? What do the battalion doctors need? Is there a trace of typhoid? Do the poles fit the stretchers? And does the driver of the Mac-Pap bus want to go home? How to tell him that he cannot go home?[13]

"Foeces," says S., "excreta and plain ordinary crap, of all sizes and colors and consistency. I've never seen so much in my life. These tours sicken me. The men have to be housebroken to latrines like dogs."

"Why not send them out into the fields and save on the Ministry of Agri-culture's bill for fertilizer? That's one good thing about war, Doc."

"Up at the front you'll find out that the ground is manured very well. . . . Feeling happy today, aren't you?"

"Well, after the good news. . . . "

"When we get up to the Front you won't be so happy. You're just about big enough"—S. looks me over from shoes to cap—"to manure a whole patch of cabbages. Now put that down in your journal."

Behind the car lies a fountain courtyard flanked by an olive mill and a flour mill. Next to the fountain bubble the three and six-foot cauldrons of

---

13. The "Mac-Paps" are the Mackenzie-Papineau Battalion of the 15th Brigade, which was named after two Canadian patriots and consisted of Canadian and some U.S. volunteers.

the Mac-Pap field kitchen, on iron tripods. Pre-Christmas pudding, sewed up in cotton bags, boil in a gigantic vessel, and two hundred liters of beef stew stirred by a wood shovel gurgle in another. I tasted the oil which was being pressed in the mill. Fifteen minutes old, it was as sweet as butter; and all of it must be exported.

Twenty feet away the Spanish company of the Mac-Paps marches in from maneuvers, singing "Red Flag" and "The Young Guard," one bayonet and one automatic rifle among the hundred of them. Nothing to sing about. English company follows them, singing Hi-ho-jorum and something about "big commissary rats in bowler hats."[14] Six bayonets.

The Mayor of this town and its population are even more strongly anarchist than those of Alcorisa. A certain class of foreign correspondents, and all left-extremist of the Trotskyist splinter-groups, believe in common that the Anarchists hate the I.B.; but the wish is not always father of the thought, and here in Mas de las Matas, the F.A.I. and the C.N.T. have vacated their headquarters to make room for us. The townspeople, I hear, have killed most of their available pigs for our men. We have imported a truckload of clothing and canned milk as Christmas presents for the children of the village. Most of the anarchists I've talked with seem baffled that the leaders in the big cities have not been able to achieve the unity which exists among the troops at the Front.

It is getting too dark to write.

The good news: this morning we heard that the Listers, afer sleeping without fires for three days in the snow, descended on the Alfambra Valley, north of Teruel, and effected a junction with the Vivancos (mostly anarchists), completely cutting the Teruel–Saragossa railroad and highway, while a mixed division is advancing on the city from the south. Good news for Spain is bad news for the 15th Brigade. So long as the Spanish troops advance, we won't be needed and we won't get to the front.

Almost too dark to write now. If it were not for the patch of blood-red sky that lies low on the horizon over which Lister marched his men, if it were not for the fires of the field kitchen, I shouldn't have been able to write this much.

I think I'll get out of my car and see what I can do about that Christmas pudding.

---

14. This line is from a song popular among American and British volunteers titled "The Quartermaster's Store."

December 23. Alcorisa. Waiting, Waiting

The thumb of the Teruel salient has been cut at the last joint. Teruel, the fingernail, is ringed. Aldehuela, Villel, Villastar, Campillo and Concud have been taken. Counter-attacks have begun, from out of Saragossa. The Army advances and here we stay, listening to Queipo de Llano tell the world over the Seville radio that the Fifteenth has been annihilated at the gates of Teruel![15] Only fifteen men in the infirmary, most grippe cases. "No matter how preposterous the lie," runs Hitler's propaganda theorem, "no matter how thoroughly disproved it may be, a certain residue remains in the minds of the people."

It is 10 A.M. I sit in my car, windows shut, bathed in the sunlight which melts the frost from my windows. Rose early this morning, tuned up engine, polished my windows and body, swept out the floor. It is as warm as a greenhouse in here. Once I replace the two rear seats with stretchers, I'll live in my car.

The scouts march by, singing, to the tune of the Doxology, "waiting, waiting, waiting . . . always bloodywell waiting . . . waiting night and waiting day . . . coffee comin' up . . . coffee never comes . . . some day we'll wait no more." The Scouts are slightly better equipped than the rest of the Fifteenth. Their rifles, all Mexicanskys, use the same shells.

Under ideal conditions it would take us two hours to pack infirmary, kitchen, medical supplies, beds, mattresses and blankets into the seventeen-car combined infirmary, Classification Post and Surgical Unit convoy. We have the bed-truck and supply truck, four big evacuation ambulances with four stretchers each and room for fifteen light wounded in their compartments; five light six-wheeled front-line ambs, each with two stretchers and room for ten light wounded; surgical and dental autochirs; light commissary truck; bug-hatcher and shower wagon, and the staff car, which is mine. The four light battalion ambs stay with the troops. All of this equipment comes from the States where it was paid for by tens of thousands of small contributions, as were our steamship fares and travelling expenses. I guess that the front-line medical service of the 15th Brigade represents an investment of at least fifty thousand dollars paid by the American workingman, liberal and small business man as premium on an insurance policy against fascism in their own country. Copic was right. Chófers have to live for their cars. Screwdrivers and end-wrenches should sprout from our finger tips, and our hands should grow hard as machine-tools. Nothing else matters.

---

15. Fascist General Queipo de Llano y Serra was one of the "Four Insurgent Generals."

My own hands have already become permanently stained by grease and carbon. Soon they will be tough as gristle; and still my radiator leaks. The radiator repair shop at Albalate is a hundred kilometers away.

J.B.S. Haldane, British physiologist heavyweight, sits in the car behind me.[16] He is the first major personality of the war and the first foreign civilian I have met in Spain. He is here as our gas-defense expert. A big man with fierce iron-gray eyebrows and duplicate mustache, morning coat and ascot tie would seem to suit him better than the heavy faded overcoat and earflap Sherlock Holmes cap he wears. He came in late last night after hitch-hiking from Barcelona over the ambulance route, and inconspicuously crawled to sleep on a mattress beside one of the Scotch cooks.

I wanted to tell the great man that I had spent two years at Oxford, and to show him that I was not an ordinary volunteer but a high-powered intellectual like himself. Perhaps he knew some of my English literary friends. Unlike the average *soldado*, I could meet him on an equal educational English plane. We would have a pleasant half hour of the profound humanitarian conversation which I had begun to crave. Perhaps Haldane had news of the outside world, in which books were still published and socio-philosophers defined, shifted and redefined their stands. Was Whitehead still clinging to the Cartesian trick by which God is produced, when the audience is not looking, like a rabbit out of a silk hat? How fast was the rate of flow of British scientists towards the loyalist cause? Could Wells be induced to come to Barcelona for the air raids and a pragmatic test of liberalism? Was it true that Shaw was slipping into Rosenberg's bed?[17] How soon could we expect a General Election in England?

The windows of the car were closed. No one could have overheard us, to discover that I was an intellectual. But I could not find the first word to say. I offered Haldane a cigarette, which he refused (he was busy scribbling mathematical and chemical equations), got out of the car, and began to paint all my nickel-work black. Yesterday I was able to obtain, after a long search, enough paint to keep my bright-work from giving me away to the planes which will soon be passing overhead. Paint of any kind is almost as rare as anything but

---

16. J.B.S. Haldane, a professor of biometry at University College, London, visited Spain as an expert on the defense against gas warfare. His wife, Charlotte Haldane, worked for the Dependants Aid Committee, assisting families of International Brigaders. She visited Spain in 1938 with Paul and Eslanda Goode Robeson.

17. "Wells" is likely British writer and historian H.G. Wells. Alfred Rosenberg was an influential member of the Nazi Party.

water and coffee to drink. Food and light commodities, almost unreplenished from abroad, are being soaked up at such a rate that soon there will be nothing left but bread, beans, gasoline, guns and gunpowder. These things are just about all we need. Morale we have by the truckload.

Discipline is increasing. The convoy lined up below the infirmary this morning. Drivers and staff stood at attention and saluted. The Major walked up the line listening to us start our cars. After that there was an inspection of the cook-shed, the store-room and wards.

First-aid bandages were issued. I have instructions to wear mine on my belt and never, never give it to anyone.

December 24. Later

Dorothy the stowaway Nightingale turned up again. Fed by chófers, she has been dodging from town to town, sleeping in ambulances, always one step ahead of Major B. The other officers have taken a tolerant attitude towards her.

Late in the afternoon I passed a peasant woman carrying two large flat loaves of fresh-baked bread. I told her that I would like to buy one of them. Very much embarrassed, she said that she had never before sold her bread, that she would be glad to give me one of the loaves. I persuaded her to take a good five-peseta Barcelona note.

Hiding the bread under my coat, I found Gus, Sana and Jack.[18] We walked out of town and climbed up through olive terraces in the cold bright Christmas weather until we found one of the rare emerald-green patches of grass that dust the terra-cotta landscape. Smoke came from the chimneys of the town below us. The tinkle of the small waterfall that came out of the terrace that sheltered us from the wind mixed with the sound of distant target practice.

"I'd like to be up here during a raid," said Sana. "You could see absolutely everything!"

"Greenland would suit me"—Jack has been at the front—"and you wouldn't watch. You'd lie at the foot of the wall or in the ditch with your face in the dirt. You wouldn't watch."

"Just the same. . . . " said Sana thoughtfully.

---

18. Gus, Augustus Neblinger Towson from Harrisburg, Pennsylvania, served as an ambulance driver and secretary at Villa Paz. Rose Sana Goldblatt, a nurse at Beth Israel Hospital in New York City before going to Spain, later lived in San Francisco, California.

I took the bread out from under my coat and laid it on a sweater.

"Jesus Christ!" said Gus, "real bread!"

I sliced the bread and we silently ate it, saving some for the evening. The sun was so warm that Jack and I peeled off our clothing down to the waist and lay on the grass, sunbathing. The reports of target practice had ceased. Sunlight and ripple of the baby waterfall were beginning to make us drowsy. But for the chill breeze that played about my shoulders, I should have slept.

"The guy over at the auto-parque who inherited a hundred and twenty-five thousand dollars . . . ," said Sana.

Gus corrected her. "It was only a hundred thousand dollars."

"*Only* a hundred thousand grand! Why isn't he going home?"

"Why did he come here? Why did you come here?"

"Well, there are too many nurses in New York, and . . . ."

"You mean," Jack said, "there aren't enough. But the people who need nurses the worst can't pay them."

"Whatever it is, I wasn't getting much work. It's true that the girls at some of the hospitals divide the calls—a while ago a few of them used to work the whole year round—but I wasn't getting very much. I got bored. You ride around on the subways a lot and you go to people's houses and drink coffee and listen to the radio and you get bored. Like most of us, I haven't any side-interests. If I had side-interests, maybe it would have been different. I got so bored giving all I made to landlords and coffee-pot Greeks that I stopped looking for work so hard and went on Relief and tried that for awhile. Relief wasn't any good, so I went back to work. Just when I had a good cancer-of-the-arm case who was going to take a long time to die, some of my friends who were radicals—some of my best friends are that way"—with a conscious smirk—"asked me was I interested in Spain. 'So I'll go over there for a while,' I thought."

Jack: You didn't even care what side you went to.

Sana: Oh! no. . . . but you can't convince me I came here out of political convictions. I haven't any politics. But Franco . . . fooey!

(*Stage directions: A siren blows in the wings. Sana, Gus and the Author first rise, then lean back on the ground, watching to see what Jack, the veteran, will do.*)

Jack: Two blasts. The boys in the church-tower think that they see something. Don't do anything. Just wait. Now you tell us why you came here, Gus. What the hell was your trade back in the States?

Gus: Me? I was an actor. . . . Say, listen, Jack, don't you think we'd better . . . .

Jack: There isn't anything better to do. You just wait. . . . An actor, hey? Well, that's a good reason for coming. . . .

Gus: For Christ's sake, shut up. (He lies flat on his back looking up into the sky.) I think I can hear something.

Jack: Nuts. That's a motorcycle. How about you, Jim? Why did you come to Spain?

Author: Tell you after the "all clear" signal blows.

Jack: So I have the floor to myself have I? Well, on the day I sailed, which must have been just about a year ago . . .

(He talks rapidly, continually shifting his eyes over the three figures that twist on the grass beside him, as if he wanted to draw their glances off the sky to his. The Author has started to pull on his sweater.)

. . . I was supposed to have gotten married. I had a good job as a commercial photographer and she didn't want me to go. I hated to argue with her. I hate to argue with girls; anything else. I guess she figured that she had some kind of rights over me because we had been sleeping together for about six months—oh! boy, was it good—she was getting about just as much out of it as I was, so what the hell. I like her well enough and we got along fine and I suppose I would have married her. On Sundays we used to lay in bed all day with the shades drawn and then get up when the heat had begun to die down and it was getting dark and go to Chinatown. Do I like to eat after a big session in bed! I like to eat almost better than anything else. We used to try all of the foreign restaurants in town. We ate more Spanish dishes than I've tasted here. When and if I get back to the States, I'm going to do nothing but eat. When I started to talk about coming to Spain, my girl saw that there wasn't anything to do about it, so she says, "Well, let's get married anyway." I hate to argue with girls. To shut her up I said, "sure." I pulled out of the harbor on my wedding day. She didn't know it. The first letter I got said that she wasn't surprised at all. And now she's supposed to be waiting for me.

Gus: What's that sound?

Jack: Don't you know the difference between a truck engine and a plane? Lie down and don't sprain your ears listening. All you can do is wait. Don't move. Just wait.

(Noticing that his audience is becoming restless, he speaks ever more rapidly.)

For six months I drove a transport truck. Those were the tough times. We never slept and we never knew where we were. For weeks at a time I didn't get out of my cab except to piss. Only one car in three ran with lights. A lot of times I would sleep at the wheel but I never had a smack-up. In the middle of the night they would tell us "a half hour for sleep, now." We would flop at the wheel. That's worse than not sleeping. I guess those six months are what took the guts out of me. Just look at me. I don't give a god damn for anything. I've seen so much and done so much that if anyone asks me about "Spain" when and if I get back to the States, I'll just say, "Let it go, let it go" and talk about something else.

For twenty-one days I drove an ammunition truck up at Brunete. That was the life. Unload the stuff before sunrise, run my car off the road—there wasn't anything you could call a tree—get some coffee and then go to sleep for a whole day in my dugout, which was a square hole covered by olive branches I carried with me. I'd strip first and sleep all day with the sun just barely coming through the leaves. Those were the best days I've had in Spain. Two hundred yards away the guns would be roaring and we were getting a lot of shelling from the other side and They were using big aerial torpedoes on us, but I didn't mind. I'd sleep all day. But when it began to get dark there wasn't two of us and we didn't dress, lift the windowshade and go to Chinatown for dinner. Then one day They got the range and too many of our gunners were killed. I helped load but I didn't know enough to keep out of the recoil, and a big bastard of a 155 kicked me in the leg. I'm no good. I don't care about anything. I don't even care about going home.

Gus: After a year over here you're entitled to apply for repatriation, aren't you?

(evidently humbled by Jack's front-line record)

Jack: Yes, I guess so. But I came over here for political reasons and I'm staying here for political reasons. I didn't tell you that, did I? Maybe I'm tired, but Franco's not.

(The nervous strain which twisted the bodies of the three men and the girl has passed its crisis. Still looking up into the immaculate cold blue Christmas day, they lie on their backs.)

Author: How much of that bread is left?

Sana: Weren't we going to. . . .

(The offstage siren blows three sharp blasts, each higher pitched than the last. All four jump to their feet and run off: Sana to her patients in the ward and the three men to their cars.)

CURTAIN

<u>Same day. Later.</u> The siren on the church tower had turned in a false alarm. No sooner had we pulled our cars out of town into the olive groves than the "all clear" signal blew.

Before going to sleep, we finished the bread.

Waiting, waiting: but would first-aid packages have been given to us if we were not leaving for the Front soon?

I'm worried about Sana. She does her work but she doesn't seem to have her heart in this fight. The house party and camping thrill have passed. She is able to stand the hardship and keep her trap shut, and she certainly ought to be able to stand the coming carnage, but suppose she starts to see her number come up?

Gus, for all of his quietness and poker-face, is all right, although he keeps much to himself and outwardly carries his moral tail between the legs. He came to Spain with the Medical Corps as an ambulance driver. It happened that there was no offensive, so we had drivers to burn. Gus was sent to Albacete and put on a big Russian transport camion. He had no complaint until things began to warm up north of Madrid and his transport division got ready to go to the Front. Gus refused to go with his car. Insisting that he had come to Spain to serve with the Medical Corps and that he wasn't going to work anywhere but in the Medical Corps, he was finally transferred to Villa Paz. Ever since then, Gus has behaved like a little boy who cannot forget that he once messed his pants in public. Remorse and a desire for atonement are screwed into his tight Scandinavian features. He is now Brigade Medical Clerk but hopes some day to be given a car. No one has anything against Gus, but he will not let us forget his misbehavior.

I do not worry about Jack. He has heart enough for an entire battalion.

And how about the Author? I don't know. I'll see. If I turn yellow, I hope no one ever finds me out.

The Day Before Christmas. Still Alcorisa

Sit in the F. A. I. headquarters. Today's coffee tastes heavily of chicory, as usual, but not of sugar. Al Hawk, of the Pharoah beard (reason for the large crop of dirty-shirt hiders among the Fifteenth, the poor quality of razor blades and the absence of hot water), says, "War is tough? Hell, I'm eating better than I ever did in my life. You never rode the freights much, did you? No boss to fire you, something to eat three times a day, no questions asked and no worries but stopping a handful of slugs. Hell, I'm having the time of my life!" Al is a product of Brookwood Labor College and the Albacete sharpshooter school.[19] After the Belchite campaign, the rheumatism he contracted from sleeping on cold damp ground for weeks at a time became so severe that he was given a "soft" job driving a camion. His is the Matford captured in September which the Major and I picked up that night in Ambiete.

The papers say that the entire city of Teruel has now been captured with the exception of the Civil Guard barracks, the Seminary, the Bank of Spain, the lunatic asylum and several smaller fortified buildings. Franco, who by this time has slaughtered the entire International Brigade over the radio for the tenth time, now announces that Teruel will be a second Toledo.

From all accounts, street fighting is a long and tedious business. Last August it took the boys a week to mop up Belchite, which was less than half the size and importance of Teruel. One house was taken only after a barrel of gasoline had been rolled into the cellar and set off with a grenade. Captain Carl Bradley (real name), a former San Francisco longshoreman, tired of having his men shot jumping from doorway to doorway and bayoneted in the throat in dark cellars.[20] His section drove through the walls of six houses with pickaxes, climbed a stair and came quietly out on a roof. There in the courtyard beneath the Washington-Lincolns were fascists smoking, sleeping, firing at loopholes. Merriman, the Commander, arrived.[21] "Sh!" says Bradley. Both men tiptoe to the cornice. "Give me a gun, somebody," begs Merriman.

---

19. Brookwood Labor College was an educational institute in Katonah, New York, supported by various labor unions.
20. Carl Bradley, a native of Newport, Kentucky, worked as a steelworker before going to Spain, and died c. 1970.
21. Robert Merriman, a graduate student in economics at the University of California, Berkeley, when the war broke out, commanded the Lincoln battalion at Jarama until

I have seen Bob Merriman a good deal. He has the physique of an Oregon crew-man. Pale gray eyes flash through horn-rims. He is perpetually agitated but never nervous. Everything and everyone interests him. He has a way of infecting the entire brigade with his almost too boyish enthusiasm. Dave Doran, the commissar of the Fifteenth, is as somber as Merriman is excitable. He has the profound respect of the men but not their devotion. Fred Copeman, Commander of English (at present in a hospital after an appendectomy performed by Major B.), is the best hated and loved man in the Fifteenth.[22] He drives and curses his men in genuine British Army style—"but Copey's a bloody fine soldier," denunciations of him always end. Copeman was a marine engineer before he came to Spain. A few days ago I listened to an English Company Commissar speak to his men. The speech was short and fluent: "Comrades; you bloody hoores talk too ——ing much about your officers. Keep your bleeding mouths shut. The General isn't going to ask you ——nts how your ——ing asses feel before he gives you an order. Anybody who has a ——cking remark to make about a comrade officer, me or anybody else, make it at a ——cking meetin'. Who wants the ——cking floor? . . . Well, that's all."

After coffee at the F. A. I., Al and I went shopping. He bought the town's last towel, to be used as a muffler. I got two of the last handkerchiefs. Not one solitary thing to eat on sale in this town, not even a toothpick on which to chew. I have formed the habit of pocketing a piece of bread during mealtime. Occasionally Danny, one of the Scotch cooks, can be persuaded to give you the crust used to clarify hot olive oil, if you can get past the door of the cook-shed and arrive at the right time. Interminable brewing of coffee from home goes on over primus stoves in our quarters. My god I wish I had a bar of chocolate. The package which is issued every ten days with my pay goes in one gulp.

4 P.M. Christmas Eve

It is beginning to get dark. Peasants come back from the fields, some of them carrying small heads of winter cabbage. Burros are loaded with limbs torn from the cemetery cypresses and aromatic rosemary thorns for kindling. The

---

he was wounded. After recovery, he became Chief of Staff of the 15th Brigade. He was captured and killed during the Retreats in 1938.

22. Fred Copeman commanded the British battalion of the 15th Brigade at Jarama and Brunete. He returned to England for a speaking tour in 1937, then returned to Spain, where he fell ill and never resumed command.

prunings of olive trees are also used for firewood. All but the top branches of the former Bishop's incredible cedars have disappeared into the village fireplaces. The arid hills are full of the small cactuses and succulents sold by New York florists at a dollar a pot, but these are too fleshy to be used as firewood. What this town needs is a good bombing.

Tonight we are invited to a dance in the Andorra schoolhouse. I will put on my necktie.

Teruel is Christmas present enough.

Christmas Day 1937. Alcorisa

The radio in the ward, which is my newest studio, purrs peace across the Western hemisphere. Organ music from half the great cathedrals of Europe rolls over the coughing figures on the beds. I am very glad for the cold which seems to have permanently crippled my sense of smell. From Finland to Greece, Church dignitaries, ministers of Education, senators and cabinet ministers sob their two cents' worth of heavenly peace over the air, with the piety of whores on a holiday.

Nevertheless, that stained-glass purplish Christmas feeling is inescapable. It is difficult not to feel sorry for yourself. All of the world is calm and pure on December 25th.

The dance last night at Andorra was no riot. I cannot boast of a hangover. The medical alcohol ran short.

I spent most of the evening standing with Finn and Jack and Smitty on the sidelines watching the dancers who shuffled over the cement floor to the music of guitar, violin and cornet. The floor was crowded with International drivers—always to be recognized by their pistols—Spanish *soldados* on leave, village boys and grandfathers. The orchestra played *jotas* with an occasional Bavarian-sounding waltz, and once, "Four o'Clock in the Morning," always a great Iberian favorite. Most of the nurses had changed from their blue ski-pants into skirts.

Andrea, one of the Spanish nurses of the Divisional Sanidad Militar, is one of the most beautiful women I have ever seen. Her tall shape is at once full and thin, tapering long curves at the wrists, waist, knees and ankles. She has close-cut blue-black hair and long eyelashes over the agate-colored eyes in her smooth dark face. A single look at her convinces you that the photographers who work for the cold-cream companies do not betray us, nor do sex magazine cover artists. I like to watch her move; to see her lift a cigarette to her lips, to take a step or to sit. Every motion she makes contains the sum of her beauty. Unfortunately Andrea knows all about herself. I was unable to get near her or even to find the range of her eyes, all evening.

The rationed and guarded refreshments consisted of one cup of coffee, three dry sweet biscuits and a square of chocolate.

I grew tired of the dance and walked outdoors. A dim light shone in the windows of one of the large ambulances in the schoolyard. I knocked and was admitted. Half a dozen 35th Division drivers, in the tall Caucasian-looking headpieces of reddish fur made here in Andorra, were brewing coffee over a primus. A can of Russian bully beef and a bottle of grain alcohol were being passed. All of these drivers had seen service at the Front. The conversation therefore consisted of stories of narrow escapes. Dorothy, the stowaway Nightingale, tended the coffee. This was her newest hideout.

" . . . and how many more times were you killed before sunrise that night?" Wild Bill, so-called because of his blond beard and mustache, interrupted.[23] "I'll bet you've never even seen something like this. . . . "

He reached under the stretcher, pulled something out and threw it on the floor. In the dim blue light of the primus stove, I could see a dried human head.

"I was walking around the cemetery where it had been bombed and I saw this lousy fascist staring at me, so what could I do but pick him up.[24] Here, Franco, have a drink. . . . "

"The Lord God alone redeemeth," came a voice from one of the upper stretchers, "though he speak through the mouth of Mohammed, of Zeus, Buddha, Vitzliputzli or. . . . "

"We've got Vitzli with us right here," said Wild Bill Cody, pointing at the dry hard lips of the head on the floor, "and he hasn't said a word. How about giving us the lowdown of life, Vitz, what's the answer?"

"For Christ's sake, go bury that thing somewhere."

" . . . or through Mary, his daughter. God has been worshipped under many names, and though His prophets have written divergent scriptures, all contain the same message of brotherly love. . . . "

"He's drunk."

"He's not drunk. He's celebrating. Teruel."

---

23. Wild Bill, Lieutenant James "Jim" Edgar Cody, aka George Cody, was chief of scouts in the 15th Brigade. He died during the Retreats in March 1938.

24. In a 1953 letter, Ernest Hemingway described a similar, and to him, repugnant, incident of soldiers playing football with human skulls around Tarancón.

"Well, somebody give him another drink. Maybe he'll pass out."

I had a last shot of Christmas cheer and walked out into the schoolyard.

There in the moonlight was Dorothy, motionless, leaning against a fence. This was my big chance.

"Oh. Hello."

"It's nice out here, isn't it, Dorothy. Why aren't you at the dance? Major B. isn't there."

"Oh, it isn't that. But somehow I can't think of dancing . . . "—perhaps she really was a fanatic—"to that funny music. I keep thinking of the Colony floor back in London, the evening dresses and champagne and sandwiches and the perfume. You can't help thinking of those things sometimes."

"No, you can't."

I found nothing to say. For half an hour we stood looking, looking at the white modern walls of the schoolhouse, whiter than the moonlight, and the roofs that descended as jerkily down hill as the graph of a depression.

"The schoolhouse looks new, Dorothy." I hoped she would not resent the use of her name.

"It isn't even finished. The Aragon is full of half-finished Republican schoolhouses. By the time that the peasants were putting on the roofs, Franco knew that the jig was up. It was now or never: so he revolted."

I was sorry that the conversation had taken a political turn. Dorothy sensed this and was quiet.

A little later she said, "Don't the stars lie low on the horizon."

This would be the signal I would have waited for back in the States. Here in Spain things were not the same.

"How is Bob?" I asked.

"He's not here. They sent him to Caspe with a load."

Because I was very cold, I left Dorothy at the fence-post.

I spent the rest of the evening carting drunks into Smitty's car, for the return to Alcorisa. Three of the thirty-five of us had taken one drink too many: the two Scotch cooks and a German stretcher-bearer.

Christmas Afternoon. In the Ward

Commandante Crome (real nom de guerre), Major B.'s superior, has just addressed us. C. is the son of White Russians, educated in Scotland.[25] His rid-

---

25. The British Dr. Leonard Crome served as Chief Medical Officer of the 35th Division, of which the 15th Brigade was part. During World War II, he earned a Military Cross for service with the Royal Army Medical Corps.

ing boots are the only perfectly polished leather I have seen in Spain. Some of us think that C. is a Prince or a Duke. He could step into the leading role of a Hollywood Zenda romance. Why has he come to Spain?

"I am glad to have good news for you on Christmas Day.

"All Teruel is ours, with the exception of the Seminary, the Bank of Spain, the Civil Guard barracks and two small fortified houses.

"The expected counter-attacks have begun. The first ones have been beaten off. At Celadas, troops advancing in storm-troop formation were turned back, with five thousand casualties. Two hundred Civil Guards died at Teruel.

"The counter attacks will come heavier and heavier.

"Thus far we are proud to say that no International troops have been used. This has been an exclusively Spanish victory. For the first time the newly organized People's Army has shown its strength. The campaign which was conducted for a Unified Command has been justified.

"You, as part of the 35th Division, are being held in readiness. From Alcorisa we can reach either the Saragossa front or the Teruel front with equal speed. The order may be given any day.

"You must remember that the infantry think as much of the Medical Corps as they do of their helmet. You are their shield. You must also remember that each of you is personally responsible to the anti-fascist men and women of the world who sent you here. They are your commanders. We officers are here to organize rather than to command. With the discipline you shall impose on yourselves, we shall win.

"Are there questions?"

December 26. Out in My Car, After Inspection

Christmas lunch, yesterday, was to be served at 12:35 A.M. At noon I was fifteen miles away, in Aguaviva.

"Thanks for the ride," said Dave Doran, the Commissar of the Fifteenth. "You'd better hurry over the mountains and get your lunch. How long will it take you to get back?"

"About three quarters of an hour, what with the ice on the road at the top of the pass. . . . " I knew I could be back at the Alcorisa cook-shed in half that time.

"Let's see . . . perhaps you'd better stay with us. I'll take you to the Quartermaster and he'll fix you up."

I was thus the first man to taste the Washington-Lincoln's turkey, cabbage and fried potatoes. I ate so fast that by the time I reached Mas de las Matas, the English had hardly sat down to dinner.

"Hello," said Walter Tapsall (real name), Commissar of the English, looking up from his plate, "what the bloody hell brings you here?"[26]

"Well, I've just been to Aguaviva and I'm going back to Alcorisa and I thought that perhaps you had a message for B. or sick to carry."

"I get you, brother." Tapsall, proud of his knowledge of the latest American slang, calls all Americans "brother." "Why didn't you say you'd missed your dinner? The Quartermaster will take care of you. Now scram."

I packed away the ham, the cabbage, fried potatoes and pudding of the English so quickly that I arrived in Alcorisa just in time to finish off the last of our sardines, green salad and fried potatoes, and bread with jam. There was also wine.

The big meal of the day came several hours later. We cleared our quarters and set up tables and benches borrowed from the Town Hall. Clean sheets served as tablecloths. We began with brandy and free French cigarettes. After that came soup, fried sweet potatoes, fresh string beans and roast pig, with white and red wine. For dessert we had cinnamon cake, almonds, figbread and Soviet candy. For the first time since I left Villa Paz, I ate sitting down. We have been swilling our rations standing up in a small dark crowded smoke-filled room ever since we came to Alcorisa.

There was not much drinking. The food was intoxication enough. After dinner we cleared away the tables and danced to the radio. Major Umberto Galleani (real name) took the floor with a scullery girl.[27] Earlier in the evening, he had waited on the table. Major Crespo Y Poyes, of the Fifteenth's General Staff, visited us. He was formerly the owner of many printing plants in Madrid and the possessor of some kind of title. His wife came in a militiaman's costume. Another officer, black-bearded and long-armed as a gorilla, wore his wife's dress, lipstick and rouge. She was in his uniform.

Towards the end of the evening, Merriman's driver—a bull-necked Alaskan miner called Irv—and I put on a wrestling match which ended after I had pulled a tendon in my back.

---

26. Walter Tapsall, commissar of the British battalion, was killed during the retreats in March 1938.

27. Umberto Galleani left his editorial post at an Italian-language newspaper in New York to head the first Garibaldi column of Italian volunteers in Spain in 1936. He returned to the United States in 1937 for a speaking tour to raise support for the Republic, then went back to Spain. He testified about Communist activities in Spain before the House Committee on Un-American Activities in 1940.

December 26. Night. About to go to bed

Nothing whatsoever happened today. In spite of the four Christmas dinners I ate yesterday, by lunch time I was as hungry as ever.

Nothing new about Teruel. It appears that the five Alcazars inside the town are still holding out. Rumors spread that the fascists have retaken a few towns from us; Concud, notably. Italian newspaper reproduced in Barcelona journals says that the taking of Teruel which is now acknowledged was due altogether to surprise and the snowfall which prevented Franco from bringing up reinforcements. If we surprised Franco, then our army is better than his, because surprise has always been the greatest weapon in ancient and modern warfare. It is even more so today. Surprise enables and alone enables a weaker force to overcome a stronger or a more mechanized one.

Pointers for Good Sleeping:

1) Get as many blankets as possible and hold on to them night and day. The best are Mexicansky. The others are small gray cottonish things. Many are in use as overcoats with a hole cut through the middle for the head. A string will do for belt.

2) Get a rubber poncho or a rubber sheet to lay on the ground or the floor.

3) Go to sleep near a stove or a fire, if there is one.

4) If you undress, lay your clothes on top of the blankets.

5) If you are able to buy five yards of any kind of cloth, have this sewn into the shape of a mattress, open at one end. Straw or cornstalks can generally be found.

The siren blew again today. Again we had our cars out of town and under olive trees or in sunken roads within three minutes, and again the alarm was false. No one has shot at me yet. I am not worried or frightened. I worry only about my car, and about cigarettes.

December 27. Alcorisa

Nothing new from Teruel. Five Alcazars still holding out. Counter attacks heavier every day. Lister still holds the Alfambra valley. I suspect that the Franco-Brigade and the Thaelmans, secretly bivouacked in this neighborhood for the past few days, have gone in to relieve the Listers.

Packages arrived from the States today, just two days late for Christmas. None for me. I sit in Smitty's Harvard amb club, full of Indian nuts and chocolate, with two packages of good American cigarettes in my pocket.

Somebody just threw me an orange drop. ("What are you writing, Jaime?" my friends call. I tell them that I am writing a long letter to my girl, that I so mistrust the Spanish mail system that I am waiting until I get to Paris, where I will dispatch the entire epistle, and that I keep a carbon copy because of the danger of being sued. Real reason for the carbons is that I will thus be able to send sections of my account back to the States as it is written. In case I get mine, parts of the writing will live and be useful, I hope. But not one is satisfied with my explanations. "What are you writing, what are you writing?" the chófers ask.) Of the thirty of us, only five got packages. Tonight we will look at dinner in a different way, for once.

Description of the Act of Being Wounded

"I was walking up to the lines when I noticed that the dirt under the olive trees was beginning to jump, as if big rain drops as angry as hornets were stinging the ground. All of a sudden, I felt as if somebody had hit me a hell of a wallop on the hips with a big lead club. The shock took me off my feet. There was no real pain. My legs go numb fast. In five minutes I had to stop crawling. Pretty soon the stretcher men got me."

Thus Sanford (real name), former San Francisco electrician and hospital orderly, got his "ticket home"; but since he wants to see the war out, he has been assigned to us as a male nurse.[28] The base hospitals send their best people to the front-line medical unit: the brigade, its weakest. I begin to feel like a slacker.

Most of the patients in the infirmary have pneumonia or dirt fever. This type of grippe comes from perpetual wet feet, from sitting around fires and from cold damp sleeping. When there are no means to heat quarters, the windows are closed. The moisture of many bodies collecting on the walls swarms into the air. Soon the dark chambers become virtual aquariums with vague figures in many kinds and combinations of uniforms floating about over the slippery floors. Dirt fever comes not only from living in the contagion of this atmosphere, but from the necessarily dirty way in which we wash, eat, sleep and take care of the calls of nature—let alone the constant contact with disease centralized in and about the hospitals, the infirmaries and barracks but in the air itself, during wartime. And yet, of the thirty members of our surgical group, there are at present twenty-five effectives.

---

28. Alfred Byron Sanford was a sergeant wounded at Belchite.

Jaundice comes from our unbalanced diet. Diarrhea results from diet and dirt. It seldom progresses to dysentery. Constipation and piles come from not being able to relieve one's self at natural moments.

We have run short on aspirin.

Eczemas and boils come from dirt and diet.

Because of the excellent work of the Medical Staff officers, epidemics have been few. Bill Pike (real name), Crome's assistant and a former New York psychiatrist, vaccinated hundreds of men in the Jarama trenches, long ago.[29]

There was nevertheless a small epidemic of typhoid at Grañen on the Huesca front last summer. The brigade was at the point of moving back into reserve. All hospital equipment was packed. Everything had to be taken apart and set up, in the driving rain, to handle the first five hundred cases.

Today's routine. Up before sunrise. Started car, cleaned engine, and tightened up body bolts and loose bumper. Inspection at 8. Evacuated three patients in the morning. One jaundice and two stomach ulcers, to Alcañiz. After late lunch, asked the Major for time off. I wanted to climb the hill back of the church and lie in the sun. He refused. "Suppose we got orders to move, or there is a raid? Drivers should stay with their cars." I was allowed to go to my quarters, where I spent the entire afternoon trying to sleep, while I listened to rumors and counter-rumors. When do we move, Oh Lord, when do we move?

Another stowaway. Harry Wilkes*(real name), pharmacist, arrived via the ambulance route, with the notion of wedging himself into the Front group.[30] He was sent back.

December 28. Alcorisa, on the Uttermost Frontier of All, Waiting, Waiting

Chocolate was issued this morning and tobacco after lunch: danger signals or

---

* dead [all asterisked footnotes appeared in Neugass's original typescript]

29. A graduate of Rush Medical College in Chicago, William Winston Pike served with the Lincoln Battalion at the battle of Jarama, and later with the 35th Regiment. Known affectionately as "Captain Shitty" because of his insistence on good hygiene, he used his psychiatric experience to treat war-shocked volunteers. He eventually became chief medical officer or the 15th Brigade. During World War II, he was a Colonel in the Army Air Corps.

30. Harry Wilkes, a pharmacist attached to the first AMB unit, was allegedly executed for theft and black market sales in 1938.

Christmas largesse. Morale = Cigarettes plus chocolate plus warm food plus a place to sleep away from the cold. Nothing else matters.

Everything: the troop camions that sizzle up the road to the Front, the armored cars, the ammo trucks, the tension among the officers, the serious news from Teruel, the issuance of first-aid bandages, the more and more frequent alarms from the church tower, and the final appearance of some of our planes—everything points towards a sudden and soon departure for the lines.

Maneuvers were nevertheless held today. The English and the Mac-Paps defended Mas de las Matas (Thornville, in English) from the L.W.'s who attacked out of Aguaviva (Runnelton).[31] The hearse I drive played the role of Medical Corps liaison car. We toured the battalion first-aid posts. Both battalion ambs camouflaged by cornstalks were stationed at the bottom of hills, presumably just out of machine-gun fire. The stretcher-bearers worked between the lines on top of the hill and the cars. We have no powder to waste on blank bullets. There was no movement under the raw gray skies, no sound and no one to be seen but for officers at the roadside field telephones and fast-running motorcycles. At mid-afternoon a whistle blew. Instantly, ragged dust-colored figures rose on the ridges and streamed down to the field stove. The sight of gun-barrels against the skyline evokes emotions which I am not prepared to analyze. I can remember part of Copic's analysis of the maneuvers, although the major part of his terminology is unfamiliar to me:

"Special mention should be made of the discipline of the English. They remained in their positions all day long without lighting fires, although it is very cold. The Canadians, in spite of orders to the contrary, succumbed to the cold. The Lincoln-Washingtons executed a very good flanking motion; but they exposed themselves on a hilltop during the infiltration which followed. . . . "

Dave Doran,* the Commissar, followed the Commander:

"Unlike our European and Balkan comrades who have had military service in their own countries, the English and North American volunteers have most of them had no previous military experience. But that is no reason for the attitude which exists in the ranks of the Fifteenth, that discipline is something to be observed only in actual battle . . . and . . . hereafter. . . . "

Over beans and wine, I talked to a friend I had met. Bill Shatzberg and I

---

* now dead

31. The "L.W.'s" are the Lincoln-Washingtons.

had once worked in the same New York department store.[32] Then he was bitter, narrow-eyed and venomous. We were both part of the tiny trade-union group which was trying to organize thousands of terrified fellow-employees. He was more clever than I and managed to keep from being fired.

"All roads lead to Spain," Bill laughed, "how's the Union?"

"Right before I left I heard that we finally broke through the ice and that the boys were about to sign a contract with the management. You knew that I had been fired, didn't you?"

Bill laughed again. Spain seems to have relieved the tension which had always played about his eyes. "There are casualties in every war and it's guys like you and me who, sooner or later, get what's coming to them for sticking their necks out."

"Were you wounded?"

"Me? Hell no. I don't know what's the matter. I've been out here a year now. Of the fifteen guys who walked over the Pyrenees with me, I saw eight, nine, ten of them get theirs. At first I used to figure that it wouldn't be me, but now, at the beginning of each new campaign, I figure that my time's just about up. I can't understand it. Still, this time, this time . . . remember, we're shock troops. The only places they give us to attack are impregnable and the only things we have to defend can't be saved. That's a long way from selling linoleum and 'may I help you, moddam?'"

He seemed cheerful.

"See you later," I called at Bill.

"If we keep our heads down," he answered.

All of the infantrymen in the Alcorisa area have seen action. Five of every ten have helmets. (Tin hats drilled by bullets are un-popular, not because they bring bad luck, but for the reason that water for coffee cannot be boiled in them. French and Czechoslovak helmets perforated by sweat-holes are equally scorned. Captured German and Italian pie-plates are most in demand.) Three of every ten infantrymen have bayonets of the triangular rather than the knife type. Almost all of the rifles are of the same manufacture. Every man has a good leather cartridge belt. Canteens, gloves, blanket-overcoats are rare. Rubbers do not exist.

The machine-guns are squat heavy Maxims on small iron wheels. The automatic rifles, of different types, fire up to a hundred and fifty bullets a minute, I am told. No one seems to know where these weapons come from, although most of us call them "Mexicansky."

---

32. Jacob Schatzberg was killed at Belchite in March 1938.

The average age of the men is about twenty-four or twenty-five years old. As I looked at them, I kept wondering, "Are these really such good troops, can they be the best troops in the world, what is it they have which no men since the Knights Templars have possessed?" No single type of physique or face or voice or manner unites them. The only quality which they have in common is their silence. These were the men who had stood off against the best and most modern mechanical equipment Krupp and Vickers-Terni, Junker and Messerschmidt, Fiat, Savoia-Marchetti and Caproni have been able to develop since the World War. These cold-looking quiet soldiers, many of them under height and most under weight, many with glasses, had held off the full weight of totalitarian war-machines, even when they were less well equipped and more poorly trained than they now are. Why had they come from a rich country to a poor country with the certain knowledge that most of them would never return?

December 29. Alcorisa, Alcorisa, Alcorisa, Alcorisa

Captain Phil Detro and *Teniente* Bill Diggs* visited us this afternoon.[33] Detro, of Texas, is said to be a judge's son. Tall and lank, he carries the best automatic in the Brigade: a Spanish .45 Colt made in Eibar. Detro has just recovered from a serious leg wound. Bill, or "General" Diggs (I have given both real names), was born in New Orleans. Because he was in the U.S. Marines and because he learned Spanish so well in Panama or Puerto Rico or the Philippines, he is Brigade Clerk. General Diggs knows everything and tells everything. He appears to have been the deciding factor in every successful engagement the brigade has fought. "So I took the four machine-guns to the top of the hill, and I . . . etc. . . . etc. . . . ." The General knows everything but when we move and where we move.

December 30. Always Alcorisa

Rumors are equaled only by counter-rumors. The painfully mimeographed single sheet of the brigade daily bulletin, printed in Spanish and English,

---

* both now dead

33. Phil Detro commanded the Lincoln-Washington Battalion at Teruel, but was wounded by a sniper in January 1938 and died from complications. William Mitchell Digges, attached to the 15th Brigade, died of self-inflicted accidental wounds behind the lines in September 1938.

and the wall newspaper gotten up even more painfully by the Medical Corps Commissar, can no longer hold down our confusion and excitement.

This morning I loaded my blankets and duffle bag in my car. By nightfall, I was still parked in the same spot. Nothing happened today, nothing.

When I'm warm enough I sleep wonderfully. I haven't worried as much in the two months I have been here as I did in one single night when I was making up my mind to leave my job and come to Spain.

What day of the week is it? Is tomorrow really my father's birthday, and is the day after that really New Years?'

If my father had not died many years ago, I should probably be sharing his seat on the New York Stock Exchange. Would I?

We were paid this afternoon. The Commissar gave us each two packages of cigarettes. This must mean business. The time for holiday generosity is past.

The fiend who threw the boulder at my amb on the Mas de las Matas road has been caught. I have been able to learn nothing about him except that he has been executed.

December 31, 1937. My Father's Birthday
At 5:30 A.M. Major B. and Captain S. walked into the chófers' dormitory. Because they were dressed, we immediately understood that our orders to leave for the Front have finally come.

I chipped off the icicles that hung from my front axle and filled my radiator. She started O.K.

Drove over the mountains with a load of patients who were being sent back into the ranks. Twenty-four brand new American Diamond-T army trucks lay outside of Mas de las Matas. Twenty outside of Aguaviva.

Carried back a single private cursing the ankle he had sprained yesterday on the rifle range.

Much activity in both towns. The population had turned out for farewells.

By 9 A.M. our entire convoy had been gassed, oiled, watered and aired. The infirmary had been dismantled and loaded. Because the autochir cannot be started, I have a little time to write.

Have just been over my baby's bolts and engine. Put five pounds more pressure in the rear tires and three in the front ones. She's all set, but for that leak in the radiator. This worries me. There won't be a repair shop where we go.

My car will lead the convoy.

WHERE? We never know.

A little snow falls. If it gets warmer, the sky will loosen and more snow will come down on the frozen ground, the clustered tile roofs and the frozen road that I see through my windshield as I sit at the wheel, waiting.

The sound of the starting and the warming up of many engines reaches me through my closed windows. Sounds as if we're leaving.

WHERE?

PART THREE

Teruel: The Front

James Neugass Photographs Collection, Abraham Lincoln Brigade Archives, Tamiment Library, New York University.

Figure 5: A bullet-scarred ambulance near the front. Volunteers unidentified.

Franco wanted Teruel back under his control, and his attacks on the Re-
publican lines in the Aragon began in earnest in late December. The Re-
publicans held positions east of Teruel, but around the city itself, the lines
shifted as one side advanced, and then the other. Hitler's Condor Legion
and Italian planes provided devastating air support for Franco's troops.
Now more directly engaged in frontline activities, James Neugass and his
ambulance traveled to a dozen towns and villages northeast of Teruel over
the course of six weeks, usually within twenty miles of the front, and also
into the city itself. Extreme winter weather—reaching to eighteen degrees
below zero—made every action more treacherous. The battle of Teruel
lasted until late February.

⚬

December 31, 1937. Later. On the Road

2 P.M. Eating Indian nuts, I sit at the wheel wondering whether the snow which has already covered road and mountainsides will stick to what olive trees there are in this desolate spot.

We are an hour's run out of Alcorisa, strung out along the road behind a turnpike and a farmhouse. Truckloads of troops whiz by. Most of them take the Teruel road. Other leads to Montalbán. Which will we take?

Nothing was left in Alcorisa but our rations. Had to go back for them. Lunch was a slice of bread and half a small can of sardines apiece. The thirty of us have enough iron rations for three days.

The dental autochir is directly ahead of me. Handsome Jack bought a sheep, a lamb and two chickens before he left. Mother and child are tied under his car. Both whimper with fear of the snow and the lack of fodder.

We have been lucky. Planes seldom leave the ground in this wonderful camouflage weather.

Wonder how the troops who pass us feel about seeing ambulances. Something like seeing an undertaker's on your way to the hospital.

Why don't we move?

Too cold out here and I've finished my Indian nuts. Think I'll go into the farmhouse.

A long line of Divisional ambs lies a kilometer behind us, also waiting.

New Year's Day. 1938. 10:30 A.M. Fifteen Hours Have Passed

The name of this town is Camarillas. 71 miles from Alcorisa. 33 from Teruel. Nice little town. Prettier than a Christmas cookie-box cover, and also snowier. Took me fifteen hours to cover the seventy-five miles from Alcorisa to here and yet my speedometer showed a hundred and sixty miles.

Sit in a clean white little room, thawing out my stiff corduroy trousers, sniffing eggs frying in sweet olive oil, and they're for me. I am the only member of the 35th Division's Medical Corps in the town.

The entire thirty-car Medical Corps convoy lies busted wide open all over the Sierra Gudar. God knows where the rest of the staff and the rest of the cars are. I think I got the furthest. That was because my car was light and good. Now my sweetheart lies on her side in a ditch out in the snow. If this blizzard doesn't let up, I won't be able to find her.

The peasants whose hospitality I enjoy think I'm out of my mind, writing, writing in the notebook on my knees. The carbon paper puzzles them. Either they've never seen such a thing before or they think I'm a spy. But they wouldn't give a spy eggs, unless they're spies themselves. Maybe they're sane and I'm nuts. Maybe they think that all foreigners are crazy. Don't think they've ever seen a foreigner before. If Major B.—and I hope he's not lying stiff in some snowdrift—came in, I'd look up and say, "Mr. Livingston, I presume?"

I think I remember that the Major said last night in the farmhouse that if orders didn't come by 7 P.M. we'd take the Teruel road. We waited until 8 P.M., four hours from the New Year, and still no orders had come. B. and I then left alone, to look for Crome, our commanding officer. I suppose the Major thought that the snow had changed our plans. I'll admit that I was beginning to long for the bed I had left that morning before sunrise in Alcorisa.

Wind had risen, the snow was heavier, drifts were already four inches deep in some parts of the road, and the leak in my radiator had enormously increased. Estimated that it would have to be filled every hour. Before leaving the farmhouse I had organized a pitcher and filled it at an ice-bound spring. I could always fill my radiator with snow I imagined. No good. Won't stuff into the opening fast enough.

We had not proceeded more than half a mile up the first ramp of the approaches of the Spanish Everest which separated us from the fascists before I had to stop, jump out and push a stalled truck of ammo. "Do you think the autochir can make it?" the Major asked me. I answered that I thought it could.

Far above us lights like horizontal meteors moved across the sky. These were the lamps of cars ahead of us. Soon I had to stay in second gear. At twelve miles an hour we spiraled up a narrow precipitous paved goat-path hung halfway up the walls of a ravine for an hour until we reached the summit of the pass. Our breath and the moisture of our bodies had begun to condense on the windshield. . . . Since I had to keep both hands on the wheel at all times, the Major occasionally wiped the glass for me.

We began to pass more and more ditched and stalled cars. The Divisional autochir lay against a rock wall on the inside of the descent. Whenever I passed one of the other Divisional Medical cars, I would stop and get out to find what was the matter. Either the wheels would not pull or the radiator was steaming. The cold had contracted the metal of our cooling systems. The incessant racing of the engines in low gear while the wheels ineffectually spun had boiled what water remained. Some of the chófers were stuffing snow into their radiators. Wild Bill Cody had tried to solve the problem with his kidneys. He was successful only in burning the most delicate part of his skin. This pays him off for the dried human head gag. The combined odor of scalded urine, hot oil, and burned rubber penetrated my cold stuffed nostrils. I don't suppose I shall ever smell it again, nor will anyone else.

It soon became plain that salvage was useless, until the snow let us go, or chains were somehow gotten to us or a wrecking-car climbed the pass. Bloody, bloody, bloody. For all we knew the Brigade which had pulled out before the snow had really started to fall was already in action. And where the hell was the Sanidad Militar! Let alone the Pope, Franco has the weather working for him. Mr. Chevrolet will reap the profit.[1]

At last we reached Crome. Two Majors and two chófers were unable to move his car from the snowfield to which it had skidded. How many cars lay in the ravine?

"Are the men in action?" B. asked.

Crome did not answer. He climbed and we fought our way up over the pass. The Commandante's driver stayed with his car. Before we left, I showed him where I had gotten water out of a snow-filled torrent. Where there's a bridge, there's water.

By the time that we got back to the farmhouse, the New Year had come in. At 1 A.M all drivers were given orders to proceed to Cedrillas, 21 miles from Teruel.

2:00 A.M. Snow still falls. Visibility, fifty feet. Drifts have begun to form. The wind sweeps the dry powdery flakes off one iced track and piles it onto

---

1. Franco's close ties to the Catholic Church led Pope Pius XI to endorse the military rebellion. Italian bishops blessed planes taking off from Italian airfields on their way to attack Spain.

the other. High gear out of the question. Use second speed for climbing and first for going down. The frost on the inside of windshield becomes heavier. Halfway up. Occasional headlights behind us prove that at least a few of the cars are getting through.

3:00 A.M. Nearing the summit. Ice so heavy on the inside of windshield (automatic wiper keeps the outside fairly clear) that we opened windows, hoping that temperature inside of car would fall until moisture would no longer condense. Useless. Passed our $15,000 Divisional autochir, still slammed against rock wall. George Hooker,* the driver, was jacking the side with boulders and laying blankets under the wheels.[2]

Gearshifting dangerous. Between speeds, car gets out of control.

3:30 A.M. Passed the top. Car went off road twice. Each time engine and the two Majors got me out. Cannot go out of low gear. Average speed three miles an hour. Whether windows are open or shut frost condenses so thick on inside of windshield that wiping is necessary every thirty seconds. B. gets his arm in front of my eyes at just the wrong time. Average of one wreck and four stalled camions per mile. Towing trucks have not arrived. Are there snow-plows? Could also be used for cleaning dead from battlefields. How does blood look on snow?

4:00 A.M. Still in first gear. Car went off road only once, but each time seems to be the last. Snow flakes now big and soft and wet. Wipe windshield myself. Use the inside of my glove. Rag too hard to hold. Average speed four miles an hour. Snow is six to eight inches deep on the road with ice underneath. Chains would do us no good. Entire convoy of brand-new Diamond T's which delivered the Brigade to the Front stuck below pass on way back. Cars a hundred meters apart. Had to skid to a stop, get out at each car, wake every driver, convince him to coast a few feet backwards to the side of the road, so that I could pass. Sleepy. Pinch eyes. Right hand wipes windshield ten seconds, pinches eyelids, falls to wheel, then repeats. Radiator has to be filled every hour. Will water last to town? Where is next town? Filled pitcher with snow hoping it would melt. Froze instead. Where the hell is the Brigade and doing what? Radiator leak shows in the temperature dial on dashboard.

---

* dead

2. George Hooker's real name was Joe Coomes, driver of the mobile surgical truck.

<u>4:30 A.M.</u> Reached lower slopes. Speed went up to eight miles an hour. Leather of glove worn away from wiping the windshield. Pull it off and use hand, which melts ice faster than cold wet leather.

All other glass completely frosted. Don't know who is with me or how many; doctors, nurses all asleep. Twice all of them had to get out and push. Passed a farmhouse.

So sleepy that pinching eyelids no longer helps. Bang my jaw instead. Try not to let the Major see. He hasn't slept all night. Chin in fur collar, eyes always on the road, always on the brigade.

<u>5:30 A.M.</u> Got to town called Aliaga. Found water but no gas-pump. Evidently concealed because of raids. Knocked on many doors. Town was as dead as if it had been deserted for fifty years. Finally got answer and was admitted to the warm fragrant air of an all-night bakery. Asked to buy bread. "No, but we'll give you some." They gave us two loaves. It was good white sweet fresh bread, still warm and alcoholic. One loaf went to the eight in my car, the other to Finn, who had caught up with us, proving that at least one of our cars had gotten through.

Never such a feast. I had eaten, in twenty-four hours of sleepless hard work, four slices of Army bread, a small can of sardines, and a handful of almonds.

Finally found the gas-pump concealed in a house. The attendants were asleep and unwakeable, so I wheeled the pump out to my car and fed the tank myself. You can do anything if you have to.

Kept hoping that the Major would call a halt to the debacle now that we were in a town. What part of the casualties of four thousand men can Finn and I handle? The Major ordered us on. We were all of half way, he said, and only one more range of mountains to cross.

Blizzards do not howl better this side of Wyoming; and here we are, in the very center of Spain.

The food has been my undoing. I handed the wheel over to the Major. "I'm a surgeon and he's supposed to be a driver," I heard him say, as my eyelids sank inexorably as the jaws of a hydraulic press. "I watch the road for him while he drives. Now that I'm doing his work, he has to sleep." Good. B. was in form. The situation could not be hopeless. But some day I'll lose my temper and teach that cantankerous Boy Scout how to smile.

<u>7:00 A.M.</u> Woke up cold, wet and stiff. B. had at last pulled us into a ditch. Blizzard had turned into a gale. The land was so flat that the road was hard

to see. Visibility was lower than it had been during the head-lit darkness. Borrowed a muffler, tied it over my head, got out and walked ahead of my car, to show B. where the road was. Had to stamp hard through the twelve-inch minimum of the drifts so that I could tell, with my heels, the hard surface of the road from the bottomless snow of the ditch. Eventually we were completely halted by an enormous ten-wheeler wrecked across a bridge. Another giant truck lay in the gulley. Nurses and doctors, pushing like tugboats at the sides of an ocean liner, turned our car in her length.

In an hour we regained the town we had left behind us in the early hours. Again we thought the order to stop would be given. Finn and I found and woke the Secretary of the village committee. He found me a section of rawhide cable which we were able to bind about our wheels in place of chains. The first slope that led out of Camarillas tore the raw hide off the wheels of the two cars. Finn was ahead of me. He skidded and stalled, blocking up the road. My cargo unloaded and pushed; but there was no use. Eventually, we heaved Finn into the ditch so that we could get by.

Still walking in front of my car, I showed B. the way. My mustache and hair were stiff as shredded wheat with snow. Have to shave that mustache. No use carrying all that extra weight.

Finally the Major irretrievably ditched her. We were suddenly sorry that he had sent back Jack, who had miraculously appeared out of the storm at the wheel of the immense Harvard bus. It was perhaps the weight of this car which had held her to the road.

B., Crome, the other doctors and the two nurses got out and started to walk for Aliaga, seven miles over the mountains. "Sorry," B. said to me before he turned and a veil of blizzard fell between us, "drivers belong with their cars. I don't know what you'll do. This is very bad. From now on you're your own boss."

Would Merriman take the brigade into action without the Medical Corps? If he had to, I suppose. The Internationals have gone into battle without guns, much less without ambulances and surgical teams.

The first thing I did after I was alone was to find the can of sweetened condensed milk I had organized in Alcorisa. I opened it with a screwdriver and drank until it was empty. Strength seemed to crawl back along my bones.

The engine roared and the wheels spun until I smelled burning rubber, but she did not move. The temperature rose so high that I was afraid of burning out my bearings.

I walked back to the village. It did not take me long to find the house in which I sit. While the cook-stove was being lit, I was shown to the fireplace. Resinous, aromatic rosemary stalks thawed out ears, cheeks, nose and feet, mustache and hair. Then the eggs fried in sweet oil, the olives and the coffee.

Plan: The oil in my crankcase must be stiff. The peasants without even having asked me are heating a pail of hot water for the radiator.

Plan: Borrow a shovel, get my car out of the ditch, get her started, battle seven miles back to Aliaga, where parts of the convoy must lie snowbound. If the other cars have left by the time I arrive, all I'll have to do is to work towards Teruel, looking for the cars of the 35th Division. I have excellent maps and there are not many roads in this neighborhood.

Before I take to the road with my pail of hot water, I'll ask if other of our ambs have reached this town. Where is Finn? Where is the brigade?

The point is to get my wet sloppy leaking frozen car unditched and to Aliaga.

This is the most frequently bombed area in Spain. Thank God for the storm. Although it is 9 A.M., the morning is dark as a late winter afternoon. The wind has gone down, snow falls more lightly, and it begins to look as if the sun might shine. The warm gold of the heavens which alone can open these roads will also expose us to the planes. Wish I had thawed my clothing. Before, I was cold. Now I am also wet.

Well, here goes. Hope she hasn't burned a bearing.

New Year's Day. 10:30 P.M Aliaga (Moorish for "Waterton," I Think)
All is well.

The whirr of tires in the snow, the smell of burning rubber and overheated oil, the snow flake machine-gun pellets noiselessly striking the armor-plate of my windshield—these things still fill my head.

We were saved by Français and his bug-hatcher. The weight of his boiler and tank on double rear wheels had given him traction enough to make Camarillas by the time I had finished my fried eggs. I found The Frenchman, his Limey assistant and Finn eating eggs and olives in a peasant kitchen. We were very glad to see each other.

At the Ministry of Defense *Intendencia* we were given one day's iron rations and eighteen snow shovellers.

The bug-hatcher pulled Finn back on the road. We then loaded rescue crew, buckets of hot water and drove out to my car. On the way I noticed a low windowless building of cut rock lying squat to the earth like the hull of an overturned boat. This structure much resembled the *naus* left on the Minorca thousands of years ago by vanished sun-worshippers.[3] Here the dead were laid to be torn apart by birds and thus carried up into the sky. The *nau* was at present used as an ice house. I have no doubt that it will soon be used for a powder magazine.

Half an hour of work carved my car out of the drifts. Nineteen men picked her up like a sick cow and set the wheels in the tracks left by the bug-hatcher. I was able to start the engine after a good deal of priming and cranking. Did not want to use my battery because the water in it is running low. Where in this wilderness is there distilled water? Maybe I will melt snow.

I went off the road five times before I got to the top of the pass that leads down into Aliaga. We had to dismount, shovel, push and reload five times. Four miles in two hours.

The men of Camarillas left me on top of the mountain where those of Aliaga had come. An order had been telephoned to every village in Teruel province to put all available men to work on the roads.

The two autochirs had got as far as the ridge which leaps from one saddle-horn peak to another. Here, balanced on a knife-edge of snow, their drivers had refused to go further. Nothing could pass until both vans were gotten out of the way.

Sweating under our frozen clothes, cursing, digging, running blankets and sacking on the snow, chasing Dorothy the Stowaway Nightingale out from under the wheels, with George Hooker[*] (real name) of New York, driving, we turned forty thousand dollars of international anti-fascist surgical equipment about and saw it down the road to the next village.

The autochirs are 35 feet long, 9 feet wide and 10 high. The road was 38 feet wide. We do many impossible things. We have to. Man-power is the best of all forces when it can be had in sufficient quantity, for it can be distributed better than any machine or combination of machines.

I reached Aliaga before dark. The shadowy frozen streets, in which a little snow still fell, were full of cars, giant tow-trucks, shovelmen, nurses, and cursing but happy drivers. Only four cars—Al Hawk among them—are missing. Crome and the Major, with Surgeon-Captain Rintz and Captain Donowa, the negro Commissar, had come in by foot. Crome is in bed with frozen feet.

Donowa set up headquarters for us in a kitchen and an attic loaned by

---

[*] dead

3. The *nau* was an ancient Mediterranean sailing vessel; the author refers to a sculptured stone structure used for burial. A famous nau on Minorca dates from 1500 B.C.

a peasant family. Taking our turns at the stove, each of us tells his and her adventures. All the drivers are heroes. We are snowed in. Tomorrow we will probably try to break through the walls of the white fortresses in which we are locked.

Field-Marshal Winter, General Blizzard and Colonel Cold took more toll of Republican transport last night than all of the gold epaulets this side of Berlin and Rome have been able to list, with all their mechanical equipment, in any one week of the war.

The brigade? A feeling exists that the battalions did not go into action last night. Where are they?

I am not extraordinarily tired or hungry or sleepy. Spare tanks of energy must exist somewhere in the human body to be drawn on during times like the last thirty-six hours. I feel as if I had just swum the English Channel or slept with one of the girls all men dream they will some day meet—something supersupersuper.

The Day After New Year's. Aliaga. 11:00 A.M.

The sun is out, blue and wintry, but not hot enough to melt more than the surface of the snow. Mammoth front-and-rear-drive towing trucks, newly received from the United States, leave and enter town, as cars are being fished out of brooks, ravines and ditches. Squads of shovelmen concentrate and are dispatched in every direction. Cavalry and loads of ammunition are beginning to appear. I hear that we will leave just as soon as word is telephoned that the roads are clear.

Planes passed overhead twice this morning. The bell in the church tower is so loud that a siren is unnecessary. Each time I saw running women, I pulled my car out of town and marched into the drifts. The second time, I saw five three-engined planes, very high. We have no trimotors. This word is also used for "louse." The war is coming near. First it was Tarancon and the sound of explosions seventeen miles away. Then I heard the report of a single cannon in Madrid, three or four miles away: and a few minutes ago fascist planes passed half a mile overhead. I was struck by the fact that between their ugly anuses and my thin skull there was nowhere a sheet of armor-plate, a stone or a cloud. Thus far curiosity utterly takes the place of fear.

Same day. Afternoon. Truckloads of what first looked like snow-covered sacks of wheat pulled up in front of the village hospital. Blood dripped out of the tailboard into the snow. Planes had caught a battalion of the Listers in Escorihuela, fifteen miles from Teruel, where they had gone "on rest."

Two Days Later. The Argente-Visiedo Salient. 60 Miles North of Teruel

Parked on a good road, free of snow. Long, rolling, treeless country. Widest sky and fields I have ever seen. Strong sun, cloudless sky, pinkish-gray snow haze on the horizon.

Palomera ("Dove Lady"), our mountain, highest in this neighborhood, takes off from the rock desert in the foreground. Their mountains are further away. First time I had ever seen the enemy territory. Getting nearer, nearer.

American boys, sunburned and stripped to the waist, dig trenches on both sides of the road. Prudence and exercise. Machine-guns are tested. Sounds like motorcycle coughing to start, then fizzing out. Highly manic personalities, not like somber introspective Madrid cannon. Diamond-T troop trucks lie 300–400 yards apart. Tanker travels up and down the line, refueling. Drivers in leather coats and hats squat about thorn-fires, cooking and getting warm. Brigade hovers on the crest of movement.

Fifteenth Brigade Classification Post (junction between light and heavy ambs, morphine stopover and assortment-station), installed in a low cow-barn, only visible roof for miles. Death Valley is more fertile than this part of Spain.

The Major and I are in search of a house suitable for front-line hospital.

Crossroads at Perales had been plowed up by the teeth of the planes. Town de-roofed and feeder-roads pitted by egg holes.

Left Aliaga late last night. I get all the breaks. Finn, Marty, Français (who is really Belgian), Hoen (from Alsace), George Hooker and the rest of us drivers are stuck in town. Al Hawk and Block turned up, the last of our missing cars: engines frozen, cars ditched.[4] Drivers never leave cars. They sit and wait like Byrd at the South Pole. (Did I hear more machine-gun fire? Practice?) We lost *no* equipment.

Slush had frozen to gin-fizz consistency. Road skirted a cliff. Fog came up and coated windshield, inside and out. Had to lift it and drive with face lowered to the level of the wheel-spokes. Thank God my glasses did not frost. The Major is the world's first champion back-seat driver, excepting Leon Trotsky.

Pushed up another mountain of snow. Most dangerous of all, because of

---

4. Joseph Block, a Canadian volunteer from Winnipeg and Toronto, was born in 1908 and survived the war.

cliff, lack of snow-shovellers and stalled tank on truck at the summit. Coming down is more dangerous than climbing. You can't stop.

Slept in road-mender's hut next to fire. Not bad. In the morning, chopped down one of the eight trees in Perales ("Peartree") township to light fire for boiling water for radiator. Some day I hope to shave warm. In the end I had to stop a camion and take a tow. Organized a larger pitcher as reserve tank for radiator. Tire pump, the best in convoy, was simultaneously organized from me.

(Stage directions: construct sounds of explosives, mixed as to distance and caliber.)

What the hell. They are not shooting at me. . . . No cover in this neighborhood: not a tree, rock, wall or ditch—nothing but snowy sloping fields with stubble and thorns. Beetles, muskrats and moles may survive *homo sapiens*. These animals have been anti-fascist for aeons.

Well, I'm going to eat an organized orange and smoke an organized cigarette.

Sunset. Mezquita. ("Mosque"). Before careening up the icy streets of this town to the frozen sheep-trough, I had come up a plateau and out into sight of a valley and mountain-range, curved and white as a sky-maniac's dream of Paradise. Late afternoon silvery sun, pastel blue-gray snow-haze all along the horizon, shading upwards to the ice-blue of the deep skies. Snow was apricot in the sunset and nowhere cast over with dirt as in cities. Set on a hill deep in the long valley was Mezquita's rosy terra-cotta roofs and walls climbing up to a delicate florid renaissance steeple.

Church towers were lightning-rods to deflect the anger of a vengeful deity. They are now used for aeroplane lookouts. Whenever the Savior's trimotors cross the skies, humming like hornets, the spire of His former home screams against Him, and His children run underground.

What are my orders? Where to and when? Beginning to feel like a centaur. The road will be frozen tonight, there will be another snowfog and I will again have to drive with my windshield up.

Hear that Franco is up to his ears in snow. All operations seem to have slowed down in spite of the firecrackers this morning. Not quite all operations: two trucks, black against the road, were grenaded from the air last night. One of them was loaded with ammo. It blew up. Passed the wreckage this afternoon. I wanted to get out and go over it for bolts and spare parts, but B. is always in a hurry.

Car-camouflage no good as long as there is snow.

Why people live in this treeless rocky soil is more than I can imagine. The peasants terrace the rock hillsides for poor thin wheat. The soil also supports sheep. What do the peasants eat? What did they ever eat? Arabs and Bedouins, for all their rooflessness, are richer. *What crime did these peasants commit? What is their guilt? Why did their Pope turn against them?*

January 4, 1938. Mezquita

Slept late last night in an enormous deep bed on the second floor of a farmer's house. If I had not had to share this gigantic blanket-loaded powder-puff with a Spanish first-aid man and Archie, the English Divisional Medical Corps map-maker; if I had been able to get to bed before 2 A.M. and had not had to get up at 6:30 A.M., I should have had a perfect rest.

After I got up I put on my shoes, went downstairs and warmed my hands over a thorn fire that had been lit to heat water for my car. The rosemary and large thorn bushes which were used in Alcorisa are not to be found here. The farmers gather wagonloads of tough little plants the size and shape of coral branches. The entire end of this room, slightly raised and covered with a plaster hood leading to a pipe, is a fireplace. Every thirty seconds a new thorn bush must be thrown on the flames. After warming my hands, I went over to the powder-dump of the Mac-Paps and had very good coffee. I hope we won't set up the hospital in this town as long as the powder-dump is with us.

Captain S. Dissolves Two Goldbrickers

Scene: Classification post. Fireside in road-mender's hut. No light but the flames. Floor covered with sleeping, pitching, coughing men.

Cast: 1. Captain S. Visor screens sensitive blue eyes behind girl's long lashes, and gives over face to broken nose and boxer's chin.

2. Volunteer Healthy, American, non-college.

3. Soldado Gloomy, unshaven, featureless. Wears bandage around head.

Captain S. (to bandaged head): When were you wounded?

S.: Two, three days ago.

C. S.: Who put that bandage on you?

S.: Myself.

C.S.: You didn't see a doctor?

S.: No.

C.S.: Then tear it off.

S.: What?

C.S.: I said tear that god damn thing off. Tear if off before I do.

> (S. *lifts the soiled bandage off his unwounded head. Moves awkwardly towards the door.*)

C.S.: Wait a minute. (He pulls a form blank out of his pocket and writes on it.) This *salvo conducto* will take you back to your brigade. I have written at the bottom that if you are found anywhere else, you are to be arrested. Now clear out.

> (*Soldado takes paper, leaves, featureless and expressionless.*)

C.S.: (*to volunteer*) Stomach, again?

V.: I throw up everything I eat. At night I feel as if I had swallowed a couple of baseballs. Now Doc I'm not a goldbricker like Lock . . .

C.S.: Who said you were a goldbricker. Who said Lockwood is a goldbricker. Do you have pain in your kidneys. Does it hurt you to piss?

V.: Yes. But Doc, it's no use. The battalion doc gets me to strip, bangs my guts and tells me we have no medicine or diet for stomach ulcers. It's no use. Now I was first-aid man, and I know enough to be a male nurse . . .

C.S: Your kidneys hurt and it hurts you to piss. Did you ever notice a feeling of dizziness if you've been lying in one place for a long time and stand up?

V.: That's it. I didn't know it had any connection . . . Doc, it's no use. All of you medical men ask the same questions and look at me as if I were lying, and then send me back to the front. If this doesn't stop I'll shoot myself. I'll shoot. . . .

C.S.: How's your record?

V.: Machine-gun company, Jarama, Belchite, Fuentes de Ebro . . . ask anybody. I've been out a year.

C.S.: Who authorized you to leave the lines? The battalion doctor?

V.: Well, I hopped a truck.

C.S.: I ought to arrest you for desertion. Instead I'm going to evacuate you to the infirmary. *Salvo* will be good for three days. Enjoy yourself. Nothing wrong with your stomach. Now get out of here and hop a truck.

V: (starts to speak, blushes, then leaves) Thanks, Doc.

Author: How did you do it?

C.S.: The first was a faker. I knew that just as soon as he was willing to peel that bandage off his head. No man with a head wound would touch his bandages. He'd be afraid. The second guy was a different case. He's had too much. That's all the matter with him. He didn't want the other men to think that he was yellow so he invented this ulcer of the stomach gag. He knew a little about medicine so he figured that I wouldn't be able to diagnose stomach ulcers without instruments, which is right. I had to take a chance. If he'd answered "no" when I asked those questions about his kidneys and his dizziness, I'd have been out on a limb. Kidney trouble and dizziness have nothing whatsoever to do with ulcers of the stomach. I called his bluff and he knew it. He needs a rest. Three days in the infirmary will fix him up.

Author: Doc, I didn't expect Volunteers to turn out yellow . . .

C.S.: How long have you been at the Front?

Author: Haven't seen the Front yet.

C.S.: You have a lot to learn.

Author: What's this about "having too much"? Shellshock?

C.S.: We don't have many cases of shellshock. Concussion is more common. But the worst complaint is getting used up: burning out, getting washed up, ——cked up, anything you want to call it. That's the improvement of this war over 1914.

Author: What's concussion?

C.S.: What are you, a doctor or a driver? . . . You'll learn. . . .

I came home yesterday afternoon when the Ribas family were having dinner. Of the twelve who sat at the table, none were between the ages of ten and fifty. I was asked to eat. When I looked at the size of the single earthenware jug in the fireplace, I answered that I had already had supper. An assortment of pots and tripods hung at the side of the fireplace. A beaked olive-oil lamp of the type used by the Greeks and Phoenicians hung in the center of the combined kitchen, dining and sitting room. The iron lamp and the fireplace fittings were so well scrubbed that they looked like pewter. Unvarnished chairs and chests were worn with washing. The floor was of earth. The mother lifted the crock from the fireplace and emptied a steaming mass of potatoes smelling indubitably of meat into a large dish in the center of the table. Children and their elders took spoons and ate directly from the single plate. This method of eating is called in Aragones "*tot un plat.*" When the potatoes were eaten, the meal was over.

While I ate I tried to think of how I could organize a can of milk for the children. I could speak only to the farmer himself; the others could not understand or talk Castilian.

Ribas passed wine in a Catalan pitcher. You throw your throat back, hold the narrow spout two or three inches from your parted lips, stop breathing, and gurgle. To stop drinking, you suddenly jerk the vessel upwards and back. The fashion is to hold the spout as far up in the air as skill permits, and open the lips as little as possible. Some Spaniards extract a front tooth for great suavity of drinking.

Glasses are very rare in Spain. I don't suppose there is more than one to a house.

Conversation with Ribas After Dinner. "What is fascism?" I ask him.

The entire family strains to see how much of my Castilian they can understand. This is very likely the first time they have ever been so near to a foreigner.

"*Es una cosa horrible,*" Ribas answers, as much perplexed as if I had asked him, "what is a stone?" "It's . . . it's . . . it's a very bad thing."

"But what is fascism?" I insist.

The ten-year-old son answers "*Es matar!*" (Killing) The entire family nod their heads.

"It is killing and cold," the father adds. Everyone is satisfied.

"To what political party do you belong?" I ask.

"*Jo . . . Jo . . . Joy soy revolutionario, como todos.*" He was a revolutionary, like everybody.

"What does 'revolutionary' mean?"

"Liberty," he answers, as if he had never thought what was the meaning of "revolutionary." "*La Libertad!*" he repeated, smacking his lips. Again his family approved.

"To what political party do you belong?"

Ribas was confused.

"*De los matafascistas,*" he answered. "I believe in the fascist-killer party."

"But which party is that?"

"That is every political party," he answered, having a good deal of trouble with a word as long and as abstract as "*politico.*"

"What is communism?"

"I don't know . . . *significa, significa . . . tractors!*"

"Communism means 'tractors'?"

"And the other parties also . . . communism, socialism, anarchism. . . . "

Ribas' children and wife listened with amazement to the assembly of big words which formed on his lips with so much difficulty. Every ear was strained. At any moment we could expect to hear the final answer to the meaning of life. " . . . it all means . . . machines for the land . . . machines!" Ribas finished his sentence and slapped his legs with the gesture of a chess player who had just called "check-mate."

A long time ago Aragon was a fertile place. The wheat rose solid as bread, and not thin as the hair on an old dog's back. Four hundred years ago the mouths of the Kings became fastened at the gold which flowed in the veins of the Aztecs and Toltecs, Incas and Caribs. Farmboys left the plow and took up the matchlock. What was the use of farming if gold could be brought to Spain to purchase not only bread but palaces and gold brocade?

The stone terraces, lifework of a race, fell apart. Rain washed the soil in the *barrancos*. Stones remained. Gradually the important people in the cities who owned the land found that farming could not be turned into cash.

Ribas said that tractors could reshape the terraces, dig ditches and plow long furrows "all the way to Perales before turning." "*Cientifico!*" he kept exclaiming.

When Mezquita farmers heard, in July 1936, that a war had broken out and that the owner of the village land was with "the Germans," they started to help each other with the plowing. Herds of sheep were combined. Collectivization was not possible without tractors. For the first time in their lives, pigs could be killed without asking permission of the village *cacique*. The people of the town began to have more to eat than they had ever in their lives tasted. Later they learned that it is not possible to fight and eat at the same time.

January 5. Mezquita
Today we cleaned out the very beautiful town convent and set up an infirmary. Chief medicine is hot coffee.

At one o'clock at night, I came in after an inspection of the Classification Post and a visit to the Estado Major to find Marty, the autochir mechanic, wandering about the streets, bedless. I made the mistake of asking him to share my fourposter with me. He brought along Bernie the mechanic.

January 6. Cuevas Labradas
Between the writing of the last line and this one I have seen many dead men.

After supper I loaded steel boxes of instruments, long rolls of adhesive tape and boxes and boxes of catgut tubes. We took B.'s assistant surgeon and the two operating room nurses with us.

I now wipe ice off the inside of my windshield at night with my bare hand. The glove wore out.

We passed the rock-pile once called the village of Perales and crept over the ice of the Teruel road. Don't know when it was that I had begun to hear The Sounds, but when my engine died out in front of the surgical hospital which the Division had set up in a town called Cuevas Labradas (Cavetown), very distinct riplets of impolite machine-gun conversations came to us from somewhere up in the mountains that shadow the road.

"See," said Queen Annie, so called because she knows she is our most important nurse, "See, now we're at the Front," with a contented, nervous little giggle.

B. put on his apron and went to work. Behind the blanketed windows of the villa in which we were simultaneously setting up surgical equipment and operating were the smell of the ether, the rush of many feet, soft groans coming from stretchers, and blood on the floor, the stretchers, the stair, the aprons of the surgeons, and the blankets.

The need for sleep had dulled the edge of my memory. I know: I ought to be able to recall what I have seen and done. Phrases smooth as oil should roll off the end of my pencil. Something big and something terribly human. Pity and terror, mercy and pain, all between drawn lips.

I am very tired and there is much to do. Sleep has become more important than food.

I think I remember that Wild Bill Cody, stepping carefully between stretchers, one eye closed by a shrapnel fragment, said "this is worse than Brunete." Brunete was worse than anything else. I asked him where the lines were. "Listen," he answered waving towards the overhanging mounts, "for Christ's sake, don't ask me where the Front is, just listen to it!"

The engine of the shower-truck furnished power for the lights. Two operating tables were going full blast. A door would open, with a vision of silent figures dressed in white, and naked bare skin and the bandaged stumps of arms and legs, rags floating in slop jars of reddish liquid. Stretchers went up and down the stairs, even while pickaxes were chipping at the plaster walls to make turning easier. Why was it that nothing was being done to ease the occasional low whimpers that came from the figures under the blankets?

I helped with the stretchers until the Major told me to go back to Mezquita for additional instruments. I would have done anything, so ashamed was I to be unwounded.

Outside the doorway was a man on a stretcher, covered only with a sheet. I could see that he was naked. I ran back into the hospital and in a very agitated voice demanded blankets.

"That guy out there is dead," someone impatiently answered me, "there isn't enough room in here, so we lay them in the courtyard. Pull the sheet off of him and bring it to me. We're running out of linens. And while you're at it, take him into the woodshed. That's what we're using until we can dig a trench."

I stripped the sheet from the body. The face was dirtier than the skin. American? . . . French? . . . or English? The clay complexion of death is international. I took him to the shed where men lay like cordwood. What can you do? Go out and make more dead. I have reached the end of the road. Perhaps I am a pacifist.

The infirmary at Mezquita was being used to take the overflow of Cuevas Labradas. I carried stretchers, loads of equipment, swept and helped the nurses cut off clothing and pull off shoes until I could find no one who wished help; and then drove back to Cuevas with the instruments B. wanted.

It was not yet sunrise when I drained my radiator and went to sleep, over the wheel.

The prayers of the nuns of Mezquita and the maidenly murmuring of novenas gave way to the more urgently suppliant cries of the wounded. The soft slippers of stretcher bearers pad up and down the stair. In the convent chapel the diaphragm of an ether machine rustles the beat of evensong: in, out, in . . . out . . . barely in. He still breathes. Surgeon-Captain Byrne, as priest, administers last rites of adrenalin.[5] This flesh shall rise again.

Outside in the snow-rimmed sunset, church bells ring a warning.

January 7. Cuevas. 12 Miles from Teruel, 1½ Miles from Front-line Trenches by Bullet Flight

"It's late," I thought as I lay on straw in the darkness of an attic. "I've over-slept and I'll be late to work. I'll lose a day's pay. Where was I last night?" Something was wrong. What had I done? Had I stayed out too late or spent too much of my wages or missed something very important?

What was wrong was The Sound. Wave after wave of shells, running rip-ples of machine-gun fire and the hard crash of grenades were breaking on the beach of my heavy morning slumber. Should I go out of doors and see what was happening? Why was it that no one had warned me? Should I not get up?

I looked out of the attic window. There in the half-melted slush of the street below me was an old woman sitting in the sunlight very carefully skin-ning a lapful of potatoes. A cavalryman was grooming his horse and several militiamen walked by, smoking and talking.

I went back to sleep. If there was danger, I would be warned. When I was wanted, someone would come and get me.

I'll have to write. Tell them what it is like. What will the words be? Ir-regular but monotone and repetitive; solid and heavy, with no overlapping explosions; very definite and loud but not loud; full organ blasts with all the stops pulled out, from the double bass of the hardly audible thirty-foot pipes to cricket-like penny whistles; the rain of gravel, boulders and monoliths on sheet iron. Will this do?

Seventy-two hours later. My beat is the forty-mile stretch of road from the Cuevas hospital to the Mezquita infirmary, where surgery is now being done. The Villa Paz equipment and front-line group are split between those two towns and Cedrillas, somewhere to the south. The full counter-offensive has begun. We are on the receiving end.

---

5. Albert Barnitz Byrne, a New York surgeon, served with the AMB. Divorced from his first wife, he married nurse Thelma Erickson during the war. In 1938, he was arrested by Spanish military intelligence and held for three months for reasons that remain unclear. He died in Texas in 1978.

The invaders want the Teruel–Perales highway. We should like to have the Teruel-Saragossa road, which parallels ours, eight miles to the west. Between the two military arteries whose corpuscles are camions charged with explosives and men runs a hilly plateau. They have forced us back until our lines run at the crest of the ridge which protects our road from artillery fire. The tiers of canyon-walled mountains that rise on both the fascist and Republican sides of the plateau could seat the entire population of the earth. Every chair would be a ringside seat.

Once They cut our road or bring it under fire, one of the two large arteries which pump gunpowder blood into Teruel would be severed, and we would have to route our camions through a complicated system of minor vessels.

The Americans are at Celadas, 24 miles to the north of Teruel. The English are at the Milestone 18; the Canadians are 11 miles from Teruel, the Germans directly above Cuevas, 9 miles from the city; then the French. Don't know who has the job of defending Teruel itself. From the rate at which the intensity of the battle has been working southwards, suspect that the defense of Teruel will shortly be handed over to us. No attempt to take the city from us itself will evidently be made until the Alfambra road has been cut. We hear that Lister took the last stronghold inside the city itself several days ago, with the capture of several thousand prisoners, including the Bishop and the Civil Governor. War material captured included three complete batteries of anti-aircraft and vast supplies of food.

I carry wounded only at night. Because the enlarged goatpaths that lead down the plateau-wall to the road are under fire during the day time, casualties are evacuated only at night.

Nights. When Mezquita is full, I have to go further and further back to the other infirmaries and clinical hospitals which have been set up along the line of evacuation to Aliaga. My car would not be in use if it were not for the ever-increasing number of casualties. At one time (I know that it was night, but I cannot remember when; if it were not for sunrise and nightfall I should not be able to tell how fast and slow the days are passing) I became so angry at peddling my load of frozen feet, leg and arm cases from hospital to hospital that I forced the setting up of a new ward. There have been no planes at night because of the snow or the mountains or because I have not heard planes or have not been strafed.

The men I carry, mostly Americans, are very quiet. They talk with the gravity of people sitting in the waiting room of a railway station, about to set out on a long journey, of what happened during the day: how near the shells came, who was killed and who was wounded, and who had narrow escapes. No anger towards the enemy is apparent. The voices rise only when they touch, again and again, on the troubles of our riflemen and machine-gunners to find targets. You can't shoot at shells and tanks and planes. Where are our artillery and our planes? They are coming soon. Our thinly-strung batteries will soon be reinforced and many hundreds of planes are being unloaded in Barcelona. Soon they will be with us. We must hold the lines and wait. Not one step back. Evacuate the trenches when They get the range, then run back into them with grenades and dynamite bombs when the tanks attack. A good day: two thousand shells, God knows how much other stuff, and only four dead and eighteen wounded in the company. Reserves are in training at Tarazona and will soon fill up the gaps.

I drive as carefully as if I were carrying wet trinitrotoluene. I cannot very well crash my car when it is full of wounded. If I think I hear a plane, I hold hard on the wheel, say nothing, and keep my eyes on the road. Whenever the temperature of my engine runs up slightly above normal, I immediately stop and fill my radiator. The water that keeps sloshing over the edge of the pitcher freezes the blood on the floor of my car into a kind of raspberry sherbet. I'll have to chip it out with an end-wrench when I have time. Nobody minds blood but ice is treacherous.

Everyone is very young and so interested in the brand-new-for-us science of fighting war in the modern way that our personal problems and political convictions are all forgotten. When I mention that I just came over from the States, the wounded ask for news. Who won the elections in New York? And what is the significance of the victory? How is the C. I. O. doing (a very good part of the brigade volunteers still wear their Union buttons); what are the chances for trade-union unity? When will Joe Louis fight Schmeling? What has Roosevelt said about the Embargo? Does the Fifteenth get much publicity in the home newspapers?

Cuevas Labradas, a Front Town

Three hundred rubble and mud-brick houses huddled under a steeple a mile and a half from the front-line trenches by bullet flight. Beyond range of artillery and machine-guns because of the ridge that overhangs the Alfambra road. Frozen winter cabbage in the river bottom fields. Eight fairly fresh egg-holes in the quarter mile of road leading to the highway. A cluster of seven-feet craters in the fields under windows of the Post. Half the church and fifteen to twenty houses gone. Fully populated except for children. Town contains Estado-Mayor of the Fifteenth, Washington-Lincoln field kitchen, Surgical Hospital, Post, battalion of cavalry, and one of infantry. Caves from which town takes its name half way up cliff at its rear now being enlarged by all available male and female civilians. Sewers and electric light out of commission. Walls of sunken approach to Main Street are pocked with holes dug in clay. Sole house with a gable roof—now our hospital—formerly summer home of a Teruel lawyer who was one of the few inhabitants to skip to the fascists.

Townspeople rush busy surgeons for attention to long uncared-for ailments.

In general town resembles a pile of loose rocks and split boulders fallen off cliff which dominates it. Eight or nine wrecked houses hardly less handsome than the as yet untouched.

Diagnosis: secondary septic infection, tending towards gangrene. Patient will not live two weeks unless air is cleaned of noisy germs or town cased in a large armor-plate capsule.

The battalions have been moved to the ridge during the night. Captain S. had to find them.

We laboriously drove up a wagon-truck towards the crest of the ridge; my mind on my tires, his on the guilt of not knowing the exact location of the men. Passed an anti-tank gun being pulled up the hill by rosy-faced sweating English youths hitched to the carriage like sleigh dogs.

A round earth-colored column ten feet through and fifty feet tall suddenly appeared against the near skyline, standing in this desert like the ruins of a Roman temple in Asia. Even as I looked, the column sank gracefully to its base, from which another now mirage-like appeared. Had heard no sound. We were still driving in low gear straight for the ridge. Soon hoped to get a nearer view and a better description of the phenomenon. Obviously my car was not being fired at, so where was the danger?

Two hundred yards from the base of a splendid Corinthian column the Captain stopped me and got out of the car. I pulled her off the road and immediately went to sleep at the wheel. Don't know how long I slept. When I awoke, solemn birds were chirping dismally among the rocks. Nowhere was there anything or anyone in sight.

S. came running down the slope, climbed next to me, slammed the door and shrieked for me to turn and descend.

"Say, Doc, did you hear those birds?"

"Birds, hell! That's shrapnel. Come on, let's get out of here."

Soft, very soft musical falling sounds, like the whistles the Chinese tie to the tail of pigeons, or wind-harps set in the ruined windows of German castles. I was sure that the sky had grown very gray, yet when I looked up my eyes swooned into blueness spotted only by dust-hairs traveling on my eyeballs.

"Did you find the Washington-Lincolns, Doc?"

"I found a nice place for a grave for you if you don't step on the gas."

"But Doc, how about my tires?"

"How about your hide?"

"Say, listen, when do we eat? There's a can of beef in the car, and I haven't had. . . . "

For a moment the lavender fire died out of the Captain's eyes. Then, re-membering that he had not found the men, flames rose. He was screwed up into a state verging on hydrophobia.

"There'll be no eating in this car until we find the battalions."

"But Doc. . . . "

"Bleeding men are lying up on that ridge and all you can think of is food."

"But while I drive you can open some beef."

"Shut up."

We had reached the bottom of the slope when a figure standing on a hill-ock blew a police whistle. Men jumped off the road into ditches and little shallow dugouts.

"What do I do, Doc?"

"Keep on driving."

The police whistle blew two short blasts. As my engine died, I heard the noise of planes. Panting, I reached the shelter of a boulder. Five silver un-marked planes were between me and the sun.

We tried to ascend the frozen bottom of a canyon. In these narrow walls we were safe from the planes except in case of a direct hit. The Washington-Lincolns might lie somewhere ahead. Afraid of crashing my wheels through the ice of the deep parts of the canyon bottom, I jumped her from one hillock of dry gravel to another like a man leaping through a swamp. The stone walls began to close in so tightly that I was afraid I could not turn. I mentioned this to S. He would not listen. Finally I found a place wide enough to allow me to turn and he gave in.

Our third attempt to reach the battalion was successful. S. left me at a bat-tery of light mountain field-pieces slightly below the summit of the ridge.

The artillerymen were busy digging shallow trenches for fresh pine boxes lettered in German. The guns were marked "Krupp." Was Hitler selling us cannon? I helped with the digging because I was very sleepy and did not want to sleep.

"*Combate*," I said, looking up at the ridge three hundred yards over our heads. All about us were ragged rock-colored men digging holes.

"*Si, mucho combate.*" The sole military feature of the gunner's dress was a string tied as a belt around his soiled cotton-wool jacket.

"*Mucho, mucho combate.*"

"*Muchisimo combate. Manaña mas.*" He smiled, as all Spaniards do when they say "Tomorrow much more," as if there were some sort of joke in this statement. "*Tu tienes cigarillo?*" The gunman asked.

"Listen to the birds," I said, resting on my shovel.

The gunner was perplexed, then understood. "That kind of chicken is not good for the stomach," he said. Pleased by his sense of humor, he passed the joke along to the others. I hope he is alive tomorrow morning. You get to hope that the people you know will live. The others do not seem to matter so much.

Before nightfall the Captain and I had found all three battalions. We had handled five frozen feet, seven light wounded and one frozen ear. Heavy wounded could not be brought down until after dark. The boys were doing well. They were well dug in and their losses had been extremely light. Not yet had they seen a single fascist infantryman.

"What happens to the dead?" I asked S.

"We bury them. Not enough transportation to take them back."

Not so bad, to be buried where you fall. Something like dying in bed with Garbo.

After a fine hot meal in the Post, the first I had ever been served between meals, I was allowed to carry supplies back up the mountain to the first-aid posts. The dark paths were now swarming with officers, fortifications men, mules loaded with crates of grenades.

Since I was alone, I left my car and went up into the lines. The dark places in the snow were the mouths of dugouts, sleeping men and rocks. No fires had been lit. I was told not to smoke.

Some one asked me for one of my gloves. "Have to keep my trigger finger from freezing." I refused.

A sweet cloying smell brought my stomach into my throat. I spat, as though I had swallowed a forkful of tainted fish. The lines were a string of foxholes that ran in the gaps between machine-gun emplacements.

Down across the valley I saw a string of headlights.

"Fascist trucks. . . . "

"Well, why don't we. . . . "

"Wait a minute . . . wait. . . . "

Far below us three rockets left the earth. Twenty pairs of fascist head-lights went out.

"That's our anti-tanks. Now we'll have to move them. Don't want to show where we are and draw Their fire."

"And our artillery?"

"Well, how about our artillery?"

"This is Valley Forge."

"This is Valley Forge and Verdun and the North Pole combined."

"How is it going?"

"We got the hell shelled out of us all day and the planes don't let us alone none, but we have good dugouts and we sit and wait. Haven't seen no infantry yet. Only get a crack at them at night; bombing parties, but that don't add up to much."

Many cigarettes lit at once a mile across the valley. Just so many white flashes appeared at the bottom of the hill where our anti-tank battery was or had been.

"See? What'd I tell you. That's their anti-tank. They've got six of them to our one."

The headlights of the fascist trucks again lit.

With guilt I thought of my car. I should never have left her but there she was black against the snow in the moonlight, three men stretched out under her in the warmth of the engine.

"Sorry, fellows, I have to move."

My three cold comrades, without speaking, moved towards a rock and huddled together on the slope like puppies.

Morning. The Perales road was empty. Camions of ammunition caught out after sunrise were my sole companions. Four times in twenty miles I passed men standing still by the roadside warning me with forefingers pointed up at the air. I stopped for the first signal and got out. Since the planes were not coming my way, I drove off. After that I paid no attention to the signs of the road, not even to the jumping of soldiers into ditches.

Their avions have not noticed me yet. After the first lesson I will prob-ably be more careful. There are many objectives along the twenty-mile ridge. Why should the planes waste their time on me?

I was getting gas in Alfambra when the attendant suddenly shut off the pump and ran to a *refugio*. I followed him. The deep soggy cave in the red earth was packed with women. Ashamed, I went back to the gas-station. Crome's car was parked beside mine.

"Never leave your car so near a gas station," said Crome through the window. I saw that his frozen feet were bound up in loose sheepskin slippers. "A gas station is always an objective. No matter how little time you have, always move your car away from the pump. This is your first service at the Front, isn't it?"

The Major had sent me to Alfambra to find out what the three-person surgical team we had sent there needed.

They needed everything. For two weeks an American surgeon, his assistant and a single nurse had run an entire surgical hospital, wards and operating room, with the assistance of three Spanish *chicas* who were the only women who would stay in the village and above ground during daytime. Their outfit had light, but lacked water and a trench in which to go when the planes came over.

I came to Spain with these Americans. The leader is a small long-faced iron-gray-haired San Francisco thoracic surgeon and university professor. He is a very rich man, a former United States Army surgeon who saw service in France, a linguist and a society figure. The younger of the surgeons is also a U.S. Army man. Avemaria (real first name) was head nurse in a New Jersey hospital.[6] She has the oval face of a Cimabue Madonna, eyes as liquid as Thais' meditation, and a voice which makes me want to cry.

"Ave, what do you eat here?"

"Rations. Rice and bread and olive oil. I'm the cook."

"Where do you go when the planes come over?"

"We stay indoors. There's no place to go. We got a lot because the gas-pump is right across the street from us. When it comes too near, we lie in the corner of the rooms."

"Why can't you find another building?"

"This is the only house in town for a hospital."

"What do you need?"

"Catgut, adhesive, some more knives."

"And for yourselves?"

---

6. The thoracic surgeon is Dr. Leo Eloesser of Stanford University, who organized a complete surgical team to serve with the AMB. According to Eloesser's published report, his companions were Dr. Edwin Sherman Weisfield of Seattle, Washington, and nurse Avemaria Bruzzichesi from New Jersey.

"We don't need anything. If the wounded can endure this war, so can we."

"When the work slacks up, come over and see us in Cuevas. We'll give you a good meal."

"When we're not busy, I stay with the boys. They need me."

Avemaria is worse than a Madonna. She's a stinking Nightingale. To make things worse, she is a pious Communist Party member. If there were more like her, Spain would be an orgiastic purgatory of sentimentality. Every man in the Fifteenth would give Ave his last cigarette. We wish there were a thousand more American women in Spain like her.

Dr. E. of San Francisco laid down the viola on which he had been playing the most eclectic of Bach exercises and told me to give his regards to Major B. and to ask him for a half a dozen knives.

"And leave Alfambra fast," he said in parting. "Don't come here. Stay off those roads. This neighborhood is not safe."

On my way back to Cuevas, I passed a big Divisional amb parked under a scrawny leafless tree. I could tell that something was wrong, because of the *soldados* who swarmed about her like ants over the corpse of a stricken beetle.

Loaded to the roof with frozen feet and light wounded, she had just that very minute been strafed. Tough luck: if I had been traveling a little faster, I should have had something to write about. I stopped and loaded eight rewounded cases. The stricken amb slowly turned about and headed back to Cuevas, which she had left not half an hour before. At such times the Spanish are apt to look up at the sky and ferociously whisper *"los cabrónes!"*

Three nice fresh new egg-holes in the Cuevas turn-off. Five more houses gone. I am told that the surgical hospital has been machine-gunned every morning after breakfast and lightly bombed almost every afternoon since it has been set up.

"I sleep in Finn's car," says Phyllis in an elaborate Oxford accent, "because we have so few beds for the staff.[7] We don't need an alarm clock. Early every morning They come over so low that you can see They need a shave. One of them is my pet. He leans over the edge of the fuselage, waves and smiles at me before he turns on his machine-gun. Then They go over the mountain.

---

7. Phyllis Hibbert, an English nurse, worked closely with the eye specialist Dr. Johnny Kyszely, serving with a mobile hospital unit. According to a memo written later by another nurse, "she was always getting pregnant and had many abortions," the last of which required her to return to England.

They're really not much interested in us yet. What They're after is the artillery on the other side of the cliff."

How many bloody planes have They got in these god damn mountains? And not one of them seems to know that I have arrived at the Front.

Crome is a fool to station a hospital in a place like Cuevas. But where is he going to put us? Only one casualty thus far; a stretcher-bearer, buried asleep in the village.

It is true that we are so near the lines that the wounded reach us almost before the echo of the guns which shot them die out, but how long can our luck last? Wouldn't it be possible to put the hospital underground? Everything should be underground. Architects of the future should plan subway cities. Proserpine was right. Pluto has always been right. Gabriel's horn was really a siren.

But the boys up on the ridge take more chances than I do. At the Front you have three or four choices to make. All of them are bad.

They say that the thermometer is at 0°. Don't know if this is true but I saw the shadow of a shell frozen to the ground.

In Memoriam

George Hooker of New York, the driver of the 35th Division autochir. Asphyxiated by the fumes of his sterilizers as he worked behind closed doors.

He was the man who sat at the wheel of both autochirs as we turned them in the snow over the Aliaga ravine on New Year's morning.

George's place has been taken by Bob Webster.[8]

The Arts of War

1) How to get your laundry done. Bundle up underwear, socks and shirt (towels and handkerchiefs are thrown away), walk out into the streets of a village. The second or third woman you see will do your wash in the river in exchange for a bar of soap. You will most likely have

---

8. Bob Webster (may be aka Robert R. Webber) was a New York City bus driver, over forty years old, who took charge of the mobile surgical vehicle and was later killed at Gandesa during the Retreats of 1938.

moved to another place by the time that laundry is ready. Weeks or days later, you may come back and recover clothing, if it has not been bombed.

Pace of the Teruel Campaign. A thousand-square chess-board with fifty types of chessmen moved with the rapidity of sped-up motion pictures. Cobwebs of field telephones are the nerves which reach out to mailed fists and boot hobs. Gasoline is the food.

January 10. Between Peralejos (Our Town) and Celadas (Theirs)

Sit in car parked on high moorland, big fascist snow mountain across the valley. Battery of our 75's fired over my head into Celadas.

Just came from observation post. Sand-bagged dugouts on lip of plateau. Three periscopic range-finders (captured by the Fifteenth at Belchite) lift mantis-like arms over the parapet. Cross-hatched lines fixed on center of town two miles away and half a mile below us correct aim. A whip-lash cracks out of the vale behind us, suction rushes over our heads; we count three then a puff of white smoke mushrooms up from the town. Black shapes of running fascists distinctly visible in the lenses, hobbling out into the fields like snow-bound rabbits. One was a woman. Must have been one of ours—all dames with dough have been able to run off to some safe spot, really safe, and the poor all belong to us, every one of them.

Observers watch smoke-puffs and correct aim over telephone. (Sound goes by; like 10-ton iron fist hitting 5-foot-thick fresh sappy pine door. Our music is as sweet as a Strauss waltz.) Boys in observation post mostly U.S.A. and Finnish. Gunner is "a crazy little Frenchman" who can "knock the eye out of the fly." So good that periscopes are almost useless. (Big one came by overhead, our way.) The visiting team is trying to get our 75's with something big and strong, bigger than anything we have, but can't seem to find the range. Fires once every three minutes or so but does not find us.

New battery of ours just opened up. Celadas getting hell from all six guns now. Fascist concentration is forming across the valley.

Two or three hundred yards down the snow-patched rough earth, mottled by gray-green thorns useless for firewood, are the lines. Things are opening up a little. (Whole battery just fired, nasty-tempered crows, well imitated by rifles.) A lonely machine-gun hiccup comes from the other side of the fence. We don't answer. Single gunflash would give away our position. Waiting, waiting, for a crack at Their infantry.

This part of the Front, 15 kilometers from Teruel, is quiet. Few planes.

Warmer today but we still had to thaw out the adhesive tape at the Post fireplace this morning. By afternoon mud lay in the crossings of the Cuevas streets smooth and liquid as fresh-cured icing on a cake. What does cake taste like?

If it were not for the squads of *"genie"* (engineers) at the turns of the road winding up to the plateau, it would be impossible for munitions, ambs and the food truck to reach the men. Field kitchen back in Cuevas sends up coffee, oranges and hot beans twice every day. Also drinking water and a little wine. First-aid post is a tent pitched in the snow.

Getting dark. The 75's have ceased firing, either because of lowering visibility or shortness of shells. Blanket of shark-blue clouds drifts down from fascist mountain on us. Like to come up to this place some day after the war with a victrola and play the Götterdämmerung. Here the three Norns were born and dead Vikings fought each other all day until the same darkness which ended their sport revived the dead. But this war is no game, Celadas is not Valhalla, and our dead will rise only inside the hearts of the comrades who will always come to fill up the gaps in the ranks.

January 12? Cuevas

Up early, having counter-attacked and slain most of the 5,000,000 grippe germs (explosion on road ¼ mile away—white smoke rises—shell?—those bastards are getting the range) driving up and down my spine, churning about in my sinuses and sizzling in my lungs. Perhaps my change of bed— from straw in attic to stretcher in pharmacy, suitcase under feet—cured me. (Another white puff. What the hell. They're not shooting at us, They're aiming for the road.)

Two men of the Fifteenth have been court-martialed.[9] They had been caught by a bombing party about to enter fascist lines. Court-martial committee consisted of a Spanish Major, an International Major and an International private. Neither prisoner had good political or trade union records in their native land, although one of the deserters had risen to the rank of sergeant. Both confessed that their purpose was to be captured. The two deserters seemed to think that once they were in fascist territory, they could somehow manage to get home.

---

9. Military courts martial were summoned in rare cases of extreme insubordination and desertion. The brigade commissar, who ranked as a major, acted as prosecutor, and the tribunal met openly. According to the memoir of British officer Bill Alexander, the deserters were British.

"Even assuming," said Commissar Dave Doran to the meeting which was to vote on the recommendations of the court-martial committee, "that they did not desert with the deliberate intention of buying repatriation from Franco in exchange for giving him information, these two men knew that they would be tortured into giving the fascists the position of our lines. If they had not been caught, many of us would be dead today . . . and I believe that the recommendations of the committee should be carried. Do I hear a motion to that effect? . . . Seconded? . . . Are you ready for the vote? . . . "

Both deserters have been executed.

I drove a long way over the mountains today with my old boss, Major B., to see Fred Copeman, the English commander whose appendix B. removed three weeks ago. The Major was able to get away from Cuevas because the diminishing number of wounded which have been coming into Cuevas can be handled by the remaining two head surgeons and their teams.

At the top of the pass over which we had fought on New Year's Eve, we stopped for luncheon. There was now no snow; and nothing to limit the eye but veil-like blue-green backdrops of tiered mountains. The broad plain which lay ahead gave the illusion of sea often observed from high places.

We ate our share of a special belated Christmas issue of tinned tongue, chicken in glass and Ukranian butter. The bread was the good wheat of Aliaga bought for English cigarettes from the bakers. The mild and luminous winter sun was orchestra, entrée, desert, liqueur—but the most tasteful part of this half-hour intermission of peace and contentment was the knowledge that we were far from the pest-spots of bombing. Shepherd is the only safe occupation in Spain today.

On the way back, we stopped in Mezquita for an inspection of the infirmary. I was able to deliver my friend Ribas the tin of milk and the can of beef (which he and many of the Spanish peasants call "Russian meat") I had been saving for him these last few days or weeks.

When I look at the dates in this journal, I know that I have been at the Front only eleven days. Time is elastic. There seems to be so little of it left. Modern war and leprosy are not declared. They break out. Soon the hide of the earth not long ago infected by the swastika bacillus will swell with white death and our blood will run back into the earth.

Before sunset—and the sky always seems to turn blood-red at this touching hour of the day when even garbage piles become beautiful and moving—we ran, and ran fast, through Perales. Nothing more can happen to this crossroad town. Planes can blast day after day for weeks and blow it from one side of the road to the other and back again, but Perales will still be shoulder height. No method has yet been invented of driving the remains of houses straight down into the earth. Cities will be twenty or thirty feet high in the end, I estimate. Moral: a plane can terrorize but not cut a road.

By nightfall we had entered the fog we had left that morning. The breath of all the snow melted this week comes back at night and haunts the earth. I had to slow down to chest-case speed.

My radiator was eighty percent fixed in Alcañiz, but headlight, brakes and bumper remained smashed. Damage was done by vibration. Can't let engine noises make a hypochondriac of me.

The Major tells me to go to Valencia for repairs. First real break I've gotten; a few days to do some writing. I'll get three or four baths, go to the movies, eat all day every day, and sleep clean and quiet at night. How long is it since I took off my shirt? When did I last see my skin?

January 13

Morning. Heard we were to move. I went to the Major, told him that my car would still roll and that I would not like to leave the Brigade at a time like this. He consented to put off the repair trip to Valencia. I'm not being noble—I just don't like to miss the fireworks. Beginning to be interested in this campaign. So far everything is all right: the roads are jammed with men and equipment every night all night and things move with the energy and precision which means that Teruel is going to be ours for quite a long time. If They want this magic city as badly as They seem to, They are going to have to pour so much blood into these desert plains that the wheat will grow thicker and higher in this pauper province than it has since the Fifteenth century.

The brigades inch southwards down the ridge. Soon we will be in the city itself. The Mac-Paps have taken over the positions of a French battalion, which was very badly used up during the past week; the André Marty's, I think.

Not a plane, not a shell, no back-chat from the machine-guns this morning. A hunting party seems to be leisurely potting at rabbits this morning up on the mountains and that's all. What's up?

Night. Write by oil-lamp in Bob's amb up on a heath over Celadas where I watched shelling the other day. Drink tea and eat—Oh my God—raspberry jam supplied by Dorothy the Runaway Florence.

Participated in a little tea-party down in the lines this afternoon, while S. was making his rounds.

Know now why we shelled Celadas. "Concentration of fascists." Came out like ants but upright, the bastards, close together, in some kind of bloody "psychological" attack. Looked like thousands. Two, three, four irregular lines, wherever you looked. Eyeing a pile of concussion grenades (thin-shelled duck-eggs that kill by concussion alone, like dynamite) and fuse bombs, I waited for our 75's to open up. Not one shot came out of our lines. "Bunker Hill," I thought. Waiting to see the reds of their eyes. Then six Maxims this side of low hills far in front of our first trenches began to talk. Conversation was short. The ants, now grown to cockroach size, went back where they came from, minus how many? Fallen ones seemed too big. Was told that they lay in clumps, where the bursts had reached them. The other ants didn't come back.

Statistics. One hundred Wash-Lincs with six guns held off three to four thousand troops. Three or four light wounds on our side to that many hundred dead on Theirs.

Analysis. They had no intention of being able to take our positions from us, except by some unforeseen luck. They had wanted to provoke us into firing and to thus give away the positions of our lines which could later be shelled for the real attack.

Instead of taking Them on from our trenches and thus giving our lines away to their guns, two machine-gun companies, taken out into No-Man's Land hills, had done the job.

Troops used on us were "*reclutas*" or conscripts, all Spanish. Moors, blond or brown, would never be wasted in such a fashion. No men would be so used except by the genius of war-loving totalitarian commanders.

Emotions. We won.
Sorry They weren't the Duce's darlings, or Moors.

Why we fight. Shoot at fascists but hit Hearst, Tammany, Girdler, Harvey, lynch-Senators, Liberty League Lawyers, injunction judges, "I am the law" mayors and all those who say "what's wrong with this country is that there's too much liberty."[10]

---

10. This is a litany of right-wing politicians Neugass considered sympathetic to fascism:
    William Randolph Hearst (1863–1951), owner of a powerful newspaper chain that

Tea-party in Bob's amb is over. Dorothy pulls down the Pullman upper berth stretchers, makes ready for work tonight. She's a good housekeeper. In daytime her and Bob's home resembles a trailer. Romance.

Before I forget: the planes finally caught up with me this morning. Had my first narrow escape. Found eight men and a Commissar under the rock which my sixth sense had picked out before my eyes could operate. At the last minute I thought of the effects of a direct hit and switched to the open fields. Bronng: bronng bronng bronng; bronng bronng. Light stuff. Rose and got a full load of flesh-wounds from under the rock. Don't know what their politics were but the Commissar led off with the Internationals and the other six joined in. More blood to wash out of my car.

It keeps getting nearer and nearer. How much more luck have I left?

We haven't seen heavy action yet.

Brigade has been taking an average of one shell and one bomb per day per man per day of good weather including Transport, Medical Corps and Kitchen, with slightly less liberal rations of lighter metal. It can hardly be said that we have been in reserve.

Later. Same night. Teruel. 10, 11, 12 P.M.(?) Right in the heart of the hot-spot city.

Sit by a ruined wall of the late Civil Guard barracks, one of the last hold-outs. Firelight, four assault guards, car and myself are nicely sheltered from plateaus and rock spires from which the voices of Their machine-gun Captains and trench-mortar Colonels command.

Plenty of firewood lying all around the streets, together with odd pieces of iron and plaster; some expensive looking but wrecked electrical machinery, and three dead horses.

Write by firelight, notebook across knees. The *Asaltos* think I'm out of my mind. Maybe I am.

---

shaped public opinion through control of the media. Tammany Hall was the New York political machine, which governed through graft and kickbacks. Tom Mercer Girdler, head of the Republic Steel Corporation, refused to allow union elections, resulting in the Little Steel Strike of 1937. George U. Harvey was a Queens, New York, politician who rejected the endorsement of the American Labor Party in 1937 because of its extensive Communist membership. The Liberty League was an anti–New Deal organization opposed to labor unions. Injunction judges invoked legal orders to halt strikes.

Reasons why you see so many dead horses and mules:

1)   Their brains are supposed to be very susceptible to concussion.
2)   Once horses and mules are ever so slightly wounded, they are put out
     of misery—unlike men.
3)   Nobody bothers to drag them off—also unlike men.
4)   Horses and mules don't begin to smell as soon as men.

Dogs wander in the moonlight sniffing the carcasses.

Machine-guns infrequent. Shot at plenty, earlier—like Jew's harp, crows,
soft whistles. Sound depends on geography, barometric pressure, echoes and
many other conditions. Always varied.

Spent bullets slither redhot to the earth. Brigade getting ready to move
into ruined city. That's why I'm here. Captain S. has some sort of arrangements to make. Will we set up (pow-sw-sw-sw-ow) hospital here? Hope so.
Would like to see town by day.

Layout is difficult to understand. City seems to be at the end of Alfambra
plateau at the edge of a precipice but overhung by big rocks among which
are the Muela and Meleton (Big Tooth and Little Tooth). Something like a
volcano in the valley between two near high ranges of mountains.

Civil Guard Barracks where I sit (the *Asaltos* ask me what I'm writing. "A
letter to my *novia*," I answer. They approve, and admire my leather covered,
zipper-bound notebook) is right at the edge of precipice. Road to Valencia
takes off a few feet away across a narrow viaduct on which I see still more
dead horses. Viaduct must be under full fire during daylight. Why is it still
whole? Is it really whole? (More pow-swow'ing.)

Hear near sounds of a mountain torrent. Also, "let-me-in, Open-in-the-
name-of-the-king," say their machine guns. Ours answer "No, No." What
the hell? Where are the lines? Are there snipers still left in Teruel? This is a
mad war, made madder by the geography.

A house down the street lies buried in its own vomit. (Gongg. Big one.
Trench mortar?) Reminds me of fireworks Christmas Eve nights back in New
Orleans when I was a kid. Always hated uniforms and military music.

Trucks as unlit as rhinoceroses go by; tankers, steering carefully between
the dead horses.

This town smells like burned wood.

Scared? Too much to be scared of. You keep something between you and
the sounds and let it go at that. Still I hope we get out of here by sunrise. The

fascists can look down on us from three sides even at night. Where is Captain S.? Well, going to look for firewood.

So what.

<u>A little later.</u> No trouble finding firewood here. Also came back with a black oilcloth imitation patent leather Civil Guard's Napoleonic-looking hat. Souvenir.

"Would you like more?" an *Asalto* politely asked me. The four of them had been peacefully talking, in a Valencian dialect, about their dead and wounded friends.

The guard led me inside the barracks courtyard. Another souvenir. Here in the moonlight two or three hundred Civil Guard hats shimmered among empty cartridges. I picked up a fascist officer's torn insignia. I asked what had happened to the wearers of the hats.

"*Hamos cortado los cabezas*," I was answered, pleasantly. I understood that the Civil Guards who tried to defend their barracks had been shot. These were the same men who had led a Republican band of militia from Castellon against Teruel in the first week of the war. At Puebla de Valverde, twenty-one kilometers south of here, the men who had worn these same black oilcloth hats had suddenly turned on the Castellon militia and annihilated them.

When the outside world becomes capable of greater hatreds it will be able to understand how the poor of Spain have hated the Civil Guard. A separate caste, with special privileges, and always billeted in villages other than their own, the *Civiles* had long ago become the symbol not only of the misery of the past but the chains of the future. We Americans hate drug-peddlers and sex-murderers and white slavers with an intensity far less than the Spanish hate *Guardias Civiles*.

Relaxed. Heat of the fire makes me sleepy and writing unlooses my tight nerves. Where's S.? Will we get out of Teruel before sunrise?

<u>Few hours later.</u> Tortajada. Early morning. Fascist drew first blood. Skinned my nose.

Happened this way: something like a pine knot suddenly exploded inside of fire. *Asaltos* immediately kicked apart embers and burning sticks. Big mosquitoes were drilling down the street and biting into stone.

I spent rest of night standing asleep against a wall on advice of *Asaltos*. Before morning fell dead asleep on my face and skinned nose. First blood goes to the fascists. Also bruised shoulder and twisted wrist. But the firing had stopped.

Sleep is a worse enemy than hunger.

January 14. Tortajada

Late afternoon. Classification Post has been moved to this town, six miles from Teruel.

Slept until afternoon on floor of curiously unwrecked house until S. called me out to drive him to Cuevas. No work all day. Road getting too hot. They can't quite manage to bring it under shell fire. Too well protected by ridge.

Took an hour to drive the six miles to Cuevas although road surface was good, between egg-holes, and I was carrying no wounded. Four, five times we had to stop and get into the good deep ditch which prevents me from driving car off road at such times.

Became disgusted and suggested that S. ride on my running-board. The Captain refused. He said it wasn't dignified. I said that either he would ride on the running board or I would and I wasn't going to let him drive my car. After one more trip into the ditch he consented.

You cannot see planes through the roof of car and engine noises are too loud for them to be heard through the windows. Keep eyes on the road looking for men. When you can't see anyone, either planes are overhead or all human beings are in ditches, culverts, bomb-holes or the open fields, or up the cliff. Teruel–Perales highway is so full of road-gangs and light wounded and men waiting for a lift on a camion, or thinly strung out Companies waiting for orders to go up to the ridge, that you can be very sure, if no one is in sight, that the avions are on you. More and more and more of them. Flying fields at Berlin and Rome must be empty as a baseball park at night. Haven't yet heard that Franco makes his own. Why should he?

Entered Cuevas cut-off with heart in my throat because town had obviously just been bombed. More houses had gone, their viscera splayed into the street. Had the hospital been hit; and the Major?

Four dead cavalrymen fully dressed and unspotted by blood lay on stretchers in the hospital courtyard. Saxton, blond tall young English doctor, knelt beside one of them.[11] He had rolled a sleeve up past the elbow of a gray arm.

"What do you think you're doing, Saxton?" I asked, suddenly remembering that he was our blood-transfusion expert.

---

11. Dr. Reginald Saxton of Reading, England, headed blood transfusion services and was one of the first physicians to use stored blood for transfusions, a technique perfected during the Spanish Civil War. He served in the British Medical Corps during World War II.

He did not answer.

Angry, I leaned over the doctor's shoulder. The single vampire tooth of a big glass syringe was slowly drawing the blood out of the vein inside of the dead cavalryman's forearm. The vessel filled and Saxton stood up.

"New Soviet technique," he said, holding the syringe between his squinting eye and the late winter sun. Purple lights shadowed the glistening bar of ruby.

"Seldom we get the chance. Most of them are pretty well empty when they go out. Those four over there were in one of those clay dugouts in the wall of the main street. No timbers on the roof. Direct hit. Asphyxiated, all of them. Their comraydes dug them out before they were cold and brought them up here. Thought we could help. Their bad luck"—Saxton pointed to the four gray young faces with clay-stuffed mouths—"was our good luck. We're running short on donors and the transfusion truck is too busy."

"You mean . . . that you're going to. . . . "

"Well, first I'll have to type and then test it . . . why not? . . . have to hurry."

I touched the bright tube with my hard black fingertips. Was the glass warm with the sun or with human life?

Now I understand why we must win. Men die but the blood fights on in other veins and their purpose fills other hearts.

The hospital was unusually full of civilians. No distinction made between them and militiamen in spite of the latter's greater use. First come first served in order of emergency. But everything is urgent in the valley of the Alfambra.

I use the operating table, still warm with the heat of the body of Captain Philip Detro* of Texas. Phil has bad luck. Shrapnel smashed his other femur this time. Leg was hit in four places. Six-foot-four, he's the tallest guy in Spain—and They always get him in the legs! Major B. left holes in the waist-high plaster cast through which the other wounds may be treated. Seldom see a man wounded in one place only.

I held Phil's leg while the cast dried. The long lashes of his blue eyes were half open. He had just come out of the ether. In a sepulchral voice he asked how the lines were holding and who would take over his command. Detro smiled when he heard that perhaps Dave Reiss would fill his place.[12]

Naked but for the plaster on his leg and waist, he was motionless, but his

* dead

12. David Reiss replaced Phil Detro as battalion commander but was killed when an en-

eyes watched everything and every motion in the room. Four of our American nurses, all of them at some time secretly or openly in love with the six-foot-four Hermes, flitted about the operating room laughing and joking and talking loudly.

I have someone else hold the leg, called Queen Annie and Nora out of the room, and told them what I thought of their gayety.[13]

They laughed still more. "But Jimmy," said Anne, knowing that I hate to be called anything but Jim, "if we walk around with long faces and don't say anything, Phil will think that he's very sick. We don't want to laugh and try to say funny things, but so long as we don't seem worried, Phil thinks he has a chance."

"*Thinks* he has a chance. Hasn't he?"

"Well, no big vessels were cut, and if infection does not set in. . . . "

"Oh, I'm sorry."

I seem to make a fool of myself whenever I meddle with medicine.

Nora gets Phil's big automatic. She will keep it for him until he is well. Wish I had a gun. There's just that grenade, under my front seat. Think I'll put it in the canvas dispatch bag I organized to protect my notebook before I left Alcorisa. I saw two fascist grenades on a windowsill up at Argente but didn't want to touch them.

B. does not look well. He has been working in twelve-hour shifts and once put in twenty-four hours at the table. He never speaks of his illness. I think he must have left the States with some severe sort of stomach ailment, because he seems to be able to hold down nothing but oranges.

The two American girls are doing well, almost too well. Annie the Queen of the O.R. boasts that she hasn't yet visited the hospital trench. I asked her what she does when the planes come over.

"Oh, I just stay where I am. If we're operating we don't do anything. Then I'm in the wards, I stay there and don't lie down in a corner until the last minute. You might just as well be in one place as in another. In case of a direct hit . . . maybe I'm silly, but somehow, if there's a roof over my head, I feel safe." Annie giggled. I hope that nothing happens to her. I hope that nothing happens to Bernie and Marty and the rest of our group in the surgical hos-

---

emy shell made a direct hit on the headquarters at Belchite in March 1938. Nurse Lenora Temple accompanied Detro to a rear hospital, where he died.

13. Anne Taft, a New York operating room nurse, joined the first unit of the AMB, arriving in Spain in January 1937, and served on every battle front. She worked so closely with Dr. Barsky that he called her "Dr. Taft."

pital they have now set up in Cedrillas. I hope that Phil Detro will live. He carries a very special kind of Spanish blood.

Some of the Internationals, for example Captain Gustav Regler of the Thälman Brigade, are almost full-blooded Spaniards.[14]

Part of the cornice of the hospital came off during the day and the rear wall is pitted by bullet-hole acne. The village women who used to help with the cleaning can no longer be persuaded to come out of the caves in which they spend all their daylight hours. A stretcher-bearer was wounded today. Candlesticks have been made of the bomb-wings found back of the building. A two-foot dud, blunt-nosed as a hammer-headed shark, lies next to the trench. I did not want to lift the pretty silver and olive-green thing to look for the markings.

We have been here nearly a week. Their aim is bad but They keep trying. How long can our luck last?

"Evacuarme," cry the wounded in the ward as they come out of the ether and listen; "evacuate me!" That's all very well. We can send them back after two or three days of what might be called rest, but how is the whole earth going to be evacuated some day and whence? Pursuit ships would follow the ambulance-planes to any planet the isolationist nations choose.

Meanwhile we pay the price of Washington's and Paris' imprudence. As for London, I have seldom been in a dugout or a ditch without hearing someone say he wished the Non-Intervention Committee were with us.[15] Sometimes it seems as if we hate Eden and Chamberlain worse than Rome-Berlin-Burgos axis. The pimp is always more despised than the purchaser. Chamberlain loses much sleep satisfying the appetites of Adolf and Benito. Halifax plays the piano downstairs and Franco is the call-boy.[16]

---

14. Gustav Regler described his war experiences in *The Great Crusade* (1940), for which Ernest Hemingway wrote the preface.

15. The Non-Intervention Committee was formed by agreement of the European powers attempting to prevent the Spanish Civil War from spreading into a general war. British Conservatives, led by Anthony Eden and Neville Chamberlain, used the agreement to embargo arms sales to the Spanish Republic; Hitler and Mussolini, also signers of the agreement, openly violated its terms. The United States was not a signer of the agreement, but used neutrality laws to achieve the same purpose, barring aid to the legal government of Spain while ignoring violations that sent oil to the Rebel (Nationalist) side.

16. Lord Halifax, Eric Frederick Lindley Wood, played a significant role in British foreign policy and was an avid supporter of appeasement policies toward Hitler and Mussolini.

I have not thought of politics or of anything but doing my work and saving my hide and getting food and sleep for a long time. None of the troops at the Front talk politics. We belong to no parties and to many parties but we do not talk politics. I wish the rear-guard could copy our unity. If I get back to the States and find that the liberals have fought each other to a standstill . . . but I forget; they still call it murder, over there.

January 14. Tortajada

Plenty of time to write. It is fifteen minutes to 2 P.M. and there have been very few cars on the roads today. The weather is perfect, except for artificial man-made clouds on the brown crest of the hill a mile across the valley. Shells break white and raise pillars of stone-dust. We are not so far from Their artillery as we had thought.

I had finished shaving by 9 A.M. and was just about to go down to the river to brush my teeth when the men first ran to the *refugios*. Listening to the average explosions and idly watching shells break under the long hillcrest, I had not noticed the sounds of the first planes.

That was about five hours ago. Leaning out of the opening of a dugout like a groundhog looking for the February sun, I have seen the same two-motors, three-motors, four- and twenty-motored squadrons of bombers, pursuit and attack planes pass by tens of times. Never counted more than eighty-four fascist planes overhead at any one time, but of course I could not see the other side of the hill. One mile away by bullet flight lies a long low gap in the hills which the Thaelman Battalion is defending. That is the point through which They are trying to break.

The main kinds of noises are

1) Constant increasing rising and falling hum of great and small plane motors everywhere.
2) Shells exploding in the hills.
3) The machine-gunning of the infantry attacks and counter-attacks.
4) The drilling roar of planes diving on the town underneath which I sit.
5) The backwards gasping stutter of the machine-gun bullets they throw at us, peppered by hand-grenades.

There have been other sights and sounds, such as the white-burning glare of incendiary shells, some below the ridge and some on the road, and the twittering of birds in the riverside trees.

The air in these rat-holes dug in the precipitous bank of the river shakes and pounds. A bit of paper shudders on the floor. A dog has been wandering about the far bank of the river all morning. There are other little mongrels in the cave with us. Those birds in the dry gray trees wrangled all morning. I have never before heard such a disgusting noise except in cities at nightfall when whole ivy walls of sparrows chatter before going to sleep.

The birds are now gone. I wonder where.

At one time, Their Pavos ("turkeys" are what Aragon peasants call the German trimotors) and whole squadrons of other planes did all sorts of fancy sky-writing in white, just like advertising, back in the States. At first we thought that the lines of white smoke coming out of their exhaust-pipes were gas. Then somebody thought he saw a fascist emblem being traced out. Soon the sky was full of the Phalangist emblem—gigantic sheaves of arrows bound by a yoke. The display was supposed to constitute some sort of fancy psychological trick I suppose, as if the planes were saying "Here we are; this is our proud emblem; come and get us." Their artillery had been throwing incendiary shells against our hillside for the same pseudo-psychological purposes, since the only inflammable things on these desert hillsides are low thorn-bushes.

No ambulances could live on these roads. We will have to wait until nightfall.

I thought it best to get my car ready. Its radiator was empty. All cooling systems are kept drained since they would freeze in an hour if left full and there is no garage capable of making repairs for a hundred miles.

I went down to the river with three pitchers, filled them, then walked back up the hill. There was no one to be seen anywhere in the valley, no cars, no movement but for the smoke of the shells. Finally I was able to make out three cavalrymen winding up the hill to the pass through which They are trying to break. I felt, well, as if I wanted to get the job done. So long as you don't run you aren't afraid.

Now I am back in our underground Classification Post waiting for orders and feeling better. I should have hated to be sent on the road and to be caught with no water in my radiator.

I am worried

1) that the fascists will come through the pass, cut the road and bottle us up in the town with all our equipment and ambulances.
2) that the boys up on the hill are taking a lot of punishment.

We are at the apex of the shock-center of the fascist attack. The fall of Teruel was a slap on Their cheek which was heard all around the world. They are spending a lot of fancy dough on explosives to get it back. As far as this town is concerned, Their gunners and aviators hit nothing but Mussolini's bankroll. *Mañana mas.* They always come back. How many anti-aircraft pieces have we over the hill? Two? Three? Don't seem to do much good. Drive the *Pavos* higher perhaps but that's about all.

Well there has been a slight let-up in the fireworks. Maybe Their aviators went home for lunch. I am going to look for something to eat, myself.

<u>After lunch.</u> The crew of the Post sit on the parapet watching shells break on the ridge. A few raise dirt near the road. Tortajada, because it is higher than Cuevas, almost comes within the trajectory of the 75's They use on us. Are They shooting at us? Heard the good rich snorting of a few batteries of ours this morning.

On the way into Teruel last night I passed an unusual number of armored cars drawn up in clumps of threes near the occasional tracks that lead up to the ridge. These weapons are used either to cover the wings of the infantry during a rapid advance or to hold off the enemy if he breaks through, until the lines can be re-established. Since there is not much likelihood of our rapidly advancing, I did not much like the look of such a concentration of armored cars, as much as I enjoy seeing how many of them we have. I have been watching these horned beetles for the past few days. They move up and down the road covering the weak spots much as a fullback watches his line and his backfield. Estimate that we must have a maximum of fifty Ford cars, each with two light machine-guns, on the thirty-five miles of road from Teruel to Alfambra.

How long can this last? If our boys back up as much as three hundred yards at any one of a number of points, the road will be cut and we will have to withdraw along the entire Front. Meanwhile the men hold the lines, Major B. holds down the Cuevas surgical hospital, Captain S. hangs on at Tortajada and I hold down some of the best ditch-bottoms in Spain. Wish I could get back at Them, a little. Signs of paranoia are developing. I am too much on the receiving end. While the boys sit nice and comfortable under a steam-roller, hoping the roof will not cave in over their heads, I run these god-damn roads like a hound dog with a tin can on his tail. My car is turning into a tin can. Frame and chassis hold together, but the roads have produced many tiny splits in the body, each of them growing larger every day, like the wrinkles on a drying apple. I'd like to spend a whole day on her with a welding outfit. But there is very little acetylene. Well, so long as my morale doesn't crack, let the old can rip and tear. How is my morale? I'll have to ask the Major.

Today's narrow escape. We stopped outside of Teruel, at Kilometer 2½, to let Captain S. visit the Estado Major of the Fifteenth. I was talking to Lewis, crack negro driver of one of the best brigade trucks, pleasantly enough, with all the warmth of two men marooned on the same raft, when he collared and toppled me to the ground.[17] He had seen a school of machine-gun strays red-hot, cross the road. Kilometer 2½ is under fire at night? And during the day?

More shell-holes in the road than the night before, but nothing you can't circumvent. Roadside trees look like they had been split by ice and rent by cyclones. At K 2, a big truck lay blasted. Al Hawk's? Drive without lights, of course. There's almost a full moon so I can make up to 15 miles an hour, near-sighted eyes and all (minus 4½ in the left eye, 5½ in the right). You can get used to everything. Two weeks more of this life and I could sleep inside a long dead whale and not notice the smell, or live on borrowed money, or take a strike-breaking job, or vote for Al Smith. We become animals. Let alone the destruction of the landscape, the filth war makes of men is its real horror.

We had gone to Teruel because S. was interested in the electrical machinery I had seen outside the *Guardia Civile* barracks. I told him just how and why I skinned my nose but he did not seem to mind the prospect of danger.

The dead horses were still at the viaduct crossroad, stinking and shining and shining and stinking in the moonlight. Solitary trench mortars, rifles and grenades were playing their habitual nightly game of hide-and-seek.

Captain S. examined the machinery in the street. Using his last flashlight batteries, we explored the four floors of the narrow little clinic. From roof to cellar it was one great mare's nest of tangled linen, medical apparatus, furniture, books and clothing. The smell of carbolic acid was victor over the reek of the other drugs the cold night air blew up and down the stair from room to room.

We began to understand that this had not only been a military clinic but the lifework of a research scientist, complete to library, microscopes and white mice.

Empty cartridges of many kinds and calibers lay on the stairs and under the bullet-marked windowsills. At one of the last moments in the defense of

---

17. Lewis is probably Charles Howard Lewis, who was born in Alabama, lived in the Bronx, and was killed at Teruel.

the city, the clinic had been used to cover the left flank of the Civil Guard barracks across the street. Its front window dominated the Valencia road viaduct up which we had advanced. Yet this building had not taken a single shell. Had our artillerymen known that it was full of the equipment we so badly needed?

Hoping against hope, the professor had waited, not for the eleventh hour, but until five minutes after twelve. Not until the first guns of Lister's Special Machine Gun Battalion, shock troops of a shock Division, had climbed up the ravine under the viaduct, did this nameless scientist carry autoclaves, diathermy and operating table to the street, hoping to be able to commandeer a truck. Later, this equipment had been used by riflemen, as testified by the bullet holes in one of the autoclaves. Drilled in a dozen places, the steel operating table can still be used.

The old boy had had time to smash his vast stores of anti-tetanus and gas-gangrene serums. Son of a bitch. I wish that he had fed his canaries and white mice. What should I do with these animals? Free the canaries? What would they find to eat? Where would they fly? How should they resist the cold? What shall I do? Grenade the lot of them after the Captain and I have taken what we want out of the clinic?

What does the world think of a scientist who smashes his anti-tetanus serums rather than have them fall into enemy hands?

We loaded an armful of anatomy books, the least-drilled-autoclave, the diathermy, many embroidered linen sheets, boxes of fine cambric bandages and trays of drugs into my car. I had wanted to take along a fine beaten copper jug, but the Captain said no. Looting belongs to the fascists. By tomorrow night a bomb or a shell may simultaneously write the final obituary of a scientist's dream and solve the problem of the white mice and the canaries. Where in all this horror can I find birdseed and what do white mice eat? I can not very well feed them cartridges.

I would like to write a post-dated obituary for the white mice and the canaries of Teruel, but I believe that the aviators are coming back for lunch. . . . I think I'll . . . there it is. Don't run. Hold notebook, walk rapidly as possible to the dugout.

Next Morning. January 15, I Think

The fascist aviators must really have gone to lunch for about two hours. When They should have been eating their dessert, clouds had begun to drift across the Cerro Rojo, or Red Ridge, across the valley. The brilliance of the morning had dissolved into drifting mist and haze. I had thought that we were safe. Again the air filled with motors. During all the cloudless morning we had at least been able to see the planes coming.

Things kept getting hotter and hotter. But there was no artillery fire. I learned from the wounded I carried that night that there had been no "zero hours" and "over-the-tops." The fascist infantry had attacked all afternoon. The two armies were so closely interlocked that cannon-fire was impossible.

The air-tactics of the enemy had changed. Their planes were now traveling below the clouds. Whirlwinds of twenty attack biplanes appeared at two or three places at once, diving, machine-gunning, rising and whirling back.

From the crooked strings of small combat ships high in the heavens to the hill-jumping triangles of heavy bombers, each fascist echelon and squad had its special territory, objectives and ammunition. The diagrams on the Potsdam blackboards had come to life.

Then Our planes came. I knew that they were Ours because of black anti-aircraft puffs (ours are white), because of the sudden sheet of flame and black smoke on the lower slope of the ridge where Theirs had unloaded all at once, in flight, and because of the sounds of dog fighting.

In half an hour the air was clean.

We lost one plane and They three. This we count a defeat. Tonight Their commander will telegraph Hitler and in twenty-four hours Their three lost planes will be replaced with six brand-new ones. Last night I looted the ignition diagrams from the dashboard of a Fiat we had knocked down. All the writing on it was in Italian.

Night started to fall. We wandered back to our outdoor kitchen, where pots were boiling. Again and still again there were alarms. I found a cavalrymen's dugout. We were machine-gunned until the light failed and it was comfortably dark. Their planes seem to have orders to bring no ammunition home. Whatever They have left at the end of the day they empty on us—bombs of odd weights, grenades, machine-gun chambers. They have ammunition to waste and They waste it. I did not know how low Their planes were coming. When They dive that low, you don't look. You sit with your back to what openings in the wall there may be and wait. I thought at first that a machine-gun right outside the cellar window where I sat was firing on the avions. Then I decided that the machine-gun sound must be the starting of a motorcycle. But because the sputter invariably came simultaneously with the diving of the planes, I realized that what I was hearing was the sound of explosive machine-gun bullets striking the street outside the window. Later

I saw the scars they had made, strings of craters a foot across and two to four inches deep in the frozen road. Hand-grenades had also fallen.

The results of the day's attack on the town were hardly apparent. New-bombed houses are hard to tell from old-bombed houses and the blood of those who had been killed and wounded in them had soaked into the plaster-dust in which the ruins floated. Four new-wrecked houses and eight dead. Their aim is bad. They hit only once out of ten tries but They come back ten and a hundred times. Every day the towns of the Alfambra valley became lower to the ground and dirtier. Our faces and hands and the skin beneath our clothing became dirtier and dirtier. The dead are the dirtiest of all. Not so much with blood and dust and mud, but with the grayness that so soon darkens their faces and fingernails.

There are more ways of being crippled and maimed and killed than being hit by copper, lead, iron, zinc and aluminum.

The lines on the ridge had held. After dark, life in Tortajada began where it had been broken off by the sound of the planes that morning. Horses were watered, sheep moved through the twisted streets down to the river, fires were again lit and smells of cooking mixed with the fumes of burning damp bandages and gasoline, which are the nasal trademarks of this neighborhood and of war. Women who had spent the day with their children in the fields or in the caves of the mountains back of us came back to their houses or to what had been their houses.

The first wounded arrived soon after dark. Some of them had been carried down the mountainside to the road where they had been picked up by the first munitions trucks to come out after dark. Light wounded walked in from the lines. A great jam of ambulances, loaded and empty, developed on the lip of the gully into whose side our Post is cut, in the soft, chalky, tan clay of this region, the clay which streaked the crowns and rims of so many of our hats, our elbows and knees and the seats of our trousers.

Mules were packed with flat crates of cartridges and square boxes of gre-nades and left for the ridge. Field-telephone wiremen went out to check their lines. A fortifications brigade rose out of the earth, and the cavalrymen led their horses out of concealed stables.

Since for a reason I did not yet understand I had not been sent out to pick up a load, I helped in the cave. By candlelight, stretcher after stretcher was carried down a ramp in one side of the gully and across the frozen stream in its bottom. My job was to cut off clothing. This must be done because of the danger of infection and because we must find out very quickly all the places where a man has been hit. Very few of the wounded I saw last night or at any other time were hit in only one place. Modern shrapnel breaks into fine metal spray that spreads as efficiently as water over an expensively-groomed lawn back in the States. The modern machine-gun fires so fast that it seldom hits a man in a single place. You cannot pull off a man's clothing because this motion, however careful and slight, would grind the broken ends of his bones into his muscle. We carried the clothing out of the cave to a pit. Cartridge belt, rifle, bayonet, side-arms and shoes are dumped beside the cave's mouth. Many a man got a good pair of shoes or a revolver from a Classification Post, not to speak of knapsacks, mess tins and spoons. After the clothing comes off, the evacuation doctor makes an inspection. Fresh gauze and adhesive are applied. The case gets his anti-tetanus and gas-gangrene. He is given stimulants or sedatives, a card with his name, rank, brigade and a description of injuries and medication, and then waits on a stretcher under as many blankets as we can give him until an ambulance pulls out for the Rear. The sick are also evacuated from Classification Posts and sometimes are given a night of sleep or a day or two of rest with us.

Frozen feet and ears were still coming in.

As soon as the sun had gone down, I was ordered out to Kilometer 2½, just outside of Teruel, to the English Battalion. Without lights I drove for a few miles through troops, tanks, armored cars, mules, light artillery, until I came to a railroad bridge. The brigade which was dug in behind the bridge and the embankments on both sides of it removed sandbags from the road so that I could pass. I had an unpleasant feeling that the sandbags were being replaced after I left. If this was not No-Man's Land, it was a region open to every weapon They had.

The other side of the bridge, traffic of all kinds had ceased. There were no sounds in the light of the half-full moon but for intermittent nervous single rifle shots. If rifles are psychopaths, machine-guns are maniacs.

I began to wish I could see someone or hear a voice. There is no silence like that of red-hot spent bullets as they streak across the road at night. Tracers pass with a white light like racing supercharged fireflies but I did not see many of these.

I reached the old anti-aircraft pit in which the English were and had set up their first-aid post and was given a load of light wounded. The heavy wounded had left in a truck that afternoon. Dead lay stretched out like sausages on a griddle next to the road waiting for the camion which handles them.

I was told to go to a receiving hospital twenty miles back over the mountains. The first five miles had to be done without lights, watching for old and new shell-holes. This road must be under fire during daylight. I climbed and climbed. Just as soon as I was able to turn on my lights, I was again driving blind because I had run into the snow-fog which rises on the mountains of Aragon after a day of sunlight. There was much snow at the top of the pass.

Before morning I made two more trips to Cedrillas.

Got home at 5 A.M. perhaps, to find my mattress gone. I picked out two feet of space on the floor of the ruined house in which we were sleeping, took off my shoes and immediately went to sleep.

I did not dream. If I had, the gap in the Cerro Rojo would have flashed backwards across the burned-out arc-lamps of my eyeballs. All day long we had looked at that spot, which would be called a wind-gap back in the States. Once the fascists sit in the seat of the saddle of the ridge, not only would the main road be cut but the quarter-mile cut-off which leads into Tortajada. They could hit this town with everything They have, point-blank, but for pistols. Between raids today I made a secret trip to the back of the town to see if there were some way of getting my car out through the hills, if we should be cut off. There was none.

At about four o'clock black shapes of men had started to come over the horizon. I began to think of the grenade under the front seat of my car. But the fascists should or ought not to come down on the town without artillery preparation. Had our men broken? I rather thought so when I saw a two-bar Commissar, big luger drawn, come panting up the hill as if he had unsuccessfully tried to rally his men; but he had been shooting at planes, and the black shapes that approached the Alfambra road were the first of the light wounded.

The fascist lines are still just the other side of the gap.

What I actually did dream last night was that my sideburns had first turned gray and then fallen off. How long is it since I last combed my hair?

Got up early this morning to wash, fill my radiator and tinker with my engine before the first planes should come out. We ought to have been hearing them at half-past nine, the usual hour, but sky and earth were empty of all sounds but the distant rushing of an occasional belated camion and intermittent machine-gun fire. One of our gunners, a negro, has a habit of warming up his gun with a familiar rat-tat-tat-tat-tat-tat! Shave-and-a-haircut bayrum American rhythm. Some of our fascist playmates have copied him.

The day was sullen gray dull and quiet as a mountain lake in the Adirondacks when you can hear bacon sizzle miles across the water. What's the matter? Is this Sunday or is everyone up on the Cerro Rojo dead?

Can't stand this quiet.

The Cavalry waters its horses, the fortification brigade pulls out, a company of Internationals sets up a Dora on the porch of the church (now let them come and strafe us) and the river-bank is full of tooth-brushing parties.

Then the rush, rocket vacuum express-train sounds began to arch over us. Our new batteries? Or the old ones in a new place? No gun seems to spend two nights in the same spot.

The Pasionaria 155's generally hang out in a grove of bare cherry trees half-way to Teruel.[18] As my car passes by them, the barrels seem to be directly pointed at my windows. As much as I enjoy hearing Pasionaria's many big black throats talk blue and red sheets of flame, do not like to pass this part of the road. Suppose . . . but if I start in supposing things I will not be able to keep my eyes on the road. Speedometer has registered 1,500 miles since I arrived at the Front, half at night without lights and most of it under fire of one kind or another, or beneath the omniscient eyes of the planes.

(whup-whupwhup-whup-whup-whup) Salvo. No answer yet from the visiting team. What's wrong today? Wish this bloody gray sky would clear off. Then we could see where They were. Blindfolded.

What the hell (whupwhup-whup; that's fast reloading) are they getting ready for us? Poison gas is no use in this mountainous country. Although there is not more than one mask for every twenty men, we'd be safe because gas sinks to the lowest parts of the ground. Into our Post, for example, among the wounded. It would crawl under the candle-lit stretchers up to the faces of the wounded, like a big green snake and say, "Darling, look at me. I've come for you now and I'm never going to give you up." "Yes, dear," he answers, vomiting. "Just a minute."

In case (whup-whupwhup) They use the gas we know They have on hand—and that will be on the day Chamberlain gets the wool securely on the eyes of all the English and his hand fast about their many throats, and he never will—we have orders to climb; to piss on our handkerchiefs and breathe through them. Meanwhile we save our handkerchiefs for our noses and our urine for manure.

Give me a good 2000-shell day! This silence gets on my nerves.

In the bottom of the garbage pail ants fight each other. Or is it the garbage which fights the ants? In the belly of a caterpillar the man who wrote the Lord's prayer on the head of a glass pin fights Colonel Tom Thumb's wife's fetuses.

---

18. This powerful field artillery gun was named after La Pasionaria, Dolores Ibarúrri, a Communist leader from the Basque country whose voice and rhetorical style was renowned for its power.

Have I a hangover? When did I have my last drink? Will I ever have another? It's so quiet that you can hear maggots digging in the corpses a mile away by air, up on the ridge.

So cold that trench-mortar shells freeze into the sky at the hesitant peak of their steep orbit. In the morning Our planes come out and Our aviators collect ammunition in baskets. Break the heavy stuff free of the frozen air with crowbars, tow it back to fascist lines, let it go.

Same Day. 10 P.M. Kitchen of Cuevas Hospital

Got a load of light wounded this afternoon, mostly Germans and French, to relay to Cuevas for evacuation further back by big ambs. Cave has been getting too crowded and large slow cars are not good for daylight work.

Ten minutes out from the Post I saw a squad which had been filling a bomb-hole run into a culvert. Ee-eee-eeee-EEEEE came the sound of a motor falling straight down on me like a meteor. Could hear the noise not only through my shut windows and metal roof but right through my bones, as loud as a dentist's drill.

Couldn't leave the wounded piled high in the seats and run off into the fields. Nowhere was there a side road or even a tree.

I stepped on the gas and headed for the railroad tunnel a hundred yards ahead of me, slightly off the road.

Glad there was no locomotive coming the other way. Glad there was a tunnel. Otherwise . . . but the day is full of otherwise. That's our business. The department clerk rings up a sale, the bookkeeper writes an entry, the grocer wraps up a herring, the ambulance driver dodges a plane, but it keeps coming closer and closer. No one can play a roulette wheel more than a hundred thousand times without winning. The longer we stay out here, the worse the odds are against us. If we stay long enough in Spain, all of us will die. All of us, not excepting anyone.

Once my car was fifteen feet deep in the tunnel, I got out and listened to the buzzing of the baffled squad of hornets until they fixed on another victim, further up the road.

"*Faut-il vraiment partir?*" asked one of the wounded as I started to back up out of the tunnel. He didn't want to leave. Why doesn't Crome transfer the surgical hospital to this tunnel?

"I don't think about the past and I don't think about the future," said Al Hawk (he had his camion shot out from under him trying to run into Teruel during daylight). "I don't write letters or expect to get them. I just drive, that's all, I just drive."

When I got to Cuevas, I pulled up to the brook that runs down from the hills, mixed a basin of liquid mud, and painted my car. I had painted out the red crosses, outlined in white on my fenders and body long ago in Alcorisa. Dirt is by far the best camouflage. The elaborate surrealism used during the World War is useless, because avions can see your shadow no matter how well camouflaged you are. Mud gives our cars the same color as the roads and the landscape and prevents the sun from sending up tell-tale reflection signals. Windshield is particularly treacherous because of its outward sloping angle. Most drivers coat windshield with mud, all but a foot-wide circle in front of their eyes.

While smearing my right rear fender, I noticed a shrapnel hole. When? Where? How?

My wounded left with Parker, who now drives the Harvard bus.[19] The other chófer is no longer on his job. I can't find out what's become of him.

Park* is the ideal chófer. He drives all night, sleeps in his car all morning and works on her engine all afternoon. A quiet small fellow with black hair, deepset blue eyes and a cleft chin, he came to Spain to enter the Air Force. He seldom talks and never asks for a cigarette and denies the possession of a single end-wrench, much less a tire pump. Parker knows his business. If I had known mine, I should never have lost my own tire pump.

I had to wait until sunfall until I could get the Divisional barber (who also shaves stomachs, heads and legs for the surgeons) to cut my hair. The barber can no longer be persuaded to come out of his cave in the cliffs during the day. He and others who were with him say that this morning's planes, after going over the town with a little light stuff, heaved a bushel of grenades side-wise at the black mouth of the cave halfway up the cliff.

The field-kitchen has moved out of town. How about the hospital?

Someone calls me. Stretcher duty. Another load just came in. Where will we put them? Hardly room for my feet among the stretchers on the kitchen floor next to the open fire. The surgeons say that warmth is the best drug.

Later. Back in the Cuevas kitchen. It was Lewis, the negro chófer who had pushed me out of the way of the strays last night or the night before that at Teruel, whom we laid out on the operating table and stripped. He had

---

* dead

19. Frank Reilly Parker was born in the United States but lived in Vancouver. A March 1938 article referred to him as the "Lucky Irishman" because he had outlived many of his ambulances without being touched.

crashed his truck. You cannot drive forever on crowded roads at night without using your headlights.

The skin over his long swimmer's muscles was full of purple and golden lights under the single lamp over the operating table. Internal injuries. Major B. was about to perform a laparotomy.

Bob Hamilton put the mask over the wide-open questioning eyes.[20] For a while there was no sound but the rustle of the dilating, collapsing diaphragm. Bob advanced the needle. The breaths became longer and for the first time painful. Muffled whimpers began to come deep out of Lewis' neck, and his hands held the edges of the table so tightly that the knuckles were yellow. The eyes over Major B.'s mouth mask beckoned to Bob, who again pushed the needle. Desperation entered the profound and regular lamentation, and the fear of insanity. I might have been listening to the cries of an undersea diver about to suffocate. The light of the single lamp was so full of ether that I put my handkerchief over my nose.

Bob, perched high on a stool with four fingers of each hand under Lewis' jaw, began to shift his thumbs from the mask to the eyes, to observe the dilation of the pupils.

The barber shaved the patient's stomach. Iodine, hardly less dark or less purple than the skin, was poured over the solar plexus and then peroxide.

The hands had not relaxed although the hopeless whimpering continued. Major B. took his knife and with swift violent gestures cut a slit from the bottom of Lewis' breast bone through inch-deep whitish fat almost to the navel.

Retractors and laparotomy sponges were applied. There was so little blood that the rags turned no deeper than faint pink.

For half an hour B. reached far into Lewis' stomach, lifting out organ after organ, holding arm-lengths of intestine up to the light, and then stuffing the viscera back with what seemed to me to be sudden brutal gestures. I saw nothing of the reverence and ritualistic tenderness which I had always imagined to be the manner of surgeon's hands.

At length a small tear in the mesentery[21] (?) was found. In five minutes B.

---

20. Rob or Bob Hamilton, aka Robert Bell and Tommy Burns, was born in Scotland in 1910 but went to Spain from Canada, listing his occupation as a tailor. In Spain he worked as an operating room anesthesiologist and survived the war.
21. An anatomical term for a part of the peritoneum that attaches organs to the back of the abdomen.

had tied a few swift hard stitches and then closed the opening in the stomach with the motions of a housewife tying a roast.

We carried Lewis to the ward. One of the nurses tells me that he will be on his feet in ten days.

I have never seen flowers in our hospitals. There is no candy, no fruit, no radio, no relatives, mothers or sweethearts.

Three of our nurses, all Internationals, have had to be sent back to base hospitals. Not that they were wounded, or that they folded up or became hysterical; they burned out, that's all, and now we have three new florences.

Begin to think that the entire brigade could use a little rest. We have been at the Front for only two cold weeks, but the men could use a rest and warm food. I have not taken what they have. I feel that I'm good for the rest of the campaign. I suffer from nothing worse than lice, ten chilblained fingers, a recurrent sore throat, perpetually infected fingers, and a gnawing lust for chocolate. Lice are not so bad. They're afraid of you all day long and lie low. At night they begin to go for long walks in the woods but you are so sleepy that you let them have their way. I could undress into a pail of gasoline but I wouldn't dare to light a cigarette, not even one of the toothpick pills we have been twisting, for hours afterwards.

We kill lice, the fascists kill us, we kill Them; and what does the Pope say? Pius thinks that it's all right for us to kill lice and for the fascists to kill us, but he doesn't think we ought to fire back. What does the cub of the Roman she-wolf say? "War, the most beautiful of sports." I agree with him. War would be the most beautiful of sports, if only the other side had no guns.

Since it was a slow night, several of the chófers had gathered in the kitchen. Because of their work, drivers know more about the condition of the Front than many of their officers and most of the men. They are the town gossips of the war. The information we get from and tell only to each other is extremely useful. If I pass one of the 35th Division ambs or trucks on the road, especially if I am driving towards the Front, I always stop and ask for the latest news. This practice has saved many a car and many a life. The other drivers of the Thirty-fifth envy me because I supposedly am able to chisel cigarettes from the officer for whom I work. I envy them because they visit the Front lines more regularly than I do, because they often carry helpers, because they don't move so much and don't miss so many meals and so much sleep.

Will Roosevelt and Blum let us buy trench mortars, planes and tanks and medium artillery and good anti-aircraft?[22] We have everything else. We have

22. Leon Blum, Socialist Prime Minister of France, reluctantly accepted the Non-

more than They had, eight and perhaps six months ago, but They keep getting more and more. I estimate that They have five planes to our one, eight
cannon and tanks to our one, twenty or thirty trench-mortars of all weights
to our one, and God knows how many machine guns.

The assortment of empty shells on the staircase of the Clinic in Teruel tes-
tifies to the variety of equipment They possess. Hear of many sorts of strange
new weapons They use: infra-red airplane cameras that pierce camouflage,
double-calibre machine guns, theremite anti-tank shells. Yesterday afternoon I picked a lead slug two-thirds of an inch in diameter off the floor of my
car. It must have come in through the window, spent, or fallen out of one of
the wounded I carried. Dum-dums, hopelessly out of date and humanitarian,
have been replaced by modern explosive bullets.

Washington, London and Paris are the real battlefields, not Teruel. We
can hold out for a long time, but not forever. Negrin says, "We beat Franco
in the first three months of the war; now we will have to defeat Hitler and
Mussolini."

I should never have come so near to the kitchen fire. Getting very sleepy. I
wish that the conference which Crome and Major B. and Captain S. are having upstairs while B. operates would end.

When and if I get back to the States, I'm going to drive a taxi or a carriage.
I'll wait at the hackstand in front of the Metropolitan Opera House and drive
society couples slowly through Central Park on spring nights, in a smell of
bath salts, gardenias and dew-wet privet.

Don't feel as if I'll ever be able to make love to a girl again. Long for
the smell of something really sweet and fragrant. Sleep, real sleep, has this
aroma. Sleep and fragrance have become the same thing. Tonight before I lie
down—I wonder where—I'll allow myself a sniff at the letter from my girl I
have been carrying all this time in my breast-pocket, next to my spare pair
of glasses.

Apology. If all of the drivers and infantrymen, nurses and doctors who
appear in this account seem without individuality, that is because all but the
strongest personalities have become submerged in the common urgency of
our purpose in Spain. I have hundreds of friends but I know few of their
names and nothing of their backgrounds, lives and mental habits. No one
talks about his former life or his hopes for the future. Almost without exception all of us want to return to our countries, unmutilated if possible, but to

---

Intervention Agreement, barring war material from Spain.

our native lands. I had a notion, before I left, that I would make my future in the country for which I now fight, if you can call driving an ambulance fighting. But some day I hope to go home. We are in Spain strictly on business. The real fight is at home.

January 16. At Field Garage. Near Peralejos

Got home last night at 6 A.M. S. inspected all first-aid posts in our new positions (moving almost every night, the battalions creep up on Teruel. The adroitness with which we are moved and the positions we are given avoid many casualties. Looks as if we were being saved for the Third Act) and dispensed the cambric bandages taken from the wrecked clinic; gasoline for the battalion ambs; and a little light luxury in the way of candy, condensed milk and two thermos bottles of coffee. Slept profoundly at the wheel while S. was in the lines, dreaming or perhaps actually seeing white tracers and red-hot strays crossing the road.

When I awoke, cold and stiff as a robot, false dawn had begun to rise like the aura of a single incendiary shell, although the moon still shone on white ruined farmhouses and the fascist hills that rose across the vineyards, all very super-romantic in the style of the Bavarian posts of the 1890's. Immensee is a long way from Berchtesgaden. Gentle lake scenery in summertime, the heart-breaking summer songs at night. . . . Have to stop thinking of things like these which after all are no more forbidden to me than to many a Chicago laundry worker and a Pittsburgh scrublady.

"Some day!" . . . these secret words are the hope of many hundreds of millions of people but never were they spoken so much and with such soft and savage longing as today in Spain. Never have men hated their guns so much as we do.

The English, having left their trucks at the bottom of the hill, came up the road in the moonlight. Too tired to swear, the men were wordless. The torn blankets over heads and shoulders and tied like skirts around the waist, the shoes wrapped with rags, the rifles on their shoulders gave them the appearance of a battalion of women beggars. Ranks of stretcher-bearers with eight-foot spearlike poles added to the Biblical quality of the scene. The Volunteers flowed around my car like sheep and turned down the communication trench which leads to the Front lines. These are the men who feel that the eye of the world's conscience is on them.

Did not admire the communication trench. It had been dug deep but straight. No trench must run more than eight feet in a straight line, because of the planes. Our English are famous for their bad luck. The positions they are given seem invariably to turn into open air slaughterhouses. At Jarama a company of Moors surrendered to the English. They came across No-Man's Land singing the "Internationale," right arm hooked in the Popular Front salute. It was not until the Moors were on top of our men that we saw the grenades each of them held in his clenched fist. Since that time, all who desert from fascist lines are given orders to clap their hands as they come towards our lines. Men who incessantly strike their palms together cannot carry even tiny black and red torpedoes imported by Franco from Italy.

I was back in Tortajada before sunrise. Al G., the Post Commissar, had laid out a mattress and extra blankets.[23] After three hours of luxurious sleep, coffee, bread and jam were brought to me.

I pulled my car slightly out of town before the first air raid, put my front seat on the ground, grenade and all, and slept until lunch time, with the sunlight driving through my filthy clothes and cold-clogged head like beautiful warm antiseptic. Although I was well within the miss-zone I slept well, lulled by the regular breaking of shells on the ridge and by the spattering of the Maxim which is Tortajada's single defense against the air. After seven days of conscientious effort, They haven't yet managed to cut the bridge at the bottom of the hill.

Everything up on the ridge is in good shape. They shell us and we wait.

I write at this moment from the shade and protection of the bridge in which our field garage is installed.

At one o'clock Block, Finn and I left for Cuevas, in the order named, all cars empty, well camouflaged by mud, and three hundred yards apart. Half a kilometer the other side of Villalba Paja (South Whitton), I heard the ee-eee-eeee-EEEEE sound. No tunnel was handy this time. No cut, no trees, no side road. As I lay in the ditch, head down, the sound of the shelling disappeared and a fleet of motorcycles sped by me.

But the motorcycle sounds were streams of double-calibre M-gun bullets exploding against the hard surface of the road.

Finn's radiator was drilled. One of his tires was flat. Block had two front flats. His radiator leaked like a honeycomb in the sun. It had not been hit by the bullets but by the shrapnel and the rock splashed upwards by the road. The body of Block's ambulance was sieved.

Finn rammed a bar of kitchen soap into the hole into his radiator. Block's

---

23. Albert Gottlieb, aka Al Stone, commissar of American hospitals, left his safe job to fight with the Mac-Pap Battalion. "I didn't come here to work in a hospital," he said, "and if I ever go back, it'll only be as a patient."

was hopeless. There were three flats to fix in a hurry, with the single tire pump, the one set of inner tube patch and the two lugwrenches among us.

We did not run either car off the road because this would have ruined the tires. I lent my spare to Finn and he cleared out. In not more than fifteen minutes, I swear it, Block and I had repaired his two flats, with one eye on our work and the other on the sky. Twice we had to run. More planes on this road than speedcops on Riverside Drive.

Once Block's tires were fixed, I towed him off with the wire cable I lately organized from a Spanish camion.

That was two or three hours ago. I had come to the field garage for gas from the two drums on the platform of the wrecked railway station and for expert advice on my transmission, which began to throw oil this morning.

The mechanics were out on the road on a wrecking errand, so I had to wait. Phil Cooper (real name), the intellectual and former writer, trusted with the best truck in the Brigade, lent me the tools I lacked.[24] For a good hour he stayed with me at the railroad station which had been bombed twice that morning because of its two drums of gasoline, when he could easily have gone to a safer place.

My transmission was repaired only when Joe Foster, crack negro mechanic, arrived. We drove to a wrecked Chevvie. Foster went under her with a wrench and got what he needed.[25]

Our main auto-parque with its workshop on wheels is a hundred miles away from Alcorisa, in which the brigade *Intendencia* has also been kept. The front-line garage consists of half a dozen of our toughest mechanics and a truckload of used tires and tools. The last garage between us and the fascists is a drum of gas, a toolkit and our two best men, in the lines themselves. Chófers are continually wearing out. After one week of tag with the planes, the driver of the water tanker had to be sent back to Alcorisa. The tanker is full of welded bullet holes. A great square patch of iron is a memorial tablet to the shell which went through her, lengthwise, at Brunete, without exploding or scratching the driver.

The 15th Brigade chófers who tried to drive into Teruel three days ago were not lucky. A shell lifted both of them out of their cab, without touching the rest of the truck. I have tried to find out their names so that I might

---

24. Phil Cooper, aka Jack Leavitt, an auto worker from Michigan, served at Brigade headquarters.
25. Joseph K. Foster was a World War I veteran whose previous war wounds disqualified him for combat in Spain.

write an epitaph, but I have been unable to find out anything about these two comrades except that they were both Finnish Americans.

This place is No-Man's Land during daytime. And at night? The war's called off every sundown except for mortars and bombing parties.

Think I'll get that grenade out of my car.

Better save it. In case the side road to Tortajada is cut tomorrow, I'll blow up my car. "American Friends of Washington D.C.," reads the inscription on the door, "To the Spanish People."

January 17. Tortajada

We lost two hundred yards last night and we didn't get them back. Hear that the rebels are burying the limbers of their seventy-fives. The high angle thus obtained transforms them into howitzers. They can now shoot right over the ridge onto the Alfambra road.

Yesterday afternoon, passed the Divisional Farmacy truck. Both cars stopped as officers got out and talked.

Heard no sound but earth suddenly swished against cars and men. Stepped on the gas.

Shells break very near the Post. Cooks and stretcher-bearers grumble. Why doesn't Captain S. move us out of here before all our cars are smashed?

Later. Cuevas kitchen. Medical staff again in conference. Five men lie in a ditch listening to each plane as it flattens out of a power dive. Machine guns fire one thousand explosive bullets per minute from an altitude of a hundred feet at the road, at the car parked at its side and the five men in the ditch. One soldier shudders but does not move. The second ruins his trousers. Two others lie as limp as fresh-killed dead. The fifth runs out into the fields. What is fear? What is courage?

Late this afternoon I was called out of my dugout to rush two belly-cases five miles down the road to the surgical hospital at Cuevas. I rolled at eight miles an hour which is belly-cases speed when the road is good. On the type of road which is built out of a *barranco*-bottom or a cowpath by the engineers in one night it is impossible to haul heavy wounded faster than two miles an hour.

On the way to Cuevas I had the good luck not to be strafed. Could not have stopped. Coming back, empty, four *Transmissiones* men gave me the high-sign: forefingers pointed up at the sky awe-ful eyes opened to standing ovals. I had of course kept my door open, swinging on its hinges, and performed my usual acrobatics: cut the switch, slam on the emergency brake, roll out on the running board—so fast that I almost beat the four men who warned me into the deep part of the ditch which we had all automatically found. There we lay while a patrol of attack bi-planes turned their guns on my car and my four comrades.

I was not the one who ruined his trousers, or he who shuddered or the *soldado* who ran off into the fields. I lay there on my stomach, hands on the back of my neck, listening and wondering. Would They come over once or five times? Would it be sensible to try to find another ditch further from the road, between raids? Was there another ditch? Did I remember a good deep shell-hole in this neighborhood, or a culvert? Was it really true that explosive bullets always broke upwards and never came down? Had my car been hit, would I be able to borrow a tire-pump, should I get up and drive off the road? How long would it be before my number came up? Had I better take my first chance to goldbrick at some soft job in the Rear? How long was it to sunset? Wouldn't it be more sensible to fight my next war up at the North Pole where the sun went out for six months at a time? Was that the noise of the planes coming back? Was it really true that if you turn your face up, They can spot the giveaway color of your skin and perhaps catch the reflection of the sun on your glasses?

I am not able to say if I was afraid at this or any other time. The *soldado* who ruined his pants was not afraid. The sound of planes has the effect of emptying the bowels of many men. Neither was the guy who shuddered afraid.

As for the comrade who ran out of the ditch and gave us all away, he was afraid. *We shot him in the leg, aiming not at the man but at Fear.* There was still some hope that the planes had not seen us.

Fear is running and panic. If you can lie still or drive on or keep firing you are not afraid; no matter what thoughts cross your mind, no matter how much you shiver. If you stick at your job, you don't have the time to wonder if you're afraid. Men who break and run are temporarily insane.

Last week I drove for a tubercular Captain who sometimes thinks he came to Spain to die. Cannot believe this because he continually does everything he can to minimize the chances of being hit. In addition to his illness his nerves are so delicate and sensitive that, after thirty-six or forty-eight hours of work in and about the Front lines, he screws himself up into such a state that the least thing that goes wrong produces a frightful hideous rage. Soon after that his fever goes up and he has to sleep. I do not recommend working for a man who sometimes thinks he wants to die.

Major B. never takes a chance. Unlike many of the other medical officers, he never makes night trips to the trenches, in order to get shot at a little, to chisel cigarettes or brandy, or to use his Leica. He is a surgeon and he sticks to his table. Major B. has not been in the hospital trench more than once or twice. It is not good for the morale of the men for the officers to be the first to take cover.

On the other hand, Captain Duclos, the Belgian surgeon, sits at the hospital door reading his newspapers and never looks up into the sky when the planes come over.[26] No one has ever seen him in a trench. We think he is brave, but that he is also a show-off.

When you get "on the griddle," as the men say, pinned flat to the earth or inside it for hours while They let you have everything They've got, you begin to curse yourself for ever having come to Spain. You think that you will desert the first minute you get a chance and not mind if you land over the French border unconscious and naked, just so long as you can get away from War.

Once the firing lets up and you are able to get a little sleep or coffee, you think that you won't desert, but that you will somehow find a soft job at the Rear. But a few hours later, especially if you have gone back from the Front, you have forgotten even shame and hope like hell to get back into the fighting, fast. Life, much less war, would not be possible if it were not for this wonderful and terrible resilience which lies in us and is our greatest treasure.

More about fear. Two, three, four afternoons ago or when was it? I passed by a culvert which had just taken a bomb. Of the six Spanish who stood on the road like temporarily paralyzed maniacs, only two would help me dig for the four or five of their comrades who had just been buried alive.

All of the men who had crawled into the culvert to get away from the planes were dead and so mangled that they would be of no use to Doctor Saxton.

January 18. Tortajada

Things have become very, very serious.

Machine-gun nests are being set up all over town with much haste. Four of them constantly chatter at the sky. An anti-tank gun has arrived. No more children and very few women left in the town. Cavalry just left, crossed the Alfambra road and charged up to the ridge, spread out to minimize the shellbursts, pulled out their carbines, dismounted, went up into the lines. Never

---

26. "Captain Duclos" is likely Captain Rene Dumont, a Belgian surgeon attached to the British medical group.

heard of anything braver. Men were needed fast and mountain trail is now too much under fire to permit passage of kitchen truck, much less camions of troops.

Clouds, cold and gray, wind. Four great black trimotors rushed out of a gap in the hills, banked, unloaded fire and black smoke on the bridge before I had a chance to get underground. Missed it, for the twentieth time.

Armored cars, leafless branches stacked against their already camouflaged flanks, are parked at regular intervals on the road.

The dump of our light batteries below the ridge was hit by an incendiary shell and still burns.

The engineers came back into town saying that They could not reach our lines.

Last night the Captain suddenly set out to look for a new place for the Post. First drove to K 2½. Good. The crossroads were still in our hands. Big cannon tanks were drawn up beside the house into which S. went for a conference. Spoke to one of the drivers, twenty-two-year-old steelworker from Chicago. He was the commander of an entire company of heavy tanks. Said that there are no wounded tank-drivers; only dead ones.

Before S. came back, I looted the machine-gun belt out of a fallen Fiat. Metal. One shell blue (tracer), next red (explosive), next one black (dumdum). Black circles were painted on underside of wings.

January 19. Still in Tortajada.

No change, no news. Nothing happens.

The Gap is a beach on which combers of shells hiss and foam, break and hiss. They shell us for two days then attack for hours. Sometimes They bury Their dead. Sometimes we bury Them. For nineteen days Franco has wanted the Cerro Gordo the way a jailed dope-fiend wants heroin. In nineteen days he has pushed his front-line trenches two hundred yards forwards. Not once has he used his Italian troops or his Moorish cavalry. We therefore know that the weight of the attack is yet to come.

The two heavyweights, squared off toe to toe, trade punches with bare fists. No more rounds, no more gong, no more time out. One of the home boy's dukes is tied behind him.

We hear that the Non-Intervention Committee has again convened. Good. We know that these gentlemen spend carfare to see each other only when the Republic shows unmistakable signs of strength, in order to concoct new ways of hamstringing us.

Twice a month the Non-Intervention Committee volunteers to buy the

Republic an expensive coffin, but the corpse always rises. The Geneva ice-box in which flowers are kept fresh for the burial of minorities and the militant enemies of fascism will not just yet be unloaded on us.

How a Village Dies

The first two breaks in the telephone lines and the hole in the sewer are easily and quickly fixed. A month later the power lines are ripped down, along with the telephone wires. Repairs take longer.

No lives have yet been lost and little precious sweat is wasted at digging. When the first Grade A Day of Judgment comes, the village loses three hundred feet of power lines and two telephone poles, nine houses, the corner of the local garage, the barber shop and the empty drygoods store. Eight dead and forty wounded. Electric lights will never again be lit because a new transformer cannot be obtained. Partial telephone service stays until the fifth minor raid.

Digging has now begun in earnest. Zigzag backyard trenchlets appear, tunnels are dug from wine cellars to chambers hollowed out under the hard surface of the main street. Cliff dwellings become over-crowded. School is adjourned and children spend the day in shepherds' huts cut in the fields with their mothers.

Most of the digging is unfortunately done in earth rather than in rock and there is little timber for re-inforcement of the soft roofs of the *refugios*.

Firewood gets scarce. Coal, needed for the war industries in the big cities, no longer reaches the village. The troops billeted in town, having burned up the beams of the blasted houses and the riverside poplars, get to work on the roadside trees. Field-stoves are omnivorous and feet are always wet and cold.

The second day of major trial comes. Telephone and telegraph connections with the outside world are gone for good. The main sewer has been hopelessly smashed. Energy and material for repair will become available only after the war is over.

Houses now have none of the conveniences of city life. Water still runs in the village well, from which it is carried on foot in jugs, since all mules have either been eaten or killed or sent to the front.

Although the end is now near, people still remain in the village because they do not know where else to go, because they think their birthplace has been so much punished that it has become immune, because each family thinks that its home will not be hit no matter what happens.

After the final disillusionment, water no longer flows in the village well and the sheep trough runs dry.

As if the fountain in the main square had been the heart of the village, the town now dies. Big two-wheeled wagons leave loaded high with pots, mattresses, tin trucks, the family canary or partridge, and pulled by the remaining plow horses, dogs trotting under the axle. The father of the eldest child walks at the bridle. Women and little girls in black overcoat shawls follow the hearse.

Only the road, rough with filled and re-filled craters, now connects the ruins of the village with the ruins of the next town. Seventy-five percent of the healthy male adults are away at the Front. Ten percent of all old people, women and children have been killed. Disease and malnutrition have killed five percent of the rest.

But fifteen percent of the town's original population stay on, living like maggots in a corpse, because the site of their native village is still the best place they know.

The Militiamen so often billeted in these dead villages hate them because there are so few women to do laundry, because eggs cannot be had, because there is nothing to buy, not even wine.

At night, when fires are lit in the ruins behind open doors and glassless windows, these dead towns are wild places. Gunbarrels point over shoulders at the heavens—man's newest, greatest, and perhaps last enemy.

The barrage crawls nearer. Sky is gray, cold, deceptive. Tortajada is getting a little too hot, I think.

The lines still hold. Nothing else matters.

Call it January 22 or 23. Corbalan and Valdecebro

Intermission of several days. I am able to write because I have at last slept, I have had coffee and bread and jam and because I got up very early this morning. I use the operating table as desk.

Some day I will be able to put down the entire story of the last two or three days, during which it has been hardly less difficult to stay alive than it has to do one's work. I did both.

But the lines still hold. Franco got the two hundred yards he needed to cut the Alfambra road, but the lines still hold.

Leaving the Cuevas hospital on the afternoon of the latest and heaviest bombing, the Captain rode on the running board, eyes up.

At the Tortajada bridge we passed and stopped the Division Farmacy truck. S. and Captain Casimir, in charge of medical supplies, dismounted and talked.[27] Casimir is the best dressed, the cleanest, the most warlike and dashing, the wisest jocular bastard in the Division. As the two officers stood conversing, there was the sound of a steamroller traveling a hundred miles an hour hitting the side of a sleeping elephant. Specks of dirt peppered with fine metal sprayed against the side of my car. Mud splashed into Casimir's beautiful blond wavy hair. Before my foot had pressed on the self-starter—I am getting pretty good at starting my car fast these days—the smile had come off Casimir's face and he and his truck were a half mile down the road.

(Later, when I told this story to Major B., he asked me how many more times I was killed before sunset.)

I think I'll be glad when I go back to my old boss, the Major.

Drove back to T.—lightlessly dodging dead horses, wrecked trucks, cannon tanks, files of men crouched along the ditches and marching like Indians in blankets—in my new paint-job of mud, guaranteed proof against shine-signals to the enemy. Made trip to Tortajada back to Teruel for a load of English.

When I had returned, orders had at last come to move the surgical hospital out of Cuevas. Probably just in time. I was ordered to move the Major, his team and their baggage back over the mountains to Corbalan and then return to Tortajada, all before daybreak. Six hours of night-camouflage were left.

Took a last look at the Divisional Hospital standing there in the moonlight. A big new American Diamond T. army truck stood at the doors, loading the last of the beds. I had grown fond of this joint.

"For Christ's sake, Oscar," I asked the assistant surgeon, as we were about to leave, "have you got a cigarette?"

"Open my suitcase and take out two packs of Camels."

He actually trusted me to go into his baggage.

I drove B.'s team for Corbalan, eighteen miles away from Teruel by road and three miles by air.

Halfway up the mountains the ambulance which had been following me with the rest of the staff broke down. The sun would come up in two hours.

---

27. Casimir DeSevetskoe (aka Charles Devetsko) was an ambulance driver from the Bronx, New York. He served with Dr. Rintz and performed construction work and repairs at the hospitals in Spain.

And this part of the road would then be wide open to the fascist artillery. I made two round trips to Corbalan before I had emptied both cars of baggage and staff.

By the time the sun came up on mountain heights lofty and magnificent as the brow of a great tragedienne looking down on battlefields covered with thick velvety hoarfrost, the first white shell-puffs were already visible against the slopes beside us; and we had been unable to fix the carburetor that had betrayed us.

I towed the stricken ambulance and chófers Rosenkranz and Guilden-stern (real names, Veltford and Felton) behind a hill.[28] Again in Corbalan I found and dispatched a camion to the rescue, although one of the rules of war is that a good car should not be lost because of a bad car.

My orders had been to return to Tortajada and Captain S. before sunrise. What should I do? The sensible thing was to hide my car from the sight of all officers and go to sleep in the sun.

1) I gloriously obeyed nature on a sunlit hoarfrosted hill that overlooked the big batteries which had already begun to fire down into the belly of the fascist lines.

2) Gulped cold can of condensed milk (organized from the local *Inten-dencia*) from a hole made by my screwdriver.

3) Reported to an officer, who told me to go "back to the inferno," after I had assured him that I knew a newly built military road which led down a gully into Tortajada.

Pulled out for my noisy home. The side road was sinuous, most of it in the gulley and the rest heavily shaded. Ideal cover: but there was no one, not one military militiaman or shepherd to be seen. I would have to depend on my ears. More and more nervous, I pulled hard on my cigarette and listened.

---

28. Ted Veltfort, politicized as a college student at Princeton University, transferred to Swarthmore College, and left his undergraduate studies in 1937 to drive an ambulance in Spain. Nearly fifty years later, during the U.S.-backed Contra war in Nicaragua, Veltfort initiated a project among the Veterans of the Abraham Lincoln Brigade to raise money for ambulances for the embattled government of Nicaragua, a replay of the humanitarian aid movement of the 1930s. "Felton" is Milton Felsen, who was an undergraduate at the University of Iowa before going to Spain. Wounded at Brunete, he completed his service as an ambulance driver. During World War II, he was captured in North Africa by the German army. He published a memoir, *The Anti-Warrior*, in 1989.

Soon the sounds of my engine and my creaking springs and chasis, pierced by the rattles, squeaks and whimperings that came from two months of running over horrible roads and no roads at high speeds, began to fill not only my ears but the sky above me.

I heard all kinds of new complaints coming out from under my hood, and each began to sound like a plane. I longed for the sight of a truck or a single human being above ground. Several times I stopped. As the sound of my engine died away, I heard nothing but the buzz of insects and the crash of distant shells.

I cannot understand why this sudden fit of fear, the kind of panic we get walking alone at night in the woods or sleeping in a house whose shutters rattle in the wind, came over me as I wound among cedar trees down the brown sunlit hillside.

Perhaps I was afraid that the lines might just have changed or that Their artillery might have been dragged nearer during the night; or that Tortajada itself was in Their hands, for all I knew. The positions and the fortunes of this war change so rapidly that no officer can guarantee the safety of his chófers.

Once I hit the Alfambra road with all its grief, I was happy because I could again look at human beings. I was glad to see my friends alive (especially the two Scotch cooks) and our cars unhurt. Crawled into the deepest end of the Post cave to a stiff blood-stained stretcher. With relief I observed by the light of a candle struck into the clay wall that both men in the stretchers alongside of me were dead. If they were alive, they would have been making too much noise. The sleep which came to me like a hand at my throat was more of a ride than a rest because of the shaking of the ground and the trembling of the atmosphere. The air of these bombarded dugouts is that of a sea-level cave during a storm.

Feeling as if I had been drunk for four days and nights, I was called back to my car. After so much sleepless driving at the Front, eating becomes impossible. Your dry throat is thirsty only for tobacco. Losing interest in the tides of battle, all sights and sounds become separate, and have no reference to each other. People speak to you and you listen to their voice coming from a great distance. Everything is horrible and funny at the same time. Bruises and scratches do not hurt. Wounds would not hurt. Only one thing has importance: keeping your car on the road. If it broke down or crashed, you would have to walk and you couldn't walk. All of the problems of modern politics and the future fate of the world become solvable. Once you wake up on the farther shore of sleep, you will astonish your friends and the world with your exquisitely simple formulas for producing instantaneous paradise on earth.

My car had already been loaded with wounded. Before I mounted to the wheel, I pulled my girl's letter out of my pocket, shameless in front of Captain S., and smelled its perfume, for strength. Lentheric's "Tweed."

Another amb went with us. Several times we had to push it up the hillside of the cedars, not because of mud or snow or gravel, but because of the violence of the slope. Months ago the mind of some Colonel or General, foreseeing the present emergency, had ordered this side road to be made. But two hours of rain would wash it out. General Mud is still Field Marshal.

Towards the end of the afternoon I found that I was driving back down our artillery mountainsides with the sun shining through my dirty windshield into my eyes. We could see five miles of our front-line trenches as they wound in and out of gulleys and rides [sic] because of the smoke of the shells that were continuously being heard along the whole five mile stretch of lines, breaking not fifty yards behind our men or fifty yards in front of them, but right on top of their dugouts. How many batteries is Franco using? His 75's and 155's must be hub-to-hub. I'm beginning to understand Leicaphilia. Wish I had brought a camera with me to Spain instead of a pencil.

Andy, back on the job after two days of rest, stopped ahead of us. He said that he wanted to look at his tires before we went into the lines and unsuccessfully tried to beg my last inner tube from me.

I believe that Captain S. was glad for the halt. We were right above the crossroads at Kilometer 4. Franco, having brought the Alfambra road under artillery fire, has now decided that he wants the milestone at Kilometer 4 more than he wants his wife. All sizes of pop-pop hand-to-hand stuff were bubbling below us in the bass of concussion grenades used only in infantry attacks.

"Captain," I said, "in ten minutes or fifteen at the outside, the sun will go down."

"So?"

"So our cars won't be profiled against the horizon if we wait another ten minutes, and their gunners won't have the sun over their shoulder, and we won't have it in our eyes."

"In 'another ten minutes,'" S. at the peak of his battle-frenzied screwed-up nerves, imitating me with all the mimicry and anger at his command, "in 'another ten minutes' four belly cases will die because no ambulances have been able to get to them. Come on. Let's go."

"Suppose no ambulances do get through, Captain?"

If I had not spoken perhaps S. would have found one excuse or another to wait until the sun had gone down.

"Keep at least three hundred yards behind Andy," he ordered in a voice softened by the consequences of his decision, "and travel at a variable speed; fast, slow, fast, slow, forty to sixty miles an hour, say."

Service had gotten by the turnpike and had headed up the hill to Teruel.[29] When I was within fifty yards of the crossroads—*wham, flash, smell*, four times more, in the same spot. Fleas of earth, stone and metal, all flying at the same speed, darkened the air. A hornet stung my insensible scalp but no metal sounded against my car.

"Seventy-fives," said S.

"Reloading now?"

"Yes. Better pull out."

A whole battery of seventy-fives, trained on the crucial turnpike, had been laying for us, shooting against time, figuring the speed it would take a car to reach the spot where the shell would break as against the time it took the missile to come through the air.

She started. Was not afraid. Fear of staying in the ditch was stronger than the fear of driving off. Battery fired again, after we left. Hate artillery. Planes warn you by sight and sound and must move off of you and haven't been coming over at night. Artillery can be anywhere and stays put. No sight or sound or other warning: wham-flash out of the silent air and that's all. You never know when you're in or out of range of artillery.

The smoke of the five wasted shells, black with white steam in it and a rusty reddish glare mixed with vapors of the falling sun, was so thick for a hundred years that I could hardly see the road. Only with the greatest effort did I shift from second speed into high before I got to the protection of the bank of earth at the top of the hill. Hard to shift gears while you're running away—you don't like to waste that much time.

Captain S. and I, our recent discussion forgotten, smiled at each other.

Again They had drawn blood. No sooner had my skinned nose begun to heal than my hair was parted for me. Nothing much. Scratch has already

---

29. Elman Rogers Service interrupted his undergraduate education at the University of Michigan to serve as an ambulance driver. He later earned a doctorate in anthropology, and published and taught cultural anthropology and ethnology at Columbia University, University of Michigan, and University of California at Santa Barbara.

closed up and I won't be combing my hair until Teruel is either won or lost, anyway.

Death comes nearer. Her fingernails have run through my hair, and I have smelled her ill breath on my neck.

Cannot understand why They don't blow out the whole crossroads if They're within range. Maybe They know we'd then drive through the fields and would rather save the turnpike for pot shots at cars giving us the illusion that the road is cut. How much artillery have They to waste this way? Our hard-working 75's fire only on troops and trenches and artillery and tanks.

The English were still holding to the spire called the Muleton, or Little Millstone, although their positions were overlooked from the Big Millstone or La Meula. First-aid post was in the pit in which we captured the four batteries of fascist anti-aircraft.

Ran my car between two of the tanks drawn up in the sunken hill-top road. On top of the parapet walked Captain Dunbar in a long leather coat and a beret, directing the fire of the four cannon in the turrets of the tanks.[30]

The fascist artillery was not being able to manage dropping shells into the road. Their shells fell both sides of us. They wanted us and They wanted us badly because the four tanks were shelling point-blank a concentration of fascist troops on the slopes of the Muela. Looked as if a big night attack was being prepared. Fascist tanks were drawn up, gray against the twilight lavender tan sides of the mountain like elephants in a circus parade. Through field glasses I saw fascist troops camped among boulders overlooking us.

The four pint-sized husky tank drivers did not wear helmets. The door of my car swung shut. Closed by concussion. Mud camouflage was peeling off her sides.

Dunbar, up on the parapet, puts down his field glasses.

"Will you please try an explosive shell slightly to the left of the last?"

Ivan ducks into the turret and comes up.

The gun: "zzzzzzzzz."

Dunbar raises his glasses. "Now give them another. Same place."

Ivan sniffs the evening air like a bird dog. "Karasho!" he says, and pops down into his turret.

Three more "zzzzzzzz," "zzzzzzzz" from the tanks: then "Crack, flash . . . gong!"

---

30. British officer Malcolm Dunbar (1912–63) was the last Chief of Staff of the 15th Brigade.

The author, after looking through Dunbar's glasses: "They look like bee-tles crawling over a skull. Can fire right down on us from up there."

Dunbar, in a mathematically composed English voice: "What do you *imagine* they *are* doing, comrayde? . . . oh Ivan, another round of explosives, please."

Ivan: "Karasho!"

Bill Diggs* comes running up the road, helmetless, loaded with two can-isters of M-gun ammo.

Author: "Want a hand, Diggs? What's the matter, got a cold?"

Diggs: "Caught it lugging two Maxims up to the lines yesterday. Those heavy bastards make you sweat."

Author: "Lucky the brigade is here to help you win the war, Diggsy."

Diggs: "Who parted your hair for you?"

Author: " . . . "

The four tanks: "Crackflash . . . gong!"

Scene: the Grand Canyon, during a Maxfield Parrish afterglow, except for the black smoke and flying earth.

Invisible fingers of concussion plucked at my glasses and tore them off my ears. I stepped off the parapet to find that my radiator was leaking furiously. More shrapnel. I asked a stretcher bearer for water.

"We have none, comrayde, but may I drink from your radiator?"

As the murderous sunlight faded out into greenish white light, the artil-lery fire let up. The wounded would not be coming in for another hour.

A chest case came up on a stretcher. I very carefully loaded him onto my rear seat. Before I pulled out with two arm cases, Dr. Bradsworth of the Eng-lish peeled off his overcoat and spread it over the chest case.[31]

The tank squadron divided. Two stayed to defend the hill and two left to cover a weak spot on the road to Teruel. Only the adult male gorilla rivals the tank in ugliness, sullen anger and air of concentrated violence always on the point of overflowing into rage. The stuttering bass roar of a tank engine combined with the fevered rattle of the treads against rock makes the most beautiful and reassuring sound in the world. The same sounds when they come from the other side of the trenches are the most hideous.

At chest-case speed (8 to 10 miles an hour) I ran the crossroads without drawing fire. Blackness had begun to run down the dome of the winter sky

---

* dead

31. Dr. Colin Bradsworth, a general practitioner from Birmingham, England, was the first British battalion doctor.

like water color into the poison green remnants of daylight. Should I use my lights?

Nervous at the suddenness and the depth of the shell holes among which we climbed the first slopes of Mansueto, Captain S. ordered me to flash my dims.

Reluctant to pull Their cannon on me, I refused. Again provoked, S. reached out to the dashboard. Almost instantly bulbs of smoke, whiter than the failing light, flowered on the hillside. I turned off my lamps.

When we had climbed behind the first ridge, the steady twin glow of my headlights, rocking a little as we crept over the rims of filled shell holes, seemed to bring back life and light into the lives of the two light wounded and they began to talk.

The English had had their usual hard luck. The enemy, using their 75's as howitzers, had taken six feet of rock and frozen clay off the top of the Muleton between sunrise and noon. Relays of trimotors unloaded two and three hundred pound bombs until the earth was everywhere soft and flaky. When the fascist infantry came to conquer the dead, the few living drove them off. One company of the English was cut down in six hours from eighty to seventeen.

The Internationals are shock troops.

My two light wounded had been hit at one o'clock. They started to walk back to the first-aid post. When they reached the open fields, planes came for them. Both men jumped into a frozen irrigation ditch, thankful that their weight had broken the ice on its surface. Back into the ditch they rolled when the planes came the second time. Halfway back to the first-aid post, clothing began to freeze to the skin. The two Englishmen stripped down to their underwear. Someone had loaned them blanket-coats by the time that I had arrived at the former anti-aircraft pit.

The chest-case in the back of my car sighed whenever the chasis unavoidably shook. A second voice which had opened up in his breast began to bubble. Thin and fair with a short silky blond trench beard under his hollow cheeks, he had been the only heavy wounded the stretcher bearers had been able to bring in all day long. "*Camilleros!*" he murmured, "stretcher-bearers!" This is the cry of a new world in birth. Will it be still-born? *Seventy-fives are the puerperal fever of social change.*

I gave the two light wounded cigarettes and they began to ask each other about their friends.... "Jock?"... "He got it." "Symington?" ... "Same thing." The roll call of the dead grew and grew until I pulled up in front of the new Corbalan hospital.

The I.B.'s are shock troops. Thank God Kipling is in his grave and no other Imperial slanderer exists equally capable of celebrating war and slandering the British Tommy, though Masefield tries his best.

Not all of the equipment for the new hospital had come in. Some of the trucks had been delayed by daylight. Major B., saying that he had light and a sterile knife, accepted my chest-case.

Al Hawk's truck rolled into the dark village square, loaded with ten wounded lying on mattresses.

"Not in my line," said Al with loud disgust as we lifted one half-frozen man after another, "hauling around stiffs is not in my line." Al's brand of humor is the language the boys understand. He is the most sentimental American in Spain. I offered him one of my Camels. "No," he said, "got one." The sentimental bastard has a complex on living hard, saying nothing and trying to stay alive.

I went back to K 2½ for another load. Plenty of wounded, not too many ambs. Finn, Slim and I were doing most of the evacuation. Before the attack had let up, a 155 hit one of the four cannon tanks. The crippled iron beast was being loaded on a White, back to the Rear for repairs.

By midnight the Corbalan hospital was going full blast. Light steam radiators had been connected by lengths of garden hose to the boiler of the shower truck. Rooms had been whitewashed and beds set up. The generator hummed. Every doorway breathed light and ether and the soft voices of busy doctors and nurses.

I was sent thirty miles back over the next mountain range with light wounded, a list of medical supplies to pick up and orders to rush back and then return to K 2½ for another load.

"Captain," I said, "suppose my eyes close up?"

"So long as there are wounded. . . . "

". . . I should carry them. But suppose I smash up?"

"You've got to stay on the road until the last of the wounded is brought in."

The road to Cedrillas was one of the usual precipice-hung ladders, full of munition and troop trucks. Glue formed on my lashes and white films drifted across the eyeballs. Pinching eyelids and slapping my jaw had long since failed.

Captain Byrne looked at me carefully, found a car to take my place and sent me to bed, with an orange, bread and jam, and a cigarette. I found a pile of blankets on the floor and dropped out for eight hours.

Back in Corbalan next day I was sent out to bring a tire pump. Ralph Spinner, chófer's delegate to the Estado Major of the 35th Division, was stalled with a flat at the top of the pass.[32] Planes chased us under the road twice (Ralph says he knows the location of every culvert in Spain) but with the attack stemmed, no wounded coming in, with time on our hands, we did not mind the diversion which gave us a good excuse to loaf in the sunlight.

Reached a good meal, the more enjoyable because I was back with the Major and my pals. Ate a *sausage*. Our quiet clean ward was empty but for the lung case I had brought in the night before, so I turned into a *bed*. Slept on top of the embroidered sheets sent to us along with our Rolls by Lord Farrington. Slept like a tenor after a first night, disturbed only by the commotion caused by the arrival of the evacuated population of Tortajada.

Few minutes ago ten heavily wounded *Carbineros*[33] came in. Half the Post is laid up with grippe. I helped with the first-aid work. Morphine is not always needed, because of shock. Lump of gray intestines as big as a grapefruit lay on top of one guy's stomach, but the fellow who made most of the noise had a torn thumb-nail. "*Madre mia . . . curame Virgen!*" The heavies often pray and beg God for help but seldom ask for a priest. How can I believe in God? How can men whose women are massacred in His very houses, by the stone and beams dedicated to Him, believe in God?

In fifteen minutes we had stripped, classified, dressed, ledgered and dispatched the ten wounded *Carbineros*.

All the Post does for the wounded is to:

1) warm them next to an oil stove in which, lacking kerosene, we burn a mixture of gasoline and rancid olive oil.
2) give all but stomach cases hot coffee; inject morphine and other drugs.
3) cut off clothing and apply sterile gauze and splints.
4) take the names, rank and brigade. Distribute medical cards describing the nature of the wounds and the treatment given.
5) rush the heavy cases to the surgical hospital and the others to the hospitals further back towards the Rear.

To demonstrate how war undermines the human spirit (whatever that is), there is blood all over one of my trouser legs and I'm not going to wash it off. Water too hard to get, pants already too dirty. Why, anyway?

---

32. New York volunteer Ralph Spinner, aka Robert Emmet, served as headquarters commissar of the 35th Division.
33. The *Carbineros* were riflemen.

When I washed the blood out of my car this morning, I found the bloody piece of metal that fell out of my lung-case's chest in transit.

We are holding Them. We are not retreating. The lines hold. One of the best proofs of the quality of the fight we have been putting up is the number of wounded that have been coming in. If we were disorganized or if we had retreated, the fascists would be getting our wounded. Our Posts and hospitals would be empty. A retreating army carries few of its wounded, as every General but few mothers know.

After the artillery strafed my car at the Teruel crossroads I was for the first time very much afraid for my life. While I was watching the tanks fire and waiting for the sun to go down, I decided to run the oil out of my crankcase and burn out my bearings. The Major would then be forced to send me out of the battle zone.

Once night had come and I was back in the mountains, I thought that ruining a car contributed to Spain by many hundreds of Americans, all for the purpose of saving my neck and broken morale, was indecent. I then thought of climbing into an ambulance while the driver was not looking, lying on a stretcher and thus smuggling myself to Valencia where I would show the American Consul my passport. He would send me home.

Once I had eaten and slept, I found that I had forgotten all my plans for escaping war. Those schemes are not quite forgotten: I have no doubt that I shall resurrect them from the mental cesspool in which we all keep the thoughts of which we are not proud, once the odds of surviving this war again seem so hopelessly against me. Perhaps I will never be able to make a professional soldier of myself.

I have now lost the power of being able to sleep above ground during daylight.

A horn blows downstairs. More wounded and more work.

In Memoriam

Ivan, tank-driver and gunner. A 155 found him. There are no wounded tank-drivers. His machine goes back for repairs. Ivan stays where he fell. None of us knew his real name and none of the world's newspapers, not even those of his native land, will print his name and the manner of his death. *Karasho!*

January 24. Valdecebro

Hashed-up Carabineros poured into the Post all afternoon. We must have handled over a hundred cases and hardly one was wounded in a single place. A good clean bullet hole which enters one side of a man and comes out of the other is a rare luxury common only in the tranquility of the World War. Dumdums used to go in clean but come out ragged. The modern explosive bullet does not come out. It explodes inside of you. The wounded of the streamlined twentieth century come out of the trenches looking as if they had been worked over by a hamburger machine.

In spite of the fact that we are doing good work here, our set-up is very bad. The former town hall and fascist stable (these gentlemen cleared out so fast that they left a large dump of Italian signal rockets and machine-gun belts, none of which fits our guns) still reeks of manure and rotted half-burned straw. We have no carbolic.

Captain S. lies upstairs on one of the few mattresses; silent, fever-dilated eyes staring upwards, refusing to be evacuated. Two of our Spanish stretcher bearers have gone up to the lines to replace *camilleros* killed yesterday. The farmacist, one of the Scotch cooks, and three of our chófers have been evacuated with pneumonia. Diez Soto, the Cuban doctor in charge of the *triaje*, can hardly administer a hypodermic.[34] Twenty-four hour shifts are the rule. We have barely managed to re-establish contact with the Brigade farmacy. Little but acid, milkless and sugarless coffee for the wounded and beans for ourselves comes out of the kitchen fireplace. The militiamen quartered in Valdecebro beg what little bread we get. Candles, our sole illumination, are running out.

Finn was evacuated in his own car today. Fever.

The work is so heavy and the confusion so great that it was not until late this afternoon that Danny, our one remaining cook, found time or energy to throw away the human leg which had somehow gotten into the garbage pail in the kitchen.

All water must be brought half a mile from the only spring in this wilderness. When I look at the hideous arid land of Teruel province, I wonder why we took it from Franco. In a thousand years of glorious Spanish history while the Kings were making a name for themselves in all of the courts of Europe, the peasants of Valdecebro were always too poor to buy half a mile of iron

---

34. Luis Diaz Soto was a Cuban doctor at the hospital in Albacete.

pipe. The pathway to the spring is the Way to the Cross, and the wellhead is the Calvary on which the poor of Spain, guilty only of wishing not to be poor, are being crucified; and in the name of Jesus Christ!

Why did I come to Spain?

This morning I joined the men who had stripped to the waist at the sheep trough next to the well, and scrubbed myself, more for the sensation and the pleasant smell of soap than for practical reasons. No sense bathing until I can get some clean underwear.

Then scrubbed the blood off the floorboards of my car. Getting a complex about blood inside the car. Why? When I do not mind it on my clothes. Perhaps blood on the floor is bad luck. Once the car was clean inside, I renewed her mud camouflage. After that I set a pitcher of water on the running board and began to shave in the rearview mirror. Then I heard The Sound; the sound of a thousand flies buzzing against a single windowpane. Nowhere was there cover; and I did not want to be seen running through the fields half naked, the top of my long winter underwear trailing like a tail, one side of my face shaved and the other high with lather. I therefore tilted the mirror so that I could simultaneously watch the sky and watch the pigskin of my unfamiliar facial hide appear under the razor.

Dropping nothing, not even a few light ones or a bushel or two of grenades on Valedecebro, which from the air must already look like broken tiles spread over a manure heap, the planes headed straight for the artillery which had been playing Wagnerian concert music while I shaved.

Our anti-aircraft opened up and I saw my first fascist plane go down, emptying black smoke into the dry earth like a waterfall. The rest of them did not come back for at least an hour.

During the raid I saw one of the blue-fingered women who had been beating out laundry in the stream that fed the spring run under a low bare thorntree. There she stood, protected from the sky by five pounds of well-spread dry twigs, twisting her apron, crying, while her mouth worked like that of an epileptic. Five minutes before this healthy applecheeked young woman had appeared perfectly sane.

I have nothing but the deepest admiration for the methodical and efficient way the fascists employ Their planes: no single avion is used for more than one purpose: the camera planes do nothing but take pictures; one type is used for strafing trenches, another for strafing roads. Bombings are carried out only by trimotors; artillery attacked only by the type of biplane also used for attacking troop concentrations. Irregular stings of tiny pursuit ships hang high overhead all day, assigned only to patrol the sky against our own horsefly-sized ships. Signals are given and maps of trenches drawn with sky-smoke. Planes signal artillery and cannon tag objectives for the planes.

The batteries we have hung on the upper slopes of Mansueto, dominated by the anti-aircraft placed so high that I have seen their barrels shoot downwards at planes in the valley of the Alfambra, move every night, not only to follow the changes in the lines or to cover the rapidly-shifting shock-points of the attacks and counter-attacks, and not only to give the planes a little more trouble in locating them, but to get out of the way of the guns always set up against them.

Our artillerymen have hard lives. They work their guns all day, while being strafed or bombed and shelled. After dark, when fires have just been lit, men and guns are loaded on camions. By midnight, the batteries have reached new emplacements and there are six hours left in which to roll the guns off the trucks, dig foundations for the wheels, dig trenches for the ammunitions, and last of all, dugouts for the men.

Each battery ought to have its own anti-aircraft for use against bombers and double-calibre machine guns against strafing. Unfortunately, the Non-Intervention Committee does not approve of this type of organization on this side of the trenches.

Franco has plenty of the best type of heavy electric anti-aircraft. No sooner does a squadron of our biplanes head for fascist lines than strings of black shrapnel puffs whip about them.

January 25. Valdecebro

Morning. At eight last night I loaded up with Captain S. (still full of fever), Lieutenant B. and two comrades coming back from a hospital into the Mac-Paps. Drove until five in the morning visiting ambulance and first-aid posts, delivering supplies, getting news. The moon that came out at half-past eleven helped me drive more than it helped fascist M-gunners' aim.

News is good: The Alfambra road is still open, although it is under fire during daylight.

Saw big caravan of fascist trucks across the valley, lights blazing. But the headlights went out all of a sudden and didn't come on again.

What has surprised me about the war in Spain and the Battle of Teruel is that the war ceases every night. Artillery observers cannot see through the darkness, nor can aviators. If troops attacked they would have trouble in telling who was who unless Italian infantry were involved, or Moors. Their Spanish infantry is as miserably dressed as ours. M-gunners, unable to see their front sights at night, use tracers. All but snipers and trench-mortars are silent. The mortar loves darkness. Their missiles fly half a mile into the air and drop into trenches not more than three or four hundred yards distant. Observers sent out into shell holes report accuracy with field telephones. This weapon is very deadly. Our hatred of it is almost as strong as our desire for mortars of our own.

The feature of the evening was another raid into a farmacy warehouse in No-Man's Land. The excursion yielded barrel-fulls of fine cambric bandages, cotton, adhesive, and rare drugs. Trench mortars kept looking for us.

There is no quiet so intense and so alive as that of battlefields at night. Dark figures move along the roads and fields, voices speak and fade fast. Sounds of truck and tank engines are heard. A single rifleman gets nervous. He is answered by an M-gunner who is interested but does not wish to waste many rounds. A member of a bombing party then heaves a grenade at a shadow. Both sides now open up with everything they have. After a few minutes of *tiroteo,*[35] the possession of the night air reverts to the sharp-shooter and his telescope-sight.

At two in the morning we ran across Al's commissary truck parked on the Teruel viaduct in full view of the enemy. A flat. Could not run off the viaduct to a more protected spot for fear of rim scoring the tire. Could not work without light. Afraid to use my headlights, we lit a candle. Frightened? Only that the truck would not be able to get home by daylight.

This is being written on my favorite desk—Major B.'s operating table. Operating rooms are the cleanest , driest, warmest, best lit, altogether most pleasant places I have found in Spain—but not the most fragrant.

<u>Night. Alcorisa again.</u> Back in Civilization, to get my radiator fixed. Just in time. I had to stop fourteen times at mountain torrents and springs in the course of the hundredmile run back to the nearest garage. Slightly surprised to find that Alcorisa has not been bombed in my absence, nor had Camarillas, Aguilar (Eagle's Rest), Aliaga and the other hamlets along the route. The fascist push cannot be headed this way.

Lunch was given to me by the kitchen of the *Campesinos,*[36] who are more famous as fighters than as cooks. Shared my meal with Major Candon,* Cuban

---

* dead

35. *Tiroteo*—shooting.

36. The Campesinos were troops led by El Campesino, "The Peasant" (Valentín González), commander of the 5th Regiment.

Commandante of Campesino's celebrated Special Machine Gun Battalion.[37] This super shock corps regularly loses two-thirds of its strength within three to twelve hours after it goes into action. Mostly Communists.

Candon was a mild, middle-sized, lean dark guy with deepset blue eyes overwhelming his other and average features. He had the quiet, melancholy, deferential and polite manner of a bank guard. The People's Army does not specialize in the extravagant personalities generally associated with the conduct of war.

The auto-parque of the Fifteenth will complete repairs in twenty-four hours. Wish they would take longer. I am full of dirt-fever and would not mind taking things easy for two or three days. I'd like to climb the hillside of the cedars and sleep in the sun. Always did like this burg with its many rushing streams, canals and baby waterfalls, good for both throat and roots, its olive oases and tan cliffs.

The Arts of War

1) How to boil eggs without fire: First get the egg. Then wrap it in gauze, drop down radiator of car and race engine, with blanket over hood, until water boils. Egg may be withdrawn by means of gauze.

2) Candlestick—bomb-wings from the lighter stuff or bottle or empty adhesive-tape roll.

3) Muffler—a bath towel.

4) Shoe-soles—section of tire, bound around uppers by wire.

5) Handkerchiefs—buy a yard of calico if possible; tear in squares and throw away as fast as used. An old sheet or a pillow-case may also be employed.

6) To delouse—throw away all clothing, bathe, and dress in a totally new outfit. This method is impossible because the rivers are too cold and all new or second-hand clothing, but for sleazy spiral puttees, unobtainable.

In Memoriam

The former Surgical Hospital of the Forty-Fifth Division, International Brigades, Spanish People's Army.

---

37. Major Policarpio Cardon, a Cuban described as a political syndicalist, served as a brigade commissar.

January 4th to 21st, 1938. Bombed, machine-gunned every day before and during mealtimes. Formally raided twenty-seven times in seventeen days.

Destroyed by direct hits from German Junkers' trimotors on the morning of January 21st, four hours after the last truckload of material and staff had left for Corbalan. Planes had been inaccurate until then.

The sweet smells of ether that pleasantly exuded from walls and roofs have now been replaced by acrid powder fumes. Militiamen will now come to these broken walls to obey nature.

Epitaph for the Half Dead

1. *Water tank driver.* Three weeks of hide and seek with the patrols of attack planes on the Teruel road tore the spine out of him. Brought in his car, sieved, for repairs. But human beings cannot be mended with an acetylene torch.

2. *Sam, a former marine cook.* "I'm demoralized and I don't mind admitting I'm demoralized. Seventy-one days straight in the Jarama trenches did it to me. They didn't relieve us until we passed a resolution and sent it to Gallo. I'm demoralized and I'll show you the reason why." Looking up at you earnestly, eyes as round as those of a cocker spaniel asking for a cake, he shows you the picture of the girl and the baby [that] soldiers have carried since Darius invaded Greece. "That's the reason I'm demoralized. I'll admit I'm yellow. But they've got to send me home. I'm not sore at anybody here and I've not gone back on Spain. I'll be just as good a union man as ever, but they've got to send me home."

3. *A nurse.*[38] "I can't stand it anymore. They send me back to Paris, *et je suis vrai Parisienne*, for rest and an operation to my tonsils. I came out of the ether with my eyes on the sweet sky of France, and there in the little window was a plane; a real one. I can't stand more. Escorial, Grañen, San Martin . . . when the planes come over I can't do my work. I thought it might disappear if they sent me to the Front . . . it's hopeless. The planes will rule. We will not win. The planes are already the rulers of all of Spain. The Republic is ours, but not the Republican air. When Franco wins, he

---

38. Probably Sonia Merims.

will kill all the Internationals fast, knowing that they have not the favor of their own governments, who will be glad to be thus relieved of the embarrassment of interceding for their nationals. If I hear another plane. . . . "

4. *An English cook.* "I was one of the thirty captured at Jarama.[39] The English always have bad luck. First They gave us to the Moors. When the Moors were done with us, They stood us up against a wall and shot—over our heads. Back in our cells They beat the hell out of us. They again ordered us out to the wall. This time They made us dig our graves. Up to our waists in fresh earth the firing squad again shot over our heads and we were taken back to our cells where Moors were waiting for us. This went on for twenty days. Then the English consul heard about us.

"We were immediately taken to a beautiful rest-home where the beds were so soft that I couldn't sleep and the food was so good I couldn't eat it. Franco needed good publicity in England. Some of us broke down and signed statements that we had not been mistreated, that we were disillusioned with the Republic, which was nothing more than a mask for the ugly face of Moscow, and that, if we were returned to England, we would never again take up arms against the Rebels. I refused to sign the first part of the statement but weakened enough to swear that I would not come back to Spain. When I got back to England I made some speeches saying exactly what had been done to us. After that I came back and re-enlisted in the I.B. But when I got to the Front, I couldn't handle a gun, my hands shook so much, and they made me a cook. And now I can't cook. I don't know why, but I can't fix my mind on anything. Don't know what I'll do for the rest of my life. Can't concentrate. Shouldn't have re-enlisted . . . but I had to get back at them. Especially the Moors."

5. *German Lieutenant.* "I worked in a Dusseldorf munitions factory. I wanted to come here as soon as the thing happened but The Party said that I was too valuable and would not allow me to enlist. During the earlier months of the war we were able to fill many of the shells and bombs that came to Franco from Germany with sawdust. When the Gestapo got busy, this sabotage became so hard that The Party approved of my coming to

---

39. "English cook"—probably Bernard Thomas from Birmingham. He was a member of the English machine-gun company captured at Jarama and repatriated after avowing not to return to Spain. He returned anyway in September 1937 and served as a driver, but he deserted his post and was officially called "*Inútil*" (unfit).

Spain. The Germans make good shells and good cannon. German gunners know their weapons. Those who fire on us have had four and ten years of training not only on a particular caliber of gun, but for all that time they have had the same piece to serve and take care of.

When German artillerymen fire, that's the time you see arms and legs fly! I'll be killed but I won't be captured. That's why I carry plenty"—he taps the bracelet of shells on his wrist—"of ammunition. Franco never kills the German Internationals he captures. Oh no. He sends them back to Germany. If I'm captured, I'll save Hitler the expense of . . . I want to die clean."

January 25. Alcorisa, and I Hope This Town Will Not be Assassinated

Repairs going nicely. Under the pretext of wanting to help, I attempted to supervise the work on my car but I was told that there was a rule against chófers' helping the auto-parque mechanics. Noticed that the proportion of Spanish to Americans has grown. We plan to leave our skill in Spain, not only our bodies. A Spanish expert is now being trained to take over the management of the garage. Spanish are put into responsible positions all over the International Brigades as fast as they can be secured. Have a notion that the era of the I. B.'s is drawing to a close. Not many of us left, for one thing—my guess is fifteen to twenty thousand, all told.

This morning I ran across the English nurse who sang Purcell arias that night at the Huete dance. She had left her husband behind at the base hospital and was going up to the Front to replace a compatriot who had . . . well, whatever it is happens to the unwounded when they take more than they can endure.

I walked her up through the cedars to the top of the hill that overlooks much of this part of Aragon. We lay on our backs in a bed of early flowering rosemary with the sun on our eyes and talked very little.

"Why not?" I thought. I believed that she must be thinking the same thing. Why not?

I now sit with my notebook on my knees, writing, and she still lies beside me with her eyes half-open. I have not touched her and I won't: why, I'm not sure; because I'm out of the habit? Or undernourished? Or too tired? Or because she might not feel as I thought I should feel? I don't know.

To dissolve the faint excitement that had begun to glow, and to burn my bridges behind me, I began to talk about the girl whose picture I carry in my hat-band.

I could see that the English nurse—I never knew and perhaps will never know her name—appreciated my slaughtering of the slight and unused-to tension that had grown up between us.

"Is she beautiful and do you love her?" she asked.

I showed the pictures and said that we were very much in love and that my girl would be waiting at the pier, when and if, providing that she hadn't met another guy she liked better by that time.

We didn't because we didn't really want to. At another time, or in another country . . . but then, we would never have been thrown together, never have walked up the hill, never have felt the necessity of taking what happiness we could. Here in Spain all of us are paupers.

My bombhole-jumper will be ready this evening, but if I decide that the carburetor needs taking down and the battery should be charged. . . .

And if there is an attack at Teruel? *How are the lines holding?*

Three Days Later. January 28th? Puebla de Valverde (Greenvaleton)

Back in the furnace of Teruel sizzling on the griddle, after forty-eight continuous hours of hide and seek with thousands of Liras' and Marks' worth of beautiful shiny metal. Battle lines and entire plan of campaign had changed when I got back to the war. Things are swinging around to the South. With the Alfambra road cut Franco begins to concentrate on the capture of the military position formerly called the city of Teruel. Anticipating a drive on Valencia. The Fifteenth has been shifted to the apex of the focal point of the greatest pressure, as usual.

Won't be able to remember what happened in the past two days until I'm rested, and by that time I'll be trying to remember something else, so I won't try to record a connected picture of my wanderings and incessant record-breaking narrow escapes.

Getting tired of being a rabbit chased by hawks. Either I'll get a chance to hit back or turn into a double-barrelled paranoic.

I'll let the running account go and hit only the high spots:

Lost. Took my first wrong road in the dark. No *control* (guardpost) at the intersection and no signs. High plateau overlooking battle-lit Alfambra valley. Road kept petering out. Tire tracks eventually resolved into a crisscross maze of wheel marks running in wide circles on perfectly level ground. Phantom airport. Flying fields—any flat piece of land—shift fast.

With my gas running low, eventually found my way back to the road.

The curtain falls on Corbalan. Before I left for Alcorisa, had been told to report back to the Major in Corbalan. Left this town healthily unspotted by a single bullet hole. Twenty-four hours later she was dark, smudged to the earth by a giant thumb. Straight rectangular lines of walls and roofs were out of plumb, chewed up and bellied. Hospital was deserted. Brand new battalion camped in the ruins, had taken over town from vanished peasants. Between dawn and dusk the Macbeths of the sky had played all three acts of the tragedy of Corbalan. Now that the final curtain has fallen, Banquo's ghost exhibits his bloodstained sheets to the stars.

Death ray. Driving down the alpine artillery gardens of Mansueto, the night sky suddenly lit with a vast sheet of cherry-colored mauve-red fire. I drove 5 K. without it getting larger or smaller. At first it seemed something like the far reflection of the neon lights of a very big city. Peculiar velvety cherry color full of purple and not at all like the rusty glow of an avenue nor like the tomato red of a burning town. Faint bars of white striations moved through It. The whole Thing was too big to have been started by man even at his pulp-magazine worst.

Troops moving down the mountain were terrified. Morale, uncracked by my God how many weeks of broiling in the icy Teruel furnace, was completely gone.

Whenever I stopped to enquire for the whereabouts of the Fifteenth, I asked about the meaning of the Thing in the sky.

"Flame-throwers."

"No."

"Liquid fire." "A burning munitions dump."

"Campesino drove seventeen kilometers into the fascist lines today. Took Celadas and set it on fire."

"It's a magnetic field the fascists send up to bring down our planes."

"I know what it is," whimpered a German lieutenant, tough enough looking to frighten children, horses, Tom Mix and Dick Tracy. "Hitler is trying his new Death Ray on us."

Is it possible that the Aurora Borealis visits the skies as Southern as those of Spain?

The belly-case nuisance. An officer of the Galan brigade stopped me.

"You are an ambulance?"

"Yes, 35th Division. Know where they are?"

"Try the Estado Major in Teruel. But there are two *ametrallados soldados*, in the stomach"—the officer looks in my car and sees that it is empty—"in a farmhouse 2 K. off the main road."

What shall I do? Keep trying to find the Post or carry the wounded to a hospital? My gas is low and I'm twelve hours A.W.O.L. I'm tired and quick-tempered. Anyway, the two M-gunned men don't belong to the Fifteenth Brigade. Don't the Galans have their own lousy ambulances?

Belly cases, who die as fast as May bugs, belong to all brigades. There was nothing to do but to carry them back over the heart-breaking snowy mountain road to the nearest hospital.

.70 Calibre escape. Broad daylight. No place to go: not a culvert or ditch or shell hole, dugout, or trench. I cut the engine, ran her off the road and crouched under the bicycle-gun that was protecting a half-acre of 75's against a squad of attack planes.

Double-sized M-gun. Gunner sits on bicycle seat, leans back and sights against long barrel waved by foot pedals.

Then They came down on us. Sensation: something like hanging off the cornice of a twelve-story building by your fingernails while somebody throws bricks at you. Wish you could shrink small enough to crawl under a pebble, like Alice in Wonderland.

Afterwards, felt strong, calm and invincible.

More about Teruel. Once I had found Major B. he ordered me into Teruel with an authorization for four stoves, six pitchers, all the bed-pans I could find, a sewing machine, electric light bulbs, wire, window-panes and as much linen as my car could carry.

Viaduct was still intact, still strewn with the same dead horses. Tracer-bullet fireflies racing across my hood escorted me into the town. Don't know how many followed.

Main square floating in liquid mud. The humming of the Estado Major's generator ties together the bass notes of mortar-bullfrogs.

Flashlights, concealed bonfires, swift footfalls of silent men.

I hear a hydrophobia-like human howling.

"What's that? Wounded?"

"No. The wounded are too sick to yell. Those are the lunatics in the nut factory. Out between the lines. The asylum's cut off and we've been able to evacuate only half of them."

"How do they eat?"

"We bring out food at night. The nuns cook it for them."

"Do you believe in euthanasia?"

"What's euthanasia?"

"Let it go."

I took the authorization B. had given me to the Estado Major, where it was countersigned.

"Now how do I get all this stuff?"

"What do you think we're running, a drygoods store? Go out and get it. If you have any trouble, show your authorization to the guards . . . got a flashlight?"

Hardware store. Entire stock lay a foot deep on the floor and the counters. I took two Falangist belt-buckles for souvenirs: four little coal stoves, a bundle of pipes, eight elbows, six electric light bulbs and a number of lengths of wire ripped from the walls.

Candy store. Empty, God damn it. By sniffing hard I could detect a faint but satisfying smell of sugar. Cleaned out bare as a sea shell by Lister's Special M-gun men, the swine. The Republic got much food from Teruel. The warehouses were so full of stuff the people wouldn't buy that sacks of wheat and of sugar were used to build sandbags for the defense of the streets. Ralph Spinner, the chófers' delegate, got into Teruel early and laid his hands on an entire case of anchovies, which a road guard took away from him.

Stationery store. Walked off with a ream of deckle-edged linen paper and a bundle of envelopes. Writing materials have been running very short.

Sewing-machine shop. Took one brand new Singer and entire set of carpenter's tools. Wanted to take one of the electric machines but couldn't find the motors.

Chinaware shop. Door caved in by rubble. Interior untouched. Row after row of Willow ware, Wedgewood and imitation Sevres. Saw a banquet set of Venetian glassware, complete to liqueur glasses and absinthe cups.

On the second floor, evidently reserved for special customers, was a collection of Fifteenth Century bisque and gold majolica, with blue dragons and lions; Seventeenth Century Talavera, and many blue and green portrait plates.

What I took with me was a double armful of the heaviest, most coarse soup bowls; four chamber pots and four painted tin water-jugs.

Why doesn't the Ministry of Fine Arts send up a truck for the rest of the china? The proceeds could be used to buy us some good anti-aircraft. Answer: all trucks are needed to transport men, guns and ammo; and besides, the stuff would be broken.

The seminary library. Shelf upon shelf of gold-tooled calf-bound classics and religious tracts, from 16-mo. to elephant folio;[40] hundreds of parchment and pigskin-bound incunabulae: rows of illuminated manuscripts. I opened a breviary and noted in the calendar that the patron saint of my birthday (tomorrow) is Saint. . . .

Here there were guards.

The infirmary. The ground floor dormitory of the former Falangist headquarters makes an excellent ward. The roof, four stories above the beds, is a superb target. Top floor is already wrecked. At the rate of one floor per day, infirmary will last us four days. Perhaps more; because the second story is heavily armored with concrete. Concealed M-gun emplacements in the windows could only be used for street fighting. The Falange had thought it wise to protect themselves against other fascist political parties. This is an example of the unity of the Right.

Captain S., racked by fever and coughing, has lain in the bed of the Grand Exalted Kleagle of the local Falange for the past two days.

The German medical-student male nurse and a stretcher-bearer bring in a man accused of pissing on the floor, for the Captain to sentence.

The volunteer, dressed in a luxurious blue fascist cape with a silver clasp, and a brand-new oyster-white ten-gallon Stetson, sways until we have to support him. The young eyes above his trench beard are shut. A big black louse crawls up the side of his nose.

Captain S: "Why did you do this?"

Stetson hat does not answer.

"Why did you do it, you sawed off c———r?"

Stetson hat reels. We have to support him. He collapses. A good Brooklynese voice comes up from the mess of blue cape and dirty khaki limbs on the floor.

"No . . . no sleep . . . four days . . . sleep."

We hauled him down the crowded aisles and pitched him into an empty bed; shoes, hat, cape and all.

---

40. *16 mo.* designates a specific size of book.

Soon the sun would be up. Before I left the infirmary I picked a red Carlist beret off a hatrack. Where was the owner?

The brigade is better dressed than it has been ever since its men came to Spain. Capes, Stetsons, fur vests, businessmen's double-breasted suits and fascist officers' uniforms in all combinations make us look more like comic opera troupers than soldiers.

Loot was piled up to the ceiling of my car; but I had not been able to find a stick of chocolate, a single egg or a can of sardines.

I had lit my dome light to rearrange the cargo when I heard Crome's bored aristocratic voice:

"Looting, oh my goodness, looting again! It innocently begins with"—he looks into my car—"chamber pots and sewing machines, but soon descends to women's silk stockings and perfume."

"Crome," I answered, "what have you got in your car?"

The Major's low limousine was packed high with silk dresses. For the nurses, I suppose.

I still haven't got a gun. But for my grenade, I'm completely unarmed. I haven't even got a bayonet or a good long knife.

And another narrow escape. This was the first time I had driven out of Teruel alone.

Crossed the viaduct. Ahead lay a crossroad. Right or left? One road led into the fascist lines; the other to Valverde.

Should I drive back into Teruel and ask?

Wouldn't the sun be coming up soon?

Tracers, silent as shooting stars, made me decide to move. Left was always a good direction to take. In a few minutes I saw several men sitting about a fire behind a wall. Could not recognize their uniforms.

First I turned my car about, ready to run back to Teruel, then called out, leaning out of the window, from a distance of two hundred yards, the single word "*Diga!*"

"*Qué quieres tu?*"

If I had been answered "*Ustedes*" instead of "*Tu*," I should have been speaking to fascists. On our side of the trenches, every one is called "Thou" and "Camarada." "Señor" is an insult. "Don" is a fighting word and "Señorito" is an accusation.

And still I haven't a gun. If I ever get back to Villa Paz and see a doctor losing weight lugging the big Colts not uncommon in the Rear, I'll take it from him.

The new classification post. Roadmender's hut ("*Peones Camineros*") three miles south of Teruel on the Valencia road. Partial roof, no water, no fireplace, one of the two rooms well used by the horses of departed cavalry, bullet-pocked inside and out. No trench, dugout, ditch, tree or shelter. Ideal for Hollywood set, not so ideal for the wounded. Very exposed. No cover for cars in daytime. But Valdecebro had grown impossible, with hundreds of troops walking through rooms at night, falling to sleep on top of us and each other. During the day we were virtually isolated, with all roads cut by artillery. The air was full of the vacuum swish of our shells and the bird-calls of Theirs, anti-aircraft puffs and shrapnel, the groaning of heavy plane motors and the croaking of bombs. Worst of all, the roads out of Teruel were so hideously rough, even for Spain and for war and for Teruel, that half a mile of them pulled the insides out of our heavies.

The staff of the Post has been cut down to: the cook—Canadian seaman; Potato-peeler—Scotch miner; Commissary driver—Greek; male nurse—Polish; evacuation doctor—Cuban;[41] and seven or eight Irish, Belgian, French, Spanish, English and American drivers.

The first load arrived soon after dark. Usual hour for their arrival. We lost an amb today. Machine-gunned at the first-aid post. Radiator, two front tires, windshield, as usual. Will be back in commission within twelve hours. Two such truckdrivers of the Fifteenth were killed today. Unlucky shell.

One of the wounded was a head case. He came in gray, cold, nose visibly stopped by blood, bloodstained bandage behind ear. Arms flopped down from stretcher as we unloaded him. Pulse hard to find. We put him in kitchen, head near fire, lower end of stretcher propped by water-jug, and threw so much wood on the chimneyless flames that the lieutenant had to hold handkerchief over his nose while using stethoscope. Robust, healthy young guy. Looked like a born wisecracker. When he pushed on his chest the lips bubbled. Didn't warm up in half an hour so we took papers out of pocket, carried him outside, opened up two feet of earth with shovel and pickax, one of us holding candle and the others standing about, miserably cold. Nothing fancy. No songs or speeches. Not a single word. We were cold, hungry and tired. We hurried.

Why I wish I had a camera. Driving down on Teruel in the late afternoon I

---

41. Oscar Soler, a Cuban American born in Tampa, Florida, served as chief of Evacuation and Interpretation with the rank of sergeant. He returned to New York after the war. Today the Oscar Soler Pediatric Hospital in Havana is named in his honor.

saw many miles of our trenches in which shells, after four, five days were still bursting up and down the entire line of battle.

Directly in front of my eyes was a road-sign lettered:
PRECAUCIÓN!

Before I forget: also picked up a set of plumbers' tools in Teruel. But no tire pump. The lack of a tire pump can kill a man as easily as the lack of a helmet. I haven't got one of those either. All of them are up at the lines. All of the best things in Spain are up in the lines or should be. There has always been plenty of bread. The Air Force comes first, then the men in the Front trenches, then the sick, the troops in the training camp, and finally the civilians. The entire country is organized to strengthen the thin thousand mile dam of dugouts, men and munitions which separate not only the Republic but every democratic nation on earth, from fascism.

Where the preceding pages have been written. At the wheel. Car, parked in a grassy field in the belly of a broad valley, walled by snowy pine-topped mountains on one side and by battlemented brown earth peaks on the other, rocks in the vicious winter wind. Blowing too hard for snow, rain or bombs.

Super-dramatic gray war-clouds rush overhead, loopholed by patches of blue sky.

Brand new Division hospital has been set up here. Moved twice in the past twenty-four hours. First place was a good building in Valverde, but too near gas-pump. Crome divided our equipment and staff. Half stays in a small building in town. The American unit occupies the sheepfold 4 K. from Valverde, near which I am parked. If the planes get one outfit, the other can carry on.

Present setup is the best yet. Series of low broad sheepfolds out in the open fields. Tile roofs are almost the same color as the earth. We are 1 K. of good gravel road from the Teruel–Valencia highway, 25 K. (a half hour, at heavy wounded speed) from the front, by night; 4 K. from the nearest town, and 20 K. from the Classification Post.

A copse of holly trees 400 yards from the sheepfolds furnishes good camouflage for the ambulances. The heavy stone walls of the sheds, the handhewn beam roofs supporting wattles on which tiles are spread, are good shelter from the weather. Two of the floors are of cement. The others are earth. Big stones keep the tile roofs from blowing away. Sanford the electrician now installs lights, using the bulbs and wire I brought in from Teruel. A power truck captured in Belchite furnishes all the electricity we need.

B. has had the smallest of the sheds scrubbed with carbolic. Sterile sheets

are nailed to the walls and the ceiling. These linens will keep dirt from falling onto the operating table when we are bombed.

We have cut windows in the walls and filled them with small sheets of glass
taken from Teruel, fixed together by adhesive tape. Water will be brought by
the brigade tanker.

I am happy to be back at work for my old boss Major B.

In spite of his prize-fighter appearance, Captain S. is physically weak. He
is probably tubercular. His desire to be strong-willed takes the form of petu-
lance and nervous twitching, sudden abuse, especially when he tries to force
himself beyond the limits of his endurance. His assistant, a French-Latvian
or vice-versa, gives the impression of a disagreeable spoiled child and a ladies'
man; but he is infinitely patient and understands his own weaknesses as well
as ours. Lieutenant B. has great natural courage and is happiest when living
with his men. Captain S. has false courage, of the I-can-do-it, just-watch-me
type. His worst fault is inability to make swift decisions. When in doubt he
separates himself from us and broods. Once, after one of our rapid shifting
of positions, S. didn't know the location of the Battalions. Rather than go to
the Estado Major for information, and thus admit his ignorance, he drove
all over the mountainside, in the dark and under fire, with only a rough idea
of the positions of our lines. But S. is a good guy. If he were not incessantly
struggling to keep himself out of bed, more of us would know that he is a
good guy.

January 29? My Birthday? Valverde

The new, dark and well-cemented interior of the sheepfold in which I have
for the past twenty-four hours lain in bed with dirt fever seems like the empty hold of a ship. The winter wind roars above me like a gale at sea.

I write by candle-light although it is daytime. The hospital carpenter has
been too busy to rig window-panes into the two small blanket-stuffed openings in the heavy stone walls.

Two more front-line ambs have been killed, I hear. One, speared to the
road by the planes, burned to death. The other tried to rub noses with a truck
at night. Headlights were off.

I'm just about coming back to earth after a forty-eight-hour stay in fever-
hell. Dreamed that I was back in the States, trying to decide to leave my job
and come to Spain.

Jack now drives my car. She couldn't be in better hands and feet, but this
is the first time that my sweetheart has gone out without me and I'm lone-
some for her. She's being used for fetching loot from Teruel. Our hospital has

been feeding of fascist adhesive, cambric bandages for the past three weeks. We have now heard of a steam-heated hotel in the provincial capital and plan to remove radiators and boiler. Never once has the Major left his work for a junket into the combination lunatic asylum and slaughterhouse on which the best blood in Spain and best explosives of Europe have so liberally been poured for the past six weeks.

The fighting has let up a great deal in the past two days. The war can't go on without me.

The wards are full of dirt fever and pneumonia, with suspicions of typhoid. The men have been sleeping on the ground for the past twenty-nine days. The temperature didn't rise above zero, Fahrenheit, during the first week.

When will the brigades go on rest? We're wearing out. Our equipment is wearing out. Hardly a watch left with which to take a pulse. Most of the thermometers have broken. But so long as the rifling in the barrels of the guns don't wear out, nothing much matters.

I've had to mend the tips of my shoes with adhesive tape. Where will I get another pair? Won't need my shoes just yet.

February 1. Valverde

Still in the sheepfold but not in the dark because Bastido the carpenter (a weak sister in spite of his height and physique—refused to go into Teruel to assist with the removal of the hotel boiler because he was "too near-sighted") fitted glass into one of the holes in the wall, late yesterday afternoon.

Sunlight pure as platinum now streams in a heavy bar across my bed. One of the iron stoves I brought back the other night heats me. Without damper it burns valuable fuel too fast. We'll make a damper out of the lid of a marmalade can and sardine-tin keys, if we can find them.

Give us a chance and we don't do so badly. In another week this joint will be—I can't say an "efficient" or a "well-run" or a "comfortable" hospital—but, after all, the Mayo brothers could not load their establishment into two trucks, set it up in three hours and take it down in two hours.[42] We do the best we can. There is a great deal about which nothing can be done. For example: three of our doctors were evacuated yesterday with pneumonia. And the cook overslept this morning. This is no joke. Our day cannot begin without coffee. The cook, nineteen-year-old Andalusian who crossed fascist

---

42. "The Mayo brothers" refers to the founders of the Mayo Clinic in Rochester, Minnesota.

lines to enlist in the Republican militia, has been steadily losing his morale. I don't know why. The kitchen boys and girls are a happy, carefree lot, given to singing wild *flamencos* all day long. If only they knew a war was on! They could still sing.

I feel entirely cured this morning. Did the whole thing myself, unassisted by so much as twenty grains of aspirin. Drugs have been running short and must be saved for the wounded. I am now sitting up in bed. Wait for B. to tell me that I can get up.

The ward is a rough place. Enough blankets, nurses, urinals, attention and beans. Diets out of the question. The wards of every front-line hospital are intended only to rest post-operative cases until they can be moved. Men don't eat for quite some time after they come out of the ether. Reason why this ward is so congested is that one building of the Mora railhead hospital was bombed, along with a hospital train. The last load we sent out was returned to us.

Throughout the entire system for the handling of the wounded and the sick there runs the following main purpose: to get the disabled to the main base hospitals far back of the lines as quickly as possible. It is only in permanent establishments that real treatment is given. Between the trenches and the base hospitals much surgery but little medicine is practiced. Many lives depend on our doctor's ability to diagnose correctly. It is also very important for our medical staff to be well liked by the men and to have many friends among them. The caliber of the doctors of the 35th Division is high. The lower levels of the staff are not quite so uniformly good. It was very hard to judge human fibre in the States, or in Albacete. War, especially at the Front, is an extreme test of character. Peculiar things have happened. Again and again, personnel and the training of personnel of every type, fit to undertake constantly greater and greater responsibilities, are decisive conditions necessary for the conduct of the war.

The Arts of War

1) How to tell if you have a fever—if your lice stop biting.
2) How to tell if you have lice—if your itching stops.
3) Lamp—condensed milk tin flattened to a spout, shoelace for wick, olive oil as fuel.
4) How to make toast—first find bread and a fire. Then use a wire splint as a griddle.
5) Drinking cup—empty condensed milk tin.

6)   Can opener—bayonet.

7)   How to mend a leaking radiator—Get an egg. Empty half of water.
     Let engine run until remainder boils. Break egg and pour. Holes will
     be plugged by fragments.

8)   In the absence of oatmeal, horse manure may be used.

February 2. Valverde

Haven't yet escaped the sheepfold. Germs counter-attacked yesterday afternoon. Back to liquid diet.

Dreamed that I was driving. The road was full of gigantic trucks traveling at enormous speeds and the fields were spread with the wrecks of trucks,
picked clean as chicken carcasses, as clean as the ribs of wrecked boats on
a beach. As I passed each wreck it changed into a dead man who reached
across the road like barbed wire.

The Major had ordered me to pass every truck on the road by morning.
None of the drivers listened to my horn; I was asleep at the wheel and so were
they. My wheel would not turn. With my outside tires balanced over the edge
of a cliff, I would swing out to pass the first camion only to find that it had
swollen so wide that the road was blocked. It ran like a plug into the mouth
of a tunnel at the bottom of a ravine. Floating on a torrent of anti-tetanus
serum, I swirled back into Teruel. My glasses had broken and my trigger
finger would not work as I took over the defense of the bonfire in which the
bodies of the entire 15th Brigade lay burning. The smoke of the fire turned
into shrapnel and fell on me. . . .

Stories still come in about snipers in Teruel. They hide all day in the intricate and half-ruined tunnels, take to windows and rooftops at night. It is five
weeks since Teruel has been completely ours! A sniper got Fred Mowbray[*] of
New Orleans in the base of the spine.[43] The Major operated. Paralyzed from
the waist down, urine accumulating in the kidneys, he begged to be catheter-
ized. Once we were to do this, Fred's ureter would remain inert, and he would
always have to be artificially relieved. He begged for morphine, which could
not be given him. Crying all the more pitifully because he was not delirious,
Fred was carried out of the ward and evacuated this morning. I hear that
spine cases, sooner or later, all die.

---

[*] dead

43. Fred Clarence Mowbray was born in Montreal in 1912, lived in Winnipeg, and joined
     the On-To-Ottawa Trek of unemployed workers in 1935. He served with the Mac-Paps
     and died in a Murcia hospital in March 1938.

A few of the Spanish wounded have the habit of crying out when in pain. "*Ai!*" they sigh, "*ai, ai! . . . mi madre! . . . hostia! . . . cag en la leche . . . ai madre! . . . surname enfermera . . . ai maria! . . . ai! agua!*" At first I thought that only the Spanish had the habit of crying out, so repulsive to Anglo-Saxon notions of courage. After three days of twenty-four-hour-a-day experience in this international war, I can report that whether a person yells when he is sick depends exclusively on how sick he is, how badly he wants water or help, how much self-control his sickness leaves him. I believe that Spanish mothers teach their infants that crying "*ai! ai!*" has the effects of morphine.

The doctors say that the reason why our wards and *triaje* are so silent is that almost all the wounded suffer from shock. Never, in all the trips I have made with car loaded to the ceiling with assorted wounded of all nationalities, have I heard other sounds than an occasional and low "*ai! . . . ai!*" This word is probably the Spanish equivalent for our "ow!"

One of the chief offenders in my ward is a pure bred (can anyone be pure bred?) Scotchman. He has typhoid. Strange that this disease should be floating around during winter time.

Little water for washing is to be found in this area. None for drinking. Dead bodies of men and animals are everywhere, hardly out of sight. A typhoid epidemic seems to be sneaking in on us. Bill Pike, Crome's assistant, inspected the hospital yesterday and asked me peculiar questions. Was my stomach hard? I asked him how the hell did he expect my stomach to get hard on a liquid diet.

Am I really suffering from dirt fever or from what? Shouldn't like to die with my shoes off, in this man's war. Feel weak and despondent, as if my battery had run down and needed to be charged.

Before coming to Spain I had a terror of being taken to a military hospital. My entry into this one was natural and easy. I was very grateful to be able to be sick under a roof. This sheepfold is the most comfortable and least depressing place I've yet struck in Spain, and that includes the Hotel Florida in Madrid. We have a hard time—little chance of getting fresh linen, no supply of pajamas and towels, very little water and light.

The Russian lettering on the thermometer with which my temperature was taken gave me much pleasure. Whenever we see things which have come from abroad we realize that the Republic cannot be altogether forsaken.

But where are those planes, and acres of 75's?

February 2. Valverde

The typhoid plague has become very real. The whole staff was inoculated last night with the exception of the Hungarian eye specialist (who has credit for at least ten pounds of shrapnel taken from hundreds of eyes since he came to Spain), the Californian Sergeant-Major and the New Zealand nurse, who were already ill.[44] The American machine gunner who has the bed next to me sighs and sighs, with punctured intestines. The Canadian anaesthetist is down; and Danny my old friend the Scotch Classification Post cook passed through here pretty well unconscious on his way to the Rear this morning.

It is still cold, and I guess we will survive.

The American chófer who just flopped into a bed near me belongs to the First Transport Regiment—two hundred good new trucks, three hundred fifty drivers and mechanics of whom one hundred fifty are Yanks. Ted, who comes from the state of Washington, had been driving the Fifth Army Corps' famous Special Machine Gun Battalion—three to five hundred chosen men armed only with machine guns and automatic rifles, together having a firing power of some forty thousand bullets per minute.[45] Super-special suicide squad sent in only to take an impregnable position or to defend something indefensible. Always succeed at both jobs, come out at one-third strength and immediately go right back into training. A few days ago they did a special job protecting the Teruel–Corbalan Road.

In Memoriam

Joe Stevenson (this is his right name) of Ayr, Scotland, died a few minutes ago of typhoid—punctured intestines.[46] No man can live on glucose fed him to his veins, stomach draining through his nose, and a high fever. He was a field telephone man attached to the General Staff of the English at Teruel, and reported to a doctor too late. These last days, the sounds that

---

44. The Hungarian is Johnny Kyszely, an eye specialist from Budapest, who was attached to the 35th Division medical group. The "New Zealand nurse" is almost certainly Una Beryl Wilson, the only New Zealand nurse known to have served at Teruel, according to historian Mark Derby. "She trained as a nurse in Australia and was one of four nurses who responded to an appeal in September 1936 from the Sydney Spanish Relief Committee. Headed by Sister Mary Lowson, they left for Spain the following month and worked on practically all the major Spanish battlefronts."
45. Theodore Roy Elliott, born c. 1907, was captured and killed around Gandesa between March 30 and April 4, 1938.
46. Joseph Stevenson from Bellshill, near Glasgow.

came from his throat had been plaintive and sighing. Last night, although I was sleeping heavily, I remember that his moaning had become loud and angry. When I awoke, he had gone out; emaciated hands holding hard on the sheet where he had pulled it under his chin, as if he had tried to shut off his staring and already milky blue eyes from the horror he saw coming around the corner at him.

We now have three good blankets less because those which covered Joe must be burned.

The military situation is rapidly becoming deadlocked. This is exactly what we want because the end of the Teruel campaign leaves us nine miles ahead of where we started two months ago and much better placed to protect ourselves. Franco says he wants Teruel. What he actually wants are the dugouts of Teruel. There is no more city. Last time I saw that burg it looked like a charred moth-eaten canvas painted by a drunken surrealist with hydrophobia, under the influence of hashish. Only the blind can now live in Teruel without immediately becoming psychotic.

As I see it, the tactics of the two opposing armies differ in the the following way: Franco calls his shots, names the date, takes his time, brings up mountains of everything from pea shooters and Christmas sparklers to Kaiser Bill siege guns. Then he lets fly, especially using the old-fashioned German "psychological attacks" which consist in marching deep and solid lines of men slowly in the open upon picric acid stained loose earth which had once been trenches and is now defended only by the dead in them.

The People's Army's best gifts are its mobility, its sudden and surprise attacks, won and over before Their air armadas and big guns have had time to move up. Our best arm is our morale.

A rumor that we have received a hundred new planes has come up the Line of Evacuation. A hundred planes will help us. If there were enough planes to keep Them off the first line trenches and the seaports, the rest of us would cheerfully take our chances. The only effective weapon against a plane is another plane. Forty fast pursuit ships patrolling the Teruel Front, a hundred fast pursuit ships patrolling the skies over Valencia, Barcelona and the gasoline tanks at Tarragona. . . . What will we do if no new planes arrive? We can't fight forever with one hand tied behind our backs.

Our fresh Gloriosos would not once need to cross into rebel territory. Let them keep the trimotors off of us and we would be happy. Then maybe we could get a crack at Their infantry. Meanwhile?

February 3. Valverde. Under Stand-by Orders?

Since I had no fever and there was sun and the wind had let up, I was let out
of bed this morning and have been up on my feet ever since then. Energy-
less and shaky, I walk slowly about the wards and the court. Only the planes
love sunlight as I do. Sure enough, as soon as I had pulled a mattress into the
wind-shade of a wall, there were distant explosions.

The mountains of Teruel seem to be full of granite quarries busy from
sunrise to nightfall. For what is the blasting done? Blood, bones and flesh.
All day long we have seen only four planes and these were so small that they
must have been Ours.

My hands trembled so that it took me an entire hour to shave a week's
growth of beard. All I've been able to do about my personal appearance was
to shave my moustache and to apply extra-neat thicknesses of adhesive to
my shoe-tips. I've taken in my belt three notches since I came to Spain. In
forty-eight hours of Paris, I could put back the fifteen pounds I estimate I
have lost.

This afternoon I walked slowly to the nearest farmhouse, gave out my
laundry and traded one American cigarette for three rolls of Alicante chocolate made of raw cocoa, sugar and mule fat pressed together. My linen will be
ready in three days. Perhaps I will have to carry it away wet, for the Brigade
seems to be moving out of Teruel. This is the best possible sign that the
military situation is good. The boys have been five weeks in the trenches.
The English and the Mac-Paps have taken very heavy losses—there was a
hill, vital to the defense of Teruel, on which fifty Canadians saw sunrise and
six saw dusk—but the Lincoln-Washingtons have lost few men. Considering
the five weeks spent night and day out in the open, the lack of hot food, the
frozen feet, the ears and hands, the sickness and now this nameless hushed
epidemic, the brigade ought to be ready to go On Rest. Why are we such
good troops? Why are we a match for any body of men the military preoc-
cupation of Europe can produce? Whenever I look at the men, I wonder how
this can be true. We look like any subway carful or movieful of men, slight as
to physique rather than husky. The only answer I can find for the excellence
with which even Franco credits us is that the ability of troops to undergo
the modern conditions of war depends not so much on their training and
their command but their understanding of why the war is being fought and
what they stand to lose or gain by the outcome. Once the Rome-Berlin-Tokio
cancer-axis has centrifuged war-disease into the entire world, no officer's
pistol can fire fast enough to make men stay in their trenches unless they are
given something better to fight for than "making the world safe for democ-

racy," "for race, for blood and honor," or "for God and Country," or "for the Fatherland."

"For a New World"? Yes. We will not run from the trenches if we know we are making a new world. We will hold our ground, to share in the wealth with which the world is ever more overflowing. That poverty amidst plenty should cease, we will bear against the full weight of mechanical death-machines bought by men who think that poverty amidst plenty is the natural and immortal principle of life laid down by the essential foulness of what they call "human nature."

There will be a new world. Who likes this one?

For the fiftieth time Franco has broadcast that the Internationals no longer exist. Propaganda produces liars as well as dupes. The last time Franco wiped us out we were in Alcorisa, 140 K. from the scene of war. First he says we are the best troops in Republican Spain, then he annihilates us. With each radio triumph the juggernaut of Fascist Force rears its ugly head higher. Such are Their propaganda methods.

An eighteen-year-old Valentina came in this afternoon, feet first. He had been shot at the exact moment he had pulled the pin out of a Mills bomb.

The four basins of burning alcohol set at his feet and head flame like the Everlasting Fires of cenotaphs to the Unknown Soldier. Bob, the anaesthetist-barber, shaves the head. The eye specialist takes five of the worst fragments of shrapnel out of the eyes and cleans the swollen lids. Two *triaje* nurses pour peroxide and iodine over the arms hands legs and feet, then inject anti-tetanus, gas-gangrene, and morphine. The patient is carried to the table where Major B. sews up the head while R. amputates a foot and Oscar takes off a section of arm. The probing, cutting, clipping and sewing of the legs and arms take three hours. Perhaps he will not lose the remaining hand, foot and eye.

Leaning behind Bob Hamilton and trying to learn how to give an anaesthetic, I think that perhaps it is better to let Franco win.

Yes, give the fascists the entire earth; and then blood, honor, race, instinct and the formula of solving the unemployment problem by manufacturing armaments will set the Duce at the Fuhrer's throat. Bright young men, instead of Going West, should enter the anaesthetic trade.

February 4. Valverde. Waiting. Will We Actually Be Given Three Days' Leave? And in Valencia?

The *tramontana* still blows fleeced clouds and great black dirty dishrags down on us from Teruel. Very few wounded come in. The ward is almost empty.

We are getting ready to move. We cannot leave until the brigade has gone. An end-of-the-summer, after-the-ball atmosphere of boredom is among us. We are reluctant to go back to the isolation, the gossip, the stagnation and the painful routine of Villa Paz.

The typhoid epidemic is under control. We had enough serum.

Packages from home arrived last night after following us around the Front for three weeks. We had a feast: chocolate, tuna, cheese, *butter*, *candy*, and a jar of local honey given to us as a kind of tribute by the farm lady who did my laundry.

I received two parcels. One of them contained the muffler knitted by the dame whose picture I carry in my cap band. So these Spanish women think they can knit?

The only work I have is to make one trip a day to the *Intendencia* which has been giving us *bacalao*, or dried codfish, to vary the beans. Cannot swallow this stuff. Tastes like rawhide soaked in glue then boiled in machine oil. Sugar, green vegetables and fat are what we need.

Big observation plane, Ours, zebra-camouflaged, sailed slowly overhead this afternoon. Ex-transport bus bought in the early days from the United States; the only bi-motor I have seen on our side. Although she's useless for bombing and combat, the deep throb of her two motors makes you feel warm and good inside. I suspect that she's used only for morale. Some of the boys say she was Ben Leider's* first plane.[47]

February 4. Valverde. Waiting. Rumor of Three Days' Leave in Valencia Seems to Be Authentic

Today, for the first time in many weeks, I've heard the "waiting, waiting, waiting, always bloody-well waiting" song cast its shade over our bright young hearts. There could be no more certain a sign that we will soon re-enter the reserve.

We have begun to pick up and there is a very it-was-nice-while-it-lasted, do-you-remember-the-time, I-really-don't-want-to-go-back, but-wonder-where-it-will-be-next-time atmosphere.

The men have finally come out of the trenches decorated by trench beards

---

* died on the Jarama front

47. Ben Leider was a New York newspaper reporter and amateur aviator who flew with the Republican air force. He was killed over Madrid in 1936. One of the Spanish refugee camps for children was named in his honor. His was the only American body returned to the United States for burial.

and black lice half an inch long, smeared and soiled and torn and scratched, blinking in the sunlight of the anthill of dugouts they have been given to inhabit. As long as the brigade is in this neighborhood, the surgical hospital must wait. A bombing could still light our autoclaves.

I saw three men standing on a low ridge of earth beside the road, heads up in the breeze, almost motionless, paralyzed by the absence of danger.

All of us live within the dream of being able to organize our day into eight shifts of three hours each: one hour of hot bath, one of sleep, one of eating. This morning I stripped to the waist, bathed in a basin of lukewarm water stolen from the ward and brushed the seams of my clothes with gasoline; but it was not the real thing. I am saving my nicely done laundry against the day when I will be able to climb into a marble tub in a Valencia bathhouse.

As usual, in times as slack as these, a good deal of wild talk flows around the cracker-box club which gathers about the wood stove in the ward.

Somebody says that the safe of the Banco de España in Teruel could not be opened until a few of the boys from Chicago got at it. The fifty thousand pesetas in silver *douros* they collected will be sent to our spies. So-and-so swears that we have received five hundred planes "from abroad, and I don't know how" and that we ourselves are making twelve-inch field pieces. The anti-tank guns are, as usual, much lied about. The rumor that we use them to cut our firewood persists. One of the gunners swears that he himself blew up a fifty-gallon fascist soup vat with his pet.

A Spanish comrade tells the story of the capture of Concud, early in the campaign. The rebels had not known we were in the neighborhood until four o'clock one December morning, when eight of our cavalrymen came down from the hills, blasted the only gas-pump in town with grenades and got away. This crippled the fascist transport. An hour later, our infantry and armored cars finished the job.

The morale of the nurses is beginning to split up into petty complaints and gossip, in the lack of work. We have evacuated the last two of the heavy wounded, one to a grave and the other to the Rear, and there is nothing to keep our womankind busy but two men who were slightly wounded when a fire they had lit over an unseen clip of loaded cartridges blew up. All floors, dugouts, trenches and the ground itself must be swept within fifty kilometers of Teruel before a fire can be lit.

The nurses worry that some of them work more than others, that B. caters to the Spanish *enfermeras*, that so-and-so hoarded the sardines she got from the States, that Annie the talkative Queen of the Operating Room thinks that the ward florences are beneath her, and that she ought to be awarded a corporal's stripes. Selma gets far, far too many packages from home and makes too much of a martyr of herself.[48] Rose thinks she's the Virgin Mary and she's a bootlicker because she doesn't join the others in complaining about sleeping quarters, the food and the lack of packages and mail.[49] All the florences are good girls. "God-damn it to hell," I once heard one of them say, "if the building would stop shaking, I could get my needle into the vein!" Our nurses do their work.

Ward-stove jaw fests generally end on the subject of William Carney, correspondent of the *New York Times* with the Rebels, to whom he refers as "the Nationalists." The Carneyphobiacs kill him fifty times with all of the elaborate ways we have of killing people out here, then take him from his manure pile grave and kill him again. Somebody says that Carney runs around in a Franco uniform and begs to be allowed to go on bombing expeditions.

We love Herbert Matthews, correspondent of the *New York Times* with the Loyalists, as much as we hate Carney.[50] A few hours ago he brought us a carton of cigarettes and a bottle of whiskey. We drank half and sent the rest to Merriman, at the Estado Major. Rintz, who ran the errand, says that just as he was about to enter the Estado Major, he slipped and the whole half-bottle of White Horse was smashed. That's Captain Norman Rintz's story and he sticks to it.

Matthews and Hemingway are the only non-military non-Spanish I have seen in Spain.[51] Once when I was filling in a shell hole, a small limousine came tearing down the road so fast I had to put on the ditchdiving act I use when the planes come near. "That's Hemingway," said someone pointing at the vanishing cloud of dust.

"He's a writer and I'm a writer," I thought, and went back to work.

---

48. Selma Chadwick (1904–62), a Polish-born nurse from New York, later served as a captain in the U.S. Army Nursing Corps during World War II.

49. Rose Freed was a laboratory technician who sailed for Spain with the first AMB unit in January 1937.

50. William Carney was the *New York Times* correspondent who covered the Spanish Civil War from the Franco side and with pro-Franco sympathies. Herbert Matthews was the Republican side counterpart at the same newspaper.

51. Ernest Hemingway visited Spain four times during the war, writing reports for the North American Newspaper Alliance, helping to script the documentary film *The Spanish Earth*, and gathering material for short stories, a play, and his novel *For Whom the Bell Tolls*. He also provided and raised funds for ambulances for the Republic and paid travel expenses for some drivers.

Newspaper correspondents, literary men, visiting members of Parliament, trade union leaders and lady novelists in search of a story for the *New Yorker* run through the bowels of the Front—and they are bowels—like a dose of Epsom salts. I cannot blame them. They arrive, ask a few questions, look up at the sky, then jump back into their cars.

We are all profoundly grateful to Matthews for the many times he visited us in Cuevas and Teruel and because he displays more genuine courage and more interest in us than any other newspaperman in Spain. If there are others who have come to the Front lines, male or female, I should like to thank them for their bravery.

When newspapermen visit us, we do not feel quite so much like international orphans.

Ghosts of the Civil War
Heliodoro, the Heroic Kitchen-Boy

Pistols are carried only by officers, first-aid men, transport drivers and by all chófers but myself.

Few side-arms are to be seen in battalion kitchens, but Heliodoro, hewer of wood and soaker of beans in a Fifth Army Corps field-kitchen, wanted a gun. All men at war want side-arms, although, with the exception of the Parabellums which can be transformed into a fair carbine, they are the most useless of our killing machines.

Heliodoro wanted a pistol because rifles were too common, too rare and too big for him and because there was nothing else of value he wanted and stood a chance of getting. The kitchen staff liked their apprentice, but could not help laughing at Heliodoro, one evening at the Front, when he was presented a pistol made of a bent soup spoon in a holster hammered from a willy-can.

That evening the food truck was late in leaving the cave at the bottom of the ridge on whose crest were the lines. The shelling had been very heavy.

The food-wagon slowly climbed the ladder-path lit by the reflection of experimental incendiary shells towards the crest of the Cerro. The two men in the cab talked little. Men in cars under fire do not ordinarily speak. Suddenly there was a hammering at the back of their compartment.

The driver stopped his car, and came back carrying the wriggling body of Helidoro.

"He hid in the big spare pot," the driver told his helper. "I guess he got frightened or something."

"Frightened, nothing. Look at your hands. Heliodoro has been wounded."

"Well, it's a shame he wasn't killed—say, this means we must have lost a good pot."

"The pot can be mended."

"Leave him in it. We'll stew him up in the beans for dinner."

The food wagon was now reaching the top of the hill. The attack, unusually strong, had lasted until after dark. The fascists must have thought they were about to break through.

A shell cut crosswise across the cab and took the chófer's legs and life with it. The helper was a cook and could not drive. The camion would have stayed where it was hit, drawing shells through the darkness into its heart if Heliodoro had not taken it to the top of the ridge, where the pots were taken by men as hungry as only those who have begun to think they have been betrayed, sacrificed and forgotten can be.

No one had known that Heliodoro could drive a truck. He let none of the men know that he was wounded.

It was his right leg. Ascending the hill, he had not needed it, for there was no reason to use his brakes. Coming down he kept his car in low gear and used his engine for a brake. He was no more than a mile or two from the kitchen.

Before Heliodoro had begun to roll well on his way home, men appeared on the road and attempted to hold him up. These were fascists who had accidentally slipped through the Republican lines during the height of the afternoon attack.

Heliodoro stepped as hard on the accelerator as his pain would permit. He had to slow down when his tires were shot flat.

A fascist jumped to the running board. Heliodoro drew his bent spoon gun from its tin can holster.

Crashing down the hill on two flat front tires, the cook wagon shot across the kitchen courtyard. Unable to put on the brakes because of his wounded right leg, Heliodoro died against the tree which stopped and saved his car.

On moonlit nights, when there has been much fighting, the figure of a boy may be seen wherever there is a Classification Post, bent, groping in the little piles of equipment taken from the wounded.

This is the ghost of Heliodoro the kitchen boy. He still wants a gun.

February 5. Valverde.

The Major called us together last night and told us that as soon as the brigade leaves, our group will go to Valencia on three days' leave, although he could not understand what we had done to deserve such a reward.

The lines are deadlocked and the campaign is done. What's left of Teruel is ours. The Alfambra valley belongs only to the dead. Defenses and fortifications are ranged up and down the valley down which Franco planned to march triumphantly to Valencia, last December. The onslaught which stopped him several feet behind his tracks was really a counter-drive anticipating an attack.

Every farm, shed, tunnel, bridge and sheepfold in this neighborhood is a field hospital, a dump of ammo, a mobile auto-parque, an *Intendencia*, an Estado Major, a field telephone depot or an artillery repair station. We are ready for any and all pushes against Valencia.

Yesterday, towards twilight, I was caught on the road so suddenly by the loudness of the roaring of so many planes so near the ground that I had no chance to run.

I got out and could not believe that the twenty-six small biplanes that' rocketed by like shells flying backwards were really Ours until I saw militiamen all up and down the road yelling and jumping and hooking their fists.

Our twenty-six hedge-jumping Gloriosos roared through the sunset under an early moon straight towards the fascist lines on the Muela.

We cheered and danced on the road until multiple black rings of smoke low among the hills on the horizon showed that the fascist anti-aircraft had spoken. Then came the crash of the twenty-six cargoes of bombs un-loading all at once on the same spot.

Seven minutes later all twenty-six planes came back, landed in the fields and disappeared under trees and camouflage. It was now almost night. By morning the airport would be moved.

February 7. The Last Few Hours of Valverde and Teruel

Orders to move came last night.

In a few minutes the operating table, left in place until the last moment, will be loaded.

Will have to gas up in the Puebla. Hate this pump above all others because of the dud buried up to the wings (eight inches in diameter) half a car length from the tanks. No one has felt capable of digging it out of the hard-surfaced road.

In six hours I'll be in Valencia. What will I do there?

My pockets are full of crisp new hundred-peseta notes. First I'll put up in the best room of the best hotel, then buy louse-killer, then go to a bathhouse with my laundry under my arm. Then I'll get a shave and a haircut, if I can find a barber willing to work on me.

After that I'll buy everything I see to eat and dine in every restaurant and bathe in every bathhouse. I'll buy a uniform, a pair of the most expensive high boots, a big knife, plenty of socks and anything else I happen to like. I'm going to sleep twelve hours a day, bathe for four, and eat the rest of the time.

Perhaps I'll look over the local whores.

And after the three days are over, I hope I will not go back to Villa Paz.

Teruel, we who did not die salute you!

February 8. Hotel Metropole. Valencia

<u>Segorbe-Valencia.</u> Halfway to the former wartime capital, new hills began to spring up. In their hollows we saw the first palms, evergreen *algarroberas* and healthy olive trees. In the gardens tender velvety *habichuelas* (horse beans) were already a foot high. There was more and more running water. We stopped to look at a cherry tree in full blossom, as if we had left the country of death and winter behind us and were coming back on earth, like Proserpine to the land of spring and life.

All kinds of feelings of tenderness welled up inside of me when I looked at the color of the cherry blossoms. I was very grateful that the tree should grow here like a bouquet for us and wished that our victory could have been more complete. For an instant, before I realized how valuable ripe cherries would soon be, I thought of tearing down the limbs and spreading them over the mud-smeared and metal-torn body of my car.

By the time that we were roaring down the Barcelona road to Valencia, we had peeled off coats, sweaters, gloves and mufflers and were driving through solid orchids of cherry trees, each flowering in an individual shade of mauve-pink, water-gray and rosiness as sheer as a Paris actress's freshly-laundered chemise.

Among the wax green leaves of the rows of orange trees ripe fruit burned in the intense Mediterranean sun like daylight lanterns. From time to time we passed vistas of the sea, which had been for me before the war at Mallorca and Capri, Rapallo and Dubrovnik, the end of all hopes and sleep, exercise and rest and excitement this side of paradise.

Nothing can violate the tranquility of the sunlight on Mediterranean shores and sedative purity of its prow-scarred waves, not even the men who are so anxious to show to the earth that only mankind can be completely hideous.

We hissed down the seacoast overhung by rosy-tan cliffs on which the Iberians had stood off the Romans and on which we may some day stand against Goths, with the speed of a humming-bird making for a bed of larkspur at sunset.

<u>Valencia. Late afternoon until the hours of sleep.</u> Albrecht Durer, when asked why he lived in Venice instead of Nuremburg, used to answer, "Here in Italy they think I'm a gentleman. At home I'm a bum."[52] That's the way we feel about the Front. Up in the lines we have dignity; here in Valencia, the place the I.B. ought to be able to think of as home, we feel ourselves to be strangers.

When do we go back to the Front?

There are people in civilian clothes, stores are open and full of goods, the many women wear makeup, the streets are full of automobile horns and pedestrians. People smile and gesticulate, little catspaw storms of amenities, petty worries and above all, personality are constantly breaking over their faces. Some of the girls wear manicured and painted finger nails.

Jack and I stood silent and paralyzed before a salesgirl in a department store as she put on her highly mannerized chatter. Did we want shaving cream or Florida water or a razor blade sharpener, a rubber scrubbing brush or a nail-file? There was a special sale of toilet-cases, non-wrinkling, waterproof and dustproof. I noticed that she was having a hard time keeping her eyes off the vulture-claw hands I had laid on the counter. Silently we waited for the sales talk of this roughed cockatoo to run out.

"Comrade. . . . "

The cockatoo seemed to be slightly shocked at what I had called her.

"Comrade," I repeated, "have you anything to kill lice?"

Outraged, she turned on her sales-patter, to let us know that she had never heard of lice. Offhand she didn't look as if she were lousy. Some new vegetable soap, synthetic but just as good as real soap, had just that morning arrived from Barcelona. Did we want celluloid or glass toothbrush cases, and. . . .

"Comrade," Jack spoke out of the illness that had come over him, "do you know that there's a war on?"

---

52. Albrecht Dürer (1471–1528) was a German painter.

The girl gave us a quick look and bit through the thick rouge on her lower lip.

"*Sí.* There is a war. We will win. We have shaving brushes, not made of hair but of a new kind of fibre which. . . . "

We feel like Rip van Winkles, like polar explorers, like paroled convicts, like lunatics just let out of the asylum, but not, thank God, like Crusaders. I keep wanting to tell everyone I see in the street that I have just come from the Front and that the war is going very well and that we do not mind the planes. These are the people whose homes and families and futures we have come to Spain to defend. A lot of the bastards do not even wear uniforms. The many officers with creased trousers and neat side-arms do not look as if they had been to the Front. Only the militiamen on Leave like us, who have the kind of gone frozen look we know so well, seem glad to see us. The rest of the people here avoid our long looks as studiously as if they owed us money they cannot repay. They do and cannot. Nor did we come here to be paid. We are here on business, but not to be paid.

I am so little of a hero that a bootblack, after one look at my shoes, refused to attempt to shine them. When bootblacks turn you down, you have fallen low.

Filled from bomb-proof cellar to wide open roof with militiamen on Leave, officers and the civilian men whose business and purpose worry us, the Metropole is one of the best hotels in Valencia. The Inglés used to be better but, buried by itself, died while we were at Teruel. Somewhere in the ruins is the bathtub in which I once soaked for an hour and the plate off which I ate a dish of wild mushrooms and the cup that had once held thick Spanish chocolate.

Jack and I have a good room and bath so high up that the smoke of the gasoline tank set on fire two days ago can be seen through our window, which is now shut because it is night and the lights are on. I believe I heard sirens several times today. What will we do when They really come over? The technique of behavior in a city while being bombed is new to us. We will probably stay right where the sirens find us. The many *refugios*—never too many—with the modernistic architecture entrances are reserved for women and children. One place is just about as good as another in a city. I had one bath this afternoon and I am going to take another just as soon as Jack staggers out of the black tile bathroom.

The soft bed on which I write is full of peanut shells, candy papers and crumbs of cakes.

In four hours I put away, most of it shamelessly eaten on the street:

A good two-peseta meal (Front pay for chófers is fifteen pesetas a day) at the International Brigade headquarters: soup, good Soviet noodles, beans with a slice of canned Uruguay beef, fresh thick green escarole salad, wine, bread and a handful of dry almonds.

Eight oranges and four mandarins.

Four ginger cakes I had the good luck to buy on the street (the entire stock of the seller).

A quarter-pound of half-ripe dates picked off the sidewalk palms.

A long bag of wettish peanuts.

An expensive package of chocolates.

A jar of mayonnaise made of egg powder, flour and rancid olive oil.

Five more oranges.

A bag of roasted acorns.

Dinner at the hotel: soup of sour potatoes; a slice of Uruguay tinned beef disguised as a Swiss steak by a thick sauce of tomato, onions and talc, and one roll, the size, shape, weight and color of a concussion grenade; a slice of fig bread for desert; four glasses of vermouth and four saucers of bitter little olives.

I went back to a street stand for more fig bread after dinner was over, but the stock had sold out.

We have just come home from the lobby of a theatre in which we had been told we would find whores. The few good-looking girls were taken by the many militiamen and we did not have the energy to walk to the nearest whorehouse, so we came home.

Of all the things I ate today, the salad tasted best.

I think that only one or two of the boys went to whorehouses. The clean rooms, the good food, the beds with the fresh sheets and above all the incessant bathing are more than equivalent of intercourse. I have enough money in my pockets to rent the best woman in Valencia for twelve hours, but well, I need shoes and a uniform and, well, some day, perhaps . . . but it will have to be with a girl I like. After so long I do not want it to be dirty and dangerous.

I had a date for dinner with Phyllis, one of the English nurses. She did not show up. It appears that I did not know that she and Captain Johnny, the Hungarian Divisional optician, have for a long time been in love.[53]

Well, I think I'll eat four more mandarins, read two or three more thin grey newspapers and magazines, bathe and turn in.

---

53. Johnny Kyszely.

Tomorrow I put on my clean underwear. Have to get shoes and a uniform and socks before I leave this town.

Think I will try to eat *calamares rellenos*. This is a dish which used to be my favorite when I was in Spain in 1930–1931. I doubt if my search will be successful, for very few of the fishing boats leave Valencia harbor. Before I left the States, a friend of mine who was in Mallorca at the outbreak of the invasion told me that she had seen six Italian battleships drawn up at the Palma docks, each with the name "Canarias" lettered on the stern. "Canarias" is the name of one of Franco's few cruisers. Why should our navy put out to sea?

The newspapers publish the following story: An Italian submarine of unknown nationality torpedoed a freighter. She was unable to submerge because the current in her batteries was low. Before the British and French Nyons Treaty patrol destroyers could come up, an Italian destroyer reached the Italian submarine and rammed her, thus destroying evidence which would have embarrassed Chamberlain.

On another occasion an Italian submarine was crippled by one of our armed fishing trawlers and sank in shallow water. The salvage crew we sent out to raise evidence for the Planned Intervention Committee was driven off by an Italian destroyer, although many Italian seamen's lives might have been saved.

To add the final marine touch, I might say that this is being written from the bathtub where I sit like Marat facing Charlotte Corday.[54] The knife of sleep, sharp as the bow of the Italian destroyer that sank the Italian submarine, sinks into me.

Tomorrow I will have to find a pair of shoes and a uniform.

No Military Police in Valencia. None needed.

February 9. Valencia. Hotel Metropole

Bad luck. I had not realized that today would be Sunday and that all stores would be closed.

A few of the florences persuaded me to drive them 40 miles north up the seacoast to see their florence friends. Here in Bencasim, base of all International hospitals, therapeutic institutions and rest homes, each of our girls had a string of amatory friendships among the wounded.

I bathed in Sappho's sea just as it was becoming wine-dark, scrubbing myself hard with salt cold brine. What the hot tubs of the Hotel Metropole did

---

54. Charlotte Corday assassinated Jean-Paul Marat during the French Revolution.

not do perhaps salt water will; but only a completely new set of clothing will really delouse me. I hope that the reader does not begin to itch.

Benicasim, a stretch of sandy beach protected by castle-topped mountains, has always been famous for its lemons and its mild climate. Formerly a middle-class summer resort, it has come to be known as the best place in which to be sick in all of Spain. The Casa Gorki, a fine villa in the center of the beach as House of Culture was equipped with wall newspapers in many languages, a beautiful garden, a radio and a piano, a library and a cantine in which small cups of coffee with real sugar (the coffee in the Valencia cafés was served with Soviet saccharine) were sold, and fresh orange and lemon juice.

Towards sunset many wounded walk down the palm path at the edge of the shore or stand looking out to see. The poignancy of all Mediterranean shores at sunset is for once understandable. So many of these men, wanted badly by the political police in their own countries, are maimed and unemployable in Spain. What future do disabled Internationals face?

It took me six hours to drive back to Valencia. Water in the gasoline as usual. Perhaps last night when my car was on the street someone tampered with my gas tank. Tonight I will leave my car in a garage where no one can touch her. Suppose one of the garage mechanics is a spy or a saboteur?

We never should have got back to Valencia last night if the breakdown had occurred in a place other than Sagunto. This port is a town through which all chófers drive fast, for it has been bombed, by actual count, one hundred and fifty-three times since the beginning of the invasion. My luck in having broken down there was that I was able to make a tow cable of a blasted telephone-pole guy.

I had missed both my Sunday meals. Like many beauties, Benicasim is not only bad luck but expensive.

February 10. Valencia. Stand-by Orders. 6 P.M.

Bad news. Something unpleasant has happened up at the Front. Looks as if we're going back. But where? If my car were not in a garage for repairs, I should have gone back to Villa Paz with the others this afternoon. I am the only one of our group who has not checked out of the Metropole.

I just came home from a long delirium of shopping and walking, eyes wide open and mouth generally full, shamelessly, of knick-knacks bought on the street. The fire lit by bombers three days ago shadows the street with smoke and fear. There was never a city in which people walk so quickly and talk so little.

In one of the many flourishing bookstores, I met a writer whom I had known in the States. He looked at me as Gold Star Mothers look at the American flag.[55] I was very much ashamed. He had heard that I had been very seriously wounded. That was the rumor that spread from the scratch I got on my head at Kilometer 2½. If something like that happens again, I will not tell anyone.

Not a single pair of high boots of any size was to be found in the entire city. Plenty of shoemakers were willing to make me shoes if I gave them leather. Eventually I found a shoemaker who would make me a very luxurious pair for two hundred and seventy-five pesetas, or almost three weeks' pay. The uniform I ordered will cost four hundred and seventy-five pesetas. It will be ready in two weeks. I paid deposits and will have to take a chance on coming back to Valencia some day and with requisite number of arms and legs, hands and feet to put into my new outfit when it is ready. The tailor and the shoemaker are good business men. If I do not come back, they will keep my deposit and sell my belongings.

I did not like the two fattish heavily beauty-shopped women I saw at the shoemaker's ordering very fancy slippers for themselves. Although they did not dare to wear hats (I have not seen a single hat on one woman since I have come to this country), they were obviously wives of guys who are cashing in on the war. How could these women order fancy shoes in a time like this? For whose eyes?

I had returned to the *Soldado Desconocido* for a fitting when I heard the heavy clatter of big anti-aircraft on the tops of nearby buildings and the slamming of many iron shop-fronts.

Customers and salesmen went to the rear of the store where sewing girls by the light of a single candle were chirping like sparrows under eaves awaiting a storm. One of them was crying.

It was plain that the fitting had to be postponed. I grew bored and went out to the empty half-dark streets. One place is just about as good as any other in a city.

As usual the planes had come at the hours between day and dusk, when the sky is full of shapes and swarming shadows. The Savoia-Marchettis ride in from the sea at a great altitude, cut their engines and glide down on the

---

55. The Gold Star Mothers club, founded after World War I, consisted of mothers who had a son killed in war and who, the author implies, held feelings of intense pride for their sacrifice.

fuming chimney pots of the city, impossible to hear and very hard for the anti-aircraft gunners to see, for it is too early for searchlights to be of use.

The last of the mothers and the children had fled to the refuges. Large open cars, each mounting a machine-gun, toured the empty streets at high speed.

The clatter of the anti-aircraft continued although I could hear no engines. The fascists must be riding high and silently.

Heavy crashes, more muffled and resonant than anything I had heard at the Front, came from the many hearts of the stricken city.

I felt as if I'd rather be at the Front. Not one in twenty of the people who are dug out of a murdered house are found to have been killed by metal. I would rather be at the Front, where six and seven story buildings do not stand in all their dead weight ready to slaughter everyone in, under and near them.

Our planes are not at the Front and not over the cities. Where are they?

At first I thought that it was anti-aircraft shrapnel that buzzed past me like mosquitoes in a dark room. Then I realized that I had heard several rifle reports.

I immediately found a deep doorway.

If one of the touring cars with the machine-guns whose purpose I now understood came down the street, I would stop it. Meanwhile I kept my eyes on the buildings across the way.

The vote in 1936 had been very close.

An officer came down the street. When he had almost reached my doorway, a spear of red light shot out of a second floor window. The officer wheeled into my doorway and pulled his pistol.

He did not know where to shoot. When I said that I had seen the flash of the rifle he gave me his gun. It was a good Soviet 7.65 Colt. I emptied it into the window while the officer took down the address of the house. Glass fell to the sidewalk. This was the first time I had shot at fascists. I have begun to pay them back a little of the lead they poured on my ambulance on the Alfambra road.

The officer put another clip into his gun and we crossed the street. Both doorways that led into the building from which the sniper had shot were barred with sheet-iron bomb-coverings.

I walked slowly along the streets. By the time I reached the Metropole the sound of planes, Ours, had reached my ears. Lights went on, the doors of the movies in the Plaza Castelar again blazed and the city resumed its normal, abnormal life.

Tomorrow morning a list of the casualties will appear in the newspapers.

PART FOUR

Segura: Counter-Attack

Toby Jensky Photographs Collection, Abraham Lincoln Brigade Archives, Tamiment Library, New York University.

Figure 6: From top left, nurses Sana Goldblatt and Toby Jensky and driver James Neugass with other staff and a group of Spanish children.

Franco's attacks on Teruel and the Aragon intensified, as did the brigades'
defense. The battle was carried out in the air, with artillery, machine guns,
rifles, grenades, and hand-to-hand. Every town and hill had strategic sig-
nificance. The brigade launched a diversionary attack on the Fascists in
mid-February from Segura de los Baños, a town on the front line sixty
miles from Teruel, in an effort to protect the city and the whole Aragon
front. Barsky's American medical team that had formed at Villa Paz was
now located in Muniesa, fifteen miles from Segura, where they could tend
to the many casualties. The unit was now more vulnerable to bombing. By
late February, though, everything would change.

^{crf}

February 13. Aliaga. Back at the Front

Valencia was a dream, then a hallucination; and now a dream again.

When the battalion pulled out of Teruel, we left a clean orderly house behind us. The campaign had been tied up in blue ribbon tight as the armature
of a dynamo, then stored away in mothballs for the summer.

A few hours later after the last truckload of volunteers left the reserve
positions, all the red torrents of the sky poured down on the Argente Visiedo
sector, on the Celadas positions which the Lincoln-Washingtons had once
defended with six Maxims and a hundred men, on the Alfambra road and the
town of Alfambra.

More iron per cubic foot of air came down on the Marineros who were
at the apex of the fascist attack than had filled the skies since Verdun and
Chateau Thierry. The Marineros are sometimes called the Famous Running
Marines. They ran at Cordoba, they ran at Brunete, and they now ran from
Alfambra and they did not stop running until the fascists had swallowed up
the hard-won strength of our lines to the depth of thirty kilometers, all in
twelve hours of daylight. Four, five, eleven towns were taken.

If the Campesinos had not been called out of bed, nothing but breath-
lessness should have stopped Franco. The Campesinos have already re-taken
four of the eleven lost towns.

The Division and the brigade are now back at the Front, waiting to advance. From now on, we are in for it. The concentration of artillery and
planes we had drawn in the second phase of the defense of Teruel has played
no more than the overture of the drama. The show is going to have more acts
than the bare-knuckle foot-to-foot slugging match John L. Sullivan staged
with Fitzgibbons a long time ago in New Orleans. The second stage of the

defense of Teruel was a spring rain compared to the gale which has now begun to blow. The full weight of the fascist attack, expected ever since the Fall
of the Asturias, has now begun to fall.[1]

The Aragon-to-Guadalajara-and-back-again feinting match is over, finished with, done. For four weary months we have swung all our material back
and forth up and down the Aragon-Guadalajara seven hundred kilometer
circuit. With geography on his side, Franco needed to travel no more than
two hundred kilometers to feint at us back and forth across the waist of the
Teruel salient. To block the threat of his blows we had to run three times that
distance around the mountain legs.

There will be no more feinting. Franco's mask is off. Behind it we see not
the half-hearted ferocity of von Blomberg and Fritsch, but the totalitarian
expressions of Keitel and Raeder.[2] We always had known what we were in
for when we heard that Hitler had fired the two fundamentally Army men
whom he had inherited from the Second Reich as the rulers of his forces, and
had chosen two new commanders who had the full Nazi totalitarian concept
of world war. Fritsch and von Blomberg had cramped down on the exports of
munitions and men to Spain.

Prophets, political soothsayers, militant pacifists and astronomers had
better come to Spain if they want to see what the entire earth will look like in
the coming years. If H. G. Wells could travel in the path of Franco, he would
not have to depend on an already overtaxed imagination for the writing of
his next vision of the future condition of human life on earth. We may now
call ourself Mars and let some slightly less bloody planet name itself The
Earth. A black, dripping sun has arisen. All the stops in the organ of death
have been pulled out, the last act of Götterdämerung is upon us. In a blood-
red sunset an earthquake topples and sets afire the pillars of Wotan's castle.
The waters of the Rhine engulf the ruins. Lady Macbeth has incarnadined
the multitudinous Mediterranean. Spain, the bad conscience and whipping
boy of the Democracies, suffers first.

Was I ever in Valencia? Is there such a place? When will the Fifteenth go
on a rest and what is a rest? Why did I come to Spain? The furnace of Teruel

---

1. The Nationalist (Francoist) campaign against the northern province of Asturias culmi-
nated in the capture of the city of Gijón on October 21, 1937.

2. Werner von Blomberg and Werner von Fritsch were career army officers in the German
army, both of whom were purged by Nazi leaders for alleged morals problems in January 1938. Wilhelm Keitel was a German field marshall, later tried at Nuremberg for
war crimes and executed in 1946. Erich Raeder was a German naval officer and admiral
before and during World War II.

was a flaming paper match in comparison with the fire in which Aragon and the earth will now be consumed.

Part of the Medical Corps of the Eleventh Brigade of Internationals was captured in front of Alfambra. I understand that they use the side of an ambulance instead of a brick wall for the execution of captured medical personnel. Wise drivers carry grenades for the demolition of their cars and themselves in case of capture or accidental crossing of the lines. In this mountainous country the lines are a series of entrenched positions rather than a groove of earthworks, and the lines are not infrequently crossed.

I know that the notion of taking some of the enemy with you when you get yours is childish and Mohammedan, but in case I get mine, and in case I do not, I hope that I will soon be able to say that the money the anti-fascists of America invested in sending me to Spain has been repaid with its full weight in blood. From a purely personal and scientific point of view, if I do not get back at them soon and in a satisfactory manner, paranoia will shake my hands from my gearshift lever and wheel. The revolver I emptied into that shadowy window in Valencia during the bombing—how many days ago was that?—helped steady me, but shooting at shadows is more vicarious than satiating.

If the London pimp would only cease pumping morphine into his Washington and Paris white slaves![3] If we could only give Them some of what They gave us! Let us face them on equal terms just once, just for forty-eight hours! We beat Franco in the first three months. We could finish Adolf and Benito in another three. Why are we being punished? What have we done? Twenty-three million people dreamed that they should not be poor. Twenty-three million people thought that human nature was essentially social and not anti-social, thought that they could rise from their Seventeenth Century sick beds and walk out into the scientific light of the Twentieth. That is why we are being punished.

Valencia to Villa Paz

With the consciousness that my car might any moment be needed at the Front, I drove two hundred miles in five hours and arrived at my base to find out that our front-line group, reorganized and re-equipped in six hours, had already left for the Front. Since I had been up the entire night in Valencia,

---

3. A reference to British Prime Minister Neville Chamberlain, whose policy of non-intervention in the Spanish Civil War effectively tied the hands of France and the United States.

relaying telephone messages from Major B. in Barcelona to Villa Paz, the Commandante told me to go to bed.

I ate cold mashed potatoes and cold bread pudding and then found my old bed in the ward of the Arms and Legs.

Villa Paz had changed while we were at the Front. Not only was it quiet, clean and orderly, but the precision in which it was run was evidence of the fact that both the Command and the Staff had at last understood that the biceps in the right arm of Democracy is Discipline.

Cars and personnel were reviewed in the courtyard and the Republican flag was lifted at 7 A.M. With all the talk about the strengthening of discipline, orders are somehow not given as absolute orders. It is all very well for the Commandante to read off the Order of the Day in a mock and urbane fashion that takes the edge off the military stench of his words, but we should not consider that any order given by any officer is optional.

Somehow we cannot bring ourselves to rise from our chairs or to salute when an officer below the rank of General enters the room. We never see a General. In spite of their contrary convictions, our commanders are grateful for the democratic spirit by which we thus receive them. There is still no officer's mess.

The staff of the base hospital had been much reduced while we were away. There had been a tendency for healed men to stay on for pedicures or as supernumeraries or simply because they enjoyed hospital life and did not wish to go back to their brigade. All this waste of human material has now been eliminated.

Immediately I was on my feet. I went to the Commandante and asked him for a gun. Pistols are looked upon as almost our sole personal possessions but I believe that Major F. understood that I meant to take away a pistol from one of our base hospital cowboys by force and the hell with discipline if I were not given one.[4]

He issued me a good German 7.65 taken from the fascists at Cordoba and a full clip of cartridges.

By noon I had assembled a United States Army canteen, two tin hats, a bag of raisins and a handful of dry but sweet cakes. Popeye, the blond walrus-mustached mechanic I was to take to the Front, is the best organizer in the brigade. We were entitled to draw iron rations for two men for one day. Instead we drew enough bully beef and bread and marmalade and raisins for

---

4. Major F., Abraham Irving Friedman (1908–66) of Hackensack, New Jersey, headed the American Hospital Unit on the Cordoba front before transferring to the Teruel area.

four days. While the commissary clerk[*] was searching his shelves, Popeye and I organized half a fresh goat's milk cheese, four onions, a can of stewed corn, two tins of Boston baked beans, a huge can of sweet potato and glucose jam, another and even larger tin of *carne* and a carton containing forty-eight cans of unsweetened condensed milk. The hell with the wounded. We were going to the Front and we were not going to be hungry for at least three days.

I tried to get some clothing from our pitiful supply of cottonish torn and patched garments each of them worn by at least five men who had died, but there was nothing to fit me. The only thing I can use, ready-made, is a toothbrush.

Before I left Villa Paz I visited Captain S. He lay in bed, blue eyes and cheeks bright with fever, betrayed by not only the Intervention Committee but by himself. His lungs have gone back on him. Perhaps his campaign is over. As soon as they are fit for transportation, his prize-fighter's frame and broken beak will be carried to the warm climate of Murcia. S. is angry and has always been angry because he knows and always has known that the chances of his dying in his shoes, hip artillery smoking and face towards the fascists—and this is the way Communists who have taken war as their assignment should die—are constantly smaller and smaller. S. is a better man than I am. Don't say we're heroic. Call us anything else but don't say we are heroic. We are business men coldly in Spain on business. Emotion could do no more than interfere with the deal we have assigned ourselves to clinch.

I spent the rest of the day at the Casa Lujan garage, oiling my springs, tightening bolts, cleaning out my gas-line and completing the repair job the Valencia army garage, biggest I had ever in my life seen, had been unable to finish. There was welding to be done all over the hood and the body, but we are out of *carburo*, or acetylene. I have long thought of taking a leaf out of each spring. If this were done my sweetheart would shake less and not need so much welding but the weakened springs would then probably break. These are the alternatives with which we are constantly faced. Driving a belly case faster than twelve miles an hour over the best road in Spain will kill him, but if you do not run fast enough to get away from the planes, he will be killed anyway and take yourself and your car with him. Spain cannot fight and eat at once but we have to fight and we have to starve. Ether poured into a dying man is ether wasted but we cannot let our men die without helping them up

---

[*] Joe Young, dead. [Neugass erred in this note: Young was actually a prisoner of war, released in 1939.]

to the last moment and with our last material. Plaster poured about the leg of a case who has also been hit in the head may be plaster wasted, but suppose we did not set the broken hip and the patient nevertheless recovered?

How much morphine have we let men take into their graves?

While Jack Devine, Les and Karl were putting the finishing touches on my car, I swam in the tank of hot spring water Don Lujan had long ago built for his country home, now used as Medical Corps garage and overflow hospital.[5] The mechanics lead a peaceful life in this secluded valley. The five of them pool all the food they can buy or receive from the States or steal or organize and really eat well. Evelyn, Karl's blond truckdriver wife, brings candy and other essentials from Barcelona. This Valkyrie is one of the most reliable efficient camion chófers in all of Spain.

After organizing a spare tire, two brand new inner tubes, a box of tire patch, a set of tire tools, a spare battery and a tool-kit from Karl, Popeye and I set out for Cuenca and the Front.

Since the Villa Paz Commandante did not and could not, because of the extreme fluidity of the lines, tell us how we would have to reach Major B. and the brigade, Popeye and I were pretty much on our own.

He had chosen the Cuenca road. With the car full of food and spare parts and tools, we were in high spirits. Unfortunately Popeye has been able to find no cartridges that fit his big nickel-plate revolver. He says that he'll be able to throw it at the fascists in case he never finds the right kind of shell.

I was glad that it had taken me until sunset to get free of Villa Paz. These roads are not healthy during daylight. By passing through Cuenca instead of winding back to Valencia, we should save at least two hundred kilometers. We should have to go through the pit of the Teruel furnace, but we knew we might at that very moment be badly needed and looked forward to the adventure which was sure to come.

Famous Dying Words

1) Charley Regan (real name), New York subway conductor and World War veteran, who had taught the boys so much of the "fine points of

---

5. John "Jack" Michael Devine of San Francisco was chief mechanic with rank of sergeant in the Medical Transport section of the 35th Division. Karl Rahman was an auto mechanic and husband of Evelyn Hutchins, Les Hutchins' sister, one of the few women enlisted in the 15th Brigade.

the game." His favorite saying was "you can't fool Charley Regan." At Brunete a 75 fooled Charley, and these were his dying words.[6]
2)   Wolfgang Goethe. "Light!"

Casa Lujan to Cuenca. Halfway to Cuenca when we had left the wheat-mangy arid plains of Castile behind us, Popeye and I stopped for dinner. In spite of the treasure we were carrying with us, I could down no more than half a tin of willy and a slice of raw onion.

In Cuenca we found a wine-shop and loaded a dozen bottles of watery muscatel and quinine-tasting sherry.

Cuenca to Libros (one bottle of muscatel and a can of baked beans). Road was full of trucks; full ones moving up men and guns, empties coming back for another cargo. Most of the camions were the Mexicanskys that arrived early enough in the war to carry the wounded Republic on their thousand backs until she was well enough to walk. Our new fleets are all of them American; Diamond T's, Autocar and GMC gray-green regulation army trucks, with streamlined cab, steel body, towing chains, collapsible prairie-schooner covers, short wheel-base, plenty of speed and power, easily turned, and good climbers. Each of these camions can carry forty to fifty men and all their equipment. White trucks, larger than the troop fleets, can carry a cannon tank up a shell-torn mountain road at fifty miles an hour or half a battery of light mountain guns, crew and ammunition. Whites are heroes in a country where every truck is Siegfried. I cannot say that the chófers are of the same calibre. I have passed too many of them, woken up and cursed too many, and seen too many wrecks. These drivers, most of them from the Catalan Anarchist transport trade union are great guys, but they have a lot to learn. Bakunin, unlike Karl Marx, did not write upon the inadvisability of parking in the middle of the road.

Libros to Valverde. 2 a.m. to 6 a.m. (a bottle of sherry and a quarter-pound of Minorcan goat's milk cheese). As we neared Teruel and the lines, the temperature fell and ice started to form on the inside of my windshield and white glue swam inside of my eyelids. Although Popeye is the kind of mechanic who can mend a burned out bearing with chewing gum and a hairpin while under fire and at night without lights, he cannot drive. Several months ago he

---

6. Charles Joseph Regan, born in 1892, from Toledo, Ohio, served as an auto mechanic.

drove a dispatch motorcycle head-on into a truck and not only broke an arm and a leg but killed his passenger and fractured his driving morale.

We got a flat and changed to the spare. Another flat would cripple us for we had no tire pump.

We drove closer and closer to the place where the lines should be without hearing a sound or seeing a road guard. Began to pass the wires of field telephones—a sure sign that the lines must be near. Kept stopping, looking at maps, and asking all the militiamen we saw for directions. Eventually found the cut-off for which we were looking, but not the right one it seemed.

High in the stone desert mountains of the Puerto de Escandon, we struck a wretched town, dead because it had been bombed to death or had been evacuated or was entirely asleep. There was not even a starved cur to bark at us and range the jagged road ahead of our wheels like the shadow of one of the four werewolves of the Apocalypse. I believe that the name of this place was Cascante or Cubla. We reached the main square but there were two paths out of it, one of which ended in a *barranco* and the other up against the rock wall of the mountains. The sole exit which was not blind led us up clay cliffs, through groves of jack-pine and then onto snow-fields, always climbing at such an angle that I thought I would stall and then have to turn about and back up these incessant hideous slopes.

We finally came out on a bald mountain top. Here the road was almost imperceptible. Saw more and more foxholes freshly scratched into the earth by men under fire. Began to get nervous. I was not sure where we were or where we were going. I am always nervous, driving at night without headlights near the lines when I hear nothing. I see no one and I am not sure where I am. Most of the military roads hastily built behind the lines or enlarged out of goat paths by the engineers and called *"pistas"* are not on any map.

Began to think that we had run into another of our air fields because of the crisscross of tire-tracks that led nowhere in broad circles. No hangars. The low pines would furnish the necessary camouflage. Everything must be under a tree if not under earth. I am thinking of planting some kind of fast-growing foliage in the dirt of my ears and coat-pockets for self camouflage.

Not having seen a human being or a light for nearly an hour, Popeye and I started to pull hard on our cigarettes.

Sparks flew ahead of us.

"Popeye," I said, "shut your window. Your cigarette's blowing burning ashes ahead of us."

Popeye pointed to his window. It was shut. So was mine.

"Sparks, hell! Those are strays!"

Just when I was thinking of sliding a cartridge into the chamber of my gun, we ran into the road-guard's hut. We were in Republican soil.

Late at night or early in the morning we got another flat. In not more than three minutes we had run under a pine tree, ripped open my blankets and gone to sleep. I had no tire pump on board and there was no way of moving until I could get one.

We were waked by the early sunlight that came through the cut glass palace of frosted window glass our breathing had made of the interior of my soiled butcher-wagon hearse.

Our joints, the radiator, the ground we jumped to and the ditch at the side of the road were all frozen. We lit a fire of the pine-bough camouflage that happened to be lying beside the car, then all at once began to warm beans and onions over the fire, to work at our tires, to thaw out the radiator and to flag the trucks that started coming down the roads.

A German dispatch rider lent us his tire pump and we soon were back on the road.

All the way to Aliaga we passed evidence of the gathering momentum of the counter-attack we are preparing: a grove of armored cars, a *barranco* of tanks, a field of ambulances and the hooded but unmistakable and beloved shapes of field guns mounted on camions. The road was full of cars. It was daylight. Our planes must be near.

The final stretch of the road to Aliaga took us over the mountain pass which turned us back on the night of the memorable New Year's Eve blizzard party. At its summit we passed the spot where George Hooker had turned his autochir. He was the guy whose autoclaves asphyxiated him a few weeks ago, or was it months? I think that George should be buried up on this mountainside. This is a stupid idea, but there are times when you become sentimental. That reminds me:

In Memoriam

Ives Bentham, volunteer infantryman, the English Battalion, I.B. He was a publisher's proofreader and the belly case for whom I got my hair parted that hot afternoon at K 2½, the comrade with the grave blue eyes, the high cheekbones and the silky yellow trench beard.

"What can be done for belly cases," I asked the Major.

"We can do much," he answered, "but they die anyway."

In Memoriam

Who knows the name of a small red-headed twenty-eight-year-old New York fur-worker, Jewish, with a broad jawbone, a peaked chin and small gray eyes?

I took him up to the lines from the Alcorisa hospital. We ate beef and bread together and talked pleasantly about the C. I. O. while he rode on the running board and looked for planes.

Three days later I carried him back from the lines. He died before I reached the Post at Tortajada. Who can live with his . . . out of an un-understandable sense of decency I will not describe the wound I saw.

I had meant to write this obituary long ago but there has been so little time. There is always less time left.

The single main street of Aliaga was blocked with tangled 35th Division trucks. All of the transport and services of the Thirty-fifth are being reassembled in the Aliaga area; the brigades on a cliffside beyond the town; camions and field garages in a pine grove at the bottom of a gorge; transmissions, in one of the village houses. A farm building houses the *Intendencia*, and the Sanidad Militar has gathered in the disused ward of the hospital set up in half of a textile factory.

Major B. calls the drivers together and makes a speech:

"The food is bad now but it is going to get worse. It will be some time before our lines of communication have been rearranged. You had earned a rest; not that we are worried about your happiness or think you should be rewarded, but because a tired driver is not a good driver.

"The fascists waited until we moved away from Teruel. While we were drinking vermouth in Valencia, they attacked. The artillery and the planes were heavier than anything thus far seen in Spain. They broke through our lines at Alfambra and Argente but we still hold Teruel. Don't worry about that. Teruel is still ours.

"From now on things are going to get harder and harder.

"The eyes of the liberty-loving people of the world are on us. We will fulfill the purpose for which we came to Spain.

"I am going to arrest any driver I see more than fifty feet away from his car."

B. had brought me a present from Barcelona: an automatic tire pump.

I found a bed.

"We just deloused our blankets," said Jack as I looked at it.

"Does that mean that I should get in or stay out?"

Very soon fifty bedfuls of us will be asleep. The single olive oil lamp that lights the long unswept ward will burn all night. Odors steal out from the closed door of the empty morgue.

Not far from the bed on which I lie relaxed as an old bag of bones, Edna and Sam* are huddled in a mess of soiled white rough wool blankets.[7] The wife is a nurse. Sam, who was a machine-gunner, is now in the Transmissions. Although both of them have been in Spain for over a year, this is the first time they have been able to sleep together.

What does a soldier know? It is often said that a soldier at the front knows nothing about the course of the war he fights. The American Expeditionary Force doughboy may have known nothing but the casualties in his company. We know a great deal about what happens not only at Teruel but on the other battlefronts.

Rumors spread and must be stabilized. The brigade therefore publishes a mimeographed daily news bulletin printed in Spanish and English. The Commissars of every Battalion in Spain try to do the same even when their men are in motion. Educational meetings are held in dugouts. The brigade papers, the Division and Army Corps mimeographed, printed and lithographed bulletins, the newspapers and magazines which we have constantly at hand, not only educate the men and reduce rumors to ash but give us a sense of importance and a feeling that we are close to our officers. Wall newspapers complete the job. Good news as well as bad news is given us. Soldier and civilian read the same reports. Plans of future campaigns or certain types of secret information do not go beyond the General Staff, the Cabinet and the Deputies of the Cortes. The names of officers are given no prominence. I do not know what general or what generals command the Fifth Army Corps, or the name of the commander of the 35th Division. No General pretends to be a victor or a savior.

The state of the roads tells us more than the newspapers and bulletins we

---

* captured

7. Edna Drabkin Romer went to Spain as a volunteer nurse. Her husband, Sam Romer, a journalist, enlisted with a Socialist Party group called the Eugene Debs column, which never materialized in Spain, and he entered the Mackenzie-Papineau Battalion. He was taken as a prisoner of war in March 1938 at Hijar and was released after the war in 1939.

receive. An empty road means an inactive front. Men who walk back a road without rifles are men who have been defeated. When artillery and anti-aircraft move up we will most likely attack because we have few heavy weapons for defense. New trucks and types of cannon mean that our international position is improving. If tanks come back a road on White trucks, the focus of the attack is shifting. If they come back on their treads we have had to retreat. When the convoys that move towards the lines are loaded and all those that come back are empty of everything but empty brass shell-cases, conditions at the Front must be healthy.

The license plates of the big two-wheeled carts tell us what towns have been bombed and what towns evacuated.

Because of the nature of my work and the amount of time I spend either on the roads or looking at them, I know more about the state of the war on this Front than many officers. I seldom pass an International driver without stopping him and exchanging rumor and fact.

Feb 15. Obon. 12 P.M.

I have just eaten four eggs fried in sweet olive oil and half a loaf of real bread.

It is late at night. Dumont, Belgian surgeon and Commandante, and I sit inside of a clean, enormous fireplace, whose heat and fragrance we absorb as a five-day bicycle race rider soaks up sleep.

Obon is the first town I have seen in Spain which has not been touched by the war and the only one whose street lights are lit at night. In the main square old people sat talking as pleasantly as if their village, cut off from the rest of Spain and the world by its extreme isolation, were further than fifteen miles by air from Franco.

I believe that ours were the first uniforms that the village people had seen, although they have given forty of their sons and brothers to the People's Army. When I saw the lights lit, I immediately knew that there were no troops billeted in Obon nor had there ever been and that there would be eggs to buy. So there were. If Dumont is wise, he will leave his pipe and his map case behind so that we will have an excuse to return for clean-up. This fat plum of a village, unravaged by our militiamen locusts, ought to be good for at least a hundred eggs, not to speak of hams, cheese and sausage.

In three hours I will be back in Aliaga. Before the sun rises, the hospital convoy will be on the road to the Segura Front.

No sleep tonight.

February 16. Muniesa

Snow covers the mountains. Zero weather but no snow in Muniesa, another treeless Aragon shambles.

As usual, the only house the wind did not blow through was a convent. In twelve hours we have wired the joint, cleaned it, installed heat—the iron stoves I got from Teruel—run stovepipes through holes in the windows stopped by cardboard and adhesive tape, rigged telephones from top floor O.R. to downstairs *triaje*, set up a thirty-bed ward, sterilized all necessary material, installed the x-ray apparatus, and prepared two tables.

Grub is slim and tobacco slimmer because we have not recovered from the tremendous disorientation of our communications. Doubt if we ever will.

Two brand new ambulances came in from the States. Just about in time. Small, low, fast and maneuverable; but why don't they think of sending us armored ambulances?

Good luck. I sleep in a downy featherbed, clean as snow and nearly as cold, in a house so clean you could eat off floors, walls and ceilings. The owners are ill at ease. Loyalist Spain is full of people who voted fascist before the invasion began, who think it prudent to house troops and especially Internationals.

Keep my gun under the bed.

The American medical group is now much smaller than the picnic party that sailed out of the gates of Villa Paz in December. Our outfit consists of my car, the big Harvard evacuation bus, Finn's light front-line car, bed and supply truck and the autochir. The staff has fallen from thirty-two members to seventeen: the Major, four chófers, four ward nurses, two O.R. nurses, one assistant surgeon (Oscar, who gave me the two packages of Camels at Cuevas), one male nurse and electrician, one spare driver and photographer (Jack), one cook and two kitchen girls. Only half of these seventeen were with the previous front-line group. Not one of us was wounded. They were left in Villa Paz either to give others a chance to get up to the Front or because they folded up or because they did not turn out well.

The American group had originally come to the front with the purpose of serving the Lincoln-Washingtons. The *Sanidad Militar*, constantly being reorganized and improved like every other branch of military and civil life in the Republic, recently passed a regulation that nothing smaller than a Division may own a surgical team. Eventually, if and when the medical and surgical services are full enough, the entire Medical staff will be operated along a geographical army-corps-area basis, like the artillery and the transport. At such a time we will serve a fixed section of a Front, rather than a particular body of troops. This should be the scientific way, but it requires more human and mechanical equipment than we yet possess.

EXTRA! EXTRA! EXTRA!
LOYALISTS ADVANCE IN TERUEL COUNTER-ATTACK

"Carrying light and heavy machine guns in zero weather over the difficult terrain of the Segura de los Baños sector, the hard-hitting Mackenzie Papineau Battalion of Canadian volunteers took three strategic hills from Generalissimo Francisco Franco's troops in the early hours of the morning without artillery preparation or support, state Loyalist sources. It is also averred that. . . . "

Between their mountains and Ours there were three hills. The highest of them, which commanded the others, had first to be taken.

Towards evening Major Bob Merriman called his men together.

"Well, comrades, we are going to have a trench mortar company."

Mortars were what we needed. The men cheered and then grew silent as someone yelled, "Well, where are the guns?"

Merriman smiled and pointed towards the fascist territory.

"There's a battery of good mortars on top of that hill. At 2 A.M. three companies of the Mac-Paps will. . . . "

The first company arrived at the bottom of the highest fascist hill just as false dawn had begun to lift the lid of darkness from the mountain tops. Foxholes were dug. Two Maxims began to fire upwards.

A second hundred men skirted the bottom of the hill and advanced to its rear, where foxholes were dug and M-guns emplaced. No fires were lit and no gun was aimed.

The third company of Mac-Paps had skirted the other side of the hill and now climbed silently towards its top where a hundred Spanish recruits were entrenched with six Doras and three heavy trench mortars.

When company number three arrived at the top of the hill, the fascists were engaged in strafing the Mac-Paps who all this time had been making targets of themselves down in the valley.

Fifty fascists were killed. Fourteen were wounded and thirty-six, together with M-guns and mortars, taken prisoner. Three who tried to escape were captured by the reserve companies whose help had not been needed.

So far so good. Three fascists have already arrived at the surgical hospital here in Muniesa. The light wounded Rebels were evacuated to the Rear.

One of the wounded fascists, a chest-case, died before we were able to operate. Another of them lies unconscious in the ward, half his side torn away by a grenade. The third, a head-case, is conscious. He looks not like one of Ours or of Theirs but like anybody's. Frightened, he keeps a sheet over his eyes but lifts one corner of it whenever he hears the footsteps of those whom he is sure are bolsheviks and killers of the wounded.

Muniesa shows no signs of war. No houses on the main streets are down, there are no egg holes in the road, no sounds of gunfire and not a vestige of troops. But for the activity about the hospital door, but for our half-military uniforms and the long shadows of the ambulances, no photographers could search out evidences of war even if he had a key to every house.

Bad luck. One of the new ambulances from the States is being used as a Post car. That lets me out. Twenty-four more hours of inactivity and I'll turn in my pistol. Nothing to do all day long but to warm up my engine and shift the position of my car so that it is always in the shade.

February 17. Muniesa
The fun has begun.

There is too much said about planes in this journal. The monotony is of the fascists' choosing, not my own.

At ten o'clock I was out sunning myself on the porch of the church. The north wind that has been knifing us ever since we hit this town was blowing as hard as usual. We had been saying how glad we were that the wind was so high that planes would not or could not come over.

At ten o'clock two very beautiful avions unmarked as the rest of the fascist fleet came over. Because the Front was so far off (nine miles) and because there was no objective in Muniesa but ourselves and, because some of us still think that a hospital is sacred, we were not worried. We thought that the observation planes had come over merely to observe.

Half an hour after the first planes had floated off into the vaporized gold of the winter sunlight I heard the deep throbbing of many big engines.

Five squadrons of silver trimotors came by at fifteen hundred feet, flying in V's of three, flanked by four triplets of biplanes, all of them floating by so slowly that we could see the altitude they lost.

While the armada was overhead townspeople and medical staff stood in the streets, noses in the air, getting an eyeful of the best aircraft totalitarianism has to offer. We did not think that we would be bombed because the town had never been bombed before and because we were so smugly unimportant.

The last two biplanes signaled to the others.

Lazy as whales sunning themselves, the trimotors banked, turned and came down on us. I heard the creaking of a giant cartwheel and ran—I mean began to run and then walked fast—to the sole *refugio*.

It took fifteen trimotors five minutes to place one bomb each on the village.

Afterwards I rushed back to the hospital. It had not been hit.

"No correr, comaradas!" we cried as the peasants again ran for the church tower which they imagine safe.

I stayed in the hospital while fifteen more bombs fell. Doctor B., Oscar the assistant surgeon and the O.R. nurses remained in the operating room. The two ward nurses who were on duty stayed with their patients. Doctor Dumont, seated in the sun at the hospital door, continued to read his newspaper.

Shrapnel crashed against the rear wall of the hospital and black smoke drifted over its roof. I lay in a corner of the ward while the two nurses got under beds and the patients pulled blankets over their heads.

"Get out of here, Jim," said the Major to me, "you are not on duty. Beat it before They come back."

Crisp as the first day of autumn, the sharp smell of explosives blew down the gutters of the empty streets. High over the rooftops blew the winter wind and the clouds that had betrayed us.

I walked fast because I wanted to count the houses taken down by the first two raids. Although the half-dozen homes that lay spilled out onto the village street were so fresh-killed that they had not yet settled in the dust of their blood, their ruins seemed to be very old and mellow.

A zinc-gray dud, size and shape of the largest sausage ever made in Bologna, lay on the rough cobbles. Poison yellow powder had rolled out of its cracked side. The wings, which would have made a handsome souvenir, were missing.

Two of the brigade commissary trucks stood at the side of the village gate.

I had not seen Joe Leguera and the three other International drivers since Teruel.[8] He showed me a picture taken of himself, in a bathing suit on the

---

8. Probably José Laguerra Colina, about whom there is little information, except that

beach at Benicasim, and we began to discuss the date and the duration of our next leave.

The five drivers heard the groan of bomb wings. I ran one way, to a dug-out, Joe Leguera and the others went into the house at the side of the village gate, where they would be protected from everything but a direct hit.

When the raid had passed, we ran out of our dugout and towards the two commissary camions. They were unhurt.

Plaster dust eddied about the wreckage of the house in which Joe Leguera and the three other drivers had gone.

Lines of men formed and passed blocks of rubble, tires and shredded beams from hand to hand. The weak, heavily sanded mortar of pre-war Spain was as incapable of resisting totalitarianism as its liberalism.

By the time that we had reached the first leg from which hung a fragment of jelly-like thigh, the fifteen trimotors and the twelve biplanes whose assignment we were came back to get the rest of us; always in perfect formation, always lower and more slowly.

The wing commander signaled with sky smoke. Specks of platinum glinted in the sunlight and the air filled with the creak, constantly rising in pitch, of sharp metal against the air.

My *refugio* was a good one. It was deep but not too deep; it was covered with two feet of earth; and there were two entrances. All it lacked was timbers, but all dugouts in this woodless country lack timbers. "*Tenemos hambre de todo, hemos siempre tenido hambre de todos: We have all hunger, we have always had all hungers*," said the civilian to whom I gave the bag of roots I could not eat, in Valencia.

There never was a country in which "some day, some day" was said with such longing.

In Memorium
José Leguera (real name)

Thirty years old, heavy-set, sanguine and handsome, with a Colman mustache, Commissary buyer and driver for the *Intendencia* of the Lincoln-Washington Battalion. Formerly a counterman in a New York Child's restaurant. Some of him lies buried in the grave dug free of charge by a fascist

---

he sailed for Spain in January 1937 and served at the battles of Jarama and Brunete in 1937.

bomb in the center of the cemetery of Muniesa. The rest of Joe will remain forever beneath the ruins of the village gate that rises like a monument to his devotion and to his bad luck.

The raids were becoming longer and more intense. The trimotors had been having trouble with the high wind, had finally found the right adjustment for their bomb sights and were closing in on us like boar-hunters descending from the saddle for the kill.

To occupy less space and to make a smaller target of myself, I had curled up in a deep corner of the trench with my knees clasped between my hands. The dim light shifted as General Beckett, the Kansan who knows neither fear nor common sense, observed the sky from the mouth of the dugout.

I had a cigarette but no longer wanted to smoke. No sense being knocked out while lighting a cigarette. The *mecha* that glowed in your lighter might burn a hole in you. There was an orange in my pocket; I could not eat it. Joe Foster, the negro mechanic who had fixed my car under fire up at Peralejos, sang the "Internationale" until we shut him up. He unendurably began to whistle.

"Now is the time. . . . "

"For Christ's sake, Foster. . . . "

"Now is the time I'd like to be back on Lenox Avenue and a Hundred and Thirty-fifth Street, swinging a beer and singing 'No Pasaran.'"

"Jesus Christ! That was a big one. About three hundred yards away."

Earth had fallen on us.

"No it wasn't. It wasn't a big one far away. It was a little one right on top of us."

After that, Foster became silent. Morosely his knotted throat continued to hum the "Internationale."

General Beckett reported that all was clear.

The big one far off actually was a little one very near. A grenade had fallen directly in the center of the two feet of earth that covered the top of the trench. The sallow-complexioned earth all about us was scarred with acne pits.

Grenades. Good. That was a sign that the raid was beginning to come to an end. The curtain would shortly come down in a shower of explosive bullets and basketfuls of grenades.

Our planes had not appeared. During the morning we had seen anti-aircraft puffs from the direction of Cortes de Aragon and the Front. Muniesa did not rate protection since it is not the Medical Corps which holds the lines. The lines must always be held.

In half an hour we had dug enough of Joe Leguera and the other nameless chófers to bury. Karl, the Swedish driver (who was ordered to the Front six hours after he had married a kitchen *chica*), found a face and held it up by the moist hair, like Judith and the head of Holofernes, for us to inspect. I recognized Joe. Eventually we loaded enough arms and legs and torsos on a stretcher to establish the names of the four chófers and the fact that they were all dead. No one has ever been more dead.

We finished the job of fishing flesh from the ruins after the fifteen trimotors and the twelve biplanes had come back and emptied their machine guns and grenade baskets in one final coup-de-grace. All flesh must be dug out of ruins because of the danger of plague.

The next job was an old woman. She came out whole, black witch's hair powdered white with plaster dust and streaming out from the set expression in her face as we carried her to the enlarged morgue of the convent-hospital. A farmer and his young wife knelt on the cement floor, hands pulling at their chins and mouths, silently staring at the infant made very tiny by the enormous blood-stained belly of the stretcher on which it lay. The child had been suffocated. Major B.'s hands can do many things but they cannot repair death. Remembering his first and useless instructions, the mother again and again breathed into the lips of what had been her daughter.

Two peasant women, enormous in their many skirts, lay on stretchers. I will never know if they were shellshocked or dead or wounded. The village Presidente already stood at the door of the hospital, his car loaded with bodies.

Why did I come to Spain?

Hospital and staff came out of the raid untouched. Our luck holds; for how long? Good luck is thin armor and we have no other. Sooner or later we will get what the whole world will receive if we here in Spain do not win.

Lunch was of course late. Everyone is very shaky and friendly. Petty feuds and complaints have been buried. Continually looking upwards and sniffing the air for sounds, like bird dogs about to make a flush. We are very sensitive about all types of noises.

I could not eat. At three o'clock in the afternoon, my appetite for smoking returned. I then ate my orange.

Walking back to the hospital after the raid is something I hate to do. Never know how many of your friends might . . . there is a very sweetish taste in my mouth . . . you just sit and wait. You sit there in the darkness and wait.

You don't want to smoke or eat or think about anything but how long it will take the sun to go down. If anyone talks or above all tries to say something funny, you hate him. You sit and wait. After a while you lose all hope for the raiding to end before the sun goes down. All hopes against hopes are lost.

The peasants have not yet come out of the dugout in which I had my latest narrow escape although the air has been clean of the sounds of planes for at least three hours.

Nothing can move the black-figured peasant women away from the porch of the church about which they sit all day long waiting for the bells to warn them to go up into the room in the tower which they think will save them. The women of Spain have always dressed in black. They will wear black for many generations. Why should any other color of cloth be sold? God in Heaven, if we could only convince the women of this village and many of the men to stay away from that church tower! In case of a direct hit . . . well, we'd just have to leave them there, all in a heap, with the cross of the tower top grasping them all in its black weather-beaten arms.

How can I believe in God? If there is a God, what kind of man is He? The theoreticians and schoolmen of the Vatican should lose weeks of sleep before they could adjust their interpretations of Divine Intervention to fit not just the bombing of Muniesa, not just the sniping in Valencia, not just . . . oh well, why run through the whole bloody catechism, when not all the mitred heads of Rome can justify the slaying by suffocation of the single infant who lies downstairs in the morgue?

I admit that my nerves are shaken.

How long can this sort of thing go on?

I envy the religious. All my life I have tried to cling to the notion of the existence of a Supreme Being or Supreme Force of Superhuman Power, and year after year I have shielded my faith from the stones of logic with the hope that I might some day understand and learn how there could be a God and what His function could be.

I envy the religious because they can blame the hideous things that I have seen happen in Spain on God. I can blame them only on men. I do not like to think that men can perpetrate these horrors on each other. Who could believe that the Devil does all of the bad things and God all of the good ones and God always must be right and the Devil always must be wrong? That we predestine ourselves to one fate or another and that ten thousand women and five hundred thousand women and all the women there are should pay with their lives for the sins of an equivalent number of other women?

I could go to the village priest (there is one, although he no longer wears his medieval costume) and confess my sins. I could pray all night; the village could hum with novenas until sunrise—and the fascist planes whose mission has been blessed by the Pope will come back tomorrow morning and the next day and the day after that and bomb hell out of our God damn hospital.

Our priests bless our banners, guns and bended heads from altars set up in the olive groves. Their priests bless their banners and better guns and fewer heads; then we go out and slay each other and the same priests absolve the wounded and bless the dead. This fervid mysticism has been going on for hundreds of years not only in Polynesia and Africa but in Europe, and it is time that reason and realism should do something about it.

Either there is no God or His representatives on earth don't know what the hell religion is about.

Night. At last. (Same day. The sun has gone down). Everyone sits about the fire in the evacuation ward telling about narrow escapes. Somebody hums "oh how I like to see that evening sun go down" to the tune of the St. Louis Blues.

Epitaph for the Half Dead

Phil Cooper. Jarama, Brunete, Belchite, Quinto, Pina, Fuentes de Ebro, Teruel and Segura.[9] Machine-gunner and best of the Brigade chófers. Formerly a Greenwich Village intellectual Bohemian drunken trying-to writer. He sits at the fire in a big blue fascist cape taken at Teruel, somber eyes and dark face blazing as he thinks about himself.

"I'm through, I'm finished and washed up. Whenever those planes come over I run. I'm not disillusioned and I'm not ratting on the brigade or squawking or saying that I've lost my morale, but I've been here thirteen months and I'm through. I was supposed to go home a month ago, and then this God damn offensive had to start.

"I have dirt fever. I've had dirt fever and concussion too often. I used to be able to take anything They would throw at me but now my chin's made out of glass.

"Maybe I'm raving because I'm full of fever but I know when I've had enough.

"Tomorrow morning They'll come back and finish the job. Think this

---

9. This is a list of all the major battles in which the American volunteers fought.

town got a shellacking? Well, more stuff fell on the cemetery than hit the town. The wind was too high and they couldn't get Their bomb sights right. Tomorrow morning there won't be much wind and They'll come back and finish the job.

"What time is it? Ten o'clock? Christ, I haven't known what date it was for six months or how long ago six months was. I don't get any letters and I don't answer the ones I get. I don't even know what my name is. Tell me, somebody, and I'll call you a liar. We haven't got names any more than the carcasses hanging up in the packing houses of Chicago have names. What time is it? Ten o'clock? And what time does the sun come up? Six o'clock? Well the observation planes will come over at nine tomorrow morning. The trimotors will come back for us at ten o'clock.

"That gives us exactly twelve hours to live."

Phil was the comrade who stayed with me and lent me his tools that hot afternoon on the Alfambra road.

We gave him four of our valuable aspirin tablets.

Out in the cold and the darkness of the street below the hospital, muffled figures rush about with candles, axles creak as carts are pulled out on to the cobbles of the main street. The hooves of mules spell out the fear and nervousness of their owners.

Mattresses, bread and pots are thrown into the carts and into grass baskets flung over the backs of burros.

EXTRA! EXTRA! EXTRA! Headlines: "Loyalist sources state that the three English-speaking brigades of the hard-hitting international shock troops with the Loyalist forces who yesterday seized three strategic hills from Franco's forces today continued the attack and advanced to a maximum depth of three miles along a nine-mile front, with the capture of many prisoners and much material.

"Denying all reports of a Loyalist advance, Rebel headquarters say that yesterday's surprise attack was repulsed with heavy losses, that not a foot of ground was lost and that the land captured yesterday by the Loyalists has today been recovered. The Lincoln-Washington Battalion of American volunteers was decimated, aver the Rebels. . . . "

The number of prisoners has gone up to 350. We have captured the Segura de los Baños. Not only is there a summer hotel magnificently able to house our field hospital in Segura but natural hot baths. Natural hot baths.

We have not advanced without opposition. Shelling has now begun, and bombing. Five towns in the neighborhood got it this morning; Corbas de Aragon, Plou, Molinos and two others. The Classification Post at Cortes de Aragon caught, from the accounts of the drivers, much more iron than we did.

I begin to understand the strategy of our attack. We do not expect to be able to cut so deeply into fascist lines that we will be able to put the Saragossa–Teruel railroad and highway under fire. The territory the Fifteenth captured yesterday and today is useless to us.

What we hope to do is to draw so much of Franco's planes, tanks and artillery on us that Lister and Campesino will have an easier time defending Teruel. The Fifteenth is being used as a decoy. The more shelling we absorb, the happier our Generals will be. This type of maneuver is called a "diversion," I believe.

According to all accounts our success in diverting Franco's mechanical weight off Teruel onto ourselves grows with each hour. We are somewhat handicapped by being many hundreds of kilometers from our nearest base of supplies. Franco, to the contrary, is very near to Saragossa. He will burn a single liter of gas to our five liters.

The bombing Muniesa caught as its share of the diversion was the usual fascist crime of impotence. They can't stand up to our men, so They kill civilians and women. There is no conceivable military objective in Muniesa but the base hospital and the crossroads. Not only did few bombs fall near the turnpike, but the fascists know as well as we do that no road can be cut even by the most persistent and heaviest of bombing. The largest direct hit can be filled in by ten men with shovels in half an hour, if camions have not already started to drive around it.

Before I Forget: A hundred-kilo bomb fell on the exact apex of a manure pile the size and the exact proportions of Mount Fujiyama. The effects were something overpowering.

I am becoming tired of inactivity. My paranoia grew to such an extent today that I was incapable of writing, although there was plenty of time. I will have to find some way of getting back at Them or my morale will break. Perhaps it will break anyway.

Doesn't B. know this? Why won't he send me to the Front? Because he doesn't want to risk losing his car, I imagine. Once a Major's car is gone, the best the officer can do is hang out at the road *controls* and thumb hitches from ambulances and trucks. Perhaps B. thinks that I am getting a rest.

It is late. I had better go out, start my engine and drain my radiator. I have poured enough water into her to float a battleship, and not a Treaty one.

The fascist wounded continue to come in. I went to the *triaje* for statistics. The nurses and the doctors seemed uninterested in my curiosity.

"You want to know how many fascist wounded we receive," said Johnny Szekely, in a studious Oxford accent, "I will tell you if you will answer me a question."[10]

"What do you want to know, Johnny?"

"Look over there. You see two stretchers, two wounded men. Now tell me which is the fascist and which is the Republican."

"Let's see . . . I'm sorry, Johnny, but I can't tell them apart."

"We-ell, Jeemy, I am a doc-tor, and neither can I. Now go out to your car and do something useful."

The roosters of Muniesa crow all night. Whenever the bald turkey-buzzard that lives on an island of oyster shells in Lake Ponchartrain sails over New Orleans, settles on a necropolis in Metairie Ridge cemetery and crows three times, one of the Author's family dies. Two have died this year. One of pituitary trouble and gallstones, one of senility.

February 16. Muniesa

News.

Word has reached us that the boys are holding on to the ground they took yesterday in the face of ever-increasing bombardment and shelling. The German invaders have arrived with their 155's and automatic 75's. More expected tomorrow.

A flame-thrower was tried out on us yesterday. This Front is so well off the beaten and half-beaten tracks of newspaper correspondents, embassy agents and Intervention Committee observers that the Italian general staff thought that experimentation was possible. The boys say that the flame-thrower looked like an ordinary heavy tank with a fire hose nozzle set in the turret instead of an anti-tank piece. Throwing a sheet of flaming fluid seventy feet ahead of her, she came up the mountain like an illustration out of a pulp scientific magazine. Engine trouble or fear stopped her, combined with our anti-tank guns. The flames dribbled out and died and she returned to her lines. Tonight the beast will be dismantled and sent back to Italy and

---

10. This is a misspelling of Johnny Kyszely, the eye specialist.

Virginio Gayda will give the foreign newspaper colony in Rome an inventory of the poison gas shells shipped by Russia to Barcelona.[11] "No matter how preposterous the lie," says Handsome Adolf, "and no matter how completely it is exposed, nevertheless a residuum of belief in it remains in the minds of the public." Lying, with these gentlemen, is neither an accident, nor the occasional means to an end. It is a science, worked out as carefully as the synthetic production of rubber, dyes, gasoline and oil. For further details, read Pareto and Sorel.[12]

Because of the advance we have made, it has become possible for ambulances to drive within a mile and a half of the lines. Before the push began, they could come no nearer than five miles. Our cars had been unable to get within working distance of the first-aid posts not because of the firing which drivers disregard, but for the reason that the terrain impedes the passage of all vehicles but tanks. Stretcher-mules and chair-mules are used to help the stretcher-bearers, who have been working in groups of four. Casualties among the human and animal carriers of the wounded have been so heavy that tanks were used yesterday to get the heavy wounded out of the lines.

Famous Dying Words

The mules had not arrived. Fred Easly of Worcester, Massachusetts, had to be carried three miles over the mountains by stretcher bearers to the nearest point at which an ambulance had been able to arrive.

The four stretcher men put Fred, who had been wounded in the left arm at Brunete and had now been hit in the right arm and leg, down to rest.

"Well, I guess I'm just about through with war," he said.

At that moment a shell landed fifteen yards away and took off the back of Fred Easly's head.

In Memorium

In the same grave lie two of the stretcher men, both of them killed by the same shell.

---

11. Virginia Gayda was the pro-Mussolini columnist-editor of Rome's *Giornale d'Italia*.
12. Vilfredo Pareto (1848–1923) was an Italian economist, whose anti-democratic theories of social change were adopted by Mussolini's Fascists. Georges Sorel (1847–1922) was a French philosopher who endorsed "direct action" for social change, ideas echoed by Fascist leaders.

Chansky, one of the stretcher-bearers who survived, told me the story and showed me a hole in his winter woolen cap.[13]

I have given my pistol to Lieutenant W., the new battalion doctor of the Lincoln-Washingtons. He had none and I have no use for mine. Here I stay, day after day, tightening up my road-loosened bolts until they snap, haunting the corridors of the hospital, helping where I am not needed, and still B. does not send me to the Front.

W. is happy, at last he is at the Front and with the men.

I thought that my break had come when I heard that O., driver of the new amb which has taken my place, broke down but. . . .

Epitaph for the Half Dead

O., driver of the new battalion staff ambulance. After three days of continuous driving under fire, he got back to Muniesa and refused to go up to the lines. He has now been taken off his car and added to the Harvard ambulance, as spare driver.

We hold nothing much against O. and it's so much trouble to build and maintain a guardhouse.

So what does B. do? He puts another chófer on O.'s car, but not me. I'm supposed to be resting. I know that if I got back to the Front and found myself on the griddle I would begin to long for the peace and luxury of Muniesa, but that's life and that's war and I've been in hot water all my life and I suppose I always will be in hot water.

Someone showed Major B. a poem printed under my name in a magazine which has somehow arrived from the States. He read it very carefully, came over to me, and said in a measured voice:

"Do you know, Jim, if a chófer started to write poetry, I wouldn't worry: but when a poet begins to drive. . . . "

I am not a poet. I have many trades, all of them as dependent on a single idea and conviction as the ribs are to the spine. Perhaps when and if I get

13. Chansky is Michael Shansky, aka Shantzek, a Los Angeles volunteer who served as a medic with the transport group.

back to the States, I will apply for a job at writing obituaries for a newspaper. If we were to win the war, I should not stay in Spain. I like the United States and belong there.

If Transmissions men arrived before dark last night, the Major would now be operating by flashlight; I should be writing by candlelight, or not at all.

The last of the peasant dead were removed by their relatives in the Presidente's cart late this afternoon.

It is an ill bomb which blows no good: a shovelful of grenades landed on a chicken coop, and today we had chicken soup and chicken livers with rice for lunch. For dinner we had the dark meat. Tomorrow we will eat the light.

The only work I did today was to dig a trench for bandage, viscera and limbs.

The ten Assault Guards, who come from a body of men known and chosen for their exceptional physique and political reliability, keep coming to the hospital to donate their blood.

Picture of the convent at 9 P.M.:

Small front-line ambs from the Post pull up at the doorway and leave loads which will be assorted and later carried, all but the dead, by the big evacuation ambs, to the railhead hospital at Hijar, thirty miles away; light wounded, awaiting evacuation, swathed in blankets, sit about the *triaje* drinking coffee, sleeping and talking little; the pharmacy at the rear is busy filling orders telephoned (with apparatus taken from Teruel) from upstairs; *triaje* nurses bend over stretchers, cutting off clothing and first-aid bandages, making injections and applying new bandages; the hospital clerk takes information from the figures on the floor and hands out cards; the stair is full of stretchers going upstairs loaded and coming down empty. In the main ward the nurses are busy at injections, transfusions, feeding, carrying bed pans and urinals and putting to bed the patients who constantly arrive from the O.R., lungs projecting ether into the burned-straw smelling air (we have little paper for kindling). Staff members off duty sit about the ward stove brewing coffee and telling stories invariably relating to the peculiarities of various explosions. Downstairs in the courtyard the autochir mechanics tend their autoclaves and make coffee over a primus stove, without which no war can be fought. Next door to the ward the night staff catches sleep on beds they may at any moment have to vacate to make place for wounded. Upstairs in the O.R. *triaje* Crome, chief medical officer of the Division, has his hair cut. The Major's hands move under the intense light of the O.R. lamp, the rest of the room dark as the corners of a billiard parlor. Dumont begins to perform an autopsy (our surgeons constantly read to perfect their science, which is evidently far different from peacetime surgery), first using the fluoroscope (they let me carry the corpse upstairs, thank God, or I should not have known what to do with myself all evening) and that is about all except for the activity in the cook-shed and the tranquility of the morgue.

The fascist head-case kept us awake all night. He may have been delirious. Time and again I stood over him, looking for fear in his wide-open eyes and trying to understand his excited high-pitched words. He looked like any one of our own wounded—trench beard, close-cropped hair, average features. I kept wondering if the tremendous fear swimming in his eyes was of us or of death.

I rather think that the wounded fascist was more afraid of me than he was of death, because he pulled the sheet over his head as soon as he saw my face above his. I am supposed to look like a minister or a doctor or a professor. Children do not run from me and horses do not shy when I look at them.

Since I do not wish to exaggerate the fashion in which Rebel wounded are treated by the People's Army, I must state that we bring in our wounded before we risk our lives carrying Theirs.

For what it is worth, here is a story. I trust the teller.

Many months ago on the Cordoba Front our lines were violently attacked at night and we had to withdraw to the top of the next hill. Before morning we counter-attacked. As the Lincolns were coming up the hill on which they had left their wounded, they saw large fires burning at its top. Americans, alive, had been soaked in gasoline and set afire. Not only were there no fascist wounded brought in that night, but no prisoners were taken.

Neither side is always able to take prisoners. Guard details are not always available and rapidly advancing troops may not leave enemy forces behind them armed or unarmed. Being able to be taken prisoner depends on your luck in the first two or three seconds following the instant in which you have been hemmed in. At the instant of capture, the captor is judge, lawyer, and jury. He is able and generally willing to decide your fate, without either reflection or consultation.

All night long Captain Alexander of the English, shot through the shoulders, gives orders: *"Get the men out in camions, bring up the anti-tanks and water for the machine guns, bring up dynamite bombs, get the men out in camions."*[14]

14. Captain Bill Alexander, wounded at Teruel in February, later authored *British Volunteers for Liberty: Spain 1936–1939* (1982).

<u>Later. Same day.</u> In the afternoon I was sent to Obon to recover the map-case and the pipe Commandante Dumont had accidentally but conveniently forgotten at the inn in which we had eaten four fried eggs. First we passed the moon landscape formerly known as Cortes de Aragon. How well the fascists know that we never, never utilize a Front town for anything but hospitals! As soon as the breath of ice thaws out of the late winter air, we will take to tents, and then all towns will be completely empty of all military objectives but civilians. Tanks, powder-dumps, transport stations, auto-parques, *Intendencias*, armored cars, artillery, troops and all of the varied services of our army are kept in the thickest olive groves or the deepest *barrancos* we can find. And yet the bombing of towns continues. Perhaps the fascists know that our most fierce weapons and source of strength are our hearts, and it is those They hope to destroy when They bomb our civilians. "Kill their women and children and grandparents, and the men at the Front will understand the senselessness of trying to defend their loved ones from us," I can hear Electric Beard Teruzzi saying, and Douhet before him.[15] Their lies are not less planned than their air methods.

After several miles of curved, dipping climbing mountain road, it became apparent that we were entering through these canyons and alp-like buttresses a region which the war had not touched. Much washing was being done in the river, laundry laid out to dry on thorn bushes, vines were being pruned, old people sat in the sun. The quiet narrow road on which I had not seen a single camion or uniform was filled with many burros and women and children.

The car was invaded by a swarm of children. We admitted fifteen of them at a time. They had probably never sat in a real automobile before and begged to be taken for a ride around the village square. This I would not do, but let each baby boy and girl blow the horn, in turn. I was glad that there had been no blood to wipe off the floorboards that morning.

The people of Obon seemed very proud of their military unimportance and their many large wine cellars, each at least forty feet deep in solid rock.

I bought 250 fresh eggs for 250 pesetas, and six brooms. Ham, cheese and sausage were unobtainable. Almost forgetting to call for Dumont's map-case and pipe, I managed to shake my car free of children and soon re-entered the territory where they do not run in the sunlight, but away from it.

---

15. Attilio Teruzzi (1882–1950) was an Italian soldier who left the army in 1920 to support Mussolini. General Giulio Douhet (1869–1930) was an Italian military theorist who advocated strategic bombing.

Before I go to bed. Sit in the x-ray room writing on the fluoroscope table while I listen to the radio. We have tuned in on a fascist station. The voice of the announcer was not the super-suave persuasive oily cheery drool of the States' mike maestros, but as savage as that of an unpaid actor. After saying something about the Nationalist Government's giving nothing but the truth to the world's newspapers, he announced the imposing number of Internationals who have this day been killed at Teruel (either Franco does not know that we are at Segura, or he wants us to think that he does not want us to know he knows we are here—and decimations of the Internationals, fit to discourage the liberty-loving people of the world, always make good script for fascist newscasters), and he gave the names of the Nationalist ministers in the newest shake-up backstairs palace-intrigue dictatorship. When the same harsh voice suddenly began to plug a brand of Seville chocolate, we neither sneered nor laughed. So They have chocolate not only to sell, but to advertise!

We have often listened to fascist broadcasts, whenever we have had our radio set and power for it. Fascist programs have not been forbidden our ears; but we usually howl them down. We have a morbid appetite for the news which comes from the enemy, but once They come over the air, our dead seem suddenly among us, and we twist the dials.

Another station, probably Radio-Toulouse, now sends boisterous jazz full of sex-insinuations to us. Two couples dance by the light of the big portable autopsy lamp. The kitchen boy, the wildest and most affable of our anarchist staff members, circles among the dancers, executing a mock waltz as he beats an omelet (made of the good eggs of Obon) and pretending that the dish is always about to spill. In other parts of the room the anaesthetist gets a shave from the Division barber, and the electrician, who is incapable of ceasing work, mends a telephone taken from the Teruel hotel. The twelve persons here are of English, American, Spanish, German, French, Belgian and Jugoslav nationality.

The day has been given over to the eating of eggs. Water boils over primus stoves in between the beds and on the ward stove. Marty slips a few eggs into his autoclave (in which Annie the Queen of the O. R. plans to roast a chicken, in violation of Major B.'s order that there must be no cooking or eating in the autochir) before he screws down the lid; chófers off duty light fires under helmets, and the smell of cooking forever slides under the doors of the Operating Room and the autopsy chamber into the dark halls. I eat hard-boiled eggs in the O. R., bean omelets with Dumont, soft-boiled eggs in the ward, and onion omelets in the autochir. The best of all eggs were those I cooked under the Soviet four-barreled anti-aircraft M-gun. Sun, food, sleep—but there was no woman.

The fascist head-case had been giving us much trouble. He makes more noise than the rest of the patients and incessantly demands water. Head-cases are given very little fluids to drink because of the danger of pneumonia, I think. His arms catch at the air. He pulls the sheet over his head and stares at us from under it with a single terrible eye.

A great change came over the fascist this morning. Sana had soft-boiled a quantity of eggs for the patients. As she worked down the ward, carefully feeding liquid gold into the mouths of each man, I wondered what she would do when she got to the fascist. The sheet had come down from his face and he was for once quiet.

The eyes of even the half-conscious were on him and on Sana. Would he be fed? It would be easy for me to say "all wounded are as alike as corpses." We do not hate the fascists when they lie in our hospital, but only when they do not. It would not matter if the head-case were a German artilleryman or an Italian aviator, or William Carney or handsome Adolf or Mussolini or blind old General Milan-Astray or the *tercios* yelling "Down with intelligence! hurrah for death!"[16] All wounded should be given eggs when we have eggs. I am a poor hater of people and a great hater of ideas. If a man has cholera or smallpox or fascism, you hate, not the man, but the germs he carries. You do not hate Hearst or attempt to destroy him. His ideas may not be killed with a trench knife.

Therefore the fascist should be given an egg although the other wounded men in the ward look at him as if he were the one who shot them, and perhaps he was. If our supplies had run so low that we had only a single ounce of ether or a dram of morphine, a foot of catgut and one bandage roll left, and two patients to treat, I think that the Republican would get them and not the fascist. When the operating tables are so busy that their doors are blocked with unconscious men waiting on stretchers, who should be taken first, our men or Theirs? Two men are heavily wounded. Both of them should be operated on immediately. The militiaman's chances of living are greater than

---

16. In a famous confrontation at Spain's University of Salamanca on October 12, 1936, the philosopher Miguel de Unamuno faced the pro-fascist General Milan-Astray, saying, "You will win because you have enough brute force. But you will not convince. For to convince you need to persuade. And in order to persuade you would need what you lack: Reason and Right." To which the general replied, "Death to intelligence! And long live death!" He then drew his pistol and drove Unamuno out of the university.

the fascist's, but many hours have passed since both men should have been treated. Would the Major be justified in first operating on the Republican?

With the entire ward looking at her, Sana held the fascist head-case in her arms and fed him two soft-boiled eggs. She is not Mary Magdalen and he is not Christ. If this is religion, then I am religious.

Calm has come over the ward. The wounded fascist no longer keeps the bed sheet over his eyes. Desperation has gone from his cries. Softly he calls for the Virgin Mary to cure him. Although he no longer believes we will kill him, he may still think that we want to kill God.

But if the fascist head-case were an aviator, we should not have given him an egg. I am sometimes thankful that my job does not require me to kill people, but if I ever have a chance to get at an aviator I will strangle him, because I have only eight shells for my revolver and know that I will never be able to get new ones. The aviator should be buried in one piece, unlike so many of his victims.

I once saw four captive Italian aviators being driven through Tarragona on a truck. It is necessary for us to keep all the aviators we capture alive so that we may exchange them for ours. The truck was caught in a traffic jam and had to stop. For a moment I believed that the women of Tarragona were going to take the captured Italians apart with their fingernails.

Among the prisoners we took in Belchite were several officers. All captives are questioned before they are jailed, set free or shot.

One of the officers was a former captain in the Republican army.

"*Viva España Fascista!*" he shouted and then, pointing at his heart and his forehead, "Here for my God! And here for my country!" We let the man live but executed the uniform.

The German officer's turn came. Taken to the offices of the Estado Major, he quietly told us all he knew about the expeditionary force Hitler had sent to Spain: the caliber of the guns, the organization of the batteries, the position of the fascist lines at Huesca and Saragossa, and the name of the "schwartzer Dampfer"[17] which had brought him to Spain.

One of the officers who interviewed the prisoner was also a German.

The German International: Why did you come to Spain?

The German Fascist: I am an officer in the German Army. I have always been a military man. I have no other profession. Although I do not

---

17. black steamship

believe in all of Hitler's ideas, I became a member of the National Socialist Workers' Party in order to hold on to my job.

The German International: Why did you come to Spain?

The Nazi: I am a married man and I have a child (he unsuccessfully at-
tempts to show the court martial committee a photograph of his family). I have never been in civil life. I know no trade other than the
Army.

The German International: Tell us why you came to Spain.

The Nazi: If I had refused to sail for Spain when my division left, I would
have been dismissed from the Army. And I have no other trade. I have
a wife and a child to support, and . . .

The German International: Then you would say that the reason you came
here was purely to support your wife and child? You would say that you
came here for purely mercenary reasons?

The Nazi: (with enthusiasm and hope) Yes. I came here for money alone.

The German International's pistol: Pop-pop. Pop.

<u>Later.</u>

Note on art and culture. The craft of decorating window glass with paper
was born in Madrid. In the early days of the war, the strips of glued brown
paper which shop owners imagined effective against the concussion of heavy
projectiles were arranged in simple squares and diagonals. As time went on
not only did the designs become more complex and artistic, but this newest
form of culture spread throughout the country until the smallest window of
the tiniest toilet (there are no outhouses in Spain) became simultaneously
objects of art and of totalitarianism.

There is the Hispano-Mauresque style, the Plateresque, the Victorian
Gothic, modernistic, geometric, the crochet style and the plain screwy.

Glass has become more rare than glue-paper. Broken windows may be replaced only with accidentally unbroken panes taken from abandoned houses.
Drivers replace machine-gunned windows with wood. When the windshield
goes, the chófer drives without it, for there are no new windshields in Spain.
In summertime windshields and the telltale reflections they cast up into the

sky even at night are removed. Ambulances of the future should be made without windows.

No glass, no tire pumps, no flints for cigarette lighters, no spoons, no bayonets, no field glasses, no range-finders, no planes, no iron wire, or cooper wire, or paint, or spare telegraph poles, no whiskey, no envelopes . . . but we will continue to fight as long as we have gun powder, gasoline and beans; and a few oranges to keep off the dirt fever.

In front of the bakeries are signs saying *No Hay Pan:* "There Is No Bread." Signs lettered *No Hay Leche* hang in front of the former dairies, sun-faded boards in the empty *estanco* windows tell that There is No Tobacco. But there is Heart, and plenty of it. No one is heroic. The Spanish are normally quiet, sweet, patient and formal. These qualities have now become more pronounced. More emotion is displayed about tobacco than over life, death and love. No one loses his temper. When a Spaniard becomes angry, his face sets hard as cement and he turns away. When a gasoline pump blows up or a truckload of I.B. passports is captured, or a carload of wounded capsized or cigarette papers run out, somebody says, *"Es la guerra."* We try to repair the damage or to do without what has been lost and say "That's war for you" again, and perhaps *mañana mas.* *"Es la guerra"* is always good for a laugh, but "More tomorrow" always brings down the house.

Nuisances of the War.

Guard duty. During the day all ambulances are kept in dispersed spots well away from the hospital and in the shade. At night each chófer brings his sweetheart to the neighborhood of the hospital. Guards are posted.

We work in two-hour shifts. The road rings with your footsteps. Everything seems to be covered with hoarfrost and moonlight. There is no one to talk to, nothing to look at and nothing to do but to walk slowly among the ambulances and inspect, again and again, the familiar shrapnel and M-gun scars on their sides. You light a cigarette, take a few puffs, put it out, and light it again. Whistling bores you. There is a noise, which turns out to be no noise. Cats' eyes stare out of the darkness like incendiary shells on a distant mountainside. You wander over to the cook-shed, hoping against hope, but the door is locked and no firelight shines under the lintel.

All movement, light, color and sound has left the world but for your breathing and the swirling of your frosty breath, but for the stars and the motionless dark shapes about you.

Something seems to move and you feel for your gun and wonder if there ever was such a senseless war, in which cartridges are almost more valuable than the pistols in whose stocks they must be hoarded, against the day of capture.

The village clock punches out the fullness of an hour. You go back to your sleeping quarters to wake the next victim.

Prisoners Without Jails. One day, down at Teruel, I was looking for the battalions. The shelling on the ridge was heavy, and I was in a hurry. At last I found an American and inquired where the boys were. He knew.

"Jump in my car and come with me," I asked him. "I don't want to get lost."

"Can't."

"Why not?"

"I'm in the guardhouse."

"Where is the guardhouse?"

"Oh, that shed over there with the open door," said the volunteer, kicking at a stone with the disgust of a small boy who has been refused money for going to the movies.

"What the hell is this! You're under arrest but they let you keep your rifle, leave the guardhouse open and don't post sentries to watch it! . . . Say, what did you do?"

"I said something about the 'dirty Spanish.' I was only kidding, but our bloody Commissar hasn't got a sense of humor. I'm going to bring him up on charges, the son of a bitch."

February 21. Muniesa. Stand-by Orders.

I had rather imagined that the Segura diversion was coming to an end when I saw the anti-aircraft and a few batteries of cannon come down the road from the Front late yesterday afternoon.

Our last four post-operative cases have been evacuated. The fifth died early this morning and is now very, very open on the Major's autopsy table.

Why do they die? Why do so many of them die? Why does such an appalling proportion of our lung cases go out? The Major is profoundly humble and curious. The bistoury teeth of his brain ceaselessly bite into the problem of death.

Why do we spend so much time and material on our heavy wounded? I understand that during the World War all of the magnificent equipment and technical skill of the Medical Corps were concentrated on giving the maximum and the most quick treatment to the light wounded, so that these might be soon cured and sent back into the lines, and that the proportion of deaths among the heavy wounded was therefore very great. With us, the heavy wounded come first. We seem unable to adopt the careless attitude towards life which might help us strengthen the lines.

I have become very much interested in my job although I have had no training at it and have read no books about medical military science. I hope that the medical corps of the United States Army is learning from our own experiences in Spain. I believe that our science has changed since the World War in two principle respects:

1) *The character of wounds.* Dumdums which would enter a chest and pull a handful of flesh out of the back are old-fashioned, sissy stuff. The modern explosive rifle and machine-gun bullet enter a man but do not come out. They explode inside and surgeons find nothing to extract but a thick metallic sludge. Shell and bomb casing break, not into a few large jagged pieces but into a uniform spray of smaller stuff. Clean, single bullet wounds are not the rule. Many of our wounded come in looking as if they had been chewed up by a milling machine, as if a robot had torn out fistfuls of them, as if they had been loosely run through a meat-grinder. I think that large portable electro-magnets would be extremely useful.

2) *The change in strategy and the resultant change in equipment.* Modern surgical units have to be able to move fast and frequently. They should never, even in the depth of winter, stay in buildings or towns. Double-walled tents with oil stoves lit inside the two layers of canvas ought to be able to solve the problem of cold. Pneumatic mattresses are useless, because shrapnel holes would be difficult to find and to mend. Cork-filled mattresses are the best. Ambu-lances ought to be made of light, windowless armorplate. Hospital trains can be stopped by a single bomb laid across the tracks and offer a magnificent target for attack planes. Field surgical hospitals will have to equip themselves as completely as if they were leaving for a month at the South Pole. They should not rely on local sources of power or water or fuel. I do not think that operating rooms on wheels will be practical because no ward can be carried on wheels, and two or four tents are not much more difficult to carry and to set up and pull down than one. Each of the many small fast six-wheeled ambulances should be equipped with an automatic tire pump and spare tires and a huge camouflage cloth capable of resisting infra-red serial cameras. Each surgical unit should carry a small repair outfit. Railroad tunnels are the

best places for hospitals. Speed is the principal thing; speed, flexibility and more speed.

Portable trenches would be extremely useful; and since the world's best brains and research equipment are now preparing the solution of how simultaneously to destroy the world and save the world from destruction, I have no doubt that portable trenches will soon be invented.

The quality of the rank and file will be the decisive factor, not just in the medical corps but in all the branches of every army. Men must believe not merely that they are right and that the other side is wrong; not only that their side is humane and that the enemy is atrocious, but that the outcome of their victory will mean, for each man, a greater share of the wealth of the earth.

No troops of any age or nationality are going to stay in their trenches under the modern conditions of war unless each man knows that victory will give him a better job, better pay, more of the earth's wealth, freedom from political machines, liberty to live under the form of government which has been chosen by the majority; and in general, more to eat, better clothes and better places in which to live.

We need a new world. Who likes the old one? Who liked 1937? Who likes 1938? Who looks forward to 1939? And Hitler says that he is going to live for a thousand years.

Why did I come to Spain?

Later. Same morning. The fascist whose body was mended by Major B.'s hands and whose mind was healed by Sana's soft boiled eggs was evacuated this morning, well on his way to physical and political health.

It was painful to watch him and the three other post-operative cases being evacuated almost before they were fit to be moved; but if the whole surgical unit stayed in Muniesa to treat them, who would operate on the wounded of the 35th Division? This unfortunate situation is one of the many things which make war what it is. I have little hope of being able to convince anyone who reads this journal of the full horrors of war. I am sure that the hideous taste of war will die out of my mouth, when and if I ever get back to a country in which what is known as "peace" exists.

We are almost ready to move. Only the operating room and the *triaje* have been left in place. Where? When? Why? Ten miles or five hundred? The Intelligence department of the Estado Major has certainly done a good job in leaving us in the dark. Meanwhile, the after-the-ball-is-over dejection of spirits which always comes over us when we are ready to move has set in.

<u>A little later.</u> Just about one last raid. Disgusted and bored, we paid no attention to the shaking of the air and the earth as we loaded the operating room.

February 22. Cedrillas. 21 Miles from Teruel. 4 A.M.

The Fifteenth is somewhere near. Has not taken up positions. We therefore do not know where to set up the hospital. The two Commandantes wait for orders in this hot-spot town. Rest of convoy pulled out for a quieter place as soon as the first warning glow of daylight lifted on the mountains.

Drove all night over Aliaga route memorialized by our New Year's Eve blizzard party. All towns along the way have now been bombed. House where I slept New Year's night in Aliaga was down on its knees, and also house in Camarillas where I had eaten my first eggs in Spain. Rubble drools from the doorway mouths of the village hearths. Clods and stones lie blown across the streets. Too bad these nice little burgs have to go. They would have looked nice this spring. The whole world is dying.

Would have to put up in Allepuz, but hospital set up in a nice summer home called "Casa del Conde" had just been bombed.

Cedrillas, once a neat clean little mountain girl, is now an old bundle of rags from which life has almost ebbed. I sit in abandoned ward of half-evacuated hospital, near fire into which, in the famine of firewood, I have just thrown a few broken chairs, writing by candle-light. Deserter from fascists lies in a near bed. Things must be bad over there when They desert even when the whole world knows they are winning.

Troops, trucks and equipment in this town equally worn; dejected and wretched as the breath of the stinking pre-dawn air.

Sun comes up very soon. Town supposed to be one of the hottest spots in Spain. When the light rises, I will go outside and listen to the sky. Soon as They come for us, the two Commandantes must be waked.

Something has gone very, very, wrong. Don't know what it is, yet, but I think it must have been Teruel. You bring up a child and then, at the age of ten, it dies. All that energy and money and love wasted.

Segura campaign wound up tight. But diversion was successful not so much in pulling artillery off Teruel but in forcing the transmittal of long radiograms from Burgos to Berlin and Rome. When the fascist infantry came up in force, the Fifteenth retreated to a high spot, waited, then turned on the Doras. Their dead fell, as at Celadas and wherever and whenever we get a crack at infantry, in clumps of four and five.

No more warming up of a cold Front. We are back in the furnace of Teruel. Franco's planes have predicted that he will drive towards Valencia in the direction of the town in which the writer sits waiting for the sun to come up. As usual, the Internationals are right in the shock center of the pressure.

No hope for rest.

Road outside the window still full of belated convoys of troops, tanks on truckback, cold cavalrymen walking beside their tired mounts, stragglers waiting for hitches up to the lines, or limping back towards the Rear.

Car is in bad shape. New, terrible rending noise of rotary scraping near water-pump. Fixed it, accidentally, in the dark with a slog of oil into the water-pump greasecup, but have no faith in the permanence of the repair. Have by now poured enough water into radiator not only to float a dreadnought but the whole British navy on which sun never sets.

Don't like the feel of this joint. It has its neck out.

And then it happened. Two silver observation Messerschmidts. Only taking pictures. Hope to get out of Cedrillas before they are developed.

The bloody sun has come up. Last of the peasants are leaving their homes. Not a child is visible above the earth for miles, or a baby boy or girl in a village, not even in the deepest reinforced wine-cellar.

I hear. . . . Have to wake up the Major.

February 24. Castellar

Teruel is Theirs. We stopped Them at Kilometer 3 on the Valencia road. We are therefore eighteen kilometers (or eleven miles) ahead of the game, since the lines, before the original attack on Teruel began, were at Kilometer 21, just outside of Valverde.

But Campesino is still in Teruel. Orders for him to evacuate the city came so late that he was cut off, with many thousands of his men. If "The Peasant," who is a Communist, has not been captured or killed, he will try to fight his way out to Valverde.

Very much maneuvering, tremendous work, no sleep, little food, and we are again under stand-by orders. Have not taken off my shoes, washed or shaved since we left Muniesa.

The snow that fell this morning has almost melted. Deep draughts of darkness fall on the earth. Not much prospect of being able to write tonight, since there are no candles, even for the dressing of head-cases. The last lead in my pencil has just about worn out.

Cold as hell. The wind blows through the only window in the huge top of the barn-like summer farm of a former Teruel lawyer, over sixty dark beds and seven patients.

There will be fewer than seven wounded by tomorrow morning.

If we shut the window, there is no light.

After dinner. Food helps. Good news helps more. Campesino and his men got their orders and fought their way out of Teruel.

In Memoriam

Major Candon, the young Cuban commander of Campesino's Special Machine Gun Battalion. The comrade with whom I ate lunch many weeks ago. He was killed while covering Campesino's retreat.

Save the pistol save the shoes and save the helmet.

The Major and I and the autochir arrived at this mountain farm to find the Catalan surgical team who had come ahead of us helpless, because of a lack of staff and equipment, to keep pace with the big loads of heavy wounded who kept coming down the hillside. The other cars of the Divisional convoy had been blocked by planes. Since there was no fuel for the autoclaves, I had to boil instruments over a fire of dry sticks.

Soon the other cars began coming in and I had to carry beds and mattresses, stretchers and surgical equipment, all over the building. I had been on the plane-swept roads for thirty-six hours by that time and my strength began to run out. First time I had ever used drink to recoup my energies. Every time I passed the wine-barrel I poured myself a big drink. The alcohol went into my arms and legs rather than my head. Stimulants seem to tap reserve tanks of energy in men. We set up the hospital in two hours flat.

Don't feel well today. No energy. Battery is running low.

Today's narrow escape. Up on magnificent defense position called the Puerto de Escandon ("Hideout Gap") I was about to descend into the town of Valbona (Good Valley) when I noticed white smoke rising from a flat field below me. The steam of forty locomotives on a winter day began to rise out of the earth. Had heard no sound. Slithered to the protection of a low roadside cliff, cut engine and rolled into the culvert I knew I would find. Three V's of trimotors came out from behind the mountain, tried to get the Valbona bridge, missed, and tore up the road over which I had been about to pass. They had just bombed an open field we sometimes use for an airport. They have bombs even for that.

From the mouth of the culvert I watched portions of Valbona go up in white smoke. The explosions did not seem loud.

By the time I had run into the town, the six-foot crater in the middle of the road had almost been filled in. Without waiting for the work to be completed, I drove off the road around the bomb hole, picked up a load of civilian women and drove them back to the Major.

The people of the town, which was wholly unevacuated, seemed to be drunk. They did not hear my horn. Little girls ran down the street, crying, looking up into the sky and swearing big long adult male curses.

Why had the trimotors not bombed the gas pump on the outskirts of the town? There is still more blood than gasoline in Spain. Wonder which will last the longest.

Frightful things are continually happening. A Madrid cartridge factory was blown up by spies. Seven hundred young girls and women were killed in it. The gasoline storage tanks in Tarragona were hit. Somebody wrecked a train, outside of Valencia, and over two hundred people were killed. *Mañana mas.*

February 25. Villa Carmen. Castellar. 12 Miles East of Teruel

The Fifteenth has taken over the defense of Corbalan. After loading in and out of their trucks, marching up and down hills seven times in one night, the men reached their destination. By noon Their artillery had taken off the top of the hill on which the men were entrenched. The lines held.

The last ? hours have been a mixture of the sounds of my engine and springs crashing over the military Cedrillas–Valbona road, of passing trucks and being passed by trucks, of small doses of food and sleep at the wheel, of ill rumors, stand-by orders and slowly lightening despair. So long as I can write I don't suppose I am completely gone. I do not feel well.

There has been a defeat but no flight, panic or disorganization. I know this to be true because I drove almost to Teruel over the Cedrillas road and the Valencia road last night and this afternoon. Camion loads and trainloads of troops, tanks, ammo, food, artillery, go up to the Front and come back empty.

This afternoon I saw three of Ours dive on Teruel through a voluminous canopy of black anti-aircraft puffs. There were multiple and terrific concussions. Then all three of our biplanes screamed back through the twilight.

Our few planes seem to come out like humming birds, mostly towards evening. Certain of being tackled by seven or ten times their number of Theirs, our Gloriosos evidently depend on darkness for escape.

New Post is in a road-mender's hut. No Champs Elysees hotel could be cleaner or in such good taste. White-washed walls, red floors scrubbed until the corners of the unevenly laid tiles were round, iron fireplace fillings and olive-oil lamps so rust-free that they looked like the silver for which I mistook them. Wood cupboards, knife and fork boxes and chests of unpainted and unvarnished wood, half worn away with scrubbing, were white as driftwood.

<u>Same day. In ward.</u> 10 P.M. Barn-like top of two-story farm-villa building, 50 × 80 feet, rough hewn beams cut from pine forest on overhanging hillside, tire roof supported by four rough brick columns in the dim light of the single electric light bulb to which our portable generator supplies shaky current. Also slight glow from iron stove used for warmth and to heat water. Floor is treacherous under the feet of stretcher-bearers because cement is not flush with beams.

80 beds. Eight wounded. Have already buried two. Six lung, one head, one gas-gangrenous arm. Three nurses and one chófer with dirt fever. Little treatment available here for the heavy wounded, but they are too sick to be moved to the nearest base-hospital. Two tables poorly stocked with bandages and drugs and instruments, but clean as plaster, stand out in the dim light. Surgeon with a flashlight changes dressings. Some of the staff sleep. Others undress or get up. Big long cold draughts play with the halo of heat that comes out of the single iron stove.

Patients yelling like hell. Chests, dehydrated by high fever and other things I do not understand, make endless demands for water we can't give them. Pain is very great. Two of the chests are developing mental troubles. "Mother, cure me, nurse, nurse, cure my wounds, nurse . . . give me a gun to kill myself . . . give me an instrument . . . give me a knife . . . the Republic! . . . get ready the concussion bombs. They are going to attack . . . nurse, give me a spoon, I want to choke myself." What this chest-case wants is morphine. He has had all the drugs he can take. Other wounded yell at him to shut up.

Through an open window over the bed on which I write I see white soundless flashes on top of the nearest hill. Snow begins to fall.

There are footsteps and a cough. One wounded asks to be turned and another spits. A nurse with grippe gets ready for a visit from her boy friend by making up her lips.

The water on the stove is almost hot enough for cocoa. Someone got a package from home.

My car (which now lacks two fan blades) lies, shrouded in blanket camouflage and shrubs, under a low cedar tree a quarter of a mile up the mountainside.

A farmer begged a piece of old inner tubing from me for his shoes. I cannot quite get the courage to bind the rest of it around mine although the tips of my socks have long since worn out against the ground.

Jack took a truck and went up to a village in which we had heard there was a coal mine. The owner gave him a shovel and a pickaxe, walked him to the entrance of the shaft and told him to help himself.

Pastimes of the war. Infantrymen spend much of their spare time digging and looking for firewood and sitting at fires. Reading letters is a great wartime occupation. I once drove through a town in whose main square a battalion, having just received mail, stood so paralyzed reading letters that they were more difficult to klaxon out of the path of my car than sheep.

Letters from the outside world painfully remind us of what is normal but give us a sense of importance. Some one who gets a letter feels for a moment as if he is a man and not a machine.

What is a commissar? Company Commissars wear one horizontal red bar and the red star of the People's Army. Battalion Commissars wear two red bars; Brigade Commissars, three. For every grade of office there is a Commissar. The auto-parque has a Commissar of its own, the Divisional Medical Corps, the various *Intendencias*, the Tank Corps, the Air Force, the Marineros, and every one of the units which make up almost all of life in the Republic today. Industries and establishments not directed by the Ministry of Defense—there are not many of these—have *responsables* and *contra-responsables* who fulfill the duties of Commissars.

Their Job? "The First to Advance and the Last to Retreat" runs the motto of our Commissariats. That our Commissars put these guide words into practice is proven by the frequency with which their obituaries appear. If a Commissar is asked what is his job, he will very likely tell you "I'm supposed to be responsible for the morale." This is only part of the answer.

Discipline and democracy are hard things to maintain simultaneously in a country at war. Infantrymen and street-car conductors must both obey all orders at the instant they are given without having been given either explanations or participation in the formulation of the command; and yet each man, if the war is to be won, must play his part in planning it. The volunteers of the original Abraham Lincoln Brigade had such exaggerated notions of democracy that they once proposed to hold a meeting in the Madrid-Jarama trenches which they later held for 106 consecutive days, throughout the months in which the fate of the Republic's capital and heart was being decided, to consider the acceptance or the rejection of Bob Merriman's orders.

Whenever governments have declared war, democracy has always disappeared almost before the smoke of the first shot has blown away, or before the first pacifist has been arrested.

March 1. Villa Carmen

I have been too sick to write, too sick to think or dream or eat or do anything but lie under my blankets. For three days the Alfambra road and the Teruel road, the Madrid highway and the ladder-paths of the Sierra Gudar and the Sierra de San Just have run between my closed eyelids and open irises like endless ticker-tape. I dodge a truck, duck a plane, dive into a ditch, pass a truck, dodge a plane, dive into a ditch, dodge a plane, until each second of the ward alarm clock raps out like a machine-gun bullet and there is no time left and then I dodge another truck and another plane. If we only had as many planes as we have trucks! And someone has been saying that he himself personally with his own eyes saw two hundred *chatos* being unloaded from a steamer to a Barcelona dock.

Someone is always saying that we have received three hundred planes, four hundred planes, a thousand planes.

Apology. I had intended to put more of the people of the war into this account and less of the things they did and the way they lived; but we who rolled out of the gates of Villa Paz so long ago and we who have been here at the Front for so long are no longer people, human beings, personalities and individuals.

The appearances of dogs differ but all dogs act alike. We differ but we act alike. No one is a hero and no one is a coward.

We talk little.

Those of us who are alive after the war is over and who are able to get back to their homes will turn back into people, most of them, after the rich proteins of Time bring them back to health.

A Trench mortar and a 75 have personalities. Gunners have none.

Some day I hope to be able to know people and to write about them.

March 2. Villa Carmen. Under stand-by orders?

Saw the brigade today. Did not let the Major know I was still full of fever. We may leave Villa Carmen soon and if B. thinks I am not well, he will not let me drive. There is always the danger that I might be evacuated to a base hospital or that I might have to wind up this campaign as a passenger.

The Fifteenth is back on the Valverde anthill. Red-eyed, filthy, slope-shouldered and ragged beyond all raggedness, they sat on the raw pelt of the earth waiting for trucks, waiting for planes, waiting for artillery to reach the Republic.

A truckload of replacements fresh from Albacete training camps and the British Isles came up. The new ones were a little apprehensive. They were very anxious to know where exactly was the Front. Someone answered by pointing up at the sky.

The veterans who were returning to the brigade, most of them healed wounded, seemed a little too bored.

What hope is there for rest? None, so long as the news is bad.

Nothing new. Heavy and light equipment is being cleaned and repaired on both sides of the trenches.

Time out. The last round lasted two months.

Teruel was a tie. The side that lost was the side that used up the largest quantity of irreplaceable material. Offhand I'd say that was us. Haven't got much left but our hearts and red eyes, and empty gun-sights.

Reasons why we lost the ruins of the city of Teruel:

1)   Lack of sufficient political work among the Spanish troops. Blame this on Prieto.
2)   The four-to-one mechanical superiority of the enemy in quantity and quality, as against their three-to-four inferiority in man power, nose for nose if not heart for heart.
3)   The ounce-wise and ton-silly fool's paradise of attitude of Washington, Paris and London.

March 3. Villa Carmen. Very Much Under Stand-by Orders

Our last head case and lung case were evacuated today. Lopez had to drive halfway to Segorbe because of the continued bombing of the hospital trains at Estacion de Mora.[18]

---

18. Epiphanio Lopez, a Spanish American garage owner and driver from New York, drove ambulances with the AMB.

It is again cold; but the past two days of sunlight brought out tall snow-drops, faint pink shadows of cherry blossom on the trees near the latrine, and swarms of very small yellow white and lavender grass flowers in the fields.

My faint, irregular symptomless fever persists. I am barely able to creep from the ward down to the sheepfold for meals. I should be out in the sun-light now playing *futbol* or swimming in the mountain brook. I ought not to be able to complain of bad luck. We have all of us been very lucky.

For the past three days the Spanish part of the staff have sung, night and day, in the dismantled *triaje*.

The Teruel campaign has folded up like Coney Island in winter. Sorry I'm sick. I should be resting up for the days of wrath that will soon come. This war is like crossing a brook on stepping stones. You leap like hell from one tiny islet of rest to another.

How distant is the farther bank? How many more of us will fall before we reach it?

The mountains are vastly quiet: silent as a grave. They are a grave.

PART FIVE

The Ebro: Retreat

Fifteenth International Brigade Photographic Unit Photographs Collection, Abraham Lincoln Brigade Archives, Tamiment Library, New York University.

Figure 7:   The Great Retreats. Retreat from Hijar to Caspe, March 1938.

Teruel was lost. The 15th Brigade fell back to positions near Hijar, about one hundred miles from Teruel, but only twenty-five miles from towns like Belchite and from the front. They would see action again very soon, and Hijar would be in Fascist hands again within weeks. The Aragon was becoming more and more dangerous. The Divisional Hospital was now located in Urrea de Gaen, not far from Hijar.

The war in Spain was only one component of developments in Europe. On February 4, 1938, Hitler took direct control of the German Army. On February 18, British Foreign Secretary Anthony Eden resigned to protest appeasement of the German leader. On March 13, Hitler expanded his empire illegally—violating the Treaty of Versailles—by annexing Austria without bloodshed or protest. And his bombs were still falling on Spain.

On the ground in the Aragon, the location of the lines kept shifting. The Fascist attacks were withering. Events became so frantic that after March 12, Neugass's journal was undated and written in fragments. The chaos that surrounded Neugass at this moment can be glimpsed in a brief fragment that survived with the original manuscript:

March ?? Near Alcañiz . . . Wear New Shoes

Fascists have big feet. Killed three, five, eight of them. One with knife, others with bombs. At night. May have to kill more. Still have my car. Eat olives off the trees. Hard to find in moonlight. Not sure where I am. Separated from unit. With infantry. Looking for the lines. Are there lines? Everything all mixed up. Very, very bad. Wound hurts. Have to move on, somewhere. Oh God. Very bad . . .

⌀

March 9. Lecora. 7 Miles Southeast of Belchite. Aragon

My speedometer has registered a thousand miles of road since I last wrote into this journal.

"We have troops up here and They have troops up here. We know that They have gotten together plenty of artillery. They will attack or we will attack. This campaign is going to be tough," said the Major, in one of his longest speeches.

<u>Valencia.</u> By the time that I reached the former capital my fever had gone.

Sana had slipped me four aspirins and half a dozen oranges before we left Villa Carmen.

We should not have stopped in Valencia if one of the nurses had not obtained permission to have her will notarized by the American Consul.

I spent my entire half hour of leave pouring vermouth down my neck and eating pickles and olives and Barachini's on the Plaza Emilio Castelar. I had thought that the vast marble shelves of this former palace of antipasto, lobster paste and anchovies stuffed with capers should have contained more than the six tins of Bensdorp cocoa I was offered, at 180 pesetas each, and the four bottles of Haig and Haig, at 220 pesetas. I was lucky in having found vermouth.

Half an hour of wolfing the main streets would have produced a sack full of everything from acorns to blood-oranges, red as a Teruel sunset, but the Major was relentless and we left the city of food almost as soon as we had entered it. Many of the staff had not even dismounted from the cars.

As we raced through dusty streets made more dusty by nightfall, up the bank of the river Turia at the very hour when the planes that ride in from Mussolini's sea love to cut their engines, dive and bomb, I noticed that the Miguelets tower, in which an anti-aircraft battery's ransom of paintings are stored, had not been hit.

Villa Paz. At 2 A.M. the returned Front group arrived and was given a victor's banquet of bread pudding and chile con carne straight from the States.

Before the sun came up I rolled my sweetheart over to the garage for repairs and welding. While the boys were climbing all over her, I went to the shower baths which had been built in our absence and for an hour scrubbed myself with an expensive cake of soap bought long ago on the Rue de Rivoli that smelled not like war but like sleep, home, clavichord music and congas, home-cooking and the girl I will some day walk to Battery Place to watch the waves and the boats and the stars.

By the time I had shaved, climbed into two sets of brand new long woolen underwear and put on my new uniform (picked up in Valencia by Johnny the Divisional optician on one of his frequent trips for new glasses for riflemen), written letters and postcards tinged with the atmosphere of a last will and testament, in the "it would be far, far better . . . " style of Sidney (Charles) Carton on the steps of the guillotine; by the time I had bought a bag of dry sweet cakes and a bundle of raisins at the hospital canteen, not stand-by orders but moving-orders had come.

Five mechanics were put on my car. My shattered headlight could not be replaced and there was no time to fix the leak in my radiator and no acetylene for welding the frame and body. Headlights are little used at the Front and as long as my car works she will roll and that is what counts. The main thing about a car as Bernie says is "if she works."

By midnight the Major and I were again on the road, headed south for Albacete.

The road was as clean of trucks as the sky was of planes. Not one ounce of lead or a single soldier's footprints had poisoned this landscape; and here we lay in the khaki filth of our executioner's apparel, stew-eyed on groaning nerves, impatient to reach the next theatre of war before the curtain should go up on the latest most stream-lined slaughter. For how many years will we who hate war as no pacifist ever hated war have to fight, and love to kill?

"It is very beautiful here," said the Major, breaking the silence in which we had traveled for eleven hours. Neither of us likes to talk while we are on the road. There is no need for talking. The human voice is an organ whose use is the planning of campaigns and the giving of orders.

"Yes" I answered, "it's a nice spot for a Classification Post." There were trees for camouflage, ditches deep enough to use for trenches when the planes came over and the ground was soft enough for the quick digging of graves. People are sometimes stupid enough to die in places where a pickaxe has to be used.

By the middle of the afternoon we had spiraled up to Morella, the Roman-aqueduct town that crowned the divide. Because of its isolation and warless-ness this place is famous for its meals; but we had taken on enough beef to carry me to the Front, wherever that was, and there was no use asking the Major if we were in a hurry. We are always in a hurry. I invariably drive as fast as the roads and my springs permit. The boys go over the top and where the hell is the Medical Corps? In Morella, eating an omelet.

Once we had left the divide behind us, I saw a geyser of thin brown smoke lying against the azure backdrop of the horizon. After half an hour of driving, the smoke, not the right color for a burning ammunition dump or town, had grown neither larger nor smaller. The air was as still as the roads were empty and silent. Perhaps the earth itself had caught fire.

Later that evening I passed the beet-sugar factory at Pueblo de Hijar, bombed two days since and still smoking. They now have enough planes to bomb even our sugar!

Before sunset I entered Alcañiz, whose large population, having just been bombed (I wondered why I had not heard the sounds), sat in the fields afraid to see what happened to their homes and relatives until the sun should go down.

Alcañiz is thirty-five miles from Belchite and the Front. Something big must be on. The town had been lightly raided three or four times since Christmas, but this was the first time Franco had really put his finger on it.

Alcañiz to Lecera. 6 P.M. to 12 P.M. Camions and more camions. Plenty of heavy stuff moving up: but I miss the quantities, organization and snap of the Alfambra road during the days of Teruel.

Met the rest of the American convoy, drawn up beside the road outside of Hijar, which had been bombed twice that day and was expecting to be bombed again before night and reorganization came; and Hijar voted heavily for the fascists in the 1936 elections!

Before the last of the spring light had faded from the sky, we were driving across the heath from which the Fifteenth had besieged, attacked and taken Belchite last September. There may be places more desolate than sections of the Aragon, but I wonder what country possesses more varieties of natural desolation.

We passed the positions the volunteers had held before the attack; staggered zigzags four feet deep, topped by two feet of earth-filled flour bags; artillery pits, good barbed wire, *cheveaux-de-frise* ready to string out across the road. A mile later we passed Their former lines—good seven-foot-deep trenches that looked as if they had been cut by a mechanical digging machine. I thought that they were too straight.

The town itself, torn, rocked, sieved and ripped, no house entirely perpendicular or unholed, looked like a toy village stepped on by an impatient child. Belchite used to be an oasis, in this high slightly rising desert against whose horizon denuded towns and eroded earth hills always rise.

March 10. Lecera. Stand-by Orders Are Now Permanent

Lunatic noises come out of the church tower all day long. Bells beat the hour, the half and quarter hour, the sighting of planes, the coming and the leaving of planes all at once.

No action in this neighborhood yet, but much aviation, of both sides. Has the world really allowed us to buy planes?

This town is practically whole. Was machine-gunned by low-flying trimotor yesterday, in warning. No wounded or damage whatsoever. There is one sight I still cannot endure and to which I will never accustom myself: the spectacle of parents running out to the fields with babies in their arms, hurrying, head looking back, kids of all ages skipping after them.

Lecera, which has never seen action, is so full of civilians that every window sill is full of faces and arms. Firewood is so rare that the people of the town have been grubbing into the cemetery for coffin planks.

The American group has put up with the Classification Post. Don't know where the Fifteenth is. Since we have not yet set up our equipment, we know that the men have not gone into action. Because of the activity of Their planes, we know something must be coming off around here, and soon. I suppose that we have not been bombed because the German aviators are fighting the Italians for that privilege.

Had cabbage soup for lunch two days running. Cabbage is a wonderful thing.

Outfit now consists of my car, of the big evacuation ambulance, a supply truck, and the autochir (now called the "meat wagon"). The staff has been cut from thirty-two to fifteen, since we first came to the Front. Oscar, Annie, the Major, Jack, Bernie and I are the only ones left of the original group. The others needed rest or stayed behind to allow some of those anxious to see what the Front lines looked like to come with us and make targets of themselves (church tower bells ring an alarm . . . what the hell, I'm out of the town and there's a good culvert near). No one has been killed. How long can this last?

Don't know where Dumont and the Divisional surgical teams and staff and equipment are.

Personnel: two ward nurses and two O.R. nurses; one cleaning girl; one anaesthetist; two surgeons and one assistant surgeon; one combination photographer–male nurse–spare driver (Jack); one driver-mechanic, and four drivers.

Think we might set up in a good cement floored cave near here.

Portrait

Looie of Chi, heart, lungs, biceps and soul of the Post.[1] Always shaved, neat. Carries a pistol taken from a fascist at Belchite, where he was wounded in the hip, last September. Always working, cheerful and interested in what you have to say. About forty years old. (Alarm . . . can hear them now, but what the hell.) Fought in the Russian revolution, became disgusted

---

1. Louis Zivin, born in Russia in 1897, listed his occupation as painter.

with the government after the fight was won, came to Chicago and almost immediately made big money as a building contractor. Then got bad conscience, sold car, said goodbye to all his blondes and came here.

Major B.'s health is bad. I do not think that he should have come to Spain. Nothing but our bread suits his ulcerated stomach, and nothing but cigarettes will ease his nerves. Tobacco hurts his stomach more than the oranges he eats after he stops the car and throws up what he has mistakenly eaten. Perhaps the Barcelona job will suit him. His nerves and sensitivity and introspection are not those of the soldier [that] will-power and political convictions have made. He is so rich that he does not need to practice his profession to live, much less come to Spain. B.'s skill has become so famous that whenever my car stops, volunteers recognize his car and beg me to tell them where he is.

March 10. Urrea de Gaen. Near Hijar. Hospital Camp

Move-on orders came at 7 P.M. last night. At 7:30 we were on our way, extra supplies carried on big steel Diamond-T fresh from the States. Is Cordell Hull's bad conscience beginning to work on him?[2] After short trip found Divisional Hospital—four camouflaged tents pitched in an olive grove a quarter mile off the road between two steep hills and a canal on whose bank canes grow fifteen feet high. There is *barranco* for each of our cars. Nice place.

Heaved mattress and blankets into my car, took off shoes, slept. Someone woke me up. Did taxi-service for the rest of the night, not using lights because of observation planes sent up to clock traffic on our roads. Highway good and jammed with all kinds of heavy and light stuff, human and metal, moving up.

Came home, parked in a gorge, pitched motionless to ground, aromatic with rosemary, thyme and semi-tropical succulents, bridge of my celebrated serpentine nose pointed towards Great Dipper and nostrils towards Orion, until an apricot and salmon dawn came up full of promise of heat, cloudlessness and gun powder smoke.

Had coffee among olive trees. Then reparked car. Balanced canes and old stretcher-poles against radiator (which still leaks) and body. Threw blankets over the poles. In this way shadow will not be that of a car. Maybe you are perfectly camouflaged with mud, black paint and blankets, but They can

---

2. Cordell Hull was the U.S. Secretary of State.

still see you if you don't do something to break up the telltale shape of your shadow.

Then located good dugout halfway up a cliff. Here I sit, ready to duck.

Drivers not allowed near hospital tents. We use the light wounded room of the big evacuation amb given by the people of the State of Vermont (Harvard bus petered out) as a chófer's clubhouse, where we make bitter cups of milkless coffee in pitcher over primus stove.

Nothing to do until nightfall, after tuning up our cars, because roads are too hot and few wounded, for the same reason, can be brought to first-aid or Classification Posts until sunset. We spread blanket near mouth of a good culvert, stripped to the waist and slept until They gave us our first welcome to this spot.

Must not have been first time the people of the town of Urrea de Gaen had seen *pavos* because they have in a body left their homes, with mattresses and pots and now camp out on a sort of barren plateau full of cavelets scooped by the wind and sun.

Big planes but small bombs. Scatter-stuff, just to warm up the griddle. Big stuff and concentration come later. Tomorrow or next day my guess.

Something big must be coming off around here. Never saw Them bomb so heavily so far back of the lines (which are twenty miles away). Hospital is exceptionally distant from the men for the same reason.

We sunbathed and sewed and talked about our narrow escapes and how afraid we are of Them and of the peculiar things explosives do until They again came to look us over and then crawled into the culvert and estimated the distance and the weight of the explosions. Bravest of us, maybe too brave, is a young I.W.W. lumberjack amateur plane pilot, longshoreman, now working as driver and mechanic on our meat wagon.[3]

Nothing fell nearer than half a mile away. For once we are not in a town or a house.

Afternoon. Our camp, complete to "Please Do Not Use Branches of Olive Trees for Camouflage—It Destroys the Tree" sign, over the signature of the camp commander, is a model of efficiency, beauty and repose. The surgical tent with its two waiting tables has now been wired to our generator. Beds in ward tent are sumptuously made up, the office tent echoes typewriters. The

---

3. John "Jack" Michael Devine, a native of San Francisco, a former Wobbly, described by Dr. Rintz as "a great driver and fine mechanic," once salvaged two Ford motors from bomb debris at Tarancon.

triaje tent has been laid out with scrubbed but still bloodstained stretchers. The ground has been swept in and outside of all four tents. The seventy-five of us will take care of the wounded of eight to ten thousand men.

The dead take care of themselves.

All up the cliffs that rise on both sides of the narrow little valley grove, groups of the staff sit at the mouths of their dugouts, reading, talking, sewing. The cook-shack among the reeds of the canal, better camouflaged than any of the tents, is busy and clean—but no tremendous amount of organization or of cooking ability is necessary to produce the rice, beans and olive oil dishes, the bread and jam, coffee and wine on which we live and work.

The huge portable drinking water tank has been filled to the brim by our water truck. Nailed to the tree which shades the tank is our mailbox.

We are here and the camp is here only because of the generosity of the many thousands of people all over the world who gave money to pay for our equipment, steamship and railroad tickets.

Cherry trees bloom all along the dusty hillsides, each an individual shape of pinkish white. Grape hyacinths are out, asphodel is in bud, and just now, while lying at the mouth of my crevice in the rocks watching a dogfight high above us, I noticed that the yellow stars in the long grass were dwarf jonquils.

A smell of ether steals out from under the closed flap of the O. R. tent.

The first two wounded from the Lincoln-Washingtons have arrived from Belchite. One of them, a stretcher-bearer, had the luckiest wound of the war. The stray which he picked out of his arm will some day make a watch fob, if the stretcher-bearer's luck holds.

A big evacuation amb slowly comes off the road into our valley at belly-case speed.

Later. The wounded came in, all right. Hearing that the green young Spanish troops to whom the defense of Belchite had been given had broken, the three battalions of the 15th Brigade marched out in open formation shortly before sunset this morning. New Mausers, capable of firing tracers for night work, had just been issued; but only thirty rounds per man of ammunition.

Met by machine-gun fire, the men clawed themselves into a hilltop with their helmets and bayonets and for the rest of the day waited while all the iron bowels of the heavens fell whistling among them.

At five o'clock this afternoon, the Fifteenth still held the ridge. Why had no fortifications been dug in the six months that have passed since the capture of Belchite?

There are no hills suitable for fortifications until Hijar, eighteen miles away.

In Memoriam

The Commissar of the Lincoln-Washington Brigade and its Commander, Dave Reiss.[4] Killed by a single shell this afternoon in front of Belchite. The Commissar's head was blown off. Reiss, hit in the leg, chest, and stomach, lived for a few minutes. His last words were "Am I bleeding? Have the men enough cartridges? How are the new rifles? Am I bleeding?"

He was.

One of the Englishmen brought in after sunset, wounded in the hand and arm, was in a fearful condition; crying and twitching on his stretcher at what he had today seen done to his comrades.

Three women of Urrea de Gaen who had camped in the caves of the plateau that overhung the town were brought to the Major in the same ambulance which had carried the English. Lecera, the town in which we slept last night, was pounded to pieces today. We are still ahead of Them. How long can our luck last?

No wounded could be carried from the lines to the Post, which was itself cut off from us all day because of the planes. Only those who could walk reached help.

Rumors are many. Wounded men are always pessimistic. Never believe what a wounded man or a driver tells you.

The sunlight of the late afternoon loses its heat and turns white. There is complete quiet, but for the cars on the road. War is voiceless and lonely . . . oh yeah? More planes just went by. . . . I can't stand this silence.

Wish to hell they would send out my car to pick up wounded. This lousy business of lounging around the hospital! I asked the Major if I could go up to the Post. He said "Yes; the *responsable* will tell you to go out as soon as he tells you to leave."

---

4. The Commissar, Dewitt Webster Parker, born in Massachusetts in 1910, was promoted as battalion commissar just before the battle of Teruel and was killed by a direct hit at headquarters on March 10, 1938.

So long as B. retains the instinct for insult which he thinks is a sense of humor, things cannot be so bad.

Well . . . it looks as if . . . here is where I had better roll into my hole. Sorry there's not enough room to write in there.

March 11. Paradise Valley. Urrea de Gaen

Worked in the O.R. last night hauling stretchers and lifting patients on and off the table. Held one etherized guy on his side while edges of what looked like a tiger bite were being trimmed, probed, swabbed with iodine, peroxide and ether. Also helped to put up an old lady's arm in plaster. We do quite a business with civilians these days. Middle-aged woman from the camp on the plateau walked into *triaje* yesterday afternoon with a limp boy in her arms, Magdalen and Christ again. Civilians are all Magdalens and Christs and every hill is a Golgotha on which They attempt to nail up Liberty. The nails slip, Christ falls to the earth from which he gets and renews his strength, then mans the anti-aircraft batteries. He is a good gunner, but the Non-Intervention Committee interferes with His aim.

Almost every operation is a laparotomy or exploration. The knife follows crisscross blotched trails marked by black metallic smudges. No sense sewing up a guy's chest if there's a hole in the liver. Since livers will hold no stitches, almost all boys nicked in this organ die. They do not die fast enough to be buried in the hospital camp, but in the Rear, after we have spent much bandage and adhesive, drugs and gasoline on them.

We almost ran out of morphine, gas-gangrene and anti-tetanus serums last night. Afraid that the farmacy truck had been strafed, but it turned up in time. The conversation, laughter and general light-heartedness of the O.R. is a continual surprise. I suppose I made a fool of myself last night when I told Annie the Queen and Helen Freeman (real name) that I would kick them in the teeth if I were a patient and they giggled while I was on the table.[5]

Because I am believed to be very strong, I often play a large and excruciating part in the job of shifting the wounded from the stretchers to the table. While they are in my arms, I can hear their shattered bones grinding inside of their flesh like the ants of history gnawing away at the pillars of false wealth.

Slept on a mattress in my car, held in a vice between seats and side.

---

5. Helen Freeman, a New York operating room nurse and a member of the first AMB unit to arrive in Spain, was seriously wounded during a bombing attack in March 1938.

<u>9 A.M.</u> Have just come through a fair-sized raid and fight. Their silver turkeys are endlessly after every roof, crossroads and camion in this neighborhood.

Hijar and its fascist population are getting hell four, six, eight times a day.

Railhead hospital on the Pueblo de Hijar hilltop, in one of whose wards I spent my first night out of Villa Paz, was destroyed yesterday.

A hundred and five wounded were killed in their beds. The railroad station still lives and the hospital near Hijar has thus far received only flesh-wounds.

The raid had three phases:

First period. Theirs came by slowly and with arrogance and precision dropped the first thirty or forty big bombs. Then Ours (middle-sized single motor biplanes with red wing-tips and Republican colors painted on tails) appeared. Sharp, hissing sounds of diving, climbing and machine-gunning. Since the cartwheel creak of falling bombs and their leaden whiplash cracking on the hams of the earth had not been repeated, I stuck my head out of my cleft in the rocks in time to see two dogfights. Immediately pulled in my ears to avoid machine-gun bullets.

Suddenly I heard the air-rush of two big ones call out my name, turned, put this very leather-covered thick note-book over the back of my neck and rammed myself into the deepest part of my crevice, with the certain knowledge that I would be smeared flat as a paper bag if anything like a direct hit were scored on the thirty-ton boulder that protects and threatens me.

When it comes near, you do not hear it with your ears. The sound reaches your eardrums through the ground and then through your body, as does a dentist's drill or the sound of a surgeons' saw cutting through one of your bones, or the sound of two rocks being knocked together under water.

Agoraphobia, claustrophobia, paranoia: I have them all. Beginning to get too much of this.

And still our luck holds. I think that our time must just about have run out. Only a few grains of sand left in the hourglass.

Second period. Then the frightful crash of many bombs being dropped at once as They unloaded, to make climbing and banking easier, and ran for home.

Third period. Run they did! Ours sailed low enough for us to see their Republican colors, then disappeared.

We dug four crooked trenches last night: one for the dead, one for bandages and sheets, and two for ourselves. Over the ditches in which the staff goes when the planes come over is a good thick mantle of olivebough camouflage. Without this covering They could spot the black zigzag excavation and the color of the fresh earth.

In Memoriam

Irving, ambulance driver for the Lincoln-Washington Battalion.[6]

His new latest model smooth front-line Chevvie, whose speedometer had registered hardly a thousand miles, took a wrong road, yesterday afternoon. It was full of wounded.

Irving was a big bull-necked guy with fine regular features. Nobody knew much about him. He told me that he had been a railroad worker in Alaska, that he had been a professional wrestler (he was the fellow who nearly broke my back at the Alcorisa Christmas party) and a real-estate salesman in Florida.

I had arranged, three days ago, to swap breeches with Irving. Wouldn't like to trade shoes with him now.

We think that ambulance drivers who take a wrong road are shot by the fascists. None of them has ever come back.

Blanco el Ranadero, stretcher-bearer and former keeper of frogs in the Barcelona zoo, went with Irving.

Franco has taken Belchite.

The Fifteenth entrenched themselves this morning on the Lecera plains with their helmets and a few shovels.

Last night the Dombrowskis, singing wild gypsy-like Polish revolutionary songs, marched up the road to the Front.[7]

The natural pessimism of the wounded spreads ill rumors; but I think that we're in for it; better take a deep breath before I dive. Hope to come up before my lungs burst.

---

6. Ed "Shorty" Irving was born in England c. 1903, lived in Regina, Canada, and died during the Retreats.

7. Dabrowski (pronounced Dombrowski) was the Polish battalion named in honor of Jaroslaw Dabrowski, a 19th-century Polish revolutionary.

<u>March 12. Urrea de Gaen</u>

Neither the first warning rays of the sun nor the raid that came in on the pale light woke me up this morning. I had returned to camp in the early hours. Slept even while I knew that the shaking of the earth above me and the pounding of the air meant that I should perhaps look for a better place or at least open my eyes and see what was going on. It was not until pebbles fell from the boulder overhead onto my face that I pried my eyelids loose from the glue which had formed on them last night.

All of the rooms in the Ritz—which is the name the chófers have given to the low ridge at the side of the gully in which we keep our cars at night— were taken. Troubled snoring, coughs and mumbled orders came from the hardly visible crevices we have for the last three days been using for bed-rooms. My hole is nine feet long and from twelve to eighteen inches high. A twenty-ton boulder is the canopy over my cork-filled mattress. Since it proj-ects slightly over the lower lip of the crevice, shrapnel cannot reach me; but in case of a direct hit, my comrades would be spared the nuisance of digging a grave. "Here lies a chófer who took a wrong road." When I get back to the States, "when and if," I'm going to rent a deep coalmine in the bootleg area of Pennsylvania. With half a mile of rock over my head, I should be able to sleep in comfort.

Was again awakened by the falling of earth on my face. This time, the flaming yellow dwarf jonquil which bloomed yesterday in my bedroom win-dow shook violently. When a petal drifted loose, I decided that the time had come to shake the sleep out of my frozen joints.

Downstairs at the curb of the Ritz's portiere was my car. Beautifully cam-ouflaged in a wild jangle of blankets strung on poles.

Paradise Valley was empty and quiet. Everyone was underground but for Slavo, the chófer of the car parked behind mine. He lay sleeping on the ground beside his running board. I called to him and he scrambled up the cliff and went to sleep with his feet in my stomach. The jonquil was again waving. I rammed myself into the end of the crevice, which was not as deep as the rest of it but still gave good shelter against what shrapnel might break in the valley.

Downstairs on the sidewalk a voice called at me. I looked out of my win-dow and saw Major C., chief of the Thirty-fifth's Medical Corps.

By the speed with which he helped me strip the blankets and poles off my car, I gathered that the military situation had changed, that it would perhaps be necessary to move the hospital and that we were going out to get orders from the Estado Major.

It was daylight and the road was empty.

Urrea de Gaen was silent and smokeless. The last of the population has now moved to the wild camp on the plateau. Just as tubercular people may seem very healthy, even when they are about to die, towns which have been bombed may seem from the outside to be whole. It is only when explosives land on the main street itself that destruction becomes apparent. Here and there in the doorways of the houses, little piles of rubble leaked from the sills like blood from the lips of a man killed by concussion.

Once we entered the plain which led north all the way to Belchite, the road began to look unhealthy. What few trucks which were going towards the Front were empty. Many of the men in the trenches that were coming back did not have guns. Soon we began to pass streams and driblets of soldiers walking back down the road, almost all of them without rifles. On their faces were the expressions of college boys drifting back from a stadium in which their team has just lost the big game of the year.

"I have seen this too often," said the Major to me, "each time I think it will be the last," with a weary smile.

Part of a battery of 76's went by us in their camions, plainly disorganized and missing much of their crews. A great tanktruck came down the road piled carelessly with empty and full crates of ammunition. The sound of heavy shells began to be audible.

Not a single cloud had drifted between us and the sun. Yet we were not being bombed!

Just before we were about to enter Lecera, we saw the entire ambulance fleet of our Classification Post ditched at the side of the road. A voice sang out of a stony cliff.

"Hey!"

I stopped my car, looked up and saw Al G., Commissar of the Post, flattened out against the base of a boulder, brown as the desert treeless landscape that ringed the horizon. He yelled again. Neither the Major nor myself could understand him. We looked in the direction of his extended arm and saw two shells break near the town which we were about to enter.

"It began this morning"—Al had left his hole and had run down to the road—"The first two shells hit the church tower. We packed up and cleared out inside of an hour. The town has been getting hell ever since. The whole thing's evacuated. We've been trying to get away, but they keep shelling the road."

"Lose any ambulances?" asked the Major.

"No, but. . . . "

"No, but you're going to lose all of them if you don't clear out of here. Do you know where the lines are?"

Al looked puzzled.

"My dear boy," said the Major "there are no lines. Now get your men together and —— out of here."

Al scurried back up the hill. I sat still, wondering where we were going, feeling somehow that I was about to drive through Lecera. I was. The Estado Major was evidently ahead of us, and we had to get orders.

Three days ago I spent the night in Lecera. It was so crowded with civilians that many of them had to spend the night in the road. In the wretched four minutes it took me to leave those powder-stinking streets behind, I saw nothing that moved—excepting odd flying stones and beams and plaster and once, a cooking pot—but for a dog or two, nosing in the ruins and probably homivorous by now, and an old man plainly as mad as the Major and I, sitting in the doorway of what had been his home.

Such are the reception committees which welcome Franco into his assassinated villages.

When we could hear polite machine-gun conversations not too far away, and when giant mosquitos had begun to play in the silver noonday sun around my soft, leaking radiator and softer tires, we came to a pitiful olive grove set like an oasis in the thorny desert of Belchite. Miserably camouflaged by adolescent thirst-warped trees were four very beautiful cannon-tanks. At the end of the grove was the white hut which must be our Estado Major.

No troops were between us and the fascists, whose cavalry and armored cars would soon arrive.

I ran my car under the largest olive tree I could find and immediately threw blankets over the radiator, the telltale windshield and headlights and the wheels. The deep sound of many engines came out of the sun. Tank-turrets slammed shut.

Because I did not wish the Estado Major to see me running, I walked at a hobbling trot towards one of the tanks, with the intention of crawling under its belly. Suppose the tank drove off while I was under it; and if a direct hit were made? In all of us was the desire to be killed by the enemy's metal, if we had to go, and not shamefully by what we had thought was protection.

I curled up in the roots of a tree with an American infantryman and a German belonging to the Franco-Belge battery. The first bombs began to fall.

"Did you see our guns?" the German asked me. He had somehow become separated from his comrades. "I heard that the men were killed and the guns captured. Did you hear about that?"

I told him that I had passed the Franco-Belge battery just outside of Lecera. He wanted to leave but we kept him with us. The bombardment was not yet over and a single man walking out from under a tree could give away a whole position to the enemy planes. "You just stay still," said the American. "This is a bad place but don't move. You just stay still. Put your hands or your helmet over the back of your neck but don't move."

These were the only words we spoke until the planes moved off us.

I put my notebook on the nape of my neck. The smell of spring had come into even this soil.

The tanks were not hit. Major C. stood beside my car eating an orange. "Where were you?" he asked.

When he told me that we were to drive back to Lecera, I felt as if I had just swallowed five long whiskies.

"Why are they shelling the town but not the road that leads into it?" I asked him, "and why aren't we being machine-gunned?"

"Here," he answered, "finish my orange."

Again we drove through the hideous town and again I saw the same old man sitting outside his ruined house, and the same dogs nosing this time in the gutter at what looked like unnaturally bulky rags. When we got to the square, the Major told me to turn left, back into No-Man's Land.

It appeared that the brigade headquarters which we had just visited had referred us to the Divisional Staff.

After a half an hour of searching the empty roads and hillsides, we came upon General W.'s long black Chrysler limousine parked in a meadow next to six cavalrymen and a motorcycle.[8] The General's car was famous because it was the only vehicle at the Front which was not camouflaged. The nickel on its hood and the windows were as prettily polished as if W. were going to be married that day, or drive down Fifth Avenue on an Easter Sunday.

We found the General seated among his staff in a cleft in the dry hills. All seven officers were freshly shaven. The creases in their trousers were perfect, boots shined, and khaki uniforms unspotted. Four sappers stood at one side, with picks and shovels. Two of them carried officers' boots and pistols. I imagine that the shoes were still warm from the bodies of the soldiers who

---

8. General Walter, aka Karol Swierczewski (1897–1947), was a Pole who had fought in the Russian army during World War I and in the Russian Revolution. Later he was an instructor at the Moscow Military School, and by 1938 he commanded the 35th Division, which included the 15th Brigade.

had worn them. Dead, an officer represents a good pair of boots, a pistol, a wrist-watch and possibly a compass.

On top of the hill, at our side, stood a Captain, field glasses in hand, searching the horizon. Every few seconds the General would look up from the map on which he was silently drawing red crayon lines and ask the two field telephone men if their machines were in order.

No Republican troops were ahead of us. The General had stayed in order to be able to plan our next defense positions.

There was a little shelling but otherwise the afternoon was absolutely quiet, except for the usual machine-gun chatter. I could not understand why we were not being bombed. It later occurred to me that we had escaped their planes because we were so far back of enemy lines that we had been mistaken for fascists.

"What do you see?" asked the Major of the Captain with the field glasses.

"Nothing."

I was so nervous that I smoked my last cigarette.

"Cavalry!" the Captain on the hill announced.

"Near?" asked the General without looking up from his map.

The officers all carried parabellums. These are Luger pistols which can be mounted on their gunstock-shaped holsters. They fire on the machine-gun principle and there is no breech-cover to slide back and ruin your aim. If you have telescopic sights parabellums are almost as good as light automatic rifles; but ten of them are not enough to hold off Moorish cavalry.

The staff officers were busy mounting their guns, inspecting the sights and testing the action of the locks. I pulled out my 7.65 and slid a shell into its barrel. My eyes, mind and every thought were all fixed on the grenade which I kept in the springs of my front-seat cushion.

"More Moors," announced the voice under the field-glasses. "A thousand meters."

I had been hearing the low roar of tank engines and could no longer contain myself.

"Captain, do you hear tanks?" I asked.

"Yes, I hear them. On our flanks."

The General put his map aside, stood up and said "Kilometer 46. We will set up a line of resistance at Kilometer 46. Has anyone an orange?"

Orders were transmitted through the field telephone and to the cavalry and motorcycle dispatch riders. The General and his staff idled down the hillside and loaded into the glistening limousine and my own mud-smeared, scarred and scorched wagon. Air clicked into the vacuums left by the paths of M-gun bullets, like the snapping of fingers. "Pluck-oo" sounds came over our shoulders. Finally I could stand it no longer.

"——— you! I said to Major C. "I don't give a bloody ——— about your ———ing neck, but I'm not going to lose my ———ing car because you have to take your ———ing time."

The officers laughed, hurried and slammed the door. "Have you got an orange?" one of them asked me. I told him that I had a pineapple, and gave him my grenade. He looked at it with fondness and gravity, tried the pin, and hooked my pet to his belt.

Swung across the meadows and drove through a shallow stream. The Moors might have cut the road. But again I had to drive through Lecera, with its insane old man and scavenging dogs. The shelling had died away. The fascists did not want to hit their own men.

Drove slowly because I did not want to lose my car. The worse the danger is, the more slowly you drive.

There was little sound. As we left Lecera behind us for the third time that day, rock-drill blasts of heavy machine guns met us, but the road took a turn and we were out of range. The most horrible things about that afternoon of anguish were the times when there was no sound. When the enemy fires at you, you at least know where he is. It was good that none of the officers had lost his head and fired on the Moors.

When I arrived at Kilometer 46, the General had already arrived. He and his staff stood across the road, guns in hand.

A truckload of men came along. One of the officers stopped it. The chófer said that he had other orders. "Is that so?" the officer answered. "Well, everybody get out" his gun waving a little.

Whenever the General found an officer among the troops that were coming back, there was a brief, very brief interview. Especially if the officer had torn off his insignia.

I was ordered to drive back, back again to Lecera, to pick up what machine guns I could find. "O.K." I said, with murder in my heart, "but give me a grenade." I was given a brand new shiny pine box of them. If your car is surrounded, you give it a bomb. We don't like to lose our women and our cars to the fascists.

Picked up two heavy Maxims, one without its mount and two Chauchats and quite some rifles before I reached Lecera. Exactly at the first house I turned back and swept down the road to K 46, where things were looking much better. The Franco-Belge battery had arrived; three guns on one side of the road and three on the other. Ahead was the full weight of Franco's war machine. I was busy helping the gunners dig when the General's Aide ordered me back to Lecera. He asked me to haul back some trucks and a new V-8 which were stalled out between the lines. I wanted to explain that my towing chain was not strong enough, but you don't argue with a General.

There were bullet holes through the windshield of the first truck and bloodstains all over the cab. The engine worked but the two front tires were flat. Mounted my automatic tire pump in my cylinder block, connected the tube with the first tire and was standing on the road watching Lecera when a car drove up behind me and stopped. A chófer jumped out and explained that, well, he had been machine-gunned that afternoon and he had, well, lost his spare man, and well, run back to the lines. He then got me to unscrew my pump, and drove off on his two flats.

I found the V-8 with three flats, glass thoroughly machine-gunned, and wheel locked. Gave her one more flat with my bayonet, so that she would tow on an even keel; hitched my chain, and started down the road.

All of a sudden there was a wham flash bang; and the V-8 towed easier. I had read that sharks often chew the body of a hooked tuna off its head before the fisherman can land his prize. I was the fisherman, the V-8 was the tuna and an anti-tank shell fired from one of the fascist tanks which had just occupied Lecera was the shark. There were a lot more whams and flashes; the bang part came a few seconds later because one of our anti-tank guns, mounted on a hill over my head, had forced the fascist to pull his ugly head back into Lecera.

Before casting the gasoline-bleeding wreck of the V-8 loose, I saw her spare tire lying fifty yards back on the road. I ran and got it, not because I wanted to be brave or because I wanted to have something to boast about to the boys back at the camp, but because a spare tire might save my life one day. A chófer loves his car not only because a car is much more valuable than a man but because cars are the best kind of legs.

When I got back to the lines, towing a nice new Dodge truck I had picked up along the way, and loaded with more rifles, half a dozen trim and heavy grenade belts, a wounded *soldado* and two old peasant women who were having trouble with their feet, things were picking up. Behind the emplacements of the roadside Franco-Belge batteries, the new pine boards of shell-boxes glistened in the late afternoon sun. Ordinance officers were searching the horizon with the waving, mantis-like uplifted arms of their range-finders, and two four-barreled anti-aircraft machine guns had arrived to protect the gunners.

In open formation Polish companies of the Dombrowski Battalion were fanning out into the hills.

I saw General W. get into his limousine and gave him a can of *carne* I had been saving.

Picked up Major C. and we drove back towards the camp. Passed families of peasants marching like queues of mourners behind carts loaded with all that was mortal of their destroyed homes.

Each vehicle was a museum of the glories of a thousand years of progress and civilization in Spain. Where was the wealth? Copper and majolica pots, casseroles and pans, half a dozen cheap bentwood chairs, pine chests almost worn out with scrubbing, crowned by huge mattresses, ready for roadside sleeping.

If there was wealth in Spain, I never saw it.

Leaving the flat heaths of Belchite behind us, we entered the red hills of Albalate. It was another of the pre-spring evenings we had been having; impeccable spring sky, silver sun full of scorchless tingle, cool breeze in the shade of fruit trees, blowing the healthy perfume of fruit blossoms across the road, new leaves in the almond orchards and algarrobas, cocoa-brown soil freshly plowed and just under irrigation.

Captain P., riding with Artie the Finn towards the lines, stopped us.[9] While he and the Major spoke, I went to sleep where I sat at the wheel. Something about the low, serious, confidential quality of Captain P.'s voice almost woke me up, and I listened, torn between sleep and curiosity . . . "just a little one, behind the tent . . . no, B. didn't get it, but one of the nurses, and . . . Webster and Crescencia . . . and one of the cars."

I asked Major C. had B. been killed?

So our luck had finally changed. There was no use asking C. what had happened.

In a few minutes we both would be able to see all we wanted. Thank God the sun was beginning to go down.

The shadow of hills on the winding road made the darkness seem more intense. Not even the sight of four great cannon-tanks rushing up the road on the backs of enormous trucks could cheer me. The death of a single good friend is more disturbing than the sight of bodies lined along the road or of naked corpses piled on the tarpaulin-covered camion which carries them to the Rear, than the merciful butchery of our operating tent, or of the pyres of burning dead which sometimes light the highway at night, black hands and

---

9. Dr. William Winston Pike.

legs sticking out of the flames like hooves of cattle or the stumps of pruned willow-trees. When your friends get theirs you feel as if the war is getting very near to you.

Paradise Valley was so full of shadows that I was unable to make out the scars of the bombs that had just fallen.

Drove up to our four camouflaged tents. The sounds of my engine died out of my ears and I heard no voices. Then I saw Slim, the Canadian chófer of one of our big evacuation ambulances, leaning up against the trunk of an olive tree, his finger pointed up at the darkening sky. I listened and heard the sound of planes.

Part of the hospital staff was still in the trench which we had dug two nights before between the operating and the ward tents. Helen lay in the deepest part of the zigzag ditch, bandages on her head. "How are you, Helen?" I asked. There was no answer.

Slim told me the story.

"The planes were over all day," he began, "a two hundred pounder landed next to my car but it was a dud. At about 2 P.M. They let us have a shower of light stuff. A ten-kilo bomb went off thirty-five feet behind the operating tent. Friedman had been doing an amputation and Broggi a skull case.[10] Both cases would have gone out if we had gotten into the trench so the eight who were there continued with their work. Helen, who's over in the trench—"

"I know."

"—Helen got it in the head and the arm. We won't be able to do her until it gets dark and the planes move off and we can use the tent—but I don't know, there are so many rips in the roof that the light would shine through—but the generator's smashed anyway—"

The noise of the planes had become louder. Someone was yelling for me, I ran towards my car. Major C. was sitting in the front seat. "Come on," he said, "let's —— out of here."

Slim had run up to my car with me. As I started the engine, I asked him who else had been hit.

"B.'s O.K.," he said, "but two patients were killed in the ward tent and Crescencia and Bob Webster and Jack—" My car had begun to move. Slim jumped on the running board. "Jesus Christ," I said, "Jack got it?"

"A slug smashed his hip-bone and we couldn't either do him or evacuate to"—through the combined noise of my engine and those of the planes which

---

10. Dr. Moises Broggi-Valles, a Catalan surgeon, worked closely with American medical personnel.

must now be directly over our valley, I couldn't make out what Slim was saying. He sensed this and hopped off the running board.

"What was that about not being able to evacuate Jack?" I asked the Major.

"We can't evacuate anybody," C. answered. This morning the other hospital up at Hijar was smashed.

I reached the highway. Then I heard a crack-slash-whipping oversized explosive machine-gun bullets spouting from overhead at the road.

Stepped on the gas, reached a place where banks of earth rose on both sides of the road, cut my switch and rolled out. We were being machine-gunned and bombed at once. I crawled under my engine, shoulders jamming between the front axle and the stone-surfaced road. Something like an earthquake, not in the ground but in the air, shook a pain into my lungs. I got myself loose in time to stand to be thrown eight or ten feet against the side of the road by the next air-earthquake, back first. Through white smoke stippled with black specks, I saw a shallow dugout.

C. stood in the ditch, looking up at the sky. I yelled at him to come in with me. He came. We sat so close together that our knees touched. I thought I heard a car climbing the road, in great agony of choking engine-sounds. Then heard a noise like a lead whip a hundred meters long hitting the solid flesh of the earth.

There was a dull sensation in the small of my back, exactly where the belt crossed the spine.

"I'm hit," I yelled at C.

He put his hand on my shoulder.

I reached behind me and pulled a disc of hot iron, half an inch thick and as big as a fifty-cent piece, partly out of my belt, my shirt and sweater, and the flesh of my back.

"Take your hand off me," I said, and showed him the present Hitler had initialed for me. It was still so hot that I put it in my pocket. We drove a hundred yards down the road and again had to dive out of the car.

Found a culvert filled with men. C. came after me. At the mouth of the culvert stood a motorcycle driver in some sort of frenzy. He would fiddle with the belt of his magnificent calfskin breeches, then look up at the sky, then fiddle with his belt again, without seeming to be able to get up the courage to take down his pants. If he kept his trousers on and came into the culvert with us, his life would be reasonably safe but he would ruin his pants. If he stayed out in the open and saved his pants, his life would be in danger. He chose to risk his life and ours also since his squatting figure might have given us all away to the planes; but we were so amused at his heroism that we didn't mind a little more or less danger. Anyway, in case of a direct hit . . .

A new sound, whipping upwards from below the road, alarmed us. Then we knew that one of our anti-aircraft guns must have just set up. Laughing, we wriggled out of the culvert, each man smearing himself in the low brown monument the heroic motorcycle driver had left at its mouth. C.'s expensive Madrid breeches were the best this side of Hollywood.

Camouflaged by the black and white smoke of the last bombs to fall and by the clouds of red dust they had raised, we drove off, our ears tingling with the rocketing of the anti-aircraft shells. The earth itself was spitting back at Their avions.

A drop of blood ran down the lower part of my spine.

"Where are we going?" I asked Major C.

"Back to Lecera," he answered.

South of Lecera at the latest hours of the night a tidal wave of gunfire broke on the six 75's at Kilometer 46. Surf of gunshots hissed up the flanks of the line of resistance constructed at sunset with the rumble of cannon-tanks and broke in its rear. Five of the six Franco-Belge 75's were loaded to two White camions pitched down the road lit by stars and powder flashes.

The sixth gun stayed in its emplacement. The first fascist tank then shoved its black fire-spouting nose up to K 46, got a shell head-on the snout and lay sodden and shapeless in its blood of gasoline, oil and water. When the 75 and its crew had died, one more tank had been destroyed.

When the sun came up, the skirmish lines of the Dombrowski which had fanned out into the hills at midnight walked, like field crickets, into the whirling jaws of a steel threshing machine.

The Harvester paused. The tanks to which it was hitched formed into a column of twenties and started down the road, in the direction of the surgical hospital at Urrea de Gaen.

❧

"The fascist tanks are coming!"

Three hundred volunteers of the Lincoln-Washington Battalion raced back the road past the nearly dismantled Classification Post, ran up a hill and without digging foxholes set up light machine guns, laid out bombs and waited.

Below them on the road an ambulance chófer called Slim crawled into a culvert and caught his breath. The noise of the fascist tank engines was no longer in his ears. The key of Slim's ambulance was still in his fist. The smell of excrement that closed on him in the narrow concrete coffin of the culvert reminded him of his shame. It takes a man to stand his ground, get into his ambulance, start the engine, turn it about when three hundred volunteers race down the road yelling, "The fascist tanks are coming."

But why had he locked his car? No other chófer would be able to drive her off so long as the key was in his hand. Jarama, Brunete, Escorial, Villaneuva de Canada, Belchite, Teruel, Segura; and now she was out on the road, with her long and glorious history written all over her sides in shrapnel and machine-gun Braille, hogtied for the fascists.

Slim crawled out of the culvert. Pistol in hand he worked his way up the ditch, taking the curves of the rough ground like a caterpillar to his car.

Before Slim started his empty ambulance on its toboggan slide back to the Republican lines or in the direction in which there ought to be Republican lines, he picked up a Maxim and threw it on a stretcher.

❧

Lightless, the first five cars of the 35th Division's field surgical hospital crept up out of Paradise Valley under the sound and the eyes of night observation planes, and started for Hijar.

Bob Webster still lay where bomb shrapnel had torn off the back of his head that afternoon. Eroded rock covered his sightless eyes.

The five-car convoy stopped at the Hijar river. Half of the heavy stone center span had been ripped down by a bomb.

The chófer of the Major's car, remembering that he had seen tanks push up the road earlier that night, knew that they must have come over the bridge. If the bridge could carry tanks, it could support the autochir. The staff members he was carrying got out and stood by the roadside. In the light of the stars, the chófer drove his car over the bridge, reached the farther bank, stopped and yelled at his companions.

The five cars, rocking and slipping through rubble, brushed by telephone and power wires, inched along the edges of bomb-hole craters and penetrated to the limits of the former town and the beginning of the road to Escatron.

❧

False dawn rose over Paradise Valley like a white veil of poison gas. The last truckload of supplies and staff made ready to leave.

"Come on. Get in," said Captain Pike to the four Spanish doctors and to Lola, the apprentice nurse.

The five last staff members to remain among the trampled earth sites of the hospital tents shook their heads.

"Get in!" ordered Captain Pike.

The sun was exploding all up and down the horizon in salvos of shells. The position of roads reached Paradise Valley camp audibly as the air belled out with the first early morning bombs breaking on them.

"We do not wish to go on the roads," said the spokesman of the four Spanish doctors.

"Get in," shouted Captain Pike, "this is an order!"

"*Somos todos iguales*," answered the spokesman quietly—"we are all equal and I do not accept the order. Stay with us, Capitano. Do not go on the road. It is daylight. Stay away from the roads."

A lonely machine gun spoke from a hill. Others answered it.

"All right," said Captain Pike, taking his hand off his holster, "stay here and take your chances. Maybe you are right. Try to meet us at . . . oh hell, at Escatron, or anywhere else. Salud!"

"Salud y vic . . . Salud!" said Lola and the four doctors.

Captain Pike's camion climbed to the road.

⚬⚬

Before brass band music of the rising sun had faded out of the sky, the first lines of Monasterio's Moorish cavalry rode down the hillside into Paradise Valley.

Three hundred men of the Lincoln-Washington Battalion waited, in foxholes dug on a hilltop outside of Hijar.

Fascist cannon tanks forged through the Moors at equal intervals, like killer sharks coming through a school of barracuda.

An infantryman lost his nerve. A single rifle shot came from the top of the hill.

As one English anti-tank gun and four Russian tanks opened up on the fascist tank section, three light Republican field pieces shot shrapnel shells into the Moorish cavalry. Three hundred Czech mausers speared into the stew of horses and turbans.

When it was all over a squad of Lincoln-Washingtons went out and cut shoulder-loads of fresh warm beefsteak from the flanks of the fallen Arabian horses.

Fires were lit.

❧

Blankets and great olive limbs heavy with unpicked purple fruit went up on the sides and the roof of the cars of the hospital convoy parked deep among the aisles of a venerable grove planted by the Moors.

Four drivers carried Helen, the wounded nurse, so deep among the trees that they soon came to a parapet where the terraces sloped down into the valley of the young, idle and silver Ebro. The spring green of the olive leaves, the silver of the river, the yellow ore of the sands and the blueness of the immaculate early morning sky were the sole colors, and the only sounds were the tremors of near light bombs or distant heavy bombs.

The four stretcher bearers laid Helen on the ground beneath the thickest of the trees. Water for tea boiled over a fire of dry olive leaves. Wild onions were stewed with olives in pork fat.

❧

"I'm sorry," said Major B. to the Chófer, "but you will have to go back to the hospital camp for Lola and the four Spanish doctors. Back into the inferno."

"Do you know where the lines are, Doc?"

"I don't know that there are any lines. There may be no troops between us and Franco. Use your judgment."

❧

Outside of the Hijar inferno the Chófer was stopped by Captain Pike's camion.

Raising his voice above the roar of explosives, the Captain ordered the Chófer to turn about. Hijar was already Franco's.

❧

Two silver observation planes came out of the sun.

Tanks and tank trucks, having betrayed the position of the field hospital convoy which was waiting for orders, moved out from under their heavy camouflage.

The first heavy stuff fell.

A doctor, two stretcher-bearers and the Chófer carried the wounded nurse through five hundred yards of screaming olive limbs and powder-scorched air to the nearest deep ditch.

Orders had not come.

As drivers tore fresher and heavier olive limbs from mutilated trees, the staff lay in a long straight ditch, waiting.

Annie, the O.R. nurse, caught the hand of the Chófer.

"I can't stand it any more. I could stand it until They got Helen but I can't stand it any more."

"What happened to Jack?"

"We had an amputation on one table and a head-case on the other, so we couldn't go into the trench. Jack's leg . . . do you think They have gone?"

"What happened to Jack?"

"We heard that the hospital train he was put on was bombed."

The avions came back. A stake of olive wood streaming with sap drove through the chest of a stretcher-bearer.

Orders came.

"Come on. Get the hell into my car," said the Chófer to the four nurses who were to ride with him.

Machine guns were speaking from the hills that overlooked the orchard.

"I don't give a God damn where you left your windbreaker. Get in! Load!"

"But where's Pepe?" giggled Fanny, "where's my dog? I can't leave without my puppy."[11]

Major B. riding on the running board of the Rolls left with Helen and the two collapsed nurses for a hospital and his new job in Barcelona.

"I'm sorry," he said to the Chófer, " but you will have to give me my gun. Report to me in Barcelona as soon as this business . . . "

"Sure," said the Chófer, unstrapping his Soviet Colt, "here you are. I have another one . . . keep your head down, Doc."

"Keep yours down, Jim . . . so long."

After all of the cars had left the hideous grove and gone out into the hideous sun-flooded shadeless road, Natividad woke up.

She had climbed down the parapet almost to the edge of the Ebro. While

---

11. Fanny Golub, a nurse educated at New York's Bellevue Hospital, arrived in Spain in April 1937.

the girl slept she had heard neither the bombing of the orchard nor the order to leave.

Singing "The Four Generals" and picking and eating olives, she disappeared on foot down the long cathedral aisles of this Aragonese green hell.

⋐⋑

At sunrise Escatron had been a clean quiet village on whose streets sounded only the footfalls of women going to the town well for water, of old men in Catalan costume padding on rubber-tire slippers out to the fields for *sarmiento* or dry vine-prunings good for kindling, of shepherds and their sheep.

By noontime the narrow steep main street of Escatron was clogged with peasants, carts, refugees, loaded and empty camions, rifleless field militiamen, stoves and heavy military equipment in many stages of complete and partial disorganization. Clots of unarmed soldiers, their hair white with dust of the road, crowded at the well. An axle had broken, and a hopeless jam of camions and carts filled the street with the shouts of drivers, racing of engines and cries of peasants. The bells in the church-tower ceaselessly jangled a warning that planes were coming.

The car that had caused the congestion was pushed into the gutter. Traffic loosened. A chófer slowly drove his ten-wheeled camion through the center of a flock of sheep that leaped from one wall to another of the narrow street and fell back under his heavy front wheels.

At one o'clock a dispatch driver entered Escatron, stood on the well-curb and announced:

"The fascists are coming."

On the outskirts of the town, the Chófer, eyes and nerves strained on the slowly moving tailboard of the truck that was holding up him and his load of nurses, said to his new Commandante:

"Take out your pistol and hold it between your knees. Pull mine and lay it on my lap."

A woman ran up and down the road, hands in her red hair, screaming that the fascists were coming.

The Chófer's car sagged to the iron rims of his wheels as peasants and rifleless militiamen jumped to the running board. Groaning from the chassis gave notice that the car was about to break down.

The Chófer shoved the nose of his gun into the stomach of a woman. She jumped back to the road. The other peasants and militiamen stepped from the running board when they saw the Chófer's gun. The Commandante had cleared the other side of the car. She now floated, not as a lifeboat loaded to the gunnels, but free and easy, in spite of the human weight she carried inside her.

"Do you hear that?" said the Commandant. "Those are the machine guns of the fascist armored cars."

"How exciting," said Fanny. "I'm thrilled! Just like you see in the movies!"

"Shut up," said the Chófer.

❧

The sign on the door of a smashed farmhouse on the Hijar-Alcañiz plain read "35th Division, this way." A hand pointed to craters made by bombs that had missed their objectives.

Two Englishmen, an American and a German walked down the slope of the first hole. Here they were given coffee, bread and jam. In the second crater, rifles were issued to the two men who had lost their weapons.

The German looked at a penciled map and lifted a case of grenades to his shoulder. The four men set out for the hill from which the Lincoln-Washingtons had been shelling that morning.

❧

The four Spanish doctors met three Americans. "Where is the 15th Brigade?" asked the Americans, at the exact time the doctors asked them, "Where is the 35th Division?"

"The 15th Brigade!" answered an American as his dry throat tried to spit, "there isn't any 15th Brigade! Maybe we're not the only ones left, but there isn't any more 15th Brigade!"

The sound of plane engines subsided. Seven men left the culvert, shaded their eyes and looked upwards.

I think that the Rear must be that way," said one of the Spanish doctors pointing along the road.

"Who the hell cares where the Rear is," said an American. "You're doctors and we're infantrymen. What we want to know is where is the Front and have you any tobacco. Besides, you're cock-eyed; that way isn't towards the Rear, it's towards the Front."

The four Spanish went in the direction which they thought was the Front. The Americans went the other way.

Half an hour later the three Lincoln-Washingtons came up to the recon-centration farmhouse.

"So we picked the wrong direction after all, thank God," said one of them to the Adjunct as he received a case of grenades and a carbon copy of a pen-ciled map. "Want us to go look for the doctors?"

"Did you say 'half an hour ago?' Probably isn't enough to find of them even if you have a microscope."

⇜

Lola walked through the olive groves, parallel to the road but two hundred yards away from it, sniffing a bunch of grape hyacinths and humming to herself. She had been born not far from here and knew where she was. Her blood-spotted Alice-in-Wonderland apron glistened white as a snowfield in the afternoon sun.

She came to a river and skirted its bank until she found a bridge head. The bridge piers stood like flood-swamped tree-stumps in the stream. None of the arches remained.

Lola turned and quietly listened to tramping of the explosions that seemed to have followed her through the mountains.

Pushing a beam from the dynamited bridge ahead of her, her white apron swirled down-stream in the direction of the farther bank.

⇜

Lieutenant W., battalion doctor of the Lincoln-Washingtons, lay in a shallow basin of earth on top of the hill which his battalion had held ever since the repulsing of the Moorish cavalry that morning.

"Like trying to walk between raindrops," he thought, whenever there seemed to be a slight let-up in the shelling. "I had better stay here. There isn't a better place."

Of all the battalion doctors, he had been the only one to stay with his men. The two others were with the Classification Post.

"And a hell of a lot of good I'm doing!" he thought. "I can't move. How long is it since I last moved? The other doctors were right. They will still be alive tonight if the planes didn't get them, and when the sun falls they will come up here and help us if we are still alive. What time can it be?"

He had stared at one of the grains in the sandy earth two inches from his eyes so long that it seemed to be a gigantic block of solid ruby, big as the frozen blood of a whole brigade.

"*Camilleros!*" came a cry out of the earth. "Stretcher-bearers!" . . . the last words of those who are stupidly wounded during daylight.

No *camilleros* rose.

"This is a tin roof and the shells are the rain," thought Lieutenant W. "Rain puts you to sleep. I should be falling asleep. The shells are not so loud as they were this morning. I should be falling asleep. But if I fall asleep They will run over me with one of Their tanks, when They come up the hill to get us tonight. I should not fall asleep."

Lieutenant W. had had dirt fever for four weeks.

In gown, ermine and mortar board, a red face with a white university mustache handed him his diploma. "I swear that I will do all in my power to save my patients and never to abandon them in the utmost hour of their need. I will always observe the utmost professional secrecy . . . and faithfully observe the prospects of my profession . . . from the halls of Montezuma to the shores of Tripoli . . . we will fight our country's battles whether on land or on the sea . . . always do everything in my power to cease buying newspapers for the Spanish news, not to dream about Spain, not to go to Spain . . . what the hell are the halls of Montezuma, the whorehouse in Paris where I, for the last time . . . why the bloody hell don't They attack. What are they afraid of? When does the sun go down?"

❧

Before the sunset stilled the late afternoon breeze, the shelling ceased.

"This is the end," thought a machine-gunner from West Virginia. "This is the very end. Be good to me baby." He laid his cheek alongside of the breechlock of this Maxim. The metal was so hot that the gunner imagined he could smell the fumes of his singed trench beard. "So you're getting hot, Ella May? Anything you like, dear, but don't jam on me. Be good and don't jam on me."

He lit his last cigarette.

"Don't want one of Them to smoke it," he thought.

❧

The hilltop held but its flanks folded.

❧

Like the multitudinous cigarettes of a prizefight audience in a stadium at night, grenades burst in the valleys on both flanks of the Lincoln-Washington hilltop.

Then the rifle-fire and concussion bomb reports came from the rear of the hill and the noise of tank engines began to climb its front.

"Here is where we ——ck out" said one rifleman to another. "Take the stuff and ——ck out."

In threes, sixes, nines, elevens, in groups of all sizes, armed with many assortments of M-gun parts, light automatic rifles and grenades, armed and unarmed, plucking olives off the dark trees as they went, the Lincoln-Washingtons fought their way down the back of the hill three hundred men had defended all day long and reached the scarred highway which led nowhere.

❧

Mac pushed a dead chófer out of the cab of the Divisional autochir, wiped the blood off the windshield and in broad daylight started down what he thought was the road to Alcañiz.[12]

He was the third chófer the autochir had had in twenty-four hours. Bob Webster had been killed by shrapnel. The second driver had been drilled, out of the air, before he had left the last houses of Hijar behind him.

Twenty thousand dollars' worth of surgical equipment jangled as Mac took the egg hole bumps in the road.

He reached a crossroad. Not only were there no guards at it, but the gun-less dusty men who straggled up to the signpost knew neither where they were nor where was the Front or the Rear.

Twice in as many miles, Mac was strafed. Twice he rolled into the ditch and listened to bullets play with twenty thousand dollars' worth of surgical instruments.

Suddenly he saw men without rifles run down the road towards him. Slowly the great moving van body of his autochir backed and advanced in the narrow road as Mac tried to turn her.

When she was broadside a full orchestra of metal sounds drummed on her thin sides.

---

12. Mac Kraus (real name Maurice Krausskopf, aka Krausikoff), a native New Yorker, was in charge of transportation at the hospital in Benicàssim.

Mac got out of the cab and ran off among the trees, leaving twenty thousand dollars behind him.

⊷

Captain Wattis of the International Brigades, ex-officer in His Majesty's Army in India, drove his baby staff-car into Albalate.[13]

"Clear out!" he ordered the field-kitchen staffs of the English and the L-W's. He distributed penciled maps.

"What about the field stoves, comrade?" the cooks asked Captain Wattis.

"Both ends of the road are cut. Now clear out. Meet at K 4 south of Alcañiz."

"What about you, comrade?"

"My car can make it across the fields," said Wattis.

The cooks grenaded their wheeled stoves, flinging themselves on the earth to dodge scalding coffee.

Lieutenant Simon, battalion doctor, gave his front-line ambulance a Mills bomb.[14]

⊷

Four Canadians met a group splintered from the Lincoln-Washingtons.

"Where's the brigade?" yelled the Canadians.

"Where's the brigade?" the Americans yelled back.

"There is no more Fifteenth. We are all dead or captured. There are no wounded."

"Yes, but . . . well, if the twenty of us are still alive, we can't be the only ones left. Somebody told me to go up to the ridge over there, under that big blue star . . . an anti-tank and a 75 are supposed to be on that ridge. . . . "

A shaken-up machine-gun crew flattened out against the ground dark as the sky and waited beside their weapon.

"The worst of this is that we don't know what's happening on the other Fronts."

---

13. Captain George Wattis, a British army veteran from Stockport, England, served as an officer on the brigade staff.

14. Lieutenant John Simon left medical school in Philadelphia to go to Spain. His service as the battalion doctor included perilous duty at the front lines.

"I heard that They attacked at Guadalajara three days ago."

"Somebody told me that Madrid had been taken."

"And did you hear that Hitler's planes, six hundred of them, wiped out Vienna?"

"A driver who brought a load of ammo up from Barcelona told me that. . . . "

"He was a liar. We're cut off from Barcelona."

Well, anyway he said that Barcelona is being bombed every three hours. . . . "

"So Hitler and Mussolini have declared war on us."

"Adolf did that when he kicked out von Blomberg and Fritsch."

"You guys are all nuts . . . now look across the valley. Do I see tanks or do I see tanks?"

"You see Italian tanks."

"Anybody got a smoke?"

"Give me a drink out of the cooler, for Christ's sake, give me a drink and then I'm ready."

⌖

Two of the machine-gunners who had helped the Fifteenth make a stand on the ridge for two hours carried a third by both ends of the blanket in which he had been rolled. The last unwounded Canadian walked with his arms hooked under the shoulders of two of his comrades. The Maxim had been left behind.

Grenades burst on them. Over-ripe olives pelted to the ground.

The wounded were dropped.

The unwounded ran.

⌖

The Chófer and his car were lost.

Afraid to turn on his lights, he crept from kilometer stone to stone descending at each white miniature tombstone to read the figures. The Chófer was afraid to stop, afraid to move, afraid to call out to the many men who he just knew must be up in the hills at each side of the road.

The sounds of the battle were on all sides of him.

He wanted to turn his car off the road on which he imagined all eyes and every gun were trained, but the ditches were deep and the hazards of the fields and hillsides great.

He stopped at one more kilometer stone. When the three men who rose beside it spoke to him in English, he suddenly realized that the pistol which was in his hand had almost gone off at them.

"Both ends of this road are cut," said an Englishman. "What will we do, try to get out through the hills or drive right through them?"

"My car can run faster than we can," answered the Chófer.

"Got enough gas, comrade?"

"Well . . . come on. Load."

"First put away that silly popgun. Here, take these."

The Chófer dropped six Mills bombs into the belly of his sweater and drove off, both front doors swinging wide on their hinges.

He drew his clasp-knife, opened and laid it on his lap.

A dynamited culvert had cut the road. The Chófer sank his front wheels into the ditch. His engine sagged, heaved and pulled him out to the fields.

His three passengers ran out of the car. The Chófer thought until he heard the explosion of the first grenade that they had left the car to show him the way back to the road.

Reaching down the neck of his sweater, he lifted out a Mills bomb, pulled the pin and pitched it at the three, five, six, black shapes who were running at him. He threw himself on the ground as the shrapnel of his bomb and something very soft and wet skipped along the earth near him; knelt, drew another grenade, pulled the pin, threw and bent to the ground.

As he rose to go back to his car a desire to count the dark bundles of clothing that lay on the field came over him.

He never knew if it was one of the dead who had gotten up or if it was still another fascist who came at him, but the shape that ran onto the knife in his left hand and dropped off the broad blade lay, afterwards, as quietly as any of them.

An Englishman was trying to start his car.

"Oh, so you're back, comrade. We thought that They got you."

"Not tonight, Josephine! Let's get out of here."

Before the car had climbed to the road and cleared the dynamited culvert, all three Englishmen had to get out and push her.

Before the Chófer reached the clumps of men whose lack of rifles told them that he had regained what would be Republican territory for at least another half hour, all of the grenades in his car had been thrown out of the window at shapes whom he had run down into the ditch.

The Chófer's paranoia, claustrophobia, agoraphobia, hunger and thirst were gone. There remained an appetite for tobacco.

༄

Never, in all its long history of raids, had Caspe, headquarters of the Army of the East, been bombed at night.

One of the first two hundred and twenty pounders to hit the town fell squarely on the building of the Estado Major.

What men who were left in the town ran out to a *barranco* on the road to Escatron.

A truck drew up to the edge of the gully.

Hanging from its running board and waving a shovel, the Communist Section Organizer of Caspe asked the men in the *barranco* if they would like to dig fortifications for the troops which would soon arrive. The camion on which he stood was full of shovels.

The Fifteenth Brigade was soon expected. So were the fascists.

The 45th Division of Internationals was on its way from the Cordoba Front.

༄

An English captain and two Lincoln-Washingtons were captured. The Moors were so excited by the officer's wrist watch that they had not the presence of mind to execute the prisoners.

One of the Americans still carried, high over his head, a heavy club-shaped tin of Soviet beef.

"Bring the can down on that guy's head," the English captain directed, "then we'll all use our fists and run like hell."

༄

Driven by avions from one olive grove to another throughout the forty-eight hours during which it had not handled a single of the many wounded of the 35th Division, the Medical Corps convoy at last came to rest in yet another grove.

It had lost fourteen of its thirty-five cars, four doctors, nine drivers, eight stretcher-bearers and three nurses.

The first meal was issued. Each staff member received one slice of bread and a thin strip of raw pork.

Missing drivers and stretcher-bearers had begun to come in.

᷍

At two o'clock in the morning the surgical hospital convoy had drawn up at a riverside farmhouse and set up its operating room in a cave. By sunrise no wounded had come in. At seven o'clock orders came to move.

Three hours later the bridge across the river went down. The earth floors of the farmhouse, opened to the sun, were black with powder.

᷍

All day long the three hundred members of the Lincoln-Washington Battalion who had been able to reconcentrate before Caspe in the trenches dug under the direction of the Communist Organizer lay while diving planes drove streams of explosives and tracer bullets into them. As each plane rose, loads of light bombs and grenades fell.

All day long fascist infantry and tank attacks broke against the thin lines of the Fifteenth.

Shortly before sunset they were driven out of their trenches, driven back through the shattered streets of the city to its outskirts, where the men re-formed and made ready to counter-attack.

Preceded by three heavy cannon tanks and led by Doctor S., who had come up into the lines from his bed in the tuberculosis ward of a Murcia hospital, the men advanced at midnight towards the town. At the first houses the three Spanish tank drivers stopped their machines and refused to go further. The pistols of the officers persuaded them to resume their positions at the head of the column.

Once the main street had been entered, one of the tanks veered into an alley. Shortly afterwards a second tank disappeared. As fighting broke out in the main square, the last of the three tanks swung about on its treads and turned its machine-gun into the Lincoln-Washingtons.

The three Republican tank drivers had been members of Franco's "Fifth Column."

Caspe was not retaken.

Between midnight and morning Captain Bob Merriman and Commissar

Dave Doran went out into the olive groves in which the brigade had been scattered and one by one led groups of men back to the Maella road, where new positions were to be established.

Before the weight of the Harvester broke against Maella, Caspe had been twice retaken and twice lost.

Merriman and Doran went out into the olive groves at night once too often and did not come back.

❧

"Madrid has been captured," said one of the three naked Americans who lay on the shore of the marshy Alcañiz lake.

"The Italian navy landed at Port Bou and cut us off from France."

"And Poland marched into Lithuania after Hitler burned Vienna to the ground. Blum and the Popular Front fell, and France is mobilizing."

"Is the World War going to help us or hurt us?"

"Killing always hurts the working class. While it's true that from now on Hitler won't be able to send so much of his stuff to Spain. . . . "

"Are you so sure that this World War has really broken out?"

"Of course. And even if it helps us . . . although it's probably too late, the working class always suffers from war and we should always be against war."

"Listen to the Socialist talk . . . you guys never learned anything about dialectics. You talk as if 1938 were 1914. . . . "

"Listen to the Communist intellectual . . . say, how are we going to get out of this . . . well, anyway, that swim was good. We'll all die clean."

The three men began to pull clothing over their pink sunburned bodies.

"Anybody have an idea where the Front is? We'd better get going."

"The Front is the whole world."

❧

Two files of English walked at the sides of the Batea road in the direction of the place in which a new line of resistance was to be set up.

Fourteen fascists tanks posted on the ridge that overhung the road fired simultaneously down into them.

❧

The Chófer's car was parked under a roadside olive tree. Lieutenant W., battalion doctor of the Lincoln-Washingtons evacuated that morning to the Rear with a high fever, sat beside him.

Both men eyed the few camions that came up and down the road.

Lieut. W.: You heard that Madrid was taken and Franco took Port Bou and cut us off from France?

The Author: And a lot more. How do you feel?

W: Fever. How are you?

A: Think that some of that iron stayed in my spine. Didn't get it all out. My belt saved me. Been bringing up blood ever since I got thrown into that wall. I can't walk but I can still drive . . . is a lesion necessarily tubercular, Doc?

W: Of course not . . . how does the road look to you?

A: Not so good. The trucks go up empty and come back full.

(Five minutes of silence, complete but for distant engines of camions and intermittent sullen fire in the mountains.)

W: I've had enough.

A: Same here. I wouldn't mind if somebody threw me over the French border, naked and sick. Just so long as I get to a place where sunlight isn't hideous and night isn't hideous and you can walk down the street without being shot at. If I would wash toilets all my life I'd be happy. I'd do anything so long as it isn't in Spain.

W: Have you got your passport with you?

A: Yes.

W: So have I. How much gas is there in the car?

A: Enough to take us to Barcelona and maybe to the border.

W: I heard that there's an American battleship in the harbor. Have you got a blank *hoja de ruta?*

A: Blank and stamped. All you have to do is make it out with your fountain pen and be sure the signature is illegible.

(The two men make out a pass for themselves and their car to Barcelona.)

W: How soon will we start?

A: As soon as it's dark. In about half an hour.

W: It's dark now . . . well, we'll wait a little.

The American consulate is in the Plaza de Catalunya. You can recognize it by the big American flag. Think the consul must get there by about nine o'clock in the morning.

(Five more minutes of silence while the two men inspect every truck that passes.)

A: A few days ago I saw forty of our 75's drawn up outside of Alcañiz.

W: And in the morning, Alcañiz was Theirs. They outflanked us. The whole thing has been one outflanking after the other.

(More silence. It has grown quite dark.)

A: Do you know, Doc . . . it isn't as if this were you and I. Everybody thinks of deserting in a time like this. But hardly anybody else has a car. And they don't desert. We held Them up at Caspe, didn't we?

W: We sure did! The brigade was down to half strength and we had lost all our field kitchens and heavy equipment, but we held up the whole God damn German and Italian Army anyway, didn't we . . . look here, just because I have a fever . . . maybe we both have fevers . . .

(A giant camion loaded eight feet high with wood boxes comes up the road.)

A: I know the shape of those boxes! Good old Soviet beef and condensed milk!

W: If we are bringing up food there must be somebody to eat it! Jesus Christ, maybe there is somebody between us and the fascists after all!

A: Suppose we follow that food truck! When he stops we'll get ourselves a meal.

W: O.K. And after that, we'll look for the brigade! They must be somewhere ahead.

A: I'm sure to see a chófer I know.

(He starts his engine. The car given to the Republic by the Washington Friends of the Spanish People takes the road to the Front.)

⟶

A volunteer walked into the office of the American Consul of Barcelona and laid a passport on his desk.

"I'm an American citizen. I want to leave Spain."

"Just a minute," said the consul.

The consul walked into the next room and telephoned to the headquarters of the International Brigade:

"Diga! Diga! Diga . . . is that the commandante? . . . Well, there's a deserter in my office . . . what do you want me to do with him?"

⟶

The uniforms of the sixty bandsmen who sat beside their instruments in a ditch outside of Gandesa had, in eighteen months of war, never been so dusty or disarrayed.

With each dull explosion that echoed like distant thunder in the mountains of the Batea road, the musicians twitched, shuddered and turned silent questioning faces on each other. There had not been so much as a pistol among them ever since the regulation sending all arms to the Front had been enforced in Catalonia, ten months before.

In Barcelona, war had meant marching down the *ramblas* at the head of parades. It had meant banners, speeches, broadcasts, phonograph recording, funeral marches, bandstand concerts towards the coolness of the evening, and innumerable walks up and down the Paseos with war-excited *chicas* and *guapas*.

The musicians could not understand why they had suddenly been loaded, like so many sacks of flour, into open trucks, carted across Catalonia and then dumped into this lonely ditch where there were no civilians, no microphones, no audience.

⟶

Two three-bar Commissars and one two-bar Commissar stood at equal intervals across the road at the gates of Gandesa.

A camion load of rifleless militiamen whose hair, face and uniform were white with dust would come back from the Front. The Commissars looked at a map and directed the men where to get coffee, a rifle and cartridges.

Each piece of artillery, each armored car and tank, each field stove, water tank and gas truck that reached Gandesa was turned about and given its station and task.

Loads of shovels, cement, dynamite and munitions were trickling from Barcelona.

By nightfall the three Commissars had organized, not another position to be outflanked by Franco's armored cars and his Moorish cavalry, but the sinews of a fortified line of resistance.

Once during the long afternoon one of the Commissars had been forced to fire on a squad of men who had tried to escape into the fields.

Two civilians standing waist-deep in the leaflets stacked in a ten-wheeled truck came slowly towards the Front, whitening the road with the first words printed on paper that had reached the battle zone for five days.

All up and down the road and the olive orchards, the towns and gas-pumps, men stood reading the few roughly printed words which had at last reached them:

"*Milicianos de la Republica! Oficiales! Chóferes! Trabajadores! Campesinos!* . . . *Tenemos mas de armas que hemos tenido en Guadalajara* . . . We have now more arms than we had at Guadalajara. One hundred men, well entrenched, can stand off a thousand fascists. . . . the rumors spread by the Fifth Column that Madrid has been taken and that Barcelona has decided to capitulate are false. War has not been declared in Europe. Vienna has not been destroyed. The Republic has received important quantities of planes and munitions from a foreign source and this new weight of metal will soon be felt by the fascists . . . . Not One Step Back! To Resist Is to Conquer!"

Giant truckloads of bread, Soviet beef and milk and coffee reached the Front. The engines of Republican planes were heard up and down the valley of the Ebro at night. In the morning the lines of men formed to read the leaflets and newspapers they had dropped. Editorials and foreign news were read aloud at automatic mass meetings.

Assault guards arrived to unsnarl the confusion of traffic in many a crowded village street. A load of new dispatch motorcycles arrived at the headquarters of the Army of the East.

Wounded at last began to reach the camp of the 35th Division's reorganized front-line surgical hospital.

When the first patient was being lifted to the table, the opening bars of the "Hymno de Riego" reached the amazed operating team. For a moment they raised their heads and listened, not to a phonograph or a radio but to the music of Barcelona's finest and largest brass band.

As the orchestra marched from grove to grove, men came out of dugouts and ditches, from under trucks and out of culverts to listen. Peasants camped among carts containing all they had been able to take from their homes, stood and looked towards the village from which they fled.

The music reached the Rolls Royce ambulance which was carrying the Chófer to Barcelona and it stopped.

Tears swelled into the Chófer's eyes, balanced on his eyelids, and sank back into his heart, where they turned to warm blood.

Long yellow crocuses pierced the eyesockets and grape hyacinths grew through the ribs. It was now spring. Wheat, fragrant as yeast and solid as bread buried the white bones which fell to powder and made fertile the lean earth. Classless men gathered the ripe and sunsoaked sheaves to their naked chests with the motions of lovers who at last have reached everlasting security.

There were no more dreams, for it had become possible to sleep.

PART SIX

Barcelona: Demobilized

Veterans of the Abraham Lincoln Brigade Photographs Collection (image #15:5:42:1), Abraham Lincoln Brigade Archives, Tamiment Library, New York University.

Figure 8: Memorial "To Our Fallen Comrades." Installed after the Battle of Jarama, June 1937.

The Fascist attacks and advances in March that Neugass experienced firsthand led to what became known as the Great Retreats. Many members of the 15th Brigade, and volunteers in other units fighting in the Aragon, found themselves running for their lives. Hundreds were killed or captured, while others made it to the Ebro River and swam to the safety of Republican lines. James Neugass's war was over.

⌖

March 22. Barcelona

I have written the preceding pages at the desk of a villa in Sarria which overlooks all Barcelona and much of this part of the Mediterranean. The Major and I have shared, for the past week, half of the home of a lawyer in the former residential district, far above the city.

As soon as my passport and International Brigade papers are ready, I will leave Spain.

I am very lucky. My lungs occasionally throw up blood into my throat, I have a hernia, the weakness of my legs is probably due to small pieces of metal that remain in or near my spinal column, and I carry various shrapnel scars on my left leg and my scalp. I am very lucky.

"What do you want to do?" the Major asked me, "Stay here and drive my car or go back to the States and write that book?"

I told him that I would rather go back to the States and write what I had seen in Spain.

"O.K., I'll send you out. But who the hell is going to send me out?"

The Major is not very well. He lives and fulfills the obligations of his new job, not on the little bread and the few oranges his stomach will retain, not on the many cigarettes he smokes, but on the power of his will.

Barcelona has recovered from the immemorial three-day bombing it received while we were at the Front.

For three days at intervals of two hours Italian planes from Palma de Mallorca or from Sardinia itself sailed in high from the sea, cut their engines and let go a brand new type of heavy time-bomb. This new missile does not explode on contact with a roof. It plows into the cellar before it goes off.

Towards the end of the three days, the city was in an extremely demoralized state. Men had rushed so often from lathes and work benches on which munitions were being made, so often run into cellars, dugouts and trenches, that they became unable to concentrate on their work and more and more stayed underground.

No ship moved in the harbor. Trains stayed outside of the stations. Families left the streets where each bomb brought an echo of rooftop Fifth Column machine guns and camped in tents made of sheets and shelters of brush on the hills behind the city.

After the first two days, a leaflet was dropped. The million and a half people of the city read that bombings would continue until they surrendered. All Republican planes, outnumbered by ten to one, were at the Ebro trying to help the men hold the lines. Anti-aircraft was ineffectual.

The news from the Front became worse and worse. A rumor spread that the cabinet members—all but Negrin, Uribe and Hernandez—had voted to ask Franco for an armistice.

Pasionaria, at the height of the raids, spoke in the Plaza de España against all compromise. The thirty-five thousand people who came to hear her formed into delegations and visited the government officers.

All talk of compromise, armistice and surrender was dropped.

The planes dropped a final leaflet. Raids would cease for twenty-four hours. The city was given twenty-four hours to consider surrender. At three o'clock on the afternoon of the following day, aviation would come back and stay over Barcelona until the war was over.

Next day at three o'clock the streets were empty. The city was silent. Much of the population was up in the hills.

The sound of engines was heard, but no siren sounded and no bombs fell. *Nuestras*, Ours, *Nuestras Gloriosas*, had at last arrived. Our aviators had met the Italians over the sea. After one trimotor was downed, the rest had fled.

That night the local broadcasting station gave orders for all unemployed or partially employed union members to report in front of their headquarters, with a blanket, a cup and a spoon, to be taken to the Front for work on fortifications.

The next day camions decorated with banners and placards and filled with young men with shovels toured the city, singing, and gathering new recruits off the sidewalks and the streetcars.

That evening a dozen new searchlights wove plaids across the sky. The dark air was full of the hum of the night patrols.

Barcelona had become Madrid.

FAREWELL

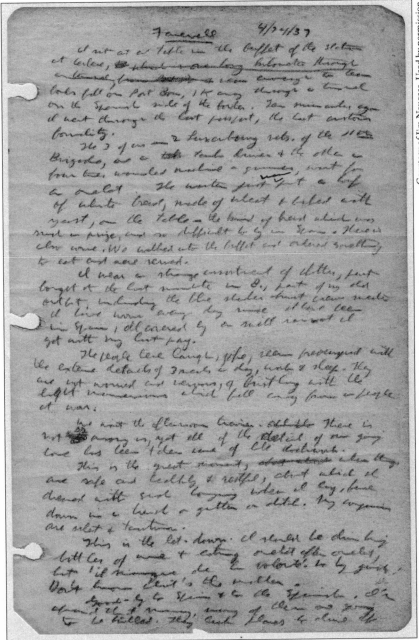

Courtesy of Jim Neugass. Used by permission.

Figure 9: "Farewell." A page from James Neugass's handwritten journal, the first page of the final chapter of this book. He dated it incorrectly. The year is 1938.

March 24. Cerbère, France. 8 A.M.

I sit at a table in the buffet of a French railroad station near enough to Spain to hear bombs fall on Port Bou.

Ten minutes ago I passed through the last passport, the last customs formality. My good luck had held to the end. I even had a rainy night on which to travel. Because almost all Barcelona stations were out of order, it was two hours before train time until I located the windowless bullet-scarred dark day coach which was to take me to the border. It took us eight hours to cover the eighty miles to Port Bou.

In the morning I saw an average of three enormous French diesel trucks to the mile. Those going to Barcelona were full. The trucks that came back towards the border were either empty or loaded with oranges.

Many sealed freight-cars stood in the Port Bou sidings and tunnels. There can never be enough of them.

The four of us who sit at this table—a tank driver and a machine-gunner from the Luxembourg, a Czech aircraft mechanic and myself—wait for an omelet. The waiter just put a bottle of wine and a large loaf of bread, made of wheat and baked with yeast, on the table.

I wear a strange assortment of civilian clothing bought at the last minute with my final Army pay in Barcelona. I was lucky enough to have been able to buy a raincoat. The merchant who sold it to me had been bombed out of every size but mine.

The people on this side of the border laugh, joke and seem preoccupied with the details of work, sleep and three meals a day. They are not worried and nervous, and bristle with the light mannerisms which so soon fall away from a people at war. No one looks as if he listens to the sky and no one suddenly stops and looks upwards.

Everything is very clean and peaceful.

We await the afternoon train. I have twenty francs, or sixty cents, in my pocket. Yet I know that the details of my getting to Paris, the details of the medical treatment I will receive there and the arrangements which will take me back to the States will be as efficiently executed as was my entry into France.

This is a great moment. This is the instant at which everything has become safe and healthy and peaceful.

The let-down has come. I should be drinking bottles of wine and eating omelet after omelet, but *il manqué de la volunte. No tengo gusto.* Do not know what is the matter.

Goodbye to Spain and the Spanish. I am afraid that many, many more of them are going to be killed. They lack planes, guns and skill. The Spanish are too young at war to stand off, unaided, German and Italian experts.

When the Italian bombs and German shells have mixed our bodies with the earth that should have defended them, Franco goes over the top and kills them again, in the name of a class whose traditions are of silence, cruelty, blindness, vainglory and possession. These were and are the traditions of the Few.

The traditions of the Many are of kindness, self-control, patience and a profound conviction that the ever-increasing wealth of the world is to be shared by the people of the world. I never heard a Spaniard lift his voice. I never saw a drunken Spaniard. I never had a favor refused. More discipline, more orders and an atmosphere of greater and more blind obedience would have and will help us win. The decisive conditions for the winning of the war are not being fought in Spain but in Washington, London and Paris.

The profundity of the Spaniard's belief that men are essentially good has softened the manner in which the war is being conducted. In eighteen months of fighting the Spanish learned how to close their open hands into fists, which became hard, but are not yet mailed by the automatic weapons by which democracy can alone exist and progress in Spain.

To those who believe that pacifism is possible, that fascism is not an anagram for "war," to those who think that their countries are really not parts of the world, to the man who says to himself, "well, if the worst comes to worst, the next guy may get it but not me," to all of these people for whom the front ranks of anti-fascists have no contempt and with whom they are so anxious to collaborate, I advise:

Immediately dig a trench in your back yard, with eight-foot zig-zags at 60-degree angles, allowing four feet of trench per person; and do not forget to camouflage the fresh earth lifted in the digging, as the Field Surgical unit of the 35th Divisions's Medical Corps forgot at Urrea de Gaen.

A long time after I have forgotten everything else about these months in Spain—if I am able to forget about any part or instant of them—I will remember the time when I mistook the sound of my own lips puffing on a cigarette for the sound of a falling bomb; and the spectacle my headlights picked out one cold night miles from the nearest lines, of a very old woman hobbling back to the Rear, alone, on a cane.

We have finished the omelet the waiter brought us, and the bottle of wine. My three comrades sit silent and taciturn about the table. No one speaks of ordering more food.

The heel of the loaf we ate fell to the floor. Four hands reached out to pick it up. Suddenly realizing that we were in France and not in Spain, in peace and not in war, we smiled foolishly at each other, leaned back in our chairs and again were silent.

-*End*-

"Neugass has driven for me for the past five months, extremely loyal, willing and worked very hard. He drove at the front for four months under tremendous stress and danger and he also deserves every praise which he has rightly earned."

—Dr. Edward K. Barsky to the American Medical Bureau
April 1, 1938

SOURCES

For biographical information about the people mentioned in James Neugass's journal, we relied on the extensive archival holding of the Abraham Lincoln Brigade Archives (ALBA) at the Tamiment Library at New York University (www.nyu.edu/library/bobst/research/tam). Particularly valuable are the papers of nurse Fredericka Martin, who corresponded with many medical personnel about their experiences in the Spanish Civil War. Colleagues around the world helped us fill in details about individuals from other countries. The best description of American participation in the events of late 1937–38 in Spain is in Arthur H. Landis's *The Abraham Lincoln Brigade* (New York: The Citadel Press, 1967). For additional contextual and biographical information, see Peter N. Carroll's *The Odyssey of the Abraham Lincoln Brigade: Americans in the Spanish Civil War* (Stanford: Stanford University Press, 1994). ALBA's own website is also an invaluable resource and research tool, with details on the American volunteers, teaching aids, historical documentation, and visuals (www.alba-valb.org).

GLOSSARY OF FOREIGN WORDS

algarroberas. carob trees

ametrallada. full of metal; machine-gunned

Asaltos. Assault Guards, Guardias des Asalto

auto-parque. car park

bacalao. dried codfish

barranco. gully, canyon

cabo. corporal

cabrones. bastards, pricks

cacique. boss, local strong man, capo

calamares rellenos. stuffed squid

camilleros. stretcher bearers

cantina. canteen (as in a bar)

canto. song

copitas. drinks, glasses of wine

carburo. acetylene

carne. meat

cheveaux-de-frise. sharp spikes laid across roads to impede cavalry or trucking

chicas. girls

chófer. driver

cigarrillo. cigarette

Comandancia. Headquarters

combate. combat

Comisario. Commisar

Delegación. Delegation

douros. silver coins, currency, from Portugal

enfermeras. nurses

enlace. liaison

Estado-Mayor. brigade headquarters

etapas. road and bridge guards, also stages, phases

evacuarme. evacuate me

flamenco. flamenco music, a style of Spanish singing, and dancing

Gloriosas. name used for Republican aircraft; glorious

Guapas. beauties, referring to women

Guardia Civile. Civil Guard

habichuelas. beans

hojas de ruta. road map

intendencia. quartermasters

inútil. useless, wounded

jotas. traditional folkdance from Aragon

mañana mas. "tomorrow, more"

matrimonio. marriage

mecha. fuse

mecheros. lighter, with a long, yellow cord of punk that smolders

novia. girlfriend, bride

obreros. workers

pantalones. pants

pavos. Henkel He 45 (German warplane used by Nationalists); literally: "turkeys"

posada. inn

Presidente. President

reclutas. draftees

refugio. refuge; bomb-shelter

regular. regular army, not a draftee

responsable. person in charge

salvo conducto. safe-conduct

señoritas. women

soldado. soldier

Soldado Desconocido. Unknown Soldier

surtidor. gas pump, also fountain

Teléfonos. telephones, also central telephone building

Teniente. Lieutenant

tiroteo. shooting.

tramontana. Italian—north wind

Transmisiones. Communications

triaje. triage

voluntarios. volunteers

ACKNOWLEDGMENTS

Rescuing this manuscript required cooperation and assistance from numerous individuals. First, we must thank the author's wife and sons, Myra Neugass, Jim Neugass, and Paul Neugass, who generously granted copyrights for the unpublished work to the Abraham Lincoln Brigade Archives (ALBA), a non-profit educational organization, which will receive the royalties for this work. We happily acknowledge the pro bono services of Rick Pappas and Fredda Weiss, who assisted in various aspects of the negotiations.

In providing research assistance to contextualize the manuscript, we benefited from numerous colleagues and friends around the world, especially Richard Baxtell in England; Christopher Brooks, the master of ALBA's biographical project; Robert Coale in Paris; Mark Derby of New Zealand; Amirah Inglis in Australia; Jyrki Juusela in Finland; John Krajlic, expert on the Slavic volunteers; Gail Malmgreen and Michael Nash of the Tamiment Library; Fraser Ottanelli who knows all about Italians in Spain; Michael Petrou, a specialist on the Canadians; Juan Salas, who knows the photographic sources and assisted with the images; Elizabeth Compa, also versed in the photographic record of the Spanish Civil War; Richard Bermack, who assisted with both the images and the map; and Erika Gottfried, from the Tamiment Library, who facilitated the permissions process for many of the images. Tony Geist provided translations for the glossary. Jim Neugass kindly gave us access to photographs and texts from his father's papers. Research support was also provided by the Program for Cultural Cooperation between Spain's Ministry of Culture and U.S. Universities, and by the Associate Professors' Research Grants Program at UC Berkeley, funded by a generous grant from the Andrew W. Mellon Foundation. Research and technical assistance with the original typescript was provided by Marc Boucai and Alexander Kort.

Our welcome at The New Press has been remarkable, thanks to our intermediary Patricia Bauman and the Director of the Press, Diane Wachtell. Priyanka Jacob provided enormous and timely assistance.

On the home front, Jeannette Ferrary and Jennifer Howard DeGolia gave a different kind of sustenance, enhancing the pleasure of the process.

BOSTON PUBLIC LIBRARY

3 9999 06200 965 7

WITHDRAWN

No longer the property of the
Boston Public Library.
Sale of this material benefits the Library.

Allston Branch Library
300 N. Harvard Street
Allston, MA 02134